The Naval Heritage
of
Portsmouth

John Winton

Foreword by Admiral Sir John Woodward GBE KCB

Ensign
PUBLICATIONS

© John Winton 1989

Published in 1989 by
Ensign Publications
2 Redcar Street
Shirley
Southampton SO1 5LL
England UK

Edited by Michael Burns
Design & Typesetting by Robert Antony Design
Film Origination by M R M Graphics
Colour reproduction by Fotographics

British Library Cataloguing in Publication Data
Winton, John
    The naval heritage of Portsmouth.
    1. Great Britain. Royal Navy, history
    I. Title
    359'.00941

ISBN 1-85455-002-0

CONTENTS

Foreword

Although Portsmouth was not the first place the Royal Navy sent me to, I did first go to sea from there, as a Cadet, aged 15, in a destroyer. Thereafter, as it has been for so many of us, it was frequently my home, my operational base and my support over a career spanning forty-four years. So Porstmouth has a special place in my heart, as therefore must any book which can put my own experience into historical context. From Portsmouth, I have commanded at various times, two submarines, one destroyer, a whole Flotilla, a Task Force, and finally the Naval Home Command. So I think I can fairly claim first hand knowledge of one small period of the historic connection between the Royal Navy and the City of Portsmouth. If I had to pick out one single period when the relationship was most important to me personally, it would obviously have to be the Spring of 1982, when, though I attended none of the sailings, I had good cause to be glad of the sterling support, and witnessed many of the heart-stopping returns from the South Atlantic. It is no hard-nosed commercial connection alone between Portsmouth and the Navy but something much deeper than that, richly based through shared good times and bad.

"First the Nab and then the Warner, Outer Spit and Blockhouse Corner" is the phrase that submariners in particular remember, but the Heritage Area, close to the centre of the big Naval Base, has more history to it, not least the still strong and lively associations of Admiral Lord Nelson, and HMS *Victory*, supported by the Royal Naval Museum which reveals the history of the Navy through the centuries just as this book reveals how that history is bound up in the history of Portsmouth.

Thus I am very glad to introduce this excellent record and to commend it to readers.

Sandy Woodward.

Admiral Sir John Woodward GBE KCB

Chapter 1

'Every item is redolent of the Navy and its belongings,' wrote Captain David Beatty to his wife when he went down to Portsmouth to take the senior officers' war course in 1911, 'which gives one the feeling as of going home, and I seem to recognise everybody in the streets . . .'. But Joy Packer, a native-born South African coming to Portsmouth for the first time after her marriage to a Lieutenant Commander at Whale Island in February 1925, thought of what she called 'the great naval arsenal, sprawling between the Portsdown Hills and the wintry sea' as 'a muddly sort of place where I'll never find my way!'

Portsmouth was always a sailors' town. Captain Stephen Martin-Leake, writing to a friend in January 1729, said that Portsmouth Point 'has one good street through the middle, from the Point Gate to the water side, is full built, and very populous and thriving, being the Wapping of Portsmouth. Here the Johns carouse, not being confined to hours, and spend their money for the good of the public, which makes ale houses and shops thrive mightily upon this spot. Some have compared it with the Point at Jamaica, that was swallowed up by an earthquake, and think, if that was Sodom, this is Gomorrah; but it is by no means so bad as some would make it, though bad enough.'

The sailors may have made Portsmouth into a Sodom or Gomorrah or both but they always gave it a certain style. The Elizabethan writer Thomas Nash, in his 1599 pamphlet *Nash's Lenten Stuffe*, praised the sober habits of Great Yarmouth and its fishermen, saying that when he walked through the streets he did not meet 'with any of these swaggering captains (captains that wore a whole ancient (i.e. a flag) in a scarf, which made them go

heavy-shouldered it was so boisterous) or hufti-tuftie youthful ruffling comrades, wearing every one of them three yards of feathers in his cap, for his mistriss' favour, such as we stumble on at each second step at . . . Portsmouth'.

This image, of a bustling town made prosperous by the armed forces, prevailed in the nineteenth century. Sir Robert Steele wrote of Portsmouth in 1803, when war had broken out again and he himself had just been commissioned into the Royal Marines at the age of fourteen, that 'he could hardly walk for the groups of officers in beautiful and rich uniforms, Army and Navy, horse and foot, Hanoverian and British, who were to be seen singly and together, arm in arm, loitering, laughing, and quizzing, while every non-commissioned officer or soldier who met or passed an officer stopped, turned, and saluted, by bringing his hand with a sort of flourish to his cap'.

Not everybody in the Navy thought so highly of Portsmouth. Even Nelson called it 'a horrid place'. Samuel Pepys said of Portsmouth men: 'They are as I understand from everybody that has to do with them, the most debauched, damming, swearing rogues that ever were in the Navy . . .'. When Vice Admiral Holburne was appointed Commander-in-Chief at Portsmouth in 1758 he at once wrote to the Secretary of the Admiralty Board, pleading in the most obsequious terms to get the appointment cancelled for, he said, 'I shall be very unhappy at that villainous Portsmouth'.

There was a price to be paid in law and order for the money the 'carousing Johns' spent in the ale houses 'for the good of the public'. Henry Capper joined the *St Vincent* training ship as a boy aged fourteen in 1869. He came from a naval family and his father was an official in Portsmouth dockyard. Capper's earliest memories of men-o-warsmen were as a child, clinging in terror to his mother's skirts as a crowd of seamen just paid off after a long foreign commission held a posse of police at bay, flinging stones at the policeman's shiny top hats, in the usually quiet Portsmouth street where his family lived.

There was another price to be paid, in loss and grief. When the official communiqué of Jutland was published, it gave a long list of the ships lost. Many of those ships were Portsmouth-manned. Women ran out into the streets on that warm June evening and wept openly. 'A Stricken Town', said the newspaper headlines.

Joy Packer came back to Portsmouth in 1943, when the town had been badly bombed. She had thought there was 'little beauty' there in 1925, but now she wrote 'there is in this battered port a quality greater than beauty. There is grandeur. "Pompey" the bluejackets call their city, but it might be Pompeii now, so bitter is the ruin of the city, so cruel the devastation . . . The Guildhall is burned out, so are barracks, schools, churches, hospitals, cinemas and music-halls, and so also are homes where once the worst menace was the mother-in-law and the lodger. The children are gone from Portsmouth now, but the women have stayed on in the mean streets with the sinister gaps and windows boarded up. They are the wives and mothers and sweethearts of sailors, and when *he* comes home, "unexpected-like", he will find them there — if home is still standing'.

Certainly, experience with the Navy over the years has given Portsmouth a certain civic stoicism. The loss of the destroyer HMS *Sheffield*, a Portsmouth ship, with twenty-one of her ship's company off the Falklands in May 1982 was as great a shock to the city as it was to the Task Force. The Lord Mayor at the time summed up his city's temperament and its history very well when he said 'Portsmouth is a naval city. We've had shocks like this before and we'll have them again, we must just get on with it'.

Portsmouth's own geography determined its history. It had a huge natural harbour, much of it deep water at all states of the tide, and a superb offshore anchorage at Spithead, with ample space for the world's largest fleets. The bulk of the Isle of Wight shielded the harbour entrance and the anchorage against the worst of the weather. These advantages, with its comparative closeness to the Saxon capital of Winchester and to London, meant that Portsmouth had to be a major seaport and naval base. The Romans called it Portus Magnus, the Great Port. They fortified Portchester, which they called Portus Adurni, and built a road from it to Venta Belgarum (Winchester).

The Romans steadily increased their naval power in Britain to safeguard the coasts and surrounding seas against the raids of Teutonic tribes, the Franks and Saxons, whom the Romans considered no better than pirates. Eventually, in about AD 284, the Emperor Maximinian appointed a *Comes Littoris Saxonici*, literally a 'Count of the Saxon shore', to take charge of operations against the pirates.

The first holder of this office, and thus the first recorded admiral to use Portchester as a base, was Caius Carausius. He was probably a Dutchman or a Fleming, from Batavi, an

Reverse of Carausius coin, with galley to left, with ram, seven oars or groups of oars, soldiers on deck, and an eagle with spread wings on the poop.

Coin of Carausius (AD 287–93), with bust to left in crested helmet and cuirass.

area of Holland around what is now Rotterdam. He was almost certainly a pirate himself and was very probably chosen on the principle of setting a thief to catch a thief.

If so, then the plan worked too well. Carausius was a very able and successful sea captain who waited until the pirate ships were laden with booty and then, instead of preventing them landing, captured them and appropriated their loot. Soon, Carausius had become so rich and powerful that a jealous Maximinian tried to have him assassinated. When the attempt failed, Carausius retaliated by seizing the great port and stronghold of Gesoriacum (Boulogne) in AD 286.

Maximinian built a large fleet in the mouth of the Rhine and together with his brother Emperor Constantius besieged Gesoriacum from the sea. Constantius blocked the harbour with a barricade of earth and sand, reinforced by trees driven in as piles, but Carausius escaped overland and crossed to Portchester. He was very annoyed to discover he need not have taken so much trouble; the siege works across the harbour were blown away by a storm on the day after he left.

As Carausius' naval base and dockyard, Portchester, or Caer Peris as it was called locally, enjoyed a period of great prosperity. Hearing of Carausius' reputation, men flock-ed from all over the Atlantic seaboard to serve under him. Carausius proclaimed himself Emperor of Britain and, through force at home and treaties in the Mediterranean, ruled the seas from the Channel to the Bosphorus.

Constantius assembled a fleet, reputedly of a thousand ships. After crushingly defeating a fleet of the Franks near the Straits of Gibraltar, he prepared to land against Carausius. However, Carausius was treacherously killed in York in AD 293 by his friend and fellow commander Allectus.

Forewarned of the approach of Constantius' ships, under their commander Asclepiodotus, Allectus assembled a much larger fleet at Spithead and sailed to intercept. However, what would have been the first ever recorded battle off Spithead was thwarted by thick fog, in which both fleets sailed past each other. It seems that Asclepiodotus had no great faith in his own abilities as an admiral. When he landed he set fire to his ships, so as to impress upon his people that they must stand or fall where they were.

When Allectus returned he fell in with some Roman troops and was killed. Some of his followers, most of them seamen, went up to London and seized the town. It so happened that part of the Roman fleet, which had become separated from the rest in the fog, arrived in the Thames, and landed a strong party who rounded up Allectus' men (many of whom, it was recorded, were foreigners) and cut them to pieces. So ended the rebellion.

A harbour like Portsmouth was bound to attract predators, of whom the most persistent were the Danes. The Anglo-Saxon *Chronicle* records that in AD 501 a Dane, appropriately called Port, with his two sons, Bieda and Maegla, 'came with two ships to Britain at the place which is called *Portesmutha* and immediately seized land and slew a young Briton, a very noble man'. The Saxon ships were from 70 to 100 feet long, and from 16 to 18 feet wide, without decks, and had a single mast and yard, with a large square sail.

The *Chronicle* also gives details of the earliest properly recorded English sea engagement, known as 'King Alfred's Naval and Beach Battle with the Danes', which could well have taken place in and around Portsmouth harbour. Alfred may or may not deserve the title of 'Father of the Royal Navy', but he certainly grasped the strategic truth that maritime foes like the Danes had to be fought and defeated at sea.

According to the *Chronicle*, there was a good deal of naval activity around the English coasts in the ninth century. Probably the first engagement in which Alfred himself took part was in 875 when 'in the summer King Alfred sailed out to sea with a fleet, and fought against seven ships' companies (of Danes) and captured one of them and put the others to flight'. Again, in 881: 'King Alfred went out to sea with ships and fought against four ships' companies of Danes and captured two of the ships, and the men aboard were slain; and two ships' companies surrendered to him, and they were badly cut about and severely wounded before they surrendered'.

Three years later, in 884, the *Chronicle* tells the story of a battle with more detail. In the *Chronicle*, 'pirates' are synonymous with 'Danes'. 'And the same year King Alfred sent a naval force from Kent into East Anglia. As soon as they came to the mouth of the Stour, then they met sixteen ships of pirates and fought against them, and captured all the ships, and slew the crews. When they were on the way home with the booty, they met a great fleet of pirates, and fought against them the same day, and the Danish were victorious'.

King Alfred's battle took place in 896 AD (although an error by some unknown scribe rendered the date in *The Parker Chronicle* as 897): 'This same year (896) the (Danish) hosts in East Anglia and Northumbria greatly harassed Wessex along the south coasts with predatory bands, most of all with the warships they had built many years before. Then King Alfred ordered warships to be built to meet the Danish ships. They were almost twice as long as the others (the Danes); some had sixty oars, some more. They were both swifter, steadier, and with more freeboard than the others (the Danes). They were built neither after the Frisian design nor after the Danish, but as it seemed to himself that they could be most serviceable.'

The King's Ships, larger and more seaworthy, were evidently a considerable advance in design over their opponents, which, as the *Chronicle* says, were obsolete warships 'built many years before'. Alfred was clearly a pioneer in ship-building, as he was in so many other fields. It is typical of him that he should build ships to *his* design, and not follow the Danes or the Frisians who were the two great rival maritime nations of the period.

Scholars and naval historians have long speculated about the exact site of the battle. Various harbours along the south coast, and particularly Poole in Dorset, have been suggested. There are references in the original Anglo-Saxon to *Wiht* (Wight), *utermere* (open sea, or outer bay), *mutha* (harbour mouth) and *ufeweardum mutha* (upper end of the harbour). The scene described, of an open sea or wide outer bay, which could well be Spithead, narrowing to a river mouth, with an inner harbour inside, does not preclude Portsmouth.

The battle was fought between six Danish ships and nine of the King's new ships. The old chroniclers were so free with their pronouns it is difficult to know who all the 'hes' and 'hims' and 'theys' and 'thems' are. But the Danish ships can be lettered, A to F, and the King's Ships numbered, 1 to 9.

'Then on one occasion the same year came six ships (A–F) to the Isle of Wight and did much harm there, both in Devon and almost everywhere along the coast. Then the king ordered nine (1–9) of the new ships to put out, and they blockaded the entrance from the open sea against their (the Danes) escape. Then the Danes sailed out with three ships (A,B,C) against them, and three of their ships (D,E,F) were beached on dry land at the upper end of the harbour, and the crews had gone off inland. Then the English seized two (A,B) of the three ships at the entrance to the estuary, and slew the men, but the other (C) escaped. In her also all but five (men) were slain; and they escaped because the ships of the others (any number from 1 to 9, perhaps even all nine) were aground.' (The narrative does not mention (C) again.)

The battle had almost a Royal Marine

flavour. So far it had been PER MARE. Now for PER TERRAM. 'They (the English) were also very awkwardly aground. Three (1,2,3) were aground on the side of the channel where the Danish ships (D,E,F) were aground, and the others (4-91) all on the other side, so that none of them (4-9) could reach the others (1-3). But, when the tide ebbed many furlongs from the ships (D,E,F: 1,2,3) the Danes went from the three ships (D,E,F) to the other three (1,2,3) which were stranded on their side, and then there they fought'.

A bloody battle took place: 'There was slain Lucumon the King's reeve, and Wulfheard the Frisian, and Aebbe the Frisian, and Aethelhere the Frisian, and Aethelfrith of the King's (personal) household, totalling sixty-two killed of English and Frisians, and one hundred and twenty of the Danes'.

Lucumon the 'King's reeve' was a very important official, possibly even the English commander. The chronicler thought it worth mentioning the deaths of two prominent Englishmen and three Frisians, a casualty list which may suggest that there were more Frisians than English serving in Alfred's navy. However, together they slew nearly twice as many Danes. 'However, the (flood) tide came first to the Danish ships (D,E,F) before the Christians (the crews of 1,2,3) could push off theirs, and hence they (D,E,F) rowed away out to sea. They were so sorely crippled that they were unable to row past Sussex, but there the crew cast two of them (D,E) ashore. The men (the crews of D,E) were led to the King at Winchester, and he had them hanged there. The men who were on the single ship (F) reached East Anglia badly wounded. This same summer no less than twenty ships perished with all hands along the south coast'.

The 'Sussex' which ships D and E could not row past was probably Selsey Bill. The original text says 'hie ne mehton Suth-Seaxna lond utan berowan' which, literally translated in the same word order, is 'they not could South Sussex land around to row'. If it were not Selsey Bill, then the next headland is Beachy Head, some fifty miles further on — a long way for wounded men to row. Selsey Bill, and the closeness to Winchester, tend to support the theory that the battle was at Portsmouth.

Alfred's brisk way with Danes/pirates, i.e. hanging them, laid the foundations of a peace which continued under his grandson, Athelstan, and his great-grandson Edgar. Athelstan won the first real sea-fight in English history when he routed a great fleet of Danes which had been plundering Sandwich. In 937 he won a great naval victory over a Danish and Celtic alliance at Brunanburh in the north. The site of Brunanburh is unknown but the battle was commemorated by a triumphant Saxon war-song.

Edgar had a fleet variously estimated in strength as being between nine hundred and four thousand eight hundred ships. He maintained three squadrons, to watch the east, south and west coasts of his realm, and he made an annual tour of inspection by sea of all his ships and his ports — the first C-in-C's inspections in English naval history.

When Edgar died in 975, the *Chronicle* hymned his praises in an admirable statement of sea power. While Edgar ruled the 'gannet's bath' — a Saxon poetic epithet for the sea:

No fleet however proud, no host however strong,
Was able to win booty for itself
In England, while that noble King
Occupied the royal throne.

But, in 991, Ethelred the Unready paid the first Danegeld — ten thousand pounds of silver, a fantastic sum for that time. Needless to say, Danegeld did not get rid of the Danes, for whom Portsmouth continued to have a special attraction. They returned again and again to plunder, and burn, and butcher, with one especially violent raid on Dorset and Hampshire in 998. By 1016, the Danes had conquered the whole country and Canute, who had succeeded his father Sweyn in 1014, became sole monarch of England that year. Ironically, this brought about peace and order at sea.

In the eleventh century, Sandwich rather than Portsmouth was the chief naval base of the Saxon Kings. It was at Sandwich that King Harold mustered his household troops in 1066. The *Chronicle* says he waited a long time for them to be mobilised. Eventually they embarked in ships — some seven hundred of them — and sailed to the Isle of Wight, to Spithead in fact, where they waited, cruising around the Solent and the Isle of Wight, expecting an invasion by William of Normandy, throughout the whole of that summer and autumn.

Some accounts say that Harold was misled by false intelligence into believing that William's expedition had been abandoned and therefore sent his crews home. The Anglo Saxon *Chronicle* gives another, wholly believable, version of what was the first recorded mutiny at Spithead. On 8 September, the Festival of the Nativity of St Mary, the sailors' provisions had run out and, as the *Chronicle* says, 'no one could keep them there any longer'.

The *Chronicle* says that 'they were therefore given permission to return home. Then the King rode up and the ships were sailed to London, but many were lost before they arrived'. It seems likely that the sailors would have gone home anyway, with or without permission. They had already served in the ships for some six months — a very long time indeed for the eleventh century — and King Harold himself had just left them to 'ride up', as the *Chronicle* said, to Stamford Bridge in Yorkshire where, on 25 September, he defeated his outlawed brother Earl Tostig and King Harold of Norway.

Thus, William the Conqueror was able to land his troops from his ships unopposed at Pevensey on St Michael's Day, 29 September 1066. Harold returned from the north, to be defeated and killed at Senlac on 14 October. Had his ships still been on station three weeks earlier, the history of England might have been very different.

In the twelfth century, Portsmouth was a regular port of arrival and departure for kings and those who hoped to be kings. In August 1101, Robert Duke of Normandy landed at Portsmouth to assert his claim to the throne, unsuccessfully, against his younger brother Henry I.

It was Henry I who built a castle at Portchester on the foundations of the old Roman fort. Henry embarked for Normandy from Portsmouth in 1114 and again in 1123, after spending Whitsuntide there. It was almost certainly from Portsmouth that he set out on his last expedition in 1133. According to the contemporary account by Florence of Worcester, in the thirty-third year of King Henry's reign, on Wednesday, 2 August, (the anniversary of the death of his elder brother William Rufus), the King was ashore waiting to embark when there was an eclipse of the sun.

Clouds appeared, bigger and thicker than anybody had ever seen before. Darkness fell, and people had to light candles at midday. To the astonishment of the King and his attendants, the sun looked like the thin crescent of a new moon, but becoming first broader and then narrower, sometimes shining steadily as normal, and sometimes flickering 'as if it were liquid, quivering like quick silver'.

At the same time, several stars appeared in the sky, and there was an earthquake. The sea was calm, and there was only a gentle breeze blowing, the account says, when suddenly the large anchors of one of the ships were wrenched out of the ground by some unknown cause, so that the ship drove into the next. Eight ships were dashed against each other and all were damaged. Shortly afterwards, very possibly in thanksgiving for his deliverance from danger, Henry founded a church dedicated to the Virgin Mary inside the walls of Portchester Castle; this also suggests that the scene of the King's embarkation, the eclipse, and the earthquake, was Portsmouth.

After Henry's death there was a dispute over the succession, between Henry's only daughter Matilda, or Maud, widow of the Emperor Henry V, and Stephen, a grandson of William the Conqueror. Portsmouth played a part again. At the end of September 1139, Matilda, her bastard brother Robert Earl of Gloucester, and one hundred and forty knights, landed there without opposition. In 1153, King Stephen landed safe on the western side of Portsmouth harbour in a fierce storm and, so it is sometimes said, called the place 'God's Port' — Gosport.

Henry II, Henry I's grandson and the first Plantagenet King, embarked at Portsmouth for Normandy on 8 August 1174, taking with him as a prisoner William the Lion, King of Scotland. He returned to Portsmouth after a successful campaign on 26 May 1175. In 1182, Henry II made his will at Portsmouth before sailing for France.

After Henry's death in France in 1189, his eldest surviving son Richard the Lionheart landed at Portsmouth as King of England on 12 August. In 1194, he granted Portsmouth a Charter. Towards the end of April that year he assembled a fleet of a hundred ships in the harbour for an expedition to France. The King inspected his ships closely, in what was probably the first ever Royal Naval Review. He was eager to sail but the weather was foul and delayed him for several days. On 2 May, although the weather was still bad, he could wait no longer. He ordered the troops and horses to embark, and put to sea himself in a 'long ship'.

It was just as well Richard's fleet did not sail with him, or many of the ships would have been lost. Richard himself had to take shelter in the Isle of Wight before returning to Portsmouth again. He finally embarked on 12 May and crossed to Barfleur. He never returned to Portsmouth or to England again. After years of campaigning, he was killed by a stray arrow in April 1199 at the siege of the Castle of Chalus in France.

The new King John, Richard's younger brother, was one of the most frequent of all Royal visitors to Portsmouth. He embarked and disembarked there, usually from the shore between the Sally Port and the Round Tower, almost annually and especially in the early years of his reign when he was dealing with his kinsman and rival claimant to the throne, Prince Arthur, whom he eventually kept in prison until he died.

In the thirteenth century, for the first time, there are ample written records of events. In March 1205, John awarded the first prize money, granting to his galleys' crews half of anything they captured from the enemy. In 1208, he ordered the Bailiffs of Portsmouth, Shoreham, Southampton and other places to select their best and strongest men and, such of them as were armed, to man the King's galleys. This was the earliest form of impressment of men for the Navy.

John was the first English King to lay claim to the lordship of the sea. For instance, he ordered that vessels should strike or lower their sails whenever they encountered the 'lieutenant of the King or the admiral of the King or his lieutenant on any voyage ordained by Common Council of the realm'. Merchantmen still dip their ensigns to a passing Queen's ship to this day.

It was during John's reign that Portsmouth took over from the Cinque Ports the position of the principal naval base of the Kingdom. The Cinque Ports were too small to shelter a fleet large enough to mount a foreign expedition or to defend home shores, and their harbours were already beginning to silt up through the action of the sea, a process that has gone on until today when it is very hard to credit that they were ever thriving sea ports.

Portsmouth, however, remained a magnificent harbour large enough for any fleet, and some of John's fleets were very large. In 1205, he gathered a fleet of five hundred ships for an expedition to France. He sailed on 13 June but, in the event, he had to abandon the project because of the discontent of the nobles who were supposed to take part.

By then, Portsmouth had become a great shipbuilding centre. Records of the thirteenth century abound with references to Portsmouth, to notices of payments to masters of ships there, orders for the release of ships arrested at Portsmouth, and grants of money paid at portsmouth for furnishing, victualling and manning of the fleets. For example, in 1212, the King ordered 'a hundred casks from our stores of wines which is at Portsmouth' to be delivered to the Archdeacon of Durham. In 1213, there were orders for thirty seven-foot long anchors for the King's galleys to be sent to Portsmouth, for fifty-four suits of chain armour and hauberks from Bristol to 'be at Portsmouth by the feast of St Hilary', and 'of all the horses which you have in your keeping — let them be at Portchester by the day appointed'.

In 1212, Portsmouth had its first dockyard in the modern sense of the word. Galleys had always been drawn up on shore for repairs. But on 20 May, the Sheriff of Southampton was directed that the *exclusa*, the slipways at Portsmouth should be enclosed with a good strong wall for the preservation of the King's ships and galleys. (The slipways were actually situated at the entrance to the Mill-pond, a site now occupied by the shore establishment HMS *Vernon*). The Sheriff was also to have penthouses built for their stores and tackle. The job was to be done at once, lest the galleys or their stores be damaged during the coming winter, and store-houses to be built on shore.

Portsmouth was the main assembly point for ships from other ports. In 1214, King John sent to William de Wrotham, Archdeacon of Taunton and Keeper of the King's Ships, Galleys and Seaports, a sort of medieval First Lord of the Admiralty: 'Get ready ten of our best Gallies which are at Portsmouth and prepare all the ships which are there with Pontoons and other necessaries of war, and gather together the Ships of the other ports so that they may be there by the feast of the Circumcision of Our Lord promptly to transport troops for our service into Angiers. The same of Robert Bloet — send all kinds of provisions — pork, ship's stores — to Portsmouth by the Feast of St Hilary'.

John has a reputation as a bad King, but he had a continuing interest in naval affairs. He published the first primitive form of Navy List, awarded the first prize moneys, introduced a new method of impressing seamen, ordered the first enclosed dockyard, laid down regulations for the assembly, organisation and dispatch of large fleets (which always sailed in convoy) and, above all, was the first to claim the lordship of the seas. Many aspects of the history of the Navy and of Portsmouth began to take shape during King John's reign.

Chapter 2

King John won one major sea battle in April or May 1213 (the exact date is not known) when he sent a fleet of five hundred sail and a force of seven hundred knights under the Earl of Salisbury to the coast of Flanders. They found a French invasion fleet at a place called Damme, now a small town some miles inland north-east of Bruges, but in the thirteenth century a seaport with a large harbour.

It so happened that many of the French crews were ashore. Salisbury attacked at once. The English seized three hundred French ships and burned a hundred more, but then Salisbury rashly landed and was himself defeated by the French King Philip Augustus. Two thousand English were killed or drowned.

Despite this tactical victory, Philip Augustus had suffered a serious strategic defeat. He had made an error in attempting an invasion by sea without first defeating a powerful opposing 'fleet in being'. Damme gave the English command of the sea, and prevented Philip from either evacuating his army from Flanders or supplying by sea.

John was anxious to follow up his advantage. After one abortive expedition which only got as far as Jersey, he ordered William de Wrotham to prepare all the King's galleys for sea in November. They were sent to Portsmouth early in 1214 and, on or about 9 February, John sailed from the Isle of Wight, with his Queen Isabella, his bastard son Richard and a large army.

This final expedition, made possible by command of the sea, was disastrously defeated in France. It was followed by further defeats, on land at Runnymeade in June 1215 when his barons forced John to sign the Magna Carta, and at sea, in 1216, when another French invasion fleet of six hundred ships and eighty cogs, commanded by the renegade privateer Eustace the Monk, who had until only recently served John, sailed to put Prince Louis of France on the throne of England. Eustace the Monk's fleet was dispersed by bad weather but Louis himself landed at Sandwich.

John died on 19 October 1216 and was succeeded by his elder son Henry III, who was then nine years old. Henry's reign began with a great English victory, the first ever at sea. Louis of France had been defeated at Lincoln in May 1217, but in August Eustace the Monk sailed again with an invasion fleet of eighty ships, with galleys and small craft.

The English commander was Sir Hubert de Burgh, Governor of Dover Castle, who had sixteen large and well-equipped ships from the Cinque Ports, and about twenty smaller vessels. When the English ships put to sea from Dover on 24 August 1217, Eustace's fleet was already in mid-Channel, some miles out of Calais and heading almost north on a brisk-south-south-easterly wind, steering to round the North Foreland and enter the Thames.

Sir Hubert did not head directly for the enemy but steered across the Channel. Eustace thought he meant to attack Calais, but was unworried, knowing it was well defended. Sir Hubert had no intention of attacking Calais. He was gaining the weather gauge — one of the earliest examples of this primary fighting tactic in the days of sail. Once he had his enemy in his lee, Sir Hubert altered to the north and his ships bore down on the French rearguard.

The English began by flinging unslaked lime downwind into the eyes of the French —

a tactic actually pioneered by King John (he also smeared his ships' gunwhales with soft soap to make boarding more difficult). The English followed up with grapnels to prevent their enemies escaping. Whilst the English archers fired a stream of flaming arrows into the French ships, the English men-at-arms swarmed on board and cut down the French rigging and halyards with axes, before engaging the blinded and bewildered defenders in desperate hand-to-hand combats which were mostly short and brutish and ended in immense slaughter amongst the French.

Some of the English ships were fitted with iron beaks, which also did tremendous execution. Most of the French ships were sunk or captured. Only fifteen escaped. Twenty-five French knights and more than one thousand soldiers were taken prisoner.

Eustace the Monk was found shivering and cowering in the hold of his ship. There seems to have been something in his personality and behaviour which excited especial revulsion and hatred amongst the English. It could be said that Eustace the Monk was the first man to arouse that Francophobia which exists in this country to this day. He was dragged out and taken ashore where his head was lopped off and exhibited on a pole throughout southern England, to general acclamation.

Eustace the Monk had paid the penalty for attempting a seaborne operation without first making sure that a hostile fleet, no matter how inferior on paper, had been eliminated. He had, in fact, committed the same error as Philip Augustus, an error which Napoleon Bonaparte himself was to repeat.

It was this basic concept, command of the sea, which Portsmouth was so well placed to implement. Sir Hubert de Burgh's defeat of Eustace the Monk off the South Foreland in August 1217 brought the war to an end. One of the conditions of peace was that lands in France lost by John would be returned to the English crown.

King Henry III's 'great ship', based at Portsmouth, was called the *Queen*. From the accounts, she was clearly a large and very important ship. In 1225, the Bailiffs of Southampton were ordered to buy cordage for the King's great ship, under the inspection of an eminent mariner called Stephen Crabbe; if there were not enough ready, they were to have it made in all haste, working day and night, and send it to Portsmouth. They were also told to have three good cables made for her, together with four dozen 'theldorum', and procure two hundred yards of cloth to repair her sails.

A year later, the Constable of Portchester was ordered to supply Friar Thomas with three boatloads of firewood, one for the King's two galleys, and two for the King's great ship. He was also given twenty-two and a half marks to buy canvas for the sails, and to make 'celtas' for the great ship, carts being sent to carry the 'celtas' and 'heyras' to Portsmouth.

In November 1227, £11 was paid to the Master of the King's great ship and to ten mariners for keeping the King's ships and galleys at Portsmouth, at the rate of sixpence a day to the Master and threepence to each sailor. In 1229, £40 was paid to the King's clerk for the repairs of the King's galleys and great ship at Portsmouth.

There were operational reasons for all this activity and expense. In 1223, Prince Louis succeeded his father Philip Augustus but failed to keep the terms of the agreement made in 1217. Henry III had to make several attempts during his long reign of fifty-six years to regain what he looked upon as his rightful inheritance. Once again, Portsmouth became a frequent port of embarkation.

In 1224, the year the name of 'Portsmue' first appeared as one of the principal ports of the kingdom, Henry III began to prepare a great expedition to Poitou. In 1225, such Barons as were at Portsmouth, intending to go to Gascony for the wine, were ordered to choose from the whole of the King's fleet the best and safest ship for the convoy of armour and baggage to Richard, the King's brother, in Gascony. They were also to see to it that the best sailors and masters were appointed to the ship, they were to keep close to it and protect it during its crossing and were not to leave it until it had arrived safely in a Gascon port.

Preparations, many of them centred on Portsmouth, went on throughout 1226. The

Queen was fitted out and placed under the command of Friar Thomas of the Temple. On 20 February, all the great ships at Southampton were ordered to Portsmouth. In March, seven of the ships at Portsmouth were assigned to the Earl of Salisbury to convey horses and equipment to Gascony. The great ships at Shoreham were sent to Portsmouth.

Mobilisation for war continued, but it took time. In May, all shipping was directed to assemble at Portsmouth by the end of the month. On 30 November, all shipping in every port in England was commandeered for the King's service.

In 1227, Henry was ready. On 2 June, he issued precepts to all the ports in the Kingdom, declaring that he was about to cross the sea in person, and ordering bailiffs to send their ships, properly manned and well found with arms and provisions, to Portsmouth before St James's Day, 25 July.

But the King never sailed because, so the old chronicles said, he was advised not to by an astrologer. Nor did he sail the next year, 1228, possibly because of a shortage of transports. There was a further setback in May when the docks King John had built 'in the pond of the Abbess' were flooded by the sea. The docks were ordered to be filled in.

Henry wanted to sail in 1229, but again there was a shortage of transports. The King blamed Sir Hubert de Burgh, calling him an 'old traytor', in spite of his long and distinguished service, and accusing him of accepting a bribe of five thousand marks from the Queen of France. The King was so furious he drew his sword and might have killed Sir Hubert had the Earl of Chester not restrained him. He later had the grace to admit the wrong he had done his old servant.

Finally, on 30 April 1230, everything was ready. In fact, there were so many ships that one hundred and eighty of them were surplus to requirements and their masters were permitted to return in them to their home ports. Henry embarked and arrived at St Malo on 3 May. However, after all the preparation, his campaign achieved nothing and was very wasteful of resources. The King was back at Portsmouth by the end of October.

When ships were not needed for war, they were hired out for commerce. In 1232, John Blancboilly was given the custody of the *Queen* at Portsmouth, with all her anchors and tackle, for life, to trade wherever he pleased for a rent of fifty marks a year. He had to keep her in good repair at his own expense so that when he died she could be returned to the King in as good a state as when he received her.

Henry continued his campaign, on and off, for many years. In April 1242, he sailed from Portsmouth again, with his Queen, and Richard Earl of Cornwall, seven other earls and three hundred knights, and thirty casks full of money, but he returned to Portsmouth in September 1243 after another futile campaign. In June 1253, Henry collected a thousand ships. After many muddles, delays and bad weather, he sailed in August but returned, without achieving much, to Dover in December 1254.

A five year truce with France was concluded in 1269. In August the following year, Prince Edward, Henry's eldest surviving son, sailed from Portsmouth with thirteen ships to take part in a Crusade. He was actually on his way home when, on 16 November 1272, his father died and he became King, although his homeward pace was so leisurely that he did not reach England until August 1274.

The three Plantagenet Edwards, Edward I, his eldest surviving son Edward II, and Edward II's eldest son Edward III, between them reigned for one hundred and five years. They were somewhat precarious times for Portsmouth. The town was often raided from the sea, looted and burned to the ground, first by Cinque Port pirates and then several times by the French, probably because both thought that Portsmouth was the source of the punitive expeditions against them — which it normally was. The old records are full of occasions when Portsmouth was excused paying farm rent or taxes because of the damage these raids had done to the town.

In March 1327, in the first few weeks of Edward III's reign, some French galleys under Nicholas Behuchet approached Portsmouth under cover of an English flag, with crews dressed as Englishmen, and landed troops, possibly on Southsea beach. They captured Portsmouth, slew many of the people, and burned almost the whole town except the Parish Church and the Hospital (the Domus Dei), which were possibly spared for religious reasons, but more probably because they were made of stone.

According to one contemporary account, the surviving people of Portsmouth rallied and drove the French off with enormous losses. However, Behuchet's force was still strong enough to go on to sack and burn Southampton.

Of the three Edwards, Edward III was the most successful at sea. He personally commanded the English fleet at the great victory over the French invasion fleet at Sluys on 24 June 1340, and again in the defeat of the Spanish fleet in the action known as 'L'Espagnols Sur Mer' on 29 August 1350. Sluys was a particularly bloody defeat for the French and their allies, who lost some twenty-five thousand men. Amongst them was Nicholas Behuchet, whom the English had the satisfaction of hanging from the mast of one of his own ships, in retribution for the atrocities he and his men had committed at Portsmouth.

Despite his own victories at sea, Edward III still regarded his fleet primarily as a means of transporting his army to where the really decisive battles would be actually had. Two lines of a poem supposedly by Adam De Moleyns, Bishop of Chichester, in 1436 or 1437, refer to a gold noble of 1344, in Edward III's reign:

For four things our Noble sheweth to me
King, Ship and Swerd, and power of the See.

But these lines suggest that the poet had a much better understanding than Edward or any of the Plantagenet Kings of the influence sea power could exert upon history.

In 1343, when Edward III was assembling a fleet to invade France, Portsmouth contributed five ships and ninety mariners to the 'Sowth Flete'. The invasion was postponed until July the following year, when between one thousand and one thousand one hundred large ships and five hundred small craft had assembled in the Solent. After reviewing his fleet, the King embarked from the Isle of Wight on 10 July and sailed the next day, accompanied by the Prince of Wales, many noblemen, ten thousand archers, four thousand men-at-arms and a number of Welsh and Irish footmen. The King landed at La Hogue on the 12th and the campaign which followed led to the victory at Crecy on 25 August.

The French continued to raid Portsmouth later in the fourteenth century until, in 1385, Portsmouth joined with Dartmouth to retaliate. The citizens of Portsmouth fitted out at their own expense a small squadron which not only beat off the French, but crossed to the Seine and there sank four French ships and captured four more, including a barge containing twenty thousand florins.

Seventy-five years after Crecy, another fleet assembled in the Solent under another King before another great victory. Henry V always took a great deal of interest in his Navy. He ordered large ships to be laid down, such as the *Holy Ghost*, the *Grace Dieu* and the *Trinity Royal*.

In 1415, Henry V began upon a campaign which he intended would enforce his claim to the throne of France. He embarked at Portchester in the *Trinity Royal* on Saturday, 10 August 1415, and ordered her yard to be hoisted to the middle of her mast, as a signal that he was ready for sea, and that all ships in the neighbouring ports were to join his fleet.

Before sailing, on 11 August, the King reviewed his fleet of one thousand four hundred vessels — ships, carracks, barges and ballingers — carrying his army of some six thousand men-at-arms and twenty-four thousand archers. This was very probably the first Royal Naval Review in any modern sense of the term.

Fair stood the wind for France and the fleet crossed without opposition, entering the Seine on the afternoon of Tuesday, 13 August. It besieged and took Harfleur before going on to the historic victory at Agincourt on St Crispin's Day, 25 October 1415. However, the tables were turned in the following year, when Portsmouth had the humiliating experience of seeing the English fleet blockaded in the harbour by a French marauding squadron.

Throughout the Navy's history, periods of

success and naval expenditure have been followed by times of neglect. After an expedition was over or an emergency had passed, ships reverted to trade or were sold off. When Henry V died in 1422 there were over thirty vessels of 400 to 600 tons but the Council of Regency for his only son, the nine-month-old infant Henry VI, sold off almost all the ships. By 1430, the Navy had only the *Trinity Royal*, *Grace Dieu* and *Jesus*, all dismantled, unrigged and laid up at Bursledon.

Sailors have always been suspicious of those who feed and pay them. In January 1449, discontent over pay led to murder. Adam de Moleyns, Bishop of Chichester, and author of *The Libel of English Policie*, was sent to Portsmouth by the King to pay 'certain soldiers and shipmen for their wages', those wages being considerably overdue. But, according to the chronicle, 'so it happened that with boisterous language and also for abridging of their wages, he fell in variance with them and they fell on him and cruelly there killed him.'

To make the murder even more heinous, 'there' was actually outside the Domus Dei where the Bishop had been conducting a service. As punishment, the Pope imposed upon all the people of Portsmouth, not just the murderers, the 'Greater Excommunication'. This prohibited the celebration of the Mass in the district, the ringing of church bells, the public saying of the liturgy, and the solemn burial of the dead. The Excommunication was not lifted until April 1508.

In 1415, Henry V had ordered a tower to be built for the defence of the town and the ships. Work began on this, the Round Tower, in 1417, but it was not finished for another ten years. In 1431, work began on a tower on the Gosport side of the harbour.

Henry V also ordered land up harbour from the Pond of the Abbess to be bought for the enlargement of the dockyard, to be called 'The King's Dock'. A 'dock' in those days was made by digging a trench in the mud of the harbour or the river estuary somewhere near the high water mark. The ship was placed in the trench and walls of timber and brush, banked with mud and clay, were then built up to keep most of the water out at high tide.

This traditional method of 'wet docking' persisted until the later years of the fifteenth century when Henry VII, the first Tudor King, ascended the throne after the defeat and death of Richard III at Bosworth Field in 1485. Henry VII never had a large fleet, but he knew that the strength of a country was reflected by the strength of its fleet and he acted upon that principle in a way that was new in England.

Henry seems to have appreciated at once Portsmouth's geographical advantages as a naval base. He began by improving the fortifications, so that it might be a secure base for a permanent Navy. In 1494, he paid £2,068.11s.1d. to William Cope in part payment for the construction of the Square Tower (at the end of the High Street) and the adjacent bulwark. In 1495, he instructed Robert Brygandine to make a dry graving dock at Portsmouth — deciding, once and for all, the town's destiny as a naval port.

It was the first dry dock ever known in this country. There is still a mystery over where the King got the original idea. One reference to Sir Reginald Bray, who was the King's Treasurer at War and the architect of St George's Chapel at Windsor and the Henry VII Chapel at Westminster, records that the original supervisor, John Nest, was superseded after three weeks by Robert Brygandine, on Bray's orders.

This suggests that Sir Reginald was in charge as the chief architect of the dock and the work was carried out from his plans, but it is not known whether those plans were original or based on plans for some other dock at home or abroad. Brygandine, the Clerk of the Ships, who supervised the work on site, was not an engineer. Yet, from the start, the work seems to have gone forward as though building a dry dock was a normal occurrence and everybody concerned knew exactly what he had to do.

The work began on 14 June 1495 and took forty-six weeks. The first twenty-four weeks, until 29 November, were spent in building the dock itself. Work stopped during the winter. It started again on 2 February 1496, going on until 17 April, during which time the dock gates were made and fixed in position. There was then a long pause after the gates had been installed, until 8 July 1497, which suggests the dock had some unforeseen weakness in its structure. Certainly, eleven weeks from 8 July were spent in 'ffortyfying' the dock head by backing it, and probably the dock itself, with 664 tons of stone and gravel.

King Henry VII's Inventories give many details of the dock's construction and materials. The main body of the dock was made of wood. At least 158 loads were brought from the Royal forests for the cost of carting it, and it is possible some wood was given by neighbouring landowners. Very little of the dock's materials were obtained locally. Almost everything was bought elsewhere and brought to the site. Four tons of iron were purchased and converted to bolts, bars and spikes. There was a forge on site, and at least one storehouse. There was also one 'Ingyn to draw water owte of the seid dokke', but buckets were still needed as well.

The gates required 113 loads of timber, sawn up into 4,524 feet of plank. In one case, materials were used 'as well for the inner as the uttermost gates of the dokke aforesaid'. From the wage bills, it seems that an average of from thirty-eight to thirty-nine men were at work during the twenty-four weeks the dock was in hand. Only seven or eight men were employed by the week on the gates and, apparently, only two on the 'fortifying'.

Portsmouth dock was built entirely by native English labour. No experts from abroad worked on it. There were no accidents during the building and no undue delays after that initial interval for 'fortifying'. The total cost was £193 0s.6 3/4d.

The first ship known to have gone into the new dock, on 25 May 1496, was the 600 ton Sovereign, built under the supervision of Sir Reginald Bray partly from the remains of the broken-up Grace a Dieu. Docking and undocking her were evidently major labour-intensive undertakings. One hundred and twenty men were employed by 'a day and a neght' in addition to the ship's crew to bring the Sovereign into dock. For undocking, twenty men worked for twenty-nine days 'breking up of the dokke hede at every tide both day and night weying up of the piles and shorys and dyggyng of the clay and other Rubbysh bytwene the gates for hauyng owte of the Soueraigne'.

The Sovereign was in dock for more than eight months, until 31 January 1497, almost certainly because there was no pressing need for her services and it was generally thought that a ship lasted longer in dock than afloat. She was shortly hired for a trading voyage to the Levant.

The next ship in dock was the Regent, of about the same size, built under the supervision of Sir Richard Guldeford. For her, there was a much greater need for urgency. She was only in dock from 4 March to 23 April 1497. She was at Portsmouth on 1 May and on the 14th she became the Earl of Surrey's flagship in the fleet operating against James IV of Scotland.

Henry VII was a King with the heart and soul of a merchant. He believed in making every penny count and, whenever possible, making other people, and especially his noblemen, pay the bills. He is credited with being the founder of the Royal Navy. In fact, although he did lay down the foundations for building and repairing ships at Portsmouth, he built few ships himself, preferring to hire Spanish ships instead, because their rates were lower.

Apart from the Sovereign and the Regent, Henry VII seems to have built only two other small warships in his reign, both described in the Inventories as the 'Kynges New Barke': the Sweepstake, built at Portsmouth, and the Mary Fortune, also almost certainly built there. They cost £120 3s.2d. and £110 17s. respectively in 1497. They were three-masted, with a main topmast, a mizzen mast, a sprit sail on the bowsprit, and eighty and sixty oars respectively. Sweepstake's crew was given in 1513 as sixty-six men and four gunners.

Although they had oars, and Sweepstake was sometimes actually called 'The King's rowbarge', they were not galleys. They were ships, smaller but similar to Sovereign and Regent, which could use sweeps when necessary. There was no armament in their inventories but they certainly carried powder and shot, probably for hand-guns. They both served in 1497 in the fleet under Robert, Lord Willoughby de Broke, against the Scots. *Mary Fortune* used up fourteen bows and thirty sheaves of arrows, out of the thirty and sixty of each on board, and all her powder, shot, lead and tampions, while *Sweepstake* expended twenty-five of her sixty sheaves of arrows, and all her powder, shot and lead.

The King thought it suspicious that both ships used up the exact totals of many of the types of stores supplied to them. The sailors blamed this on articles 'ravenously despoiled' by the army and 400 lb of powder taken by the gunners 'by clayme of duty'.

Sweepstake survived into Henry VIII's navy, and was rebuilt in 1511, being renamed *Katherine Pomegranate* in honour of Katherine of Aragon. (The pomegranate formed part of the coat of arms of the city of Granada; the capture of Granada from the Moors was a resounding victory for Christendom and after Katherine of Aragon's arrival in England, the pomegranate was often used as a badge).

In 1523, another *Sweepstake* joined the Navy. Although *Sweepstake* and *Mary Fortune* could be, and were, hired out as merchant ships, they can fairly be said to have been the first two men-of-war to be built at Portsmouth.

The next two, built in 1509, were the *Peter Pomegranate* and the *Mary Rose*. *Peter Pomegranate*, the smaller of the two at about 400 tons, was armed with sixty obsolete serpentynes (small calibre swivel guns, weighing about 250 lb), but the 600 ton *Mary Rose* was, with the recently rebuilt and re-armed *Sovereign*, one of the most formidable warships of her time. She had seventy-nine guns, besides another six in her tops: thirty-three serpentynes, twenty-six stone guns (i.e. firing stone shot), ten murderers, five brass curtalls and five brass falcons. The curtail, or curtow, was a heavy gun of some 3000 lb, until then used only on land as a siege weapon. *Mary Rose* and *Sovereign* were the first English ships to mount curtalls and their use at sea was a considerable advance in naval gunnery.

Named after Mary Tudor, Henry VIII's sister, *Mary Rose* was 122 feet 4 inches long at the water-line, 37 feet 5 inches in the beam and drew 14 foot 9 inches. She was strongly built, with wooden diagonal braces in her hull, and almost entirely of oak but with her 105-foot long keel made of two pieces of elm scarfed together. She had four masts: fore, main, mizzen and bonaventure mizzen; and five decks: hold, orlop, main, upper and gun decks, with guns on the top three decks, firing through ports on the main and upper decks. She had a crew of twenty gunners, one hundred and eighty sailors and two hundred soldiers.

She was an excellent sailer and could point closer to the wind than any other ship in Henry VIII's fleet. Lord Edward Howard, whose flagship she was in the war against France of 1512-13, wrote to the King of her as 'your good ship, the flower I trow of all ships that ever sailed'.

The King himself rode down to Portsmouth in August 1512 to review the twenty-five ships which had been assembled to reinforce Lord Edward Howard, who was already cruising off the coast of Brittany. Like all Henry's ceremonial events, the review held on 2 August was a spectacular occasion. The King appointed Sir Thomas Knivet, Master of his Horse, captain of the *Regent*, with Sir John Carew of Devonshire as second-in-command, and Sir Charles Brandon to command the *Sovereign*, with Sir Henry Guilford. Sixty of the 'tallest yeomen of the King's garde' were put in the *Sovereign's* crew and 'many other gentlemen were made captains'.

Before they left, the King gave all his captains a great banquet at which 'everyone swore to another to defend, aid and comfort one another without failing, and this they promised before the King, which committed them to God'. Then, with the sailors all specially dressed in white gaberdine suits, emblazoned with the badge of the Tudor rose and a red cross on a white ground on breast and back; and all the ships flying their flags, pennants and bannerets showing the rose and the pomegranate, the royal arms of England and emblems of the saints at their mastheads and yard-arms; and so, 'with great noise of minstrelsy', they sailed to war.

Howard, with his reinforced fleet, met the French fleet of thirty-nine sail off Brest on 10

August. During the battle the *Regent* grapped with the 'great carrack of Brest' the *Marie la Cordeliere*, which either caught fire after a gunpowder explosion or, as one account says, 'a varlet gunner, being desperate' set fire to the powder. The flames spread rapidly to the *Regent* which was to leeward and both ships were destroyed. Only one hundred and twenty of the eight hundred crew of the *Regent* were saved and only twenty Frenchmen of the reputed one thousand five hundred on board *Marie La Cordeliere*.

Henry VIII's response to this disaster was typical: 'on hearing of the loss of the *Regent*, (he) caused a great ship to be made, such another as was never seen before in England, and called '*Henry Grace de Dieu.*'

The *Henry Grace a Dieu* was laid down at Woolwich in the autumn of 1512, and completed and commissioned in 1514. She was of 1000 tons, with a complement of four hundred soldiers, two hundred and sixty sailors and forty gunners, and armed with over one hundred and twenty guns. She also was a good sailer; Admiral Sir William Fitzwilliam reported to the King in 1522 that she sailed as well as, or better, than any ship in the fleet, 'weathering all save the *Mary Rose*'.

In 1523, the *Henry Grace a Dieu* docked in Portsmouth, after the dry dock had been specially enlarged. It was an occasion of some ceremony, with the ship flying flags and banners and streamers from her masts and upperworks. Of her ship's company of sailors and gunners, more than half had come round from the Thames in her. The ship had cost £8,708 5s. 3d., of which about a quarter had been given by peers, private persons and religious bodies. Representatives of these were present to witness the docking, together with gentlemen and yeomen of the district, dockyard officials and workmen.

The ship's arrival was timed for one hour before high water so that she could enter the dock on the last of the flood tide with the maximum depth of water. About a thousand mariners and workmen were involved in the work which took all day, during which the workers consumed eight quarters of beef, forty-two dozen loaves of bread and four tuns of beer.

After the actual docking, the shoring and filling of the dock head and pumping out the dock took some days. As there were very few skilled artisans resident in Portsmouth, the shipwrights and others came from all over the country, from Plymouth, Dartmouth and the west country, and from Ipswich, Yarmouth and Hull on the east coast. They received a half-penny a mile and a shilling a day travelling expenses. The carpenters, 141 of them, were given free coats, which cost the King two shillings and fivepence each. The average wage was ninepence a day. Cooks were hired to cook quantities of cod, hake, herring and oatmeal. Beds for two or three man, and sometimes ten, were provided under rough shelters.

Henry Grace a Dieu was a splendid ship, and she is forever associated with Henry VIII's name and reign. But she was only one of eighty-five warships which Henry either built (forty-six), bought (twenty-six) or acquired as prizes (thirteen). He also built thirteen 20-ton 'rowbarges', making a total of ninety-eight warships of various types and sizes added to the Navy in Henry VIII's reign. Of 7,780 men in the fleet in 1547, 1,885 were soldiers, 5,136 mariners and 759 gunners.

Henry took a close interest in guns and gunnery and during his reign more and ever smaller warships were armed with an ever greater variety of guns. He had a 'pond made and cast' at Deptford large enough to make the *Mary Rose*, which were the beginnings of that yard, and founded Woolwich yard, which more or less grew up around the *Henry Grace a Dieu*.

Henry introduced and enforced new regulations for the control and manoeuvring of fleets at sea and the discipline of their crews. He reformed the administration of the Navy, changing it from the medieval pattern under one official to a committee, known as the Principal Officers of the Navy, and later the Navy Board, a system of Admiralty which, albeit in a greatly changed form, exists today.

He confirmed Portsmouth's position as the premier naval port of the kingdom. Nine acres of land were purchased for the Dockyard, at 20 shillings an acre, in 1527. Of fifty-three ships in the Navy at Henry's death in

1547, forty-one were based at Portsmouth. To supply his sailors with beer, he ordered four great brewing houses, the 'Lyon', 'Fragon', 'White Hart' and 'Rose' to be built in Portsmouth on the north-east side of the town near a fresh water spring. To improve Portsmouth's defences, in 1522 he had a great chain of iron, with links three feet nine inches in length and three inches in cross-section, stretched from the Round Tower across to Blockhouse. Its weight was supported by lighters and it was raised and lowered by capstans.

John Leland made his celebrated 'Itinerary' in Henry's reign, between 1536 and 1542, and probably visited Portsmouth in about 1540. He said: "The land here, on the east side of Portsmouth Haven, runneth further by a great way straight into the sea, by south-east from the haven mouth, than it doth at the west point. There is, at this point of the haven, Portsmouth town, and a great round tower, almost double in quantity and strength to that which is on the west side of the haven,

right against it; and here is a mighty chain of iron to draw from tower to tower. About a quarter of a mile above this tower is a great dock for ships, and in this dock lieth part of the ribs of the *Henri Grace a Dieu* (a mysterious reference; at that time the ship was still complete and operational), one of the biggest ships that have been made *in hominum memoria* (in the memory of man). There be above this dock creeks in this part of the haven . . . The town is bare, and little occupied in time of peace".

Under Henry VIII the Navy took the first steps towards becoming a powerful offensive instrument of policy in its own right rather than an ancillary and a mere means of transport for the army. Thus, in his own way, Henry VIII is much more entitled to be called the Founder of the Royal Navy than his father. Yet it was Henry, for all his flamboyance and authoritarian pride, who had the humiliation of watching one of his ships sink before his eyes in one of the most dramatic mishaps in all naval history.

Chapter 3

The *Mary Rose* was rebuilt, uprated to 700 tons, and armed with new cast bronze muzzle-loading guns in 1536.

She was in Henry VIII's fleet in 1544 when, in alliance with the Emperor Charles V of Spain, he was once more at war with France and Scotland. Henry himself landed at Calais on 14 July with an army of thirty thousand men and besieged Boulogne, which surrendered on 14 September.

In October, Sir Thomas Seymour was appointed vice admiral in command of a fleet to take winter stores to the garrison of Boulogne, who were themselves now besieged by the French. After delivering the stores he was to cruise off Etaples on the river Canche, capture or burn French vessels and generally to cause the French the maximum annoyance. However, Seymour's ships were blown away by storms and he had to return to Portsmouth with the loss of all his boats and two storeships. Henry was furious but accepted Seymour's explanation. However, Boulogne had no stores.

Meanwhile, the French King Francis I decided to retaliate by seizing the Isle of Wight, going on to attack Portsmouth and Southampton, and eventually to march on London. He began to assemble every available warship on the Normandy coast. By the end of spring 1545 he had a fleet of some one hundred and fifty large merchant vessels (*gros vaisseaux ronds*) and sixty oared coasters (*flouins*), under the Admiral or France, Claude d'Annibault, Baron de Retz. He also summoned from the Mediterranean twenty-five galleys under Paulin, Baron de la Garde, and Leone Strozzi, Prior of Capua, Admiral of the Galleys of Rhodes, and the best galley commander of his time.

Realising the danger, Henry VIII decided that attack was the best form of defence. He dispatched his fleet on a raid along the French coast. It was commanded by the Lord High Admiral, John Dudley, Lord Lisle (later Earl of Warwick, Duke of Northumberland, and Lady Jane Grey's father-in-law). Lisle entered the Seine estuary, where the French lay, and exchanged shots, but it came on to blow and both sides drew off, the French galleys because of the weather and the English because of shoals. Lord Lisle returned to Portsmouth.

The French fleet sailed from Le Havre, Honfleur, Harfleur and other ports in the Seine estuary on 6 July, carrying a vast invasion force of more than sixty thousand men. As one historian commented: 'So great a host had not appeared upon the Narrow Seas for centuries'. The Emperor Charles was no longer an ally. England stood alone.

Henry VIII had already had news of the French invasion fleet. As a contemporary account said, he 'fretted and his teeth stood on an edge to see the bravery of his enemies to come so near his nose, and he not able to encounter with them, whereby the beacons were set on fire throughout the whole coast.' The King's ships were ordered to Portsmouth with all speed.

Henry himself left Greenwich on 12 July. He and his retinue arrived in Portsmouth on 17 July and were billeted either in the town or under canvas on the common. The English had about sixty ships and some small craft, and sixteen thousand men, many of them assembled on Southsea Common. The guns of the town's defences, including the newly completed Southsea Castle, were all manned. The watchword in the fleet that night was

'God Save The King'. The answer was 'Long to reign over us'.

The French arrived off the Isle of Wight on 18 July, and d'Annibault sent Polain in with four galleys to reconnoitre the English fleet. During the day, d'Annibault brought his entire fleet round St Helens Point. His ships stretched in a long line from Brading Harbour almost across to Ryde. That evening, fourteen English ships stood out on the light wind to cut off the French galleys, which at once fell back towards their main fleet.

Sir George Carew, Vice Admiral to Lord Lisle and captain of *Mary Rose*. From a portrait by Holbein.

The King was dining with Lisle on board the flagship the *Henry Grace a Dieu*. Present were Sir Peter Carew, who flew his flag in the *Venetian* of 700 tons and four hundred and fifty men, Sir George Carew, the Vice Admiral, flying his flag in the *Mary Rose*, and Sir Gawain Carew. Whilst at dinner, the King 'willed someone to go up to the top, and see whether he could see anything at the seas. The word was no sooner spoken but that Peter Carew was as forward; and forthwith climbed up to the top of the ship and there sitting the King asked of him what news? who told him that he had sight of three to four ships but as he thought they were merchants; but yet was not long but he had ascried a great number, and then he cried out to the King that there was, as he thought, a fleet of men-of-war'.

Henry ordered 'the board to be taken up', told everybody to go to their ships, and sent for a 'log boat' to take him ashore. He had 'secret talks' with Lisle and with Sir George Carew, after which he took from his neck a 'great whistle' of gold on a chain and presented it to Carew, with 'many good and comfortable words'.

The rest of the English ships weighed and slowly approached the French. Some desultory shots were exchanged at long range. The English tried to lure the French into the shallows on the Spit Sand, and within range of the town's guns, but d'Annibault refused to be drawn, and both sides broke off as night fell.

D'Annibault retired to St Helen's Road, where he found his biggest ship, *La Maitresse*, making so much water he had to send her back to Le Havre for docking. During the night he recast his battle plan, dividing his ships into three squadrons, himself commanding thirty ships in the centre, with two squadrons, of thirty-six ships each, on the right and left. The galleys under Polain were to form a separate striking force, in the van of the main fleet, with orders to engage the English ships closely and to fall back so as to try and draw them out into the open.

On 19 July, the sun rose on a perfect English summer's morning. It was slack water and flat calm. The sea lay like a sheet of shining glass. There was not a breath of wind. The sails hung flat and motionless on the English yards. Such conditions were ideal for the French galleys and for an hour, during which they were handled very brilliantly, they had some excellent shooting practise against the stationary hulls of the English. By some accounts, the *Henry Grace a Dieu* was one of the English ships badly damaged.

At last a brisk wind sprang up off the land and the English ships began to weigh anchor.

The *Mary Rose* had just weighed when she was seen to heel slightly. She was manned and stored for war, with a full complement of men and a full outfit of guns and shot. She would be drawing her maximum draught. Her lower guns might already have been run out for action. Whether or not the order was ever given to shut the gun-ports, it was certainly never carried out. Water flooded in through the openings and the ship rapidly filled and sank. Sir Walter Raleigh, writing in the early years of the next century but very probably using the testimony of eye-witnesses, said that *Mary Rose*: 'by a little sway of the ship in casting about, her ports being within sixteen inches of the water, was overset and lost'.

There seems also to have been some insub-ordination. Sir Gawain Carew, passing the *Mary Rose* in his own ship at that moment, called out to Sir George 'asking him how he did? who answered, that he had a sort of knaves whom he could not rule'. It also seems possible that the *Mary Rose* suffered from what in modern terms would be called the 'too many Chiefs and not enough Indians' syndrome. Nobody thought it their duty to see to such mundane matters as shutting gun-ports when going to sea. It seems the crew had been selected for the *Mary Rose*, the Vice Admiral's ship, because they were especially good sailors and therefore, as Sir Peter Carew said of his brother's crew, they 'so maligned and disdained one the other that refusing to do that which they should do were careless to do that which was most needful and necessary and so contending in envy perished in for-wardness'.

There were only about forty survivors. Sir George Carew and most of the four hundred men on board were drowned, many of them trapped between decks. Watching from the shore were Henry VIII, and Lady Carew, who fell in a dead faint at the sight. 'All over, and the cry of mun, and the screech of mun,' went one account of the loss. 'Oh sir! up to the very heavens! And the King he screeched right out like any maid, 'Oh, my gentlemen! Oh, my gallant men!' And as she lay on her beam ends, sirs, and just "a-settling, the very last souls I seen was that man's father and that

man's. Iss! Iss! drowned like rattens! Drowned like rattens!"

Meanwhile a somewhat anticlimatic battle was in progress. As the English ships advanced on the wind, so the French galleys retreated. They had been ordered to lure the English on and they had, in any case, the galleys' dread of being rammed and having their oars broken by the great beaks of the sailing ships.

The galleys were very adroitly handled and all rowed clear. Then, to their amazement and consternation, they were pursued by a flotilla of small 'roo-barges' (row-barges) which shot out from behind the larger ships. Galleys had no guns aft, so the roo-barges followed close astern, firing into their unprotected poops. Only the great Strozzi himself turned his galley and chased his tiny tormentor, but in a moment the roo-barges had gone about and withdrawn out of danger.

D'Annibault landed troops on the Isle of Wight, hoping Lisle would respond. But Lisle refused to be drawn. D'Annibault then con-sidered whether he could attack Lisle, but decided it was not feasible and anchored off Bricklesome Bay for the night. Lisle, too, considered whether he could make use of a westerly wind to drive the French down on to the Owers sands, but the wind dropped and so, also, was the plan.

D'Annibault re-embarked his troops after they had looted and burned a few villages. He decided, wisely, not to land in force and carry on with the invasion while the English fleet was still in being. He retired to France. Lisle did not follow. There the invasion ended for the moment.

French historians, understandably, claimed later the *Mary Rose* was sunk by the French, either by gunfire or by the galleys, but there is no doubt that her loss was an accident. It had been a mortifying experience for Henry VIII who had watched from Southsea Castle one of his best ships sinking and the French galleys attacking with apparent impunity.

In an attempt to deal with the French galleys, Henry took what seems to be the reactionary decision to have his own galleys or 'oared pieces'. By August 1545, the French fleet under d'Annibault was once more at sea, cruising up and down the Channel. They were met off Shoreham on 15 August by Henry's fleet, commanded once more by Lisle.

This time, however, the fleet also had a windward vanguard squadron under Captain William Tyrrell consisting of the new galleasses powered by sail and by oars, *Grand Mistress* (Admiral) and *Anne Gallant* (Vice Admiral), the *Galley Subtille* and the *Greyhound*, with nine Royal pinnaces, twenty pinnaces from the Western Ports and seven boats from Rye. The English fleet was Tyrrell's forty sail of 'galleasses, shallops and boats of war', twenty-four heavy ships in the van, under Sir Thomas Clere, Vice Admiral of England, and Lisle the Lord Admiral himself, with forty sail in the 'battle': one hundred and four sail in all.

The French attacked with Paulin's galleys but, as Lord Lisle reported to the King, 'your Highness's shallops and rowing pieces did their parts well, but especially the *Mistress* and the *Anne Gallant* did so handle the galleys, as well with their sides as with their prows, that your great-ships in a manner had little to do.'

The only English casualties were some of Tyrrell's oars broken. D'Annibault did not get up to support his galleys until the evening but after a shift of wind both sides anchored. Lisle wanted the wind to strengthen so that it would favour his ships and disadvantage the galleys, but in the morning the French had vanished. Lisle gave chase but could not catch them.

It seemed an inconclusive action but it had long term effects. Francis I did not attempt another invasion. Also, it seems to have been the very first battle in which English ships fired broadsides in action. In 1574, a Spanish agent in England wrote to the Governor of the Netherlands about the 'new' English tactics. 'If the fleets come to hostilities it would be well to give orders, when they (the Spaniards) approach them (the English) that the ordnance flush with the water should be at once discharged broadside on and so damage their hulls and confuse them with the smoke. *This is their own way of fighting, and I have many times seen them do it to the French thirty years ago'.* Thus, clearly these forgotten sea

battles in the waters off Portsmouth laid the foundations for the great age of Elizabethan naval tactics under Drake and Hawkins.

As for *Mary Rose*, it appears that Henry gave orders almost at once that she should be salvaged. She lay in some forty feet of water, which was not an insuperable depth for recovery. By 1 August, plans had been made to pass cables down from hulks and through her ports, or fasten them to her masts, and then hoist her bodily. On 5 August, Lisle reported to Sir William Paget, a Secretary of State, that her yards and sails had been removed and 'to her masts there is tied three cables with other engines to weigh her up and on every side of her a hulk to set her upright'.

Two days later there was a general air of confidence at Portsmouth, and a feeling that *Mary Rose* would be raised within twenty-four hours. But, on 9 August, Lisle was reporting that the 'Italians' who were weighing *Mary Rose* were now saying that they could not recover her, for they 'had already broken her foremast'. They now wanted to try another method, to drag her into shallow water (evidently by hulks, using tidal lifts).

This was no more successful, and work was suspended, after an expenditure of some £500, which probably included payments to Peter Paul, one of the Italians, for recovering some of the guns. It certainly included the cost of the 22 tuns of beer consumed by the salvagemen (a tun being 252 gallons). Finally, after four years, in August 1549, salvage and hope were abandoned. (*Mary Rose* lay undisturbed until 1836 when two divers, John and Charles Deane, rediscovered the wreck site off Brading and recovered several guns, including a bronze demi-cannon, probably made at a foundry at Salisbury Place, London, by Archangelo de Arcanis in 1542).

From the accession of Edward VI in 1547, Portsmouth's position began to decline again. The local economy was still very precarious, being not much more than that of a small rural town. Certainly the dock and its ancillary buildings gave no financial security. It was not only Italians for salvage work who had to be brought in from outside but workers in almost every shipyard craft and trade. Portsmouth began to face stiff and growing competition from the Thames and Medway ports, and especially from Chatham whose dockyard began in the 1550s. In 1547 one Henry Huttoft said that Portsmouth was 'utterly decayed, and no man comes there with victuals and merchandise'.

Misfortunes followed each other. There was plague in the ships at Portsmouth in the autumn of 1545 and in the town in 1563. King Edward VI himself toured Portsmouth in 1552 and found its defence 'weak in comparison of what it ought to be'; however, he did review the fleet. The Navy storehouses were burned down in June 1557, and again in August 1576. By April 1586, the Mayor, Aldermen and people were petitioning Queen Elizabeth to be excused paying customs and other dues because of 'the great ruin and decay of the town'. There is no record of any reply from the Queen. It took another threat of invasion to restore Portsmouth fortunes, at least to some extent.

The decade of the 1580s, like the 1930s, was a time of increasing tension. In 1582, Queen Elizabeth reviewed a squadron at Spithead, where yards were manned and gun salutes fired for the first time. Two years later, work on the fortifications of Portsmouth was being hurried ahead.

In 1584, Portsmouth was the chief rendezvous for the forces being mobilised for the defence of the Narrow Seas. There were twenty-one of the Queen's ships in the harbour and ten pinnaces, manned by 3,559 mariners and 1,646 soldiers. The pace of preparations for war accelerated. By February 1587, eight hundred men were employed on Portsmouth's fortifications, making new defence lines and installing additional guns sent down from the Tower of London. To clear lines of fire, all hedges and other obstructions were removed for a distance of forty to fifty yards from the ramparts. A new wharf was built in the dockyard.

The Marquess of Winchester wrote to the Council in February 1587, drawing attention to the need to strengthen the defences of Browne's Down and Stokes Bay 'where 1,000 ships might land at one instant 30,000 men'. The Earl of Sussex, Lord Lieutenant of Hampshire and in charge of the general defence of the county, also wrote to ask that the tower and Platform might be repaired. They were in such a state, he said, that at the Queen's Coronation he 'durst not shoot off one piece, the Tower was so old and rotten'. The Earl personally supervised the drilling of the trained bands. On 20 November 1587, every trained band in the Hundred of Portsmouth took part in the first ever Volunteer Review at Portsmouth.

Three Queen's ships, *Hope, Nonpareil* and *Advice*, were fitted out at Portsmouth and joined Drake in January 1588 when he called on his way from the Thames to Plymouth. But these were Portsmouth's only contribution in ships to the Armada Campaign. In April, Lord Howard, the Lord Admiral, was complaining to Burghley of the shortage of victuals in Portsmouth.

On 5 July 1588, Mr Gilbert Lee, captain of the *Rat of Wight*, arrived in Portsmouth to report that on 25 May (by the Spanish calendar) one hundred and three score sail of small and great ships had departed from Lisbon. Portsmouth's defences, incomplete though they might be, were manned. Some merchant ships put to sea to join the Lord Admiral. On 19 July, the beacons on the Isle of Wight announced that the Spanish Armada had arrived in the Channel. The signal was repeated by a fire in a cresset on the tower of St Thomas, Portsmouth, and by another beacon on Portsdown Hill. Next day, sixteen thousand men arrived in Portsmouth to man the defences. Town and people were astir as they had not been since Henry VIII's arrival before another threatened invasion more than forty years earlier.

After engagements off Plymouth, on Sunday 21 July, and off Portland on Monday, 22nd, there was a brisk encounter between Drake's *Revenge* and the straggling Rostock hulk, *El Gran Grifon*, flagship of the supply squadron, west of the Isle of Wight on 24 July. The Duke of Medina Sidonia had to send galleasses back to rescue her.

On that Wednesday evening, 24 July, the Armada and Howard's ships lay becalmed, and quite close to each other, off the Needles. (Wednesday, 24 July was Wednesday, 3 Au-

Sir Francis Drake.

gust in the Calendar introduced by Pope Gregory XIII in 1582, used by the Spaniards but not by the English; English dates are therefore ten days in arrears, although the days of the week remain the same).

Four days of fighting had left the English ships very short of ammunition. Howard send 'divers barks and pinnaces unto the shore' for supplies. He obtained some but not enough. The English ships were also very short of direction. Until then the battles had developed more or less as individual ship's captains had decided. There was little sense of the ships being components of a corporate fleet or squadron.

That night, 24 July, Howard held a council of war on board his flagship *Ark Royal*. As a result, he organised his fleet in four squadrons. He himself as the Admiral was in the centre. Drake, as the senior vice admiral, was on the right or seaward end of the line, with Hawkins, Rear Admiral, in *Victory*, inshore and to port of him. On the port landward wing was Frobisher, the junior flag officer, in the great galleon *Triumph*.

A critical point in the campaign was now approaching. The English reasoned that Medina Sidonia was certain to make some move into the Solent and seize the Isle of Wight. It would provide him with a large harbour of refuge whilst he established communications with the Duke of Parma. He could safely wait there until he received word that Parma was ready. Once past the Isle of Wight, there was nowhere else he could take shelter. He could land troops on the Isle of Wight, as d'Annibault had done, and possibly invest Portsmouth or Southampton. He had with him the flower of the Spanish army, the finest infantry in Europe. Finally, the political advantages for his King of having some firm foothold on English soil would be enormous.

King Philip II of Spain's instructions to Medina Sidonia had been specific and inflexible: he was to proceed directly and join the Duke of Parma. However, it seems that Medina Sidonia's advisers strongly urged him to capture the Isle of Wight. It seems that he did make some move in that direction, although his own account is silent on the point.

Dawn broke on Thursday, 25 July with the Armada off Dunnose Head and both fleets still almost becalmed in very light airs. Soon the wind picked up a little from the southwest and the Armada was under way, keeping as close to the shore as it could. The English followed, intending somehow during the day to slip as many ships as possible through to landward of the Armada and block the entrance to the Solent. The cliffs and beaches of the Isle of Wight were packed with spectators, and some troops. For years, the people of England had dreaded the possibility of a Spanish invasion. It seemed to many that that day might have arrived at last.

At dawn, the ships of Frobisher's landward squadron were off Dunnose Head, to the north and east of the Armada, and ahead of its van. As the light strengthened, two ships, the *Santa Ana* and the Portuguese galleon *San Luis*, could been seen straggling astern of the Armada. They were engaged by Hawkins and then by Howard. Medina Sidonia sent ships including his own flagship, the *San Martin*, back to help the stragglers.

San Martin was herself hotly engaged by Frobisher and it was while he was thus occupied that a breeze sprang up from the south-west, leaving the *Triumph* in the Armada's lee and cut off. It was a perilous situation for Frobisher and very similar to one he had experienced off Portland a few days earlier.

The great galleon *Triumph* was, of course, a tremendous prize for the Spanish ships. Gleefully they crowded on sail to bear down and capture her. *Triumph*, still becalmed, got out her longboats to try and pull herself clear of danger. Lord Sheffield's *White Bear* and the *Elizabeth Jonas* came round the Armada's flank to assist *Triumph*. Even so, *Triumph* might still have been taken but, luckily for her, a wind suddenly got up, veered and freshened. Shaking out her sails and casting off her boats, *Triumph* got under way and slipped clear.

Although there is no admission in the Spanish accounts that Medina Sidonia did divert from the course ordered by Philip and entered St Helens Road, it seems very likely that he did, perhaps even reaching as far as Spithead. The wind freshened and stayed in the south-west, ideally for his purpose, and then as he steered for Spithead the wind changed, again very suitably, to north-east. He was followed and harried as he went by Howard, who must have thought his worst fears of invasion were about to be realised and by Frobisher. Then, seemingly inexplicably, Medina Sidonia turned back to the south-east and appeared to abandon any attempt to reach Spithead.

Hawkins and Drake, commanding the two most southerly and seaward English squadrons, also drop out of the English narratives for a time, but it was certainly those two who attacked the Armada's right wing later in the forenoon. The wind had backed to south-west again and Drake and Hawkins, by steering out to sea, gained the weather gauge of the Armada.

The brunt of the attack was borne by the Portuguese galleon *San Mateo*, supported by the 52-gun *Florencia*, the most heavily-armed Spanish ship. However, as the battle developed and more ships were involved, *San Mateo* and the other ships were forced backwards, slowly giving ground as they retreated into the middle of the supply squadron which they were escorting, and throwing them into confusion.

Wind, tide and the chivvying and harassing English ships, gradually edged the Armada's seaward wing of the array northwards and eastwards, across the eastern entrance to the Solent, thus making sure they could never now enter the Solent, and driving them ever nearer the dangerous shoals and rocks of the Owers Bank, which stretched out from Selsey Bill. These were the same shoals on which Lord Lisle had intended to drive the French forty years before and it seems clear that this was exactly what Drake and Hawkins now had in mind.

The leading Armada ships were within forty minutes of striking and disaster. The discoloured shoal water ahead, with seas actually breaking over uncovered black rocks, could be clearly seen, when Medina Sidonia noticed, or more likely had his attention drawn, to the imminent danger to his ships. He fired a gun from his flagship and bore away to the south-east. The ships in his landward wing, some of whose captains had already been very reluctant to follow him to the north because they knew and feared the Owers Bank, turned away from Spithead and followed the seaward wing to the south and east.

Medina Sidonia later wrote in his 'Relation', enclosed in a letter to the King, that: 'The Duke seeing that in the proposed assault the advantage was no longer with us, and that we were now near the Isle of Wight, discharged a piece and proceeded on his course, the rest of the Armada following in very good order, the enemy remaining a long way astern.' With this passage, coming immediately after the description of *Triumph's* escape earlier that morning, Medina Sidonia thus slurred over any reference in his official account to his unofficial diversion into the Solent.

By ten o'clock that forenoon, the whole Armada was streaming away to the eastward. With the westerly wind behind them, all hope of their entering the Solent had gone forever. By three in the afternoon, the Armada was out of sight of the Isle of Wight. The gunfire which for some time had been clearly audible in Southsea Castle fell silent for good. With nothing more to see, the watchers on the cliffs began to disperse. The obvious danger past, the volunteer troops in Portsmouth began to disband and return to their homes.

The English ships had forced Medina Sidonia to take the course ordered by his master. The Duke had no choice now but to go on and meet Parma at Calais. It was a great strategic victory, a crucial turning point in the Armada campaign. 'Thanks be to God', wrote Sir George Carey, Governor of the Isle of Wight, to the Earl of Sussex at eight o'clock that night.

The Armada, which was essentially a large convoy, may have been thwarted off the Isle of Wight but it was still intact and still formidable when it reached Calais. It was not until the fireships off Gravelines had broken its formation that the Armada's defeat was finally assured. Portsmouth rejoiced with the rest of the Kingdom at the news that the Armada was fleeing in disarray up the east coast of England, although Portsmouth had actually contributed very little to the victory.

Queen Elizabeth visited Portsmouth on one of her Royal Progresses and stayed for several days in August 1591. In the same year, Portsmouth conferred the Freedom of the Borough on Lord Howard of Effingham in recognition of his services to the Navy and the country.

With the accession of James I of England and VI of Scotland in March 1603, the Navy, that great weapon forged by Henry VIII and wielded so effectively by Elizabeth and her admirals, fell into doting but feeble hands. Ironically, James was greatly interested in the Navy and its ships and actually spent more on the Navy than Elizabeth did, but under Howard of Effingham, now Earl of Nottingham, the Navy was allowed to rot. Howard may have been a capable commander in war; he was an incapable administrator in peace.

The Jacobean Navy was riddled with scandal, and disfigured by fraud, embesslement and maladministration on a scale so massive that it led to commissions of enquiry. Bribery and corruption were rife. Places were bought and sold. Charges for travel and pilotage and stores were grotesquely inflated. Worn-out ships were commissioned to use up stores and to provide places for the dependants of officials, who were themselves corrupt where they were not incompetent.

Portsmouth's fortunes followed this general decline, until it reached its lowest ebb as a naval port. Henry VII's dock fell into decay through disuse and in 1623 Portsmouth suffered the ultimate indignity for a naval port of having the 'great dock' filled up and the dock mouth rammed with rock stones 'for the better preserving of the yard against the violence of the sea'. Portsmouth had no dock for the next thirty years.

King James himself paid an unexpected visit to the Fleet at Portsmouth on 25 August 1623, and dined on board the *Prince Royal*. Named after James' eldest son Henry, Prince of Wales, *Prince Royal* was built at Woolwich and launched in 1610. At 1,200 tons she was the largest ship of James' reign and indeed the largest warship so far built for the Navy. She was also extravagantly and gorgeously decorated with 'curious paintings the like of which was never in any ship before', gilt and painted badges, arms and 'mask heads', and carvings of 'great lions' heads round the ports'. The Prince's cabin was 'very curiously wrought with divers histories'.

In October 1623, the Prince of Wales, later Charles I (his brother Henry having died of fever in November 1612) landed at Portsmouth on his return from France and Spain. James ordered a commemorative bust of the Prince to be placed in a niche on the north wall of the Square Tower in Old Portsmouth. The original inscription, now partly defaced, read 'King Charles the First, after his travels through all France and Spain, and having passed many dangers both by sea and land, he arrived here on the 5th Day of October 1623: there was the greatest applause of joy for his safety throughout the Kingdom that was ever known or heard of'.

The next freeman of Portsmouth, in 1626, was the unlikely figure of King Janes' favourite, George Villiers, Duke of Buckingham, who as Lord High Admiral unexpectedly proved to be one of Portsmouth's greatest benefactors.

Chapter 4

George Villiers, the second son of a Lincolnshire squire, came to London in 1614 aged 22, and first met the King in August that year. He was a good-looking young man and an entertaining companion who soon became a favourite. His face was literally his fortune and in the space of six years he became successively a gentleman of the bedchamber, Master of the King's Horse, a Knight of the Garter, Baron Waddon, Viscount Villiers, then Earl, Marquis and finally Duke of Buckingham.

Buckingham was made Lord High Admiral, an office he particularly wanted although he had no experience of the sea or the Navy, in January 1619. Later that year, James himself was present at Deptford for the launch of two warships, specially named by him the *Happy Entrance* and the *Constant Reformation*, to commemorate Buckingham becoming the Lord High Admiral.

The King gave Buckingham a free hand so far as the Navy was concerned and for a time Buckingham had absolute power. As a favourite amongst favourites, he could not have been expected to achieve much but, in fact, Buckingham proved a surprisingly accessible and responsive Lord High Admiral, who did improve the Navy's effectiveness — albeit from an unusually low level. The Commissioners who introduced reforms into the Navy after 1618 could have achieved nothing against the vested interests ranged against them without the active support which Buckingham gave them.

He was a man of extravagant notions and ambitions but in general they benefited the Navy and Portsmouth. He improved, enlarged and repaired docks and storehouses in naval dockyards as far as the available money allowed. He increased the number of ropehouses and encouraged Dutch rope-makers to settle in England and teach Englishmen their craft. He introduced lieutenants and corporals on board ships and set up the first practical system of regular gunnery instruction in the Navy.

Above all, he was the first seventeenth century political figure to grasp the importance of Portsmouth as a naval centre. Even with his efforts, Portsmouth still lagged a long way behind Chatham, but, from Buckingham's time onwards, warships were always stationed at Portsmouth, and increasing use was made of the port for the repair and victualling of the ships.

Whereas Elizabeth left a Navy fit to go anywhere and do anything,' wrote William Laird Clowes, 'James left one largely composed of vessels unfit for any duty whatsoever'. There was, perhaps fortunately, only one military operation of any size in James' reign and, in spite of Buckingham's efforts for the Navy, it was an almost complete failure.

Pirates from Algiers and privateers from Dunkirk and the Channel ports had been infesting waters around the British Isles for years — in fact, it was one of the charges later laid against Buckingham at his impeachment that he had failed to protect the country's shipping and harbours from these predators. A punitive expedition to Algiers, of 6,000 tons of shipping and two thousand five hundred men, left England in October 1620 and returned the following summer having achieved almost nothing.

The Algiers expedition, for which Buckingham as Lord High Admiral must bear responsibility (although Viscount Wimbledon who led the expedition was incompetent) was not quite the nadir of the seventeenth century Navy. The expedition to Cadiz in 1625, the first year of Charles I's reign, is generally reckoned to be the lowest water mark of seamanship in the whole of the Royal Navy's history.

The planning was non-existent; the organisation, if it can be so called, was chaotic. The men were mostly unpaid and hardly trained. Many were sick when they sailed, or sickened soon after, and many died. The ships were ill-found and ill-equipped. Incapable officers were chosen and there were fresh suspicions of corruption. Many of the ships could not keep proper station, and kept on colliding with each other, and some of the captains did not even know where the expedition was supposed to be going or where they should rendezvous if they became separated from the main body.

In March 1627, Special Commissioners appointed on Buckingham's recommendation to inquire into the state of the Navy came down to Portsmouth to look at the facilities of the dockyard. After they had reported, estimates were prepared for a new dock, a crane house, a saw house and other additions. One Commissioner of the Admiralty, Mr Secretary Cope, came down to Portsmouth at the King's command in May to reorganise the fleet. He stayed most of that summer in Portsmouth and heartily disliked the place, calling it 'that loathsome place subject to ague and the infection of so many poor sailors'.

On 11 June, King Charles visited Portsmouth and reviewed the fleet. He also walked about the town ramparts, now in a state of ruin, and pleased everybody by promising he would have them repaired. He stayed in the town until the 17th, held a Council and reviewed the troops assembled for the forthcoming expedition to La Rochelle. On 26 June, the day before the expedition sailed, the number of sailors on board the men-of-war in Portsmouth was reported as being 3,936, with another 594 in the victualling ships and the transports.

Buckingham himself, flying his flag in the *Triumph*, commanded the Rochelle expedition which sailed from Stokes Bay with one

George Villiers, Duke of Buckingham.

hundred ships and seven thousand troops on 27 June. It was yet another fiasco. Everything went wrong, from a lack of coordination which gave away all hope of surprise, to heavy rain storms, and time-wasting circuitous marches by the troops when they got ashore. Carelessness allowed the French to run supplies into the important fort of St Martins on the very night its besieged commander decided he would surrender the next day. From the combined effects of famine, sickness and enemy action, Buckingham lost more than four thousand of his men and returned in November having achieved nothing.

Of 7,833 men who had embarked for Rochelle at Portsmouth, only 2,989 returned, and many of these were sick or wounded or both. The Mayor, Henry Halt, lodged one hundred and fifty sick sailors in two of his old houses. After burning '20 tons of cask and ten in stacks', they pulled the houses down (presumably after removing the sick sailors) and burned everything they could. Although in December, the citizens of Portsmouth refused to allow sailors to billet ashore for fear they would bring infection, the sickness spread so rapidly through the town that Portsmouth was 'like to perish'.

When there were twenty or thirty fresh cases of sickness in the ships every day, Admiral Sir Henry Mervyn, commanding in the Narrow Seas, wrote to Edward Nicholas, Buckingham's secretary, that at this rate the King would shortly have more ships than men. Sickness was only one of the sailors' afflictions. They were starved, unpaid and ill-clothed. In James' reign, sailors used to say the galleys were better than the King's service, but in Charles' reign, they were soon saying they would prefer hanging.

In March 1626, Admiral John Pennington wrote to Buckingham that he had twenty-nine ships but neither victuals nor clothes nor men for them. The men sent down do the ships ran away, he said, as fast as they were pressed: 'I wish you were a spectator a little, to hear their cries and lamentations'. From Portsmouth he wrote that there were no hammocks in the ships, not even cans to drink or platters to eat from.

The men of the *St Peter* petitioned Buckingham direct, begging to be discharged because they could get neither pay nor food and were existing on the charity of their friends. In June, the entire crew of the *Lion* at Portsmouth, some four or five hundred men, marched off the ship saying they were going to London to state their case because their wives and children were starving and they themselves were perishing on board. The crew of the *Swiftsure* at Portsmouth mutinied and went ashore in a body but were persuaded to come back; even then, there were only one hundred and fifty men instead of two hundred and fifty, and fifty of those were raw boys. Every ship in the port was undermanned.

Dishonest victuallers cheated the sailors of what food there was. Beef sent to Portsmouth weighed only 2 lb a piece instead of the 4 lb the Crown had paid for. The attitude of some officers aggravated the situation. Captain Sir John Watts, Buckingham's flag captain in *Triumph*, described the behaviour of the ragged and starving men as 'insolent misdemeanours'. 'The common seamen at Portsmouth', he wrote, 'grew insolent for want of victuals'. He arranged with the Governor of the town to use 'shot' if necessary when seamen appeared showing their tattered clothes and making their 'scandalous speeches'. In January 1628, he was reporting to the Admiralty that the seamen of Portsmouth were in a state of mutiny. He had had to use 'much violence' to make them return to their duties and had had to put some men in the 'bilboes' (irons).

In April 1628, the Earl of Denbigh, Buckingham's brother-in-law, led a second expedition to relieve Rochelle. It too was wholly unsuccessful. Buckingham planned to lead a third expedition himself in August, but in June, when the ships were being collected at Portsmouth, there were two more mutinies, and complaints that the sailors had no shirts and the few surgeons in the fleet were always in the shoreside taverns. One party of one hundred and fifty pressed men sent down to Portsmouth in July included saddlers, ploughmen and 'other mechanics'; some of the men were old and weak and many of them were useless.

By 11 July, the troops for the Rochelle expedition were camped on Southsea Common and there were sixty ships at Portsmouth, of 4,070 tons, with 783 guns and 3,934 seamen. Buckingham went down to Portsmouth himself in August. He was by then one of the most unpopular men in the Kingdom and, with the streets of Portsmouth full of disaffected sailors, his life was in danger. He stayed at Captain Mason's house at 10 High Street. One day, as he climbed into a coach, he was surrounded by some three hundred sailors demanding their back pay.

One bold sailor tried to drag Buckingham out of the coach but was arrested and taken into the house. Buckingham managed to calm the situation and left to join the King, who was staying at Sir Daniel Norton's house at Southwick. In Buckingham's absence the sailors had the arrested man released by threatening to pull down Mason's house by force.

However, Buckingham had the man re-arrested after seeing and recognising him in the street. Again, the sailors tried to have the man released but Buckingham and his followers, on horseback and with swords drawn, drove the mob down the street to Point Gate in a 'most furious manner', killing some of them.

At a 'Council of War' on 22 August the man was sentenced to be hanged. The sentence was carried out that day on a gibbet between Portsmouth and Southsea Castle by another condemned mutineer who thereby obtained his own remission.

Buckingham seemed to have some premonition of disaster. He begged a friend to recommend his wife and children to the King, saying: 'Some adventure may kill me as well as another man'. He seems not to have thought of assassination, for when somebody suggested he wear a shirt of mail under his clothes he said that 'would be but a silly defence against any popular fury. As for a single man's assault, I take myself to be in no danger'.

After breakfast on 23 August, Buckingham stepped into the hall of Captain Mason's house, preparing to attend a meeting with the King that morning. He turned to speak to Sir Thomas Fryer. While his attention was distracted, a man standing close to the entrance to the passage leading to the breakfast-room struck him with a dagger in the left breast, calling out 'God have mercy on thy soul!'.

Buckingham drew the knife out of the wound, shouted 'Villain' at his assailant and tried to follow him but stumbled heavily against a table and fell dead. Hearing the commotion, the Duchess rushed out in her night-dress, to see her husband's bleeding corpse on the floor.

The murderer turned out to be a Captain John Felton, a discharged and disgruntled army officer, who believed he was the champion of God and his country and that by

The murder of the Duke of Buckingham.

killing Buckingham he would both right his own wrongs and rid the world of a tyrant. He was hung at Tyburn and his body exhibited in chains on Southsea beach.

Buckingham's murder deprived Portsmouth of a powerful advocate at Court and in the Admiralty. The future of the town and dockyard was now to be decided by men who had vested interests in other dockyards. In May 1630, Phineas Pett, the great shipwright, and William Burrell, the Master Shipwright, arrived in Portsmouth to conduct business concerning the defects and survey of ships, but Pett was a Deptford man born and bred, and Burrell, it was said 'desired to have all business to himself at Chatham'.

The two men disliked each other, to the verge of hatred, and they stayed in separate lodgings, Pett with John Brooke, Clerk of the Stores, and Burrell with his brother Francis, Clerk of the Check. However, they finished their business amicably enough, and 'having all ordered, settled and graved the ships' they went back to London in June.

Both men returned in August as members of a full Commission to 'take a view of the harbour and the river running up to Fareham, for the removing of his Majesty's ships to a more safe place of riding'. They also took the view that the tidal rise and fall at Portsmouth was not enough for the use of a dry dock. There was what Pett called 'much dispute and contrariety about the business, but in the end a fair agreement was concluded'.

This 'fair agreement' looked ominous for Portsmouth's future as a naval port, especially as there was also the suspicion that the harbour was infested by the ship-worm *Teredo navalis*. In a sense, however, Portsmouth had its revenge on its critics, because several of the Commissioners fell sick in the town and had to leave early. Pett got home to Woolwich dangerously ill and lay in bed for eight weeks, during which time Burrell actually died.

Pett returned with yet another Commission in November to enquire about the *teredo*. After examining shipwrights and others strictly under oath they decided that it was all a malicious rumour 'raised to hinder the keeping of any of his Majesty's ships in that harbour'. However, five years later some of the men who signed the report positively concluded 'that there is a worm in that harbour'.

Worm or no worm, Pett was back again in 1631 to 'prepare all the ships riding at Portsmouth . . . and to entertain his Majesty, resolved to view them all', which Charles I duly did, on 2 August, before going over to the Isle of Wight.

It seems from these remarks of Pett's that a decision had been taken on Portsmouth's future as a naval port. In 1636, for the first time, a pinnace named *Maria* with a crew of ten was stationed to act as a guard ship at the harbour entrance, with authority to prevent strangers entering. In 1638, a Master Shipwright was appointed to reside permanently in Portsmouth. From then on, many ships wintered in Portsmouth and came there for repairs.

In October 1634, the King issued the first writ for ship-money, requiring coastal towns to pay levy for the equipping of ships. This first writ was obeyed, albeit with some grumbling in Parliament, but the second, levied on inland towns, and the third and subsequent writs, aroused mounting fury and ever more bitter opposition from both people and parliament. In a celebrated case, John Hampden of Great Hampden was imprisoned for refusing to pay what was in fact a forced loan for the cost of a ship of 450 tons, manned and equipped for six months, or £4,500 in lieu, demanded from the county of Buckinghamshire.

In the summer of 1642, the continuing war between King and Parliament changed from words to weapons. In January that year the sailors had sworn 'to acknowledge Charles King; to stand for the privileges of Parliament', but this assumed that the King would govern through Parliament. Considering the disgraceful way the King had for years treated his sailors over their pay, food, clothing and conditions of service, it was no wonder that when it came to a choice between King and Parliament the sailors went over virtually en masse to Parliament.

The Earl of Northumberland was Lord High Admiral but, when he fell ill, Parliament appointed Robert Rich, Earl of Warwick, as Admiral in June 1642. The King's choice was Vice Admiral Sir John Pennington, but he was too much of a Royalist to be acceptable to Parliament who applied to Northumberland (in whose gift the appointment actually was) to nominate Warwick. He did so, whereupon an angry King dismissed Northumberland and appointed Pennington.

The Navy now had to choose. Four or five captains were in favour of Pennington, who was personally very popular in the Navy, but the great majority readily accepted Warwick. Warwick appointed Sir William Batten as his Vice Admiral, with a fleet of sixteen warships and sixteen merchantmen in home waters.

As late as July 1642, by which time there was a state of virtual civil war in the country, the Governor of Portsmouth, Colonel George Goring, was still accepting Parliament's money whilst corresponding with, and offering refuge to, the Queen Henrietta Maria. King and Parliament both seemed confident that Goring was their man, but in July, Goring declared Portsmouth for the King, leaving the town's citizens in the curious situation of publicly supporting the King whilst their chief sources of income, the ships and the sailors, were on the side of Parliament.

To Goring's surprise, Portsmouth was very quickly besieged by land and sea. On the night of 9/10 August, a Parliamentary cutting-out expedition went into Portsmouth harbour and captured from under Goring's nose the guard ship, the pinnace *Henrietta Maria*, his only naval vessel.

By mid-August, Portsmouth was blockaded from the sea by six Parliamentary warships, the *Paragon*, the *Charles*, the *Caesar*, the *Black James* and two others, under the Earl of Warwick, and the free-lance *Lion*, owned and commanded by Captain Lovis Dick. A member of *Paragon*'s crew later wrote to his cousin that: 'Our greatest harmony is the thundering of cannon both day and night'. In fact, the ship's guns 'did not spend a shot upon the town' during the whole siege, but they did intercept boats trying to enter Portsmouth with supplies and they landed troops to seize Carisbrooke Castle and other forts on the Isle of Wight.

From 2 September, guns from Gosport kept up an accurate fire upon prominent buildings in Portsmouth, and especially the parish church of St Thomas, which the defenders were using as a look-out post. The church bells gave warning of the approach of ships by sea or horses and riders by land. The bombardment wrecked the church tower and the nave and several houses nearby.

Goring's garrison were carrying off for their own consumption the sheep, cattle and corn of the people of Portsea. Warwick landed seamen, with two guns, at the east end of the island to hold Goring's cavalry at bay whilst the sailors ferried numerous women and children across to safety on Hayling Island.

Parliamentary troops with scaling ladders stormed the Castle in the early hours of 6 September, and the town surrendered a day later. Goring made it one of the conditions of his surrender that he and his garrison should be allowed to keep their arms and equipment, otherwise he would destroy much of the town by detonating the magazine in the Square Tower. It was just possible that a man of Goring's known reckless temperament might do just as he threatened. Thus Goring and his garrison were allowed to march out of Portsmouth bearing their weapons, with flags flying and drums beating.

In recognition of the sailors' good service during the siege, Parliament gave them an extra month's pay and sent a tun of wine to each ship. The spirit and morale of the Navy improved dramatically during the Commonwealth which was declared in May 1649. The pay of officers and men was raised and paid almost regularly, although not invariably. Compared with the sailors of the Stuart Navy, Commonwealth sailors were much better and more punctually paid, properly clothed, well fed and found, much better cared for when sick or wounded, and were promised much more prize money.

In 1645, Portsmouth was besieged again, this time by Royalists under Goring, who attacked Gosport. Gunfire from three ships, the *Fellowship*, *Swiftsure* and *Mary Rose* under Captain William Penn, helped to drive the

Royalist troops off. During all the years of political turbulence which led to the execution of the King and the establishment of a Commonwealth in 1649, Portsmouth remained generally loyal to Parliament. In 1648, Prince Rupert of the Rhine sailed with twenty-five warships to join the Prince of Wales in Holland, but eight warships at Portsmouth stayed where they were, on the Parliament side.

Cromwell, the Lord Protector, and the Commonwealth recognised that their own security in the wars against the Dutch and in safeguarding their position against the Royalists depended principally upon the Navy. Enormous sums, in some years much more than half the total national income, were spent on the Navy. In 1652-3, from a total expenditure of £2,600,000 some £1,400,000 (or over 50 per cent), or £848,000 out of £1,517,000.

The Commonwealth built more warships than the Stuarts ever dreamed of. Where James or Charles' Navy thought one ship a year a matter for celebration, the Commonwealth launched ships by the dozen: no less than 207 new warships in the eleven years from 1649 to 1659 inclusive. In one year alone, 1654, twenty-two warships were launched, in addition to the numerous merchantmen which were chartered by the Crown and the prizes fitted out for naval service.

Under the Commonwealth, the Navy began to be used on a world-wide scale for the first time. Whereas Charles I had one fleet, which after a whole year of preparation cruised peacefully up and down the Channel, the Commonwealth Navy kept one powerful fleet ready for action in the Downs, numerous warships patrolling along the coasts, a strong squadron in the Mediterranean, another in the West Indies, and even some ships on the North American Station.

Under the Commonwealth, corruption in the Navy greatly diminished. Piracy in home waters was virtually unknown. The earliest Articles of War for the government of the Navy, based on some regulations drawn up for Warwick's fleet in 1648, were enacted by Parliament in 1652. Under the leadership, ironically, of military officers, men began for the first time to regard service in the Navy as a profession, as a career for a man's working life.

Portsmouth shared in this general progress and prosperity. Naval expenditure at Portsmouth more than doubled, from £6,860 in 1652 to £13,700 in 1653 and up again to £15,700 in 1654. In June 1649, when it was decided to build five warships, Portsmouth was chosen as one of the building yards. A new ship, symbolic in name and as a token for the future, was launched at Portsmouth in the following year.

Her name was *Portsmouth*, a fourth-rate of 600 tons and 38 guns. She was designed by Thomas Eastwood, Master Shipwright at Portsmouth and was the first man-of-war to be built at Portsmouth for more than a century — the first, in fact, since the *Jennet* of 1539. She was followed by nine more ships in as many years, all designed by Eastwood's successor, John Tippets.

Portsmouth carried the town's name in many of the naval engagements of the Dutch wars. She won battle honours in the First Dutch War in the action off Dover in May 1652, off the Gabbard in June 1653, and off the Dutch coast at Scheveningen the following month. In the Second Dutch War she took part in the battle off Lowestoft in June 1665, in the Four Days Battle in the North Sea in June 1666, and at Orfordness seven weeks later.

In May 1671, she was in Admiral Spragge's squadron which attacked and set fire to the Algerine pirates' lair at Bugia Bay in north Africa. She was at the last battle of the Third Dutch War, the Texel, in August 1673. She won her final battle honour at Bantry Bay, in yet another war, of the English Succession, in May 1689 before being captured by the French Ship *Marquis* and blown up on 9 August. A successor of the same name was at Barfleur, in the same war, in May 1692.

Portsmouth had not been involved in one of the biggest battles of the Dutch wars, which began off Portland Bill in February 1653, but the town was. The Dutch fleet commander, van Tromp himself, was escorting a convoy of some two hundred merchantships homeward bound for Holland. The English fleet which intercepted him was commanded by two Generals-at-Sea, Robert Blake and Richard Deane. Blake did not go to sea until he was fifty years old, but he rapidly developed into one of the foremost admirals in English naval history.

Robert Blake, Admiral and General at sea.

The battle became a running chase up Channel almost to the Dutch coast, in which five Dutch men-of-war were destroyed and one man-of-war, many ships of the convoy and several hundred Dutch sailors were captured. On 19 February, the second day of the battle, when the fighting was off the Isle of Wight, Blake's flagship, the *Triumph*, was badly damaged and there were many casualties amongst her ship's company. Her captain was killed and Blake was seriously wounded by a splinter in the thigh.

Some of the ships, including the *Assistance, Oak,* and *Advice,* put into Portsmouth to repair their damage. The prizes and the prisoners-of-war were also brought into Portsmouth. Blake himself was carried ashore, and lay recovering from his wound for some weeks.

The prisoners-of-war were distributed around Portsmouth, Gosport, Cowes, Southampton and Winchester. Portsmouth and Gosport were full of wounded men, lodged wherever there was room, in private houses and beer halls. Fifty surgeons came down from London and the southern counties. They were not impressed by Portsmouth. 'The filthy nastiness of this place, undrained and enduring an epidemic of smallpox,' wrote one, 'showed that Portsmouth had prepared for mending ships and replacing stores, but not for the human aftermath'. The surgeons had some unexpected help, from Elizabeth Atkin, otherwise known as 'Parliament Joan'. She had nursed wounded soldiers in the Civil War and now came to Portsmouth where she treated the sick and wounded largely at her own expense.

The Commonwealth appointed commissioners to administer the shipyards. Portsmouth's commissioner, appointed in 1649, was an able and energetic Parliamentary soldier, Colonel William Willoughby. Willoughby's own records show how busy he was, not only looking after the yard and the ships at Portsmouth but the other ships escorting convoys in the Channel who called for stores and victuals. He drew up and signed contracts, bought masts and sails, chartered ships, supervised the building of the ship *Portsmouth* and, as he was also Commissioner for Peace in the county of Hampshire, arrested and imprisoned pirates.

Willoughby died in 1651 and was succeeded by another soldier, Captain Robert Moulton, who also died within a year. Colonel Francis Willoughby, brother of William, was appointed. The Dutch wars provided Portsmouth with a powerful economic stimulus. The new Commissioner was soon supervising a huge increase in shipbuilding and repairing activity. A third of the Navy was stationed at Portsmouth and Portsmouth's size relative to the other yards can be judged by comparing the number of watchmen employed: Portsmouth had thirteen watchmen and Woolwich sixteen, while Chatham, still the premier yard, had thirty-two. At one point, when there were seventeen ships in Portsmouth waiting repairs, Willoughby wrote that 'the multiplicity of naval affairs to be carried on here is such as scarce to leave us a minute's time from one week to another'.

Portsmouth yard still lacked a rope-walk and a dry dock. There were rope-makers working outside the dockyard and at least three ropers working in the yard, mending ropes and ships' tackle. Rope could be obtained from outside contractors but Willoughby felt that the Navy should be independent and that a proper rope store yard and a rope-walk were essential. He told the Navy Commissioners that he could build twenty per cent more cheaply at Portsmouth than anywhere else. He wanted permission to buy five and a half acres of land adjoining the dockyard and build a rope-walk on part of it. He also wanted to enclose the whole dockyard within a brick wall 73 perches (just over 400 yards) in length.

Willoughby built two rope-walks alongside each other, three storeys high, 1,095 feet long, and 54 feet wide. Dutch prisoners-of-war provided the labour for making the ropes. Willoughby was as energetic and conscientious as his late brother, and made frequent tours of inspection round the yard. Portsmouth yard, enclosed within its newly-built brick wall, was now an industrial complex of considerable size, with the two rope-walks, upper and lower storehouses, upper and lower hemp houses, block loft, office, nail loft, tar house, canvas room, hammock room, kettle room, iron loft, oil house, sail loft, and houses for the rope-maker, top-maker and boat-maker and senior officials such as the Master Attendant.

On 18 August 1656, the Admiralty Commissioners authorised the Navy Commissioners to order a new dry dock to be built at Portsmouth. Known always as the 'Double Dock', it was to be big enough to take a 70-gun third-rate and a 50-gun fourth-rate ship, one ahead of the other, and it was not to cost more than £3,200, £500 of which was to be provided by the magistrates and citizens of Portsmouth. Work was not to begin until this sum was produced.

There is no record of the Corporation ever paying the £500, but building work began. The dock was made of wood; an account of 1801 stated that 'on the site of the extension of No.1 Basin was an ancient dock formed of timber bolted and trunnelled together the sides being formed in many places of whole trees'. The construction was a saga, with an almost contemporary ring about it, of labour troubles and late completion.

It was forecast that the dock would be ready to take a ship in February 1658, but a long strike by shipwrights in the summer of 1657, bad weather which held up work on the foundations, the death of one of the contractors and disputes between Tippetts and all the others, all delayed completion until 8 March 1658.

Meanwhile, the Lord Protector Oliver Cromwell had died, leaving a Navy of 157 vessels, one third based at Portsmouth, carrying 4,390 guns and manned by 21,910 men. Willoughby's inventory of Portsmouth yard recorded 62 anchors, 498 masts, 70 cables, 508 loads of timber, 63.5 tons of hemp, 10,600 yards of made-up canvas and 7,650 yards on reels, 99 barrels of tar and pitch, and 2,020 hammocks.

But some things did not change. In the summer of 1654, the sailors at Portsmouth had mutinied and petitioned Cromwell about the badness of their food and the hardship of their service. The food was improved and the mutiny quelled, with some difficulty.

Chapter 5

King Charles II landed at Dover on 25 May 1660, to restore the monarchy. He took a great interest in his Navy and appointed his younger brother, James Duke of York, 'Squire James' as he was known to the Navy, as Lord High Admiral. It was Charles and James, an unlikely couple on the face of it, who disagreed with each other all their lives, but who between them laid down many of the foundations of the Admiralty and the modern Navy.

The first Royal visit of the Restoration to Portsmouth was early in January 1661. The Queen Mother, Henrietta Maria, and the Princess Henrietta (Charles' favourite sister 'Minette') sailed from Portsmouth for France after the Queen Mother had visited England in an unsuccessful attempt to dissuade James from marrying Anne Hyde. The Royal ladies embarked in the *London* on 6 January and sailed three days later. But Minette fell ill (measles was diagnosed) and at the Queen Mother's request, *London* anchored in St Helen's Roads. Whilst trying to turn back to Portsmouth in a fast-running ebb tide and a light wind, *London* struck on the Horse Sands. Luckily, she came off with the flood, with no serious harm done, and the Royal ladies continued their journey to France on 26 January, when Minette was well again.

News of the accident reached London on 11 January when Samuel Pepys recorded it in his diary, attributing the grounding to the 'negligence of the pilot'. Pepys had just been appointed Clerk of the King's Ships. As such, he was in effect secretary to the Navy Board which then consisted of a Treasurer, a Comptroller, a Surveyor, Pepys himself as Clerk, and four (later increased to five) Commissioners.

Samuel Pepys.

Pepys owed his appointment to his patron Sir Edward Montagu, whose secretary he had been, who commanded the fleet which brought King Charles to England, and to the Duke of York, whose attention he had attracted during the voyage. His duties took him frequently to Portsmouth which, unlike a great many visitors, he described as 'a very pleasant and strong place'. On 1 May 1661, he and Mrs Pepys stayed at the Red Lion and, although he did not think much of the accommodation, he was pleased and flattered that several officers from the dockyard came to visit him. He bought them drinks and they all got somewhat merry.

On 2 May, he and Mr Creed walked round the town walls. All the officers of the Yard called on Pepys at the Red Lion 'with great respect, and I walked with them to the Dock and saw all the stores, and much pleased with the sight of the place. Back, and brought them all to dinner with me, and treated them handsomely; and so after dinner by water to the Yard, and there we made the sale of the old provisions. Then we and our wives all to see the Montagu, which is a fine ship, and so to the town again by water, and then to see the room where the Duke of Buckingham was killed by Felton'. Next day, Pepys walked up and down the town again with Mr Creed and got the impression that Creed and some others wanted to make him a freeman of Portsmouth, but 'the Mayor was, it seems unwilling, and so they did not do it'.

Almost a year later, Pepys was back in Portsmouth to await the arrival there of Catherine of Braganza, Charles II's intended bride. He decided not to take his wife this time, much to Mrs Pepys' annoyance, and travelled down with Admiral Sir William Pennington and Sir George Carteret, Vice Chamberlain to the King and Member for Portsmouth. After a delay, when their guide lost his way, they arrived in Portsmouth on 23 April and Pepys put up at Wiard's the Chyrurgeon's.

After breakfast next day at Sir George Carteret's lodgings at Mrs Stephens', Pepys went to the Pay House, but the books were not prepared, so he went to a lecture in St Thomas's Church where there was 'much London company, though not so much as I expected'. In fact, it was some time before the Queen arrived. She had left Lisbon on 15 April 1662, sailing in the 80-gun *Royal Charles* flagship of Sir Edward Montagu (now created Lord Sandwich, for his part in the Restoration) and escorted by fourteen warships.

Sandwich wrote in his diary for that day:

15th Tuesday. By 6 o'clock in the morning we weighed anchor, the wind at N.W., and got out of the river to sea; as I passed by the Castles the Queen commanded me to loose the Standard, which was done. As soon as we were out at sea the Queen and all the ladies were sea-sick.

Pepys spent all day of 25 April at the Pay House. In the evening he enjoyed the company of his friend the Doctor but, he said 'I was much troubled in my eyes by reason of the healths I have this day been forced to drink'! On the Sunday (27th), Pepys saw the rooms at the Domus Dei which had been prepared for the Queen. He thought them all 'rarely furnished, and escaped hardly being set on fire yesterday. At chapel we had a most excellent and eloquent sermon. By coach to the Yard, and then on board the Swallow in the Dock, where our Navy Chaplain preached a sad sermon full of Nonsense and false Latin . . .'

Pepys visited the Mayor, Mr Timbrell, 'our anchor-smith', who showed him the Queen's wedding present from the town of Portsmouth. It was 'a salt cellar of silver, the walls christall, with four eagles and four greyhounds standing up at the top to bear up a dish: which indeed is one of the neatest pieces of plate that ever I saw'.

That evening there was a flurry of excitement when a merchantman came into the harbour, 'which we hired in London to take horses to Portugal; but Lord! but what running there was to the seaside, to hear that news, thinking it had come from the Queen'.

After two more days without news, Pepys decided to go back to London, but after dinner on 30 April Mr Stephenson, one of Portsmouth's burgesses, told Pepys that the Mayor would like to make him a Burgess. Pepys put on his best suit 'lined with silk' and went to the Town House, where he took the oath and shook hands with everybody. Then he took them all to a tavern and bought them drinks. After paying the bill at the tavern, Pepys reckoned that being made a Burgess of Portsmouth had cost him one piece of gold to the Town Clerk, ten shillings to the Bailiffs, and another six shillings for the drinks. Finally, on 1 May, Pepys went back to London and therefore was not in Portsmouth for the arrival of the Queen.

The *Royal Charles* had been much delayed

by stormy weather, especially in the Bay of Biscay. She reached St Michael's Mount on 6 May, Torbay on the 10th, where they were met by the Duke of York in his yacht *Anne*, and on the night of 13 May anchored off St Helens Roads. The Queen and her ladies had continued to be sea-sick to the end.

On 14 May, as Sandwich wrote in his diary: We weighed anchor and about 2 o'clock in the afternoon came to an anchor off the Spit Head and about 4 o'clock in the afternoon his Royal Highness (the Duke of York) took the Queen in the Anne yacht and sailed to the beach at Portsmouth next the Town gate (probably the Point Gate, a gateway in the battlements east of the Platform and the Square Tower) and then her Majesty went into the barge wherein she was brought ashore, the Duke of Ormond and the Earl of Manchester attending on the shore side to receive her Majesty, who immediately upon landing went in her own coach, the Lords, the Portugal Ambassador and myself walking afoot before the coach, to the King's House in Portsmouth.

According to a contemporary account, the nobility and gentry and multitudes of Londoners were waiting on the shore 'and the Mayor and Aldermen and principal persons of the Corporation, being in their gowns, and with a present (the salt cellar Pepys had seen) and speech ready to entertain her; the cannon and small shot both from around the town and the whole fleet echoed to one another the load proclamations of their joy'.

The Queen's retinue, of more than a hundred persons, attracted a great deal of comment, including as it did 'six frights — calling themselves maids of honour — and a duenna, another monster (old and deaf), who took the title of governess of these extraordinary beauties. Besides these there were six chaplains, four bakers, a Jew perfumer, and a certain officer, apparently without employment, calling himself her Highness's barber'.

The Queen, still weak with sea-sickness, took to her bed at once and sent a message to the King, who was still in London (and had never yet seen his bride). He had to prorogue Parliament and, according to Pepys, supped that night with Lady Castlemaine, who was pregnant by him. The Queen was still in bed, with what Sandwich called 'a great cold' when the King did arrive in Portsmouth at about noon on 20 May, for what he called 'the happiest meeting which has ever taken place'.

Catherine of Briganza was no beauty. It was said that Charles 'though they had brought him a bat instead of a woman'. However, he did write to Clarendon that: 'Her face is not so exact as to be called a beauty, though her eyes are excellent good, and not anything in her face that in the least degree can *shocque* one'. John Evelyn was more critical, writing in his diary when the Queen eventually arrived in London 'with a traine of Portugueze Ladys in their monstrous fardingals or *Guard-Infantas:*: Their complexions *olivaster*, & sufficiently unagreable: Her majestie in the same habit, her foretop long and turned aside very strangely; She was yet of the handsomest Countenance of all the rest, & tho low of stature pretily shaped, languishing & excellent Eyes, her teeth wronging her mouth by stiking a little too far out: for the rest sweete & lovely enough'.

The Queen received her intended bridegroom from her bed. The wedding was put off until the next day, which suited Charles very well. Writing next morning to Clarendon he said 'It was happy for the honour of the nation that I was not put to the consummation of the marriage last night for I was so sleepy, having slept but two hours in my journey . . .'

Charles tried to persuade Catherine to agree to a Protestant service, but she insisted on a Catholic ceremony. So, on 21 May 1662, they were married twice, first by Catholic rites in her bedroom and again in public in the Great Chamber of the Governor's House. The marriage register, which wrongly gives the date as 22 May, recorded:

'Our most Gracious Sovereign Lord, King Charles II, by the Grace of God, King of Great Brittaine France and Ireland, Defender of the Faith, etc. and the most illustrious Princess Donna Catarina, Infanta of Portugal, daughter of the deceased Don Juan the fourth, and sister to the present Don Alphonso, King of Portugal, were married at Portsmouth, on the two and twentieth day of May, in the year of our Lord God, 1662, being the fourteenth year of His Ma'sties reign; by the Reverend Father in God Gilbert, Lord Bishop of London, Dean of the Chapel Royal, in the presence of the Nobility of His Majesty's dominions and of Portugal. Anno 1662.

The couple spent the first few days of their honeymoon in Portsmouth. The King reviewed his fleet in May 1662, very probably during this period. Royal watermen were brought down from the Thames to row the King out to the ships. There is a contemporary description of the ceremonial for this Royal review. Ships were to be 'neat and ready in every part' and trimmed with all their flags, ensigns and pendants. The barge was to be well furnished with carpets and cushions, the coxswain with his whistle in the stern to steer, and the 'barge's gang in their cleanliest clothes or liveries to row'.

As soon as a ship sighted the Royal barge approaching, her decks, tops, yards and shrouds were all thoroughly manned and, as it were, 'hung with men'. As the barge came nearer, the trumpets sounded and kept on sounding until the King was less than a musket shot from the ship's side. Everyone with a whistle was to 'whistle his welcome three several times', and the whole ship's company hailed the King 'with a joint shout after the custom of the sea'.

The ships' sides and ladders were manned by the 'primest and best fashioned men'. Captains were ready to receive the King on their knee. Gun salutes were not fired until His Majesty had left the ship, but the King was entertained with music while he was on board. And, as His Majesty went over the ship's side, the trumpets sounded the 'loath to depart'.

In 1664, Portsmouth dockyard had a new Commissioner, Colonel Thomas Middleton. Middleton took over a thriving yard, busy preparing ships for the Second Dutch War, which began very well, with the taking of New Amsterdam (renamed New York after the Duke of York, who was Governor of Portsmouth). James himself as Lord High Admiral commanded the English fleet in a victory over the Dutch off Lowestoft in June 1655.

In March 1665, Charles II came down to Portsmouth to look at his ships. His retinue thought Portsmouth 'a cold and unwholesome' place but the King, as always, was interested in everything he saw. He went over the *Catherine*, the *Charles*, the *James*, the *Triumph*, the *Resolution*, the *Royal Prince* and he went twice on board the *Royal Oak*, a Portsmouth ship built by John Tippetts. The King was particularly pleased with her and dined on board with Sir George Askew her Captain.

Charles visited Portsmouth again that summer. There was a plague in London and the people of Portsmouth were afraid that the King and his Court might bring it with them. The King ordered pest-houses to be built, to isolate the infection, and certain houses of wood to be rebuilt in stone, to minimise the fire risk.

Plague did come to Portsmouth, its deadly progress charted by Middleton in his letters to Pepys. In August 1665, he wrote: 'Portsmouth is at present free from the plague, though fever and small-pox abound'. Personally, he dreaded the outbreak of plague amongst 'so crowded and miserably poor a population'. In October he wrote: 'all are yet in good health. It is a strange mercy that Portsmouth is so free from contagion'. But in November, there was much sickness in the dockyard, several men having died.

In January 1666, plague was confirmed on board the man-of-war *Essex* in the harbour. Eight men died and Middleton was afraid that the docking of the ship would 'frighten the workmen and endanger the whole yard'. In February, the plague was bad at Gosport and in March very bad. By April, it had broken out in several houses at the Point and 'people die apace in Gosport'. A physician arrived who opined that 'the air of Portsmouth is naturally so pernicious to man that the man whose body is able to be supported in this air is plague free, and no contagious distemper is apt to seize on him'.

This diagnosis was not borne out by events. Later in April there were several more deaths, and by May the plague was so bad in Gosport that 'people now make tents out of town or lie in any barns or hovels they can get'. Middleton reported a practice in Portsmouth that horrified him: 'The people are so wicked in that town that its reported they take their foul plasters from their sores and in the night throw them into the window in fresh houses'.

In June and July the epidemic reached its height: 'The sickness is spread all over the Island, and broken out in the Broad-street of Portsmouth'. In July, the people in the dockyard were healthy but fifteen a day were dying in the town. 'There is now no way left to go out of the Yard without annoyance,' Middleton wrote on 15 July, 'the pest-house being on one side within 100 feet, and the common burial ground within three or four roods of the other. The graves are left so shallow that they are commonly covered with crows and ravens, except when the grave-digger is at work'. As so often, the epidemic passed its peak, and after several recurrences, died away with the arrival of cold weather in December.

Meanwhile, Middleton had other domestic concerns in the dockyard. In March 1665, he wrote to Pepys about a fire which might have had disastrous consequences. 'Mr St John Steventon's wife being in her tyme a deboosh drunken woman, such a one as I can believe she hath not left behind her, rose from her husband in the night, or rather towards day, goeth down stayers, lyteth a candle, and withall being exceedingly drunke sat in a large wicker chayre which was set on fyre, wheare she was burnt to ashes. The house excaped, which had it taken fyre, would have burnt ships in docke, storehouse and what-not. The mantelletre of the chimney took fyre, but day being at hand, people stirringe, was quenched. It happened at lowe water, and noe water in the yard considerable to put out fyre if it should happen, which hoope will be considered of.

Pepys authorised the purchase of a fire-engine at a cost of £20.

Middleton disliked Portsmouth intensely. In August 1665, he wrote to Pepys:

For my part to you as frinde I declayr I intend not to make Portsmouth by habytation if I can avoid it. TIS TREW if the King command me to live underwater if it weare possible I must and would do it, I shall not live heare for the rent of Hampsheare. To tell yow of the strayght I have been put to sence my comynge to Portsmouth for my accommodation would be to small purposes but that I have a boddy that can indure all things I hadd been dead. Wheare I now am wee are forced to packe nyne people in a roome to sleep in, not above 16 foot one way and 12 foot the other. Wee are 26 in famyly, in the Mayoures house, nyne of which are small children. What comfort can man have in such a condition soe being together.

Pepys responded to this cry from the heart by authorising Middleton to build a Commissioner's house, which was finished in 1666.

Middleton also took what was, in view of events to come in the Thames two years later, a very wise precaution. He ordered Edward Silvester, a blacksmith in Gosport, to make 'one Substantiall chaine to replace the one made in 1522 for blocking the entrance to the harbour'.

Plans were also made to strengthen the defences of Portsmouth town. The design, which included the dockyard, the Portsbridge and Gosport, was prepared by Sir Bernard de Gomme, a Dutchman who had erected a number of town fortifications in Flanders. The work was largely carried out by Dutch prisoners-of-war and took fifteen years to complete. The town was encompassed by huge defence walls and a moat. The Landport Gate, which had two bridges, also had an outworks called a ravelin, which consisted of two walls forming an angle from which flanking fire could be directed at attackers crossing the moat. The bastions at the corners of the main walls were strengthened and the gun emplacements reinforced to take the weight of the heaviest guns. Two more forts were built, Charles Fort at Gosport, and James Fort, or Burrough Castle as it was sometimes called, on a small island in the harbour.

Strengthening Portsmouth's defences

seemed particularly apposite in 1667, when the Duke of York authorised the work to begin. In June, the Dutch admiral de Ruyter's ships entered the Thames estuary and went up the Medway. There they burned the *Royal James*, the *Royal Oak* and the *Loyal London* and, ignominy of ignominies, captured as a prize the *Royal Charles*, the ship which had brought Queen Catherine to England, which had once been called *Naseby* and which was the very symbol of restored monarchy.

De Ruyter then sailed down the Channel and appeared off the Isle of Wight. There were very few ships in Portsmouth, de Gomme's defence works were still on the drawing board, and the town's only real defence was Edward Silvester's chain. There seemed nothing to stop de Ruyter sailing up to Spithead and landing to invest Portsmouth. However, to everybody's relief he said away again, perhaps not realising how weak Portsmouth's defences actually were.

The Dutch wars continued to give economic impetus to Portsmouth. In fact, it could be said that Portsmouth owes the consolidation of its position as the premier naval port in the Kingdom to the Dutch. The scale of operations in that era can be judged by the size of the combined fleets of the Anglo-French alliance of 1672; in May that year, before the battle at Solebay later in the month, there assembled at Spithead a French fleet of thirty-three capital ships and eight fireships, manned by 10,966 officers and men, while the English fleet was sixty-five capital ships and twenty-two fireships, manned by 23,530 officers and men.

The King came down to Portsmouth specially to see the French ships. He visited the port again later in the year to inspect progress on building a new *Royal Charles*. He was 'infinitely pleased with the sight of the great new ship, for she would be the largest vessel in England'. Designed by Anthony Deane, the rising star of the ship-builder's craft and a future Commissioner of Portsmouth yard, she was a 90-gun ship, of 1,531 tons and 670 men.

Portsmouth built more of the larger warships than other yards. From 1660-86, Portsmouth built three first-rate ships and five second-rates, while Chatham built three first-rates and two second-rates, and Woolwich two first-rates and three second-rates. Ships came off the slips at Portsmouth at the pace of at least one and sometimes two or three a year. In 1673, two of Deane's ships, the 60-gun *Swiftsure* and the 44-gun *Assurance*, and the yachts *Navy*, and *Isle of Wight*, were all launched at Portsmouth.

Two years later, the King hoped to be present at the launch of another *Royal James* to replace the flagship lost at Solebay, but was delayed and the ship had to be launched without him. Knowing the ways of the sea and that tides wait for no man, not even Kings, Charles was not at all put out. When he did arrive two days later, he inspected every part of the ship, was once again delighted with everything he saw and knighted John Tippetts and Anthony Deane.

By the close of the Dutch Wars, Portsmouth was the principal naval rendezvous in the Kingdom. A list of warships at Portsmouth on 19 June 1684 gives: first-rates, *Royal Charles*, *Charles* and *Royal James*; second-rates, *French Ruby*, *Vanguard*, and *Ossory*; third-rates, *Dunkirk*, *Dreadnought*, *Edgar*, *Expedition*, *Harwich*, *Lyon*, *Monk*, *Plymouth*, *Swiftsure*, *Warspite*, *York*, *Eagle* and *Northumberland*; fourth-rates, *Advice*, *Bristol*, *Jersey*, *Kingfisher* and *Reverse*; fifth-rates, *Guarland*, *Rose* and *Swan*; sixth-rate, *Fann Fann (Fanfan)*; Fireships, *Ann and Christopher*, *Castle*, *Sampson*, *Sarah* and *Young Spragg*; Yacht, *Merline*; and hulks, *America* and *Slothany*.

In 1691, a new dry dock and two wet docks were ordered for Portsmouth. The marking and lighting of the harbour approaches were improved. When finished, in 1698, the new docks doubled the size of the yard and confirmed its status as the premier yard.

Portsmouth's prestige was such that the Freemen of the town included all the principal naval commanders of the time. The Earl of Sandwich, who had served both Commonwealth and King, was made a Freeman in 1661. He was lost at Solebay in May 1672. His great friend John Evelyn mourned him in his Diary, although he had 'I confesse serv'd the *Tyrant Cromwell*, when a young man'.

Evelyn records that Lord Sandwich had some premonition of death: 'going at *White-hall* to take my leave of his Lordship (who had his Lodgings in the Privy Gardens) shaking me by the hand bid me *god buy*, he should he thought see me no more, & I saw to my thinking something boading in his Countenance; no says he, they will not have me live'.

At the height of the battle, Sandwich's flagship *Royal James* caught fire and blew up with the loss of over one thousand lives. Sandwich himself had just transferred to a boat alongside but so many people flung themselves into it, hoping to save themselves, that it capsized and Sandwich was drowned.

Captain George Legge, who was Governor of Portsmouth from 1670, also served at Solebay. He commanded the 84-gun *Royal Catherine* with distinction under Prince Rupert in the actions against the Dutch in 1673. A cousin of Buckingham's and a friend and confidante of James, as Duke of York and as King, he was created Baron Dartmouth in 1682 and made a Freeman of Portsmouth the following year. He commanded James' fleet during the 'Glorious Revolution' of November 1688, when the so-called 'Protestant wind' drove William of Orange's invasion fleet along the Channel whilst keeping Dartmouth's ships penned in the Gunfleet.

When James sent the Prince of Wales (the future James III, The Old Pretender) to Portsmouth, Dartmouth politely refused to smuggle the infant to France as James wanted, believing that such an action would be treason. Dartmouth himself made his allegiance to William and Mary in 1689 but two years later he was arrested on the highly improbable charge of conspiring to hand over the country's defences to the French. He was committed to the Tower of London, where he died of a fit of apoplexy in October 1691.

Admiral Arthur Herbert, later first Earl of Torrington, commanded William of Orange's fleet during the 'Glorious Revolution'. He was made First Lord of the Admiralty and a Freeman of Portsmouth in 1689, but his naval career ended in failure. He failed to prevent the French landing at Bantry Bay on 1 May 1689.

Although both sides claimed to have won at Bantry Bay, William III was very pleased with his fleet. He came down to Portsmouth, stayed the night at Colonel Norton's House at Southwick, drove by coach to the town and was received at the Land Port by a hundred horsemen who saluted him, the Lord Mayor and town dignitaries.

The Mayor walked in front of the Royal coach to the Sally Port, where Admiral Herbert was waiting to take the King in his barge out to his flagship, the *Elizabeth*. The King knighted Captain John Ashby of the *Defiance* and Captain Cloudesley Shovell of the *Edgar*. He ordered every man in the fleet to be given ten shillings.

This was a very popular move indeed. Officers and men cheered the King and pledged their loyalty (which, the King knew, he might well need against the deposed but still aggressive James II).

In 1690, Herbert commanded the Anglo-Dutch fleet against the French admiral de Tourville and had the worst of an engagement off Beachy Head in June. He was court-martialled, charged that he 'had through cowardice or treachery, misbehaved in his office, drawn dishonour on the English nation and sacrificed our good Allies the Dutch'. He argued in his defence that he had kept his 'fleet in being' so that no invasion could be attempted, and was acquitted, although the King deprived him of his commission the next day.

It seems that the Freedom of Portsmouth did not bring much luck to its recipients. Edward Russell, who was made a Freeman in 1696, also served at Solebay and also came to England with William of Orange. As an admiral, he served under Herbert in 1689 and succeeded him in 1691. In 1692, he commanded an Anglo-Dutch fleet of eighty-two ships and, with the help of Sir George Rooke, gained a decisive victory over the French under de Tourville at Barfleur and La Hogue. Once again, there were repercussions and recriminations. Russell was accused of not taking proper measures to destroy the enemy fleet completely and was relieved of his command. He was reinstated in November 1693, appointed First Lord in 1694 and, in 1697, made first Earl of Orford.

George Rooke was made a Freeman in 1698, the year he also became Member of Parliament for Portsmouth. He, too, served at Solebay, as a captain at Bantry Bay in 1689, as a rear admiral under Herbert at Beachy Head, and was knighted as Russell's third-in-command when, after the fleet action off Barfleur, he led the boat attack on La Hogue and burned thirteen French ships of the line. In 1704, during the War of the Spanish Succession, Rooke captured Gibraltar, the exploit for which he is chiefly remembered, although it was a sudden raid which was almost an afterthought.

Seemingly inevitably for Freemen of Portsmouth, this victory led to Rooke's dismissal. His Tory friends, to further their own political ends, boasted that the capture of Gibraltar was a more splendid victory than Blenheim (fought a few weeks earlier) and therefore Rooke was a better commander than Marlborough, whose Whig party was then in power. This so maddened the Whigs that Rooke was relieved and not employed again.

However, Sir George was always remembered kindly in Portsmouth where, as the local MP, he used part of his prize money to pay the apprenticeship fees of poor orphans of the town and to buy a new set of bells for the Parish Church of St Thomas.

Chapter 6

The eighteenth century came in like a lion, with one of the most violent storms, perhaps even the most violent storm, for hundreds of years, in November 1703. It was preceded by signs and portents. For a fortnight that month the wind blew from the west-south-west with unusual and increasing strength. People took shelter, thinking there were thunderstorms approaching, but the thunder was the sound of the wind, blowing harder every day. Normal life in town and country became increasingly difficult, as branches and whole trees were blown down, tiles were swept off roofs, chimney stacks fell in, and stock panicked and stampeded in the fields.

Daniel Defoe, in his account of the Great Storm, wrote that it was 'the greatest, the longest in duration, the widest in extent of all the tempests and storms that history gives any account of since the beginning of time'. Some people saw strange vapours in the heavens, great flashes like bolts of lightning, and atmospheric phenomena which 'raised the nitro-sulphurous or other heterogeneous matter in the sky and exploded'.

On the morning of 26 November, the storm began to climb towards its crescendo. The sky darkened, the wind increased in strength and fury. People wondered whether it was safer to stay in their houses or to try to seek refuge in the open fields. Few ventured outside for fear of being struck by flying tiles and bricks.

The barometer fell steadily during the day to the lowest levels in living memory. One man accused his servant of breaking his barometer, because the mercury level had virtually disappeared out of the bottom of the glass tube. Water spouts appeared in the countryside. A parson followed one of them for miles, noting that it swept up trees and houses in its violent cross-country passage.

At about midnight people noticed that, unbelievably, the wind was still increasing. The earth actually shook underfoot, as though there were an earthquake, but it was the sheer force of the wind. By midnight, the whole night sky seemed to be filled with flares and fires and blazing meteors. Pregnant women gave birth prematurely, without the aid of midwives, who either could not make their way against the wind and flying debris, or had decided to stay at home. Almost the only people abroad were looters, breaking into abandoned houses.

The climax of the storm lasted for about three hours. By 3 am on 27 November the winds at last began to decrease. But at sea, where the devastation had been as appalling as on land, enormous waves pounded against the shore for days, culminating with the high spring tide of 30 November when the water rose eight feet higher than usual. Ships were blown ashore and stranded high on beaches, streets in Portsmouth were flooded, and the foundations of houses were undermined. When the waters receded from Portsmouth, the whole town seemed under a stinking layer of mud, sand, shingle, drift wood and storm debris.

At Portsmouth and Cowes [wrote Defoe], there lay three fleets; first, fleet of transports and tenders, who with Admiral Dilkes brought the forces from Ireland that were to accompany the King of Spain (Archduke Charles of Austria, called Charles III, whom the English and Dutch allies were supporting for the Spanish throne) to Lisbon; secondly, a great fleet of victuallers, tenders, store ships and transports, which lay ready for the same voyage, together with about 40 merchant ships who lay for the benefit of their convoy; and the third article was the remainder of the grand fleet which came in with Sir Cloudesley Shovel; in all almost 300 sail small and great . . .

It seemed a miracle that any of these ships survived. Many of the smaller ones were driven ashore or out to sea and were never seen again. Defoe mentioned one ship full of soldiers and two merchantmen which 'have never been heard of as I could learn'. The *Resolution* anchored off Bembridge on the 25th, lost both her anchors soon after midnight on the 26th and struck on the Owers two hours later. She drifted eastward and was wrecked beyond Beachy Head. Her crew

were saved. The fireship *Vesuvius*, moored at Spithead, was driven ashore but her crew also survived. However, when the third-rate *Newcastle* foundered at Spithead at the height of the storm, 193 officers and men were drowned; only the carpenter and 39 men were saved. The second-rate *Vanguard*, a Portsmouth-built ship, was driven ashore at Chatham.

In all, thirteen men-of-war were wrecked. According to Defoe: 'Portsmouth, Plymouth, Weymouth and most of our seaport towns looked as if they had been bombarded and the damage of them is not easily computed'. Whole forests of trees were uprooted. Eight hundred houses, four hundred windmills, seven church steeples and the Eddystone lighthouse were blown down. The lead roofing of more than a hundred churches was rolled up, innumerable houses were stripped

'Perspective View of Portsmouth and Gosport *c.* 1705' by J. Lightbody. Engraving showing the dockyard, Point, saltworkings, a variety of shipping and the growing communities of Cowes and Ryde.

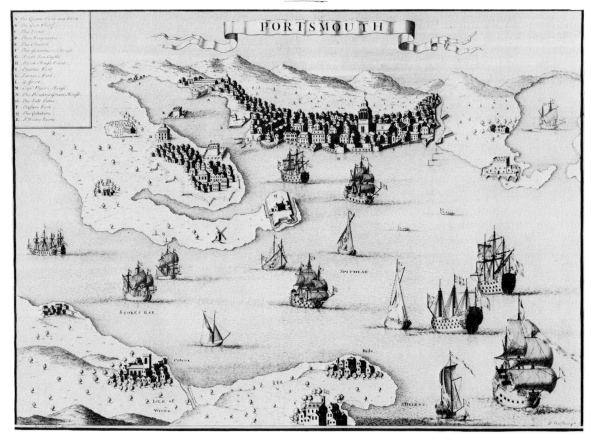

of their roofs and thousands of lives were lost.

The *Postman* of 30 November 1703 said that his 'perfect hurricane' had 'done such damage to the houses of this place (Portsmouth) that £10,000 will not make good the same, and there is scarce a man-of-war at Spithead which has not received damage'. The Great Storm was considered to be a judgement of God upon the nation and a day of national humiliation was observed throughout England on 19 January 1704.

Dilkes' and Shovell's fleets of 1703 recorded by Defoe, were only two of many eighteenth century fleets gathered at Spithead. It was a century of wars, large and small, and a time of tremendous expansion of the British Empire. There were innumerable expeditions and voyages, to the Mediterranean, to India, to the West Indies and to North America. In all these comings and goings Portsmouth played a central part, as the foremost naval rendezvous and departure point of the century.

It was to Portsmouth that Rooke returned after the capture of Gibraltar in 1704. From here Vernon sailed to Porto Bello in 1739. A year later, Anson sailed from Portsmouth on his epic voyage round the world and it was to Portsmouth that he came back in June 1744 with only one remaining ship, the *Centurion*, but with treasure valued at £1,250,000; it required thirty-two wagons and a strong naval escort to take it up to London. In 1747, Anson arrived at Spithead with the six French ships of the line he had taken in his action off Cape Finisterre and £300,000 more in treasure. He was a Freeman of Portsmouth and when in the town, lived at 74 High Street.

In April 1711, a large expedition of some fourteen men-of-war, thirty-one transports carrying five thousand three hundred troops, a hospital ship, eight storeships and a tender, all under the command of Rear Admiral Sir Hovenden Walker, sailed from St Helens for Canada. The ambitious object of the expedition was the capture of Quebec from the French. The project literally foundered on the shoals of the St Lawrence River where eight transports ran aground and over eight hundred men were drowned.

Walker and his ships returned on 9 October 1711, having achieved nothing. Six days later his flagship the 70-gun *Edgar* blew up at Spithead, killing some four hundred of her crew and about forty visitors who were on board at the time. Walker and all the ship's officers were ashore and thus escaped.

There was some mystery about the disaster and even suspicions that it had been engineered. Superstitious sailors thought it ominous because *Edgar* was the oldest ship in the fleet and some believed she was the actual ship in which King Edgar himself sailed, because some part of the original ship had been preserved every time the ship was rebuilt.

However, the explosion was certainly lucky for Walker, who was about to face a court-martial after which he would very likely have been struck off the flag list. All his papers, including the logs, reports and charts of the expedition, were destroyed and without them the court martial could not proceed. He was given another command, but a year later the Admiralty called upon him to give an account of the Quebec expedition from memory. When he declined, saying that he could not do so, he was dismissed from the Service without a pension.

Early in the eighteenth century, the Admiralty devised a scheme for the entry and training of their own nominees as young officers, as an alternative to the usual method whereby naval officer entered their own proteges as 'Captain's Servants'. An Order in Council authorised the establishment of a Naval Academy at Portsmouth in 1729. However, the buildings were not finished and the staff were not appointed until 1733, when the Academy opened for the education of 'forty young gentlemen, sons of noblemen and gentlemen'. The buildings are the present Staff Officers' Mess in the dockyard. The brig *Success* was rigged in the harbour for instructional purposes in the following year. The young gentlemen, aged between thirteen and sixteen, and were placed under a Master, three ushers and instructors in French, Drawing, Fencing, and the use of the firelock. A Latin master was appointed in 1749.

The new Academy and its 'College Volunteers', as they were called, were not well

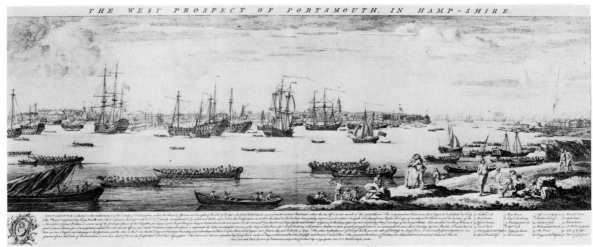

Engraving by Samuel and Nathaniel Buck 1749.

received by naval officers who felt that it undermined their own privilege of patronage, as indeed it did; nor did the nobility send their sons there, because only half the places were filled; nor was the education given by the Academy of a high standard, although it was very much better than that received by many young officers, which was often nothing at all.

The students soon gained a reputation for idleness, swearing and drunkenness and many of them were expelled. In 1766, the Port Admiral was ordered 'to enquire into a dispute which has arisen between the masters, and between the masters and the scholars'. As a result, the headmaster, the mathematics usher and a number of scholars were dismissed.

By the time James Trevenen, who was to go as a midshipman on Cook's last voyage in the *Resolution* in 1776, went to the Academy in December 1772, the number of scholars was only fourteen including himself. The rules of entry were changed in 1773 so that:

> ... none shall be admitted into the Academy but the sons of noblemen or gentlemen, who shall not be under 12 years of age, nor above 15 at the time of their admission, except fifteen young gentlemen, the sons of commissioned officers of H.M.Fleet, who are to be educated at the public expense and may be admitted at the age of 11 years.

The Commissioner of H.M.Dockyard shall be the Governor, and the Masters, Ushers and Scholars shall be obedient to and observe his directions.

The scholars are to lodge in separate chambers and all to board with the Master, at £25 a year, in consideration of which he is to keep them a decent and proper table and to find them in washing, fire, candles, towels, table and bed linen and the messing utensils of the house.

A yearly suit of blue cloth, conformable to a pattern suit lodged with the Master, to be donned on H.M. birthday at the price of £5.

The subjects studied in the 'plan of learning' included writing, arithmetic, navigation, gunnery, fortifications, dancing, 'the useful parts of Mathematick and the use of the Firelock'. However, a report of 1774 complained that the scholars were 'too talkative when under arms'. No boy was permitted to leave the dockyard without permission — although many of them did, staying out all night drinking at what Trevenen called 'bawdy houses'. No boy could stay at the Academy longer than five years to complete his education. Each boy was given a discharge certificate when he joined a ship.

These reforms seemed to have little effect on either the Academy or the number of new entries. In July 1774, William Delater, one of Trevenen's class mates, was expelled for 'eloping and for decoying Henry Wray and for having a bad character'. A report dated the same month said 'Kitchen utensils are amazingly dirty. The scholars heads abound in vermin. Scholars to have three clean shirts, etc., a week and clean sheets once a month. Not to throw stones over the wall, or to go to a billiard table'.

In December 1776, three scholars were expelled and eight 'confined for insolent and riotous behaviour when the Head Master was gently correcting Charles Hurt for ill behaviour'. Occasionally, a boy who had already gone to sea as a Captain's Servant attended the Academy for a short time when his ship was in Portsmouth. Such a boy was James Anthony Gardner in 1780 when the Master was a Mr Orchard: 'a very good man he was; but who the devil taught him navigation is more than I can say. He was a great disciplinarian, and used to flourish with direful sway an infernal horsewhip, that I have reason to remember. It was called 'black pudding', and he was no way stingy in serving it out'.

In the holidays the students used to go to Grange near Gosport and have fights with the gypsies who had a camp there. Once they caught the gypsies' donkeys and rode off on them but, Gardner said, 'the swarthy squad got a reinforcement with which they attacked us and with sticks and stones we maintained a running fight until driven into Stoke, after abandoning our donkeys and giving up the contest. The clergyman at Stoke (Mr Shield) who had witnessed that engagement said it was the defeat of the long-eared cavalry by the Egyptian infantry'.

There were sixteen scholars in Gardner's day. In 1793, when Jane Austen's brother was a scholar, there were only twenty-eight. Nor had the Academy's reputation much improved. Lord St Vincent asked a prospective parent: 'Are you so partial to that seminary as to hazard a son there?' In 1801, he was writing: 'The Royal Academy at Portsmouth, which is a sink of vice and abomination, should be abolished . . . '

It was not abolished but it was reconstituted and renamed the Royal Naval College

R.N. College, Portsmouth c. 1880.

A view of the town and harbour of Portsmouth *c.* 1755.

in 1806. The headmaster was the Rev. James Inman (of the Nautical Tables). Inman established the first school of Naval Architecture at Portsmouth in 1811. It amalgamated with the College in 1816 and lasted, with some twenty-four students, until 1834. The sons of Army officers were admitted to the College in 1828 and in the following year, commissioned officers on half-pay who wanted to improve their scientific knowledge. The College in its original form finally closed on 30 March 1837.

Portsmouth has always been an accurate gauge of the state of the Navy — what is said in Portsmouth accurately reflects public feelings about the Navy. In January 1745, four English sail of the line fumbled their attack on two French treasure ships off Ushant and allowed them to escape. The Captain of the 70-gun *Hampton Court*, Savage Mostyn, was court-martialled but acquitted with honour. However when *Hampton Court*, with Mostyn still in command, next sailed from Ports-

mouth the cry went up from the walls; 'All's well! There's no Frenchmen in the way!'

This was only one of many incidents which showed the low state of the Navy's prestige at the time, resulting in a new Naval Discipline Act of 1749. On 19 July that year, an obscure naval officer, Mr Baker Phillips, 2nd Lieutenant of the 44-gun *Anglesey*, was shot on board the *Princess Royal* at Spithead. In march that year, off Ireland, *Anglesey* had encountered a large French privateer, the 50-gun *Apollon*. In a brisk engagement *Anglesey's* Captain and Master were killed, some sixty of her men were left dead or wounded and the ship herself half-flooded. Baker Phillips, left in command, decided their position was hopeless and struck his colours.

The court martial apportioned most blame to the late Captain Elton of the *Anglesey* but also found Baker Phillips guilty and sentenced him to be 'shot by a platoon of musqueteers on the forecastle . . . ' The court recommended mercy but the sentence was carried out, very probably because England was then in great fear of a Jacobite invasion and just possibly Phillips was suspected, rightly or wrongly, of being in the pay of the Young Pretender (the same suspicion might have been the reason for the harsh treatment meted out to Rear Admiral Sir Hovenden Walker).

Eight years later, during the Seven Years War, there was another, much more famous court-martial at Spithead, which made the accused officer immortal in naval history. In 1756, Admiral John Byng was sent out to the Mediterranean to relieve the island of Minorca, which was beset by the French. The Admiralty appeared at first unaware of the importance of the island and gave Byng a small, weak and poorly equipped fleet of only ten ships of the line — although there were over fifty ships of the line in commission, which Byng was not allowed to use.

Until the expedition to Minorca, Byng had had a generally successful naval career and had held several important commands. He was a competent, conscientious and hard-working officer, if somewhat uninspired and uninspiring, and he tended to be too cautious and pessimistic about his own chances, too ready to take counsel of his own and others' fears.

Byng's tactics were severely inhibited by the current Fighting Instructions which laid down that fleets should only fight in line ahead, van opposite van and rear opposing rear, unless the enemy was clearly retiring, when the signal 'General Chase' could be hoisted and then, and only then, was room for manoeuvre possible.

Such restrictive Fighting Instructions virtually prohibited Byng from showing any initiative in battle. Furthermore, Byng had very much in his mind the fate of Admiral Thomas Mathews, who had been court-martialled and dismissed the Service for disobeying the Fighting Instructions twelve years earlier.

Byng did hoist the 'General Chase', but an inconclusive engagement followed, with some casualties and damage on both sides. However, the French had retreated, leaving Byng at least technically the victor. Byng should then have reinforced his advantage by remaining at sea and blockading Minorca. Instead, he held a council of war (often a sign of weakness and lack of self-confidence) in his flagship *Ramillies*, as a result of which he decided to bear away and return to Gibraltar. This was a gross strategical error, unworthy of any Commander-in-Chief, for which Byng should certainly have been reprimanded, and possibly never employed again. The English garrison at the capital, Port Mahon, held out for a month before surrendering, and Minorca was lost.

At this news, the Government, the Admiralty Board and the general public all awoke together to the importance of Minorca and demanded a scapegoat. Byng was the obvious choice. He was superseded and brought home. When he arrived at Spithead he was placed under arrest. He was taken to Greenwich and virtually imprisoned on the top floor of the Queen Anne building at the Royal Hospital, where the Governor spitefully had iron bars put across the windows to prevent him flinging himself out and thus 'cheating justice'.

The Admiralty, who were themselves at fault for choosing Byng and then failing to give him a sufficiently large and powerful fleet, behaved very shabbily towards him. They kept back his dispatch, admittedly a somewhat apologetic account, full of excuses, for some time and then published it with certain omissions which were calculated to prejudice Byng's case.

Meanwhile poor John Byng was viciously lampooned in the press, accused of being a coward, in the pay of the Jacobites, and having sold his country to the enemy. He was kept imprisoned until December when he was moved to Portsmouth. His court martial began on board the *St George* in Portsmouth harbour on 27 December 1756 and continued until 27 January 1757.

In short, the court found that Byng had not done his utmost to relieve the English garrison on Minorca, and had not done his utmost to take, sink, burn and destroy the enemy ships and to assist such of his own ships as were engaged. He was not guilty of treachery, not guilty of cowardice, but guilty of negligence, under the 12th Article of War:

Every person in the fleet, who, through cowardice, negligence, or disaffection, shall, in time of action, withdraw, or keep back, or not come into fight, or engagement, or shall not do his utmost to take or destroy every ship which it shall be his duty to engage; and to assist all and every of his Majesty's ships, or those of his allies, which it shall be his duty to assist and relieve; every such person, so offending, and being convicted thereof by the sentence of court-martial, shall suffer death'.

This article used to continue 'or such other punishment as the circumstances of the offence shall deserve, and the court martial shall judge fit'. But, unfortunately for Byng, during the War of the Austrian Succession, just ended, this mitigating conclusion had been removed by a new Act. So, the only sentence the court could pass on Byng was death, but with the strongest plea, signed by every member of the court, for mercy.

The verdict was farcical. That Article of War governed offences in battle. Byng had not been negligent in battle. He had done as well as any man reasonably could with the forces at his disposal. His negligence, his dereliction of duty, was in leaving Minorca, an offence with which he was not charged. In a month-long trial, nobody ever asked Byng why he had withdrawn.

All appeals for mercy to the King were refused. It was the law, and must stand. Thus, on the morning of 14 March 1757, the Marines of the *Monarch* were drawn up on the poop, along the gangways, in the waist, and on one side of the quarterdeck. On the other side was spread some saw-dust, and a cushion placed on it. Nine Marines were drawn up in three lines of three, the front and middle lines with bayonets fixed. The captains of all the ships in Portsmouth and at Spithead had been ordered to attend but, to avoid overcrowding, were directed to stay in their boats.

Byng himself behaved with great dignity throughout. Just before twelve o'clock, he retired to his inner cabin for about three minutes. The doors of the outer cabin were then thrown open and Byng walked from his after cabin with a steady pace and a calm expression. As he passed through the fore cabin he bowed to his friends there, said to the Marshal of the Admiralty, 'Come along, my friend', and walked out on to the quarterdeck.

Byng bowed to the Marshal, gave him a paper which was a vindication of his case, and said, 'Remember, sir, what I have told you relative to this paper'. A friend offered to tie the bandage over Byng's eyes, but he refused and blindfolded himself.

The Marines stepped forward two paces and presented their muskets, waiting for Byng to give the signal to fire. Byng stayed on his knees for about a minute, apparently in prayer, and then dropped a handkerchief, the signal to fire.

Six Marines fired. One bullet missed. Four bullets struck various parts of Byng's body. One bullet passed through his heart. He fell forward, dead. His body was put in a coffin nd taken to his family home at Southill in Bedfordshire. His monument was inscribed:

To the Perpetual Disgrace of Public Justice, the Hon. John Byng, Esq., Admiral of the Blue, fell a Martyr to Political Persecutions, March 14th, in the year MDCCLVII; when Bravery and Loyalty were insufficient Securities for the Life and Honour of a Naval Officer.

The bitterness in the inscription was justified. Nobody, not the King, nor the Duke of Newcastle's government, nor the Admiralty, came well out of the affair. Voltaire had sent Byng the Duke of Richelieu's account of the action off Minorca, but it was intercepted and held back until it was too late to be of any use to Byng. He mocked them all in a well known passage of *Candide* (translated from the French):

Talking thus they came ashore at Portsmouth. A crowd of people covered the shoreline and closely watched a rather big man who was kneeling blindfolded on the poop of one of the ships of war; four soldiers, standing facing him, each fired

The Execution of Admiral Byng.

three bullets into his skull in the most peaceable manner in the world, and the whole gathering went away extremely satisfied. 'What is all this, then?' said Candide, 'and what demon is it that holds sway everywhere?' 'It was an Admiral,' he was told. 'And why kill this Admiral?' 'It is,' he was told, 'because he did not have enough people killed; he gave battle to a French Admiral, and they have found that he did not get close enough to him.' 'But', Candide said, 'the French Admiral was as far away from the English Admiral as the English one was from the French.' 'That is undeniable', they replied, 'but in this country it is a good thing to kill an Admiral from time to time, *pour encourager les autres.*'

Almost the only naval figure of stature to emerge unscathed from the miserable debacle of the Byng Affair was Admiral Sir Edward Hawke, who was sent out to Gibraltar to relieve Byng as Commander-in-Chief Mediterranean. Hawke had been made a Freeman of Portsmouth in 1747, the year he became one of the two MPs for Portsmouth (the seats were in the Admiralty's gift) and he represented the town in Parliament for the next twenty-nine years. Hawke seldom or never spoke in the House, but he did take action to look after the interests of the townspeople over the years.

It was also the year of the first of his two great victories over the French, at the Second Battle of Finisterre on 14 October 1747. Hawke never received quite the same credit

Admiral Lord Hawke.

A SOUTH EAST VIEW OF PORTSMOUTH.

1. South Sea Castle.
2. The New Hospital for Sick Seamen.
3. Block house fort.
4. Gosport.
5. The Saluting Battery & Magazine.
6. The Spur Battery.
7. The King's Bastion.
8. Governours House.
9. Portsmouth Church.
10. Feltons Gibbett.

A south-east view of Portsmouth, 1765.

for his battle as Anson did for the First Battle of Finisterre in May of that year, although Hawke's was strategically the more decisive victory and was gained against a stronger opponent.

Nothing could detract from Hawke's victory over the French under Conflans in Quiberon Bay on 20 November 1759 — the 'Year of Victories' and the 'wonderful year' of David Garrick's 'Hearts of Oak'. With his legendary admonishment to the Master of his flagship the *Royal George* — 'Where there is a passage for the enemy there is a passage for me. You have done your duty in showing me the danger: now obey my orders and lay me alongside the French admiral!' — Hawke led his ships through a howling 40-knot gale and a huge swell and on a lee shore into the shoal waters of Quiberon Bay. Eleven French ships were lost and others escaped only by lightening themselves by throwing guns and weapons overboard so that they could cross the shoals. Two British ships were lost. Not for the first time in our history, a naval victory removed the threat of a French invasion.

Hawke returned from Quiberon Bay in January 1760, to be welcomed by the cheers of the people of Portsmouth. He received the thanks of Parliament and a pension of £2,000 a year but not the peerage Anson had received and which Hawke richly deserved.

Portsmouth continued to be the scene for the washing of the eighteenth century Royal Navy's dirty linen in public, with more court martials in 1779, when another war against France had just begun. In 1778, the Tory government of Lord North was looking for an officer to command the fleet. Hawke was too old. Howe was in North America. Rodney was in France and in debt. Admiral the Hon. Augustus Keppel, a Whig, was next.

Keppel was an officer of an altogether higher calibre than Byng. He had gone round the world with Anson and had been promoted Lieutenant for his services. He commanded the 74-gun *Torbay* under Hawke at

58

Quiberon Bay, led a successful expedition to capture Belleisle in the Bay of Biscay and was Pocock's second in command at the capture of Havana in 1762.

Lord Sandwich, the First Lord, offered Keppel the command, having boasted in the House the previous year that there were forty-two ships of the line in commission, thirty-five of them, he said, manned, victualled and fit for sea 'at a moment's warning'. This simply was not true. When Keppel got down to Portsmouth he found the fleet unprepared, with only six ships 'fit to meet a seaman's eyes' and the dockyard woefully short of stores. It is said that when Keppel poked the mainmast of one of these 'ready' ships with his cane, it disappeared into the rotten wood.

Augustus Viscount Keppel.

Flying his flag in the newly-completed 100-gun *Victory*, Keppel sailed from St Helens on 13 June with twenty ships. Hearing that the French, whose Navy had improved enormously in strength and efficiency in recent years, had thirty-two ships at Brest, Keppel obeyed the spirit of his orders and returned to Spithead to wait for reinforcements, thus infuriating the government who took this as a criticism of themselves. On 9 July, Keppel sailed again with twenty-four ships, later increased to thirty-two. On 27 July, miles out in the Atlantic, he encountered a French fleet of thirty-two sail.

The Battle of Ushant, as it was called, might have been a conclusive victory for the British which would have had incalculable political and military effects on the war just beginning. Instead, it was inconclusive and is now largely remembered for the behaviour of Keppel's Third-in-Command, Vice Admiral Sir Hugh Palliser, leading the rear squadron in the 90-gun *Formidable*.

Palliser's ships had suffered most during the first brush with the French. When Keppel wished to reform his fleet and signalled to Palliser to take station astern of him, Palliser acknowledged the signal but did nothing. An exasperated and puzzled Keppel finally took the most unusual step of signalling to all Palliser's ships individually, by name, to join his flag. By the time they did so, it was too late to reform the line, and darkness had fallen. Next day, the French had vanished.

Keppel generously did not criticise Palliser in his report. On the contrary, he said that Palliser's spirited conduct 'deserves much commendation'. Inevitably, the true story began to circulate in rumour and gossip and eventually appeared in the newspapers. Palliser was furious. He and Keppel were both Members of Parliament. Palliser, a Tory, accused Keppel of misconduct across the floor of the House. Keppel defended himself but was careful not to be provocative. Without too much difficulty, Palliser persuaded the Tory government to court martial Keppel for misconduct and neglect of duty — both capital offences.

The trial began on board the *Britannia* at Spithead on 7 January 1779, but after five weeks it was transferred to the Governor's House ashore because of Keppel's ill health. Keppel gave evidence on his own behalf in a quiet and convincing manner and he was supported by captain after captain who had been present that day off Ushant. The result was not in doubt. 'The charges are ill-founded and malicious', said the president of the court.

It was then Palliser's turn to be court-martialled, for the sake of his reputation. He was acquitted, but in such a manner as to be tantamount to a conviction. The people of England were delighted by this outcome. A mob tore down the gates of the Admiralty in London and broke the windows of official residences. Palliser's own house in Pall Mall was gutted. He himself was burnt in effigy and became the target of the lampooners. Even his house in St Thomas' Street in Portsmouth was attacked.

By contrast, Keppel's acquittal had been greeted by gun salutes from *Victory* and every ship in Portsmouth and at Spithead, and by thunderous cheers along the Portsmouth road as the news travelled up to London. Bonfires blazed in Keppel's honour, and riotous mobs drank his health. After a change of government, he became First Lord in 1782 and a Freeman of Portsmouth. Keppel remained so popular that — infallible sign of popular esteem in England — many public houses were named after him. There is a 'Keppel's Head' on Portsmouth Hard to this day.

Chapter 7

King George II did not, understandably, visit Portsmouth during or after the furore over Byng's court-martial and judicial murder, nor during the 'Wonderful Year' of victories in 1759. But his grandson George III, the first of the Hanoverians to pride himself upon his 'Englishness', who succeeded in 1760, realised the importance of Portsmouth as a naval base and arsenal. He paid his first visit, and reviewed the fleet, in June 1773.

The visit was in fact a formal inspection, not just of the fleet, but of the town and its fortifications, the Dockyard and the ships in ordinary. The King set out from Kew early on 22 June and reached the Portsbridge just before eleven o'clock, to be greeted by the first of many Royal gun salutes. He was met by Major General Parker who handed over the garrison keys, which the King handed back.

At the Landport Gate, the King was saluted by a 'triple discharge' of 232 pieces of cannon, mounted on the town ramparts, at Block-house Fort and at Southsea Castle. The King went to the Commissioner of the Dockyard's house, where he was received by the Lords of the Admiralty, principal naval officers and officials, and all the Dockyard workmen who gave three hearty cheers for His Majesty before dispersing to their work.

After a levee at the Governor's house, where the King met the Corporation and knighted the Mayor, John Carter, the King returned to the Dockyard, embarked in the Royal Barge and was rowed out in state to Spithead. The King was followed by a procession of barges: the Board, flying the Admiralty flag, three Admirals flying their flags, and all the Capitals of the Fleet flying their pennants.

Meanwhile, the forts fired another salute, which was taken up by the fleet of Spithead, consisting of twenty ships of the line, two frigates and three sloops, most of them ships which had fought in the Seven Years' War, and all with their yards manned and dressed overall with flags and ensigns.

The King received the flag officers on board the *Barfleur*, 90 guns, and then walked through the ship which was cleared for action, with every officer and man at his post. At 3.30 pm he sat down to 'a table of thirty covers'. When the Queen's health was drunk, a twenty-one gun salute was fired through the fleet in her honour. At six, the King was rowed through the fleet. Every ship manned yards and fired a Royal salute. It must have been a tired and somewhat deafened King who landed at 9 o'clock and went to the Commissioner's House for the night.

But the King was up early next morning to tour the Dockyard and inspect ships in ordinary in the harbour. He went on board *Barfleur* again, with the same gun salutes, and in the evening sailed to St Helens in the yacht *Augusta*. Next day, Thursday, the King himself inspected the Gunwharf, the Victualling Yard at Weovil and other parts of the Dockyard. He visited the naval bakehouse in King Street, which produced 34 cwt of biscuit a week. The King was presented with ship's biscuit which he munched as he walked through the streets with his courtiers. Later, the King held another reception at the Governor's House, and dined again on board the *Barfleur*. That afternoon, the King knighted several officers and in the evening sailed through two lines of ships in the *Augusta*.

During the visit, twelve ladies of Portsmouth asked for the honour of rowing His

Majesty from the Dockyard to *Barfleur*. The King said afterwards that his Barge had been 'manned' by twelve of the finest women in Portsmouth. The Royal party was followed the whole time by an armada of private yachts and sailing boats, while the shores on the Portsmouth and Gosport sides were lined with cheering crowds.

On Friday, the King began by inspecting the town fortifications and had another sail in the *Augusta*, when the Vice Admiral's division of the fleet weighed anchor and accompanied him. In the evening, there was a Naval levee on board the *Augusta* with more promotions and honours. At ten o'clock, soldiers and marines manned the town ramparts and fired a *feu de joie*, with a triple discharge of cannon and musketry all round the works.

The King said he was very pleased with the state of the fleet, the Dockyard, the arsenal and garrison and the many demonstrations of loyalty. To show his pleasure he left £1,500 for the workmen in the Dockyard, the Gunwharf and the Victualling Office, £350 for the crews of the *Barfleur, Augusta* and the Royal Barge, and £250 for the poor of Portsmouth and Gosport. He also ordered the debtors in Portsmouth Gaol to be released.

The King left Portsmouth, after a most successful visit, at a quarter to seven on Saturday morning, to yet another triple discharge of all the ordnance and a final twenty-one gun salute as he passed the Portsbridge.

The King's visit to Portsmouth aroused great interest in London. Responding to the public mood, David Garrick suggested to the poet and dramatist Captain Howard Thompson that he revive Charles Shadwell's nautical comedy *The Fair Quaker of Deal*, first produced at Drury Lane in 1710. A new production opened, also at Drury Lane, with the scene changed from Deal to Portsmouth and the French replacing the Dutch as the enemy, and a final tableau showing a fleet review at Spithead. At the same time, a play by G. T. Stevens called *A Visit to Portsmouth*, with music by Dibdin and scenes showing the King's visit to his ships, opened at the Haymarket Theatre.

Nearly five years later, on 2 May 1778, George III visited Portsmouth again, this time with Queen Charlotte. The five-day visit followed the earlier pattern: a thunderous multitude of gun salutes, a review of the ships as the King was rowed through their lines, inspections of the Dockyard and the 90-gun *St George* on the building slip, a public levee, a reception on board the 90-gun *Prince George*, Admiral Keppel's flagship, and a dinner under an awning on the quarterdeck of the Royal yacht, when the King drank to 'the prosperity of the Navy and to all his good subjects by sea and land'.

If the King noticed the poor state of the ships, he made no comment. He and the Queen visited the Naval Academy, the brew house at Yeovil, and the ropehouse in the Dockyard, where they watched the whole sequence of rope manufacture. One afternoon the King spent more than an hour down in a dock, watching workmen sheathe the bottom of a 28-gun frigate with copper. The Royal party left on Saturday morning to more gun salutes and cheers.

In the eighteenth century, the Royal Navy was the chief instrument of an expanding British empire, and grew to become the largest industrial organisation in Europe. Various establishments for the Navy were founded all over the Portsmouth and Gosport area. The Gunwharf, outside the dockyard, where the torpedo and mining school HMS *Vernon* would one day stand, was enlarged and improved. A hospital for seamen was begun at Forton in Gosport in 1713. The foundations of a larger hospital at Haslar were laid down in 1746. In the same year, work began on the construction of Cumberland Fort on Portsea Island, using convict labour. A magazine at Priddy's Hard on the Gosport side was authorised, with a grant of £4,000, in 1769.

But it was the Dockyard which showed the most remarkable expansion. By the time of George III's visits, Portsmouth Dockyard had grown into a considerable business enterprise. A *Guide to Portsmouth* of 1775 said that

> it resembles a town in the number of its dwelling-houses, offices, storehouses, lofts, and other edifices erected for carrying on the various purposes of the Yard. There

are never less than 2,000 men employed in it, and in time of war upwards of 2,500 who, last war, were all disciplined and formed in a regular body ready for action in case of necessity. The docks and basins are beyond anything we can conceive magnificent. Within these few years a piece of new ground of about fourteen acres, on the north side, has been added, being taken from the harbour and raised to a level with the other parts of the Yard. On this new ground are four slips, two for building large ships and two for smaller rates; besides these, two other slips are intended to be made

However, such a Dockyard, with its huge accumulations of timber, wood chips and shavings, planks, masts and spars, tar, pitch, barrels, sacks, stores full of rope and lofts full of canvas, was nothing less than a gigantic and perennial fire hazard. Minor fires were frequent, and major conflagrations occurred periodically. In July 1760, lightning set fire to the roof of the rope-house which was destroyed, with the spinning house, the hemp-house and several adjacent stores, causing damage estimated at £40,000.

Ten years later almost to the day, on 27 July 1770, fire broke out in the early hours of the morning in the building where tar and pitch were stored, and in four other place. It spread with great rapidity and for a time threatened to destroy the whole yard. Sailors from the ships, marines and dockyard workmen joined to fight the fire and, with a lucky shift of wind, had put it out by the afternoon, but not before it had caused damage estimated at £149,880.

Sabotage was suspected, because the fire had begun in several places at once, and also because war in America had just begun, 'foreigners' had been seen in the town, and French vessels previously sighted hovering about the coast disappeared after the fire. But, despite a reward of £1,000, no arsonist was found.

In 1776, there was a real arsonist in the Dockyard. A Scot by birth and a painter by trade, his name was James Hill, alias Hind, alias Aitkins, alias 'Jack the Painter'. He had gone to America at an early age and, after the American War of Independence started, returned to Britain to help the rebels' cause by destroying the dockyards at Portsmouth and Plymouth.

At about 4 pm on 7 December 1776, a fire broke out in the round-house of Portsmouth Dockyard. The whole building was destroyed and others nearby were only saved with difficulty. At first, it was thought to be an accident but, on 5 January 1777, three men working in the hemp-house found a 'machine' made out of a tin, like a tea caddy, with a wooden box containing combustible materials; it was, in fact, a home-made incendiary device.

Suspicion fell on a man called Hill, otherwise John the Painter, who had been seen lurking about the Yard. With a reward of £50 on his head, he was arrested and his examination began at Bow Street on 17 February. The chief prosecution witness was a man named John Baldwin, also a painter, who had worked in America. Baldwin said Jack the Painter told him he had inspected dockyards and fortifications around England, noted the number of ships in the Navy and their armament, and had been to Paris to inform Silas Deane, the rebel American minster to the Court of France, of his discoveries. Deane had given him money and letters of recommendation to merchants in the City of London.

In fact, according to Baldwin, Jack the Painter was a self-confessed American spy. Baldwin said he had described his incendiary devices, using hemp and turpentine and long-burning fuses. In fact, Jack the Painter had not been as successful as he had hoped. Some cheap matches a woman had sold him failed to ignite.

The trial began at Winchester Castle on 6 March 1777. Although Jack the Painter tried to discredit Baldwin's evidence, there was not much doubt he would be found guilty. He was sentenced to death, whereupon he made a full confession.

On 10 March, the day of execution, Jack the Painter was taken to the White House, as Portsmouth Gaol was called, and then to the Dockyard where he was drawn in an open

'An English Tar Giving Monsieur A Drubbing'. Robert Sayer, 1788. Also published in connection with Keppel's court-martial ten years earlier.

cart around the scene of his crime. Ironically, just before he was executed, Jack the Painter solemnly warned the authorities to show greater vigilance in the dockyards at Chatham, Woolwich, Deptford, Portsmouth and Plymouth, and especially, he said 'at the rope-house in Plymouth'!

When Jack the Painter himself gave the signal he was drawn up by pulleys to the top of a 64.5 foot high gibbet, made from the mizzen mast of the frigate *Arethusa*, at the Dockyard gate. He hung for an hour and was then taken down and suspended in chains on Blockhouse Point, at the harbour entrance. Years later, it was said, some sailors took down his skeleton and left it at a public house as payment for their drinks.

Contemporary eighteenth century memoirs give many glimpses of the attitudes of the people of Portsmouth and Gosport towards sailors. On 12 December 1781, Rear Admiral Richard Kempenfelt, flying his flag in the *Victory*, with twelve ships of the line,

encountered a French convoy carrying an army intended for the occupation of Jamaica, 160 miles south-west of Ushant. Kempenfelt skilfully outmanouvred his enemy and captured twenty ships, thus wrecking the entire expedition.

James Anthony Gardner, then a student at the Naval Academy, was standing on Gosport beach when the prisoners from some of Kempenfelt's prizes were landed. Gardner wrote: 'A party of soldiers assembled on the beach to escort them to Forton prison, a lieutenant of the navy and several midshipmen also attending, when a *posse* of women rushed out to Rime's 'noted alley' and pointing to the soldiers, sang the following beautiful ditty:

> Don't you see the ships a-coming?
>   Don't you see them in full sail
> Don't you see the ships a-coming
>   With the prizes at their tail?
> Oh! my little rolling sailor
>   Oh! my little rolling he;
> I do love a jolly sailor,
>   Blithe and merry might he be!

Then, catching hold of the lieutenant and midshipmen, they began to hug and kiss them, and it was some time before they could get out of their clutches. They then began to pelt the soldiers, who took it very patiently and seemed very glad when the order was given to march with the Frenchmen'.

Gardner, serving in the *Panther* (60 guns), was an eye-witness at Spithead on 29 August 1782 when the *Royal George* (100 guns) was 'careened' i.e. listed to port, to bring a stop-cock on the starboard side above the water-line, so that repairs could be carried out on it. *Royal George*, flying Kempenfelt's flag as Admiral of the Blue, was one of the most famous ships in the Navy. She had worn Hawke's flag at Quiberon Bay, and was presently part of Howe's fleet of forty ships of the line, forty frigates and some two hundred merchantmen, about to sail for the relief of Gibraltar, once again besieged by the French.

The careening had been done at 8 am that morning, by running all the port-side guns out as far as they would go, so that their carriages reached the gun-ports, and hauling

Above: Mary Rose from the Anthony Roll *c.,* 1546. *(Master and Fellows of Magdalene College, Cambridge.)*

Below: H.M.S. *Victory* in Portsmouth Harbour c., 1850. This contemporary print shows H.M.S. *Victory* at her moorings on the Gosport side of the harbour, close to the site of the modern ferry pontoon. She was only removed to her present berth in 1922. The paddle steamer is *Victoria and Albert,* the first Royal steam yacht, built in 1843. *(Lithograph by G H Atkins.)*

Above: Portsmouth Point by Thomas Rowlandson.
(Portsmouth Museums Service.)

Top: King Edward VII reviews the French fleet
at Portsmouth on the 9th of August 1905.
(Portsmouth Museums Service.)

Left: Sailors Head *c.,* 1934. This painting by Arthur D.
McCormick was commissioned by John Player and Sons. It was
presented to H.M.S. *Excellent* in 1980.
(H.M.S. Excellent.)

all the starboard-side guns in as near to amidships as possible, and securing them with tackles. According to a survivor, James Ingram (admittedly speaking many years later, when he was an old man) this brought the water nearly to the level of the lowest port-side gunports.

At about 9 am, a sloop of about 50 tons carrying rum came alongside *Royal George*'s port side. Ingram was one of those who began to unload her. He saw water lapping in over the gun-ports at every wave, and mice swimming in the hold, which the men were trying to catch, with 'a rare game going on'. In Ingram's view, the added weight of the rum, and the water lapping, in, brought the gun-ports level with the sea.

The carpenter went up to the quarterdeck to point the danger out to the officer of the watch, but he received, in Ingram's words, a very short answer. Water continued to slop in. The carpenter went up again. The officer of the watch was an unpopular lieutenant nicknamed 'Jib and Foresail Jack' from the habit of bothering the watch at night with orders to 'up jib' and 'down jib' and 'up foresail' and 'down foresail' every minute.

'Jib and Foresail Jack' told the carpenter, 'Damme, sir, if you can manage the ship better than I can, you had better take the command'. However, a moment later he ordered the drummer to call the hands to 'right ship'. Ingram ran down to his station on the third gun from forward on the starboard lower gun deck. He and the rest of his gun's crew tried to run their gun out but the list was too great and the gun kept on running back on them.

Everybody on board heard the sickening crack or rent as if the hull had been crushed. Water poured in through the port-side gun-ports. Ingram jumped into his gun-port and saw the other ports crammed full of heads. The ship was 'full of Jews, women and people selling all sorts of things'. One woman was trying to get out of the same port-hole as Ingram. He seized the bower anchor just above him and dragged the woman out.

Ingram could see men's heads sticking out of the ports all along the ship's side 'as though from chimneys'. But just as he threw the woman from him, the ship rolled over so far that the starboard side gun-ports were horizontal and Ingram saw all the heads drop

Sinking of the *Royal George*.

Sinking of the Royal George.

from the ports, because the men had nothing for their feet to rest on. Ingram felt the air venting out of the ship, blowing so hard it blew his hat off. The ship then 'sunk in a moment'. When going down, the *Royal George*'s main yard caught on the boom of the rum lighter, helping to bring her upright so that she sank on more or less an even keel.

Panther picked up twenty-seven of *Royal George*'s survivors, and other ships did what they could. One small boy was saved because he clung to the fleece of a swimming sheep. The woman Ingram had saved also survived. Ingram himself went down with the ship but bobbed up again with an open barrel of tar so that he surfaced as black as a negro. The admiral's baker was seen hanging on the mizzen top-mast shrouds which were above the water.

The exact number lost in the *Royal George* was never known. There were many visitors on board for the day, but some of her complement of over nine hundred men were ashore. It is probable that nearly a thousand people went down, including 'Jib and Foresail Jack', the carpenter — and Kempenfelt. It was said he had just been shaved by his barber and was writing in his cabin when the ship capsized and jammed the cabin-door shut, trapping the Admiral inside.

Bodies were still coming up, thirty or forty at a time, several days later. Some corpses surfaced 'so suddenly as to frighten anyone', but the watermen of Portsmouth, who tied ropes to the heels and towed the corpses ashore, made a good profit from the belts, buckles, wallets and watches of the dead.

The loss of the *Royal George* was a national disaster. It was still being replayed on the stage a century later. William Cowper wrote a solemn threnody to mourn the loss. 'Toll for the brave', he wrote, 'The brave! that are no more'. Cowper did not doubt the cause of the tragedy: 'A land breeze shook the shrouds, and she was overset.' 'Her timbers yet are sound,' he went on, 'and she may float again'.

Attempts were made in the following year to salvage the *Royal George*, but it was to be many years before she floated again. The court-martial on Thomas Waghorn, her Cap-

tain, who could not swim but hung on to the mizzenmast top-sail yard-arm, did not conclude that a land breeze overset the *Royal George* or that her timbers were sound. On the contrary, the court found that the *Royal George*'s hull had become badly decayed through neglect and the bottom had literally dropped out of her. But the verdict of the court, with the minutes and other documents, were suppressed to avoid a scandal.

Neither James Gardner's nor many other eighteenth century reminiscences of Portsmouth mentioned one of the most numerous types of ship in the Solent — the prison hulks. The prisoners landed from Kempenfelt's prizes joined thousands of other French prisoners-of-war, lodged in Portchester Castle, Forton, and in hulks. There were also some thousands of convicted criminals, male and female, who were also kept in hulks.

In late eighteenth century England there was, as in modern times, a 'crime wave' — real or imagined. Nearly two hundred crimes were capital offences; one could be hanged for impersonating a Yeoman of the Guard. Many sentences were commuted to imprisonment and 'transportation beyond the seas', which until the ending of the War of Independence in 1783, meant America.

But the American planters preferred slave labour, which could be kept for life, to convicts who had to be released after they had served their seven, fourteen or twenty-one year sentences. Thus, in a short time, the few prisons at home were full. The prison hulks, intended only as stop-gaps, were soon moored in long dismal lines in the Thames, the Solent and Langstone harbours, and they too were full.

Some new destinations for the prisoners had to be found. After much discussion, William Pitt's government decided on a remote bay on the east coast of Australia, which Captain Cook had visited briefly in *Endeavour* in 1770. On 31 August 1786, the then Home Secretary Lord Sydney wrote to the Admiralty that '750 of the convicts now in this Kingdom, under sentence of transportation, should be sent to Botany Bay, on the coast of New South Wales . . .'

Botany Bay was chosen very probably

because of public pressure on the government to be seen to be *doing* something, but there were other reasons. A South Pacific base would be useful for protecting British trade interests in the Pacific and the Indian ocean. The so-called 'criminal classes' would be 15,000 miles from their homes, which would surely discourage escape attempts.

There were few natives but they were supposed to be cannibals — another powerful discouragement to escapers. There were believed to be a good climate, fertile land and ample local resources, so the penal colony could be self-supporting. Norfolk Island, halfway to New Zealand, had stands of tall timber, good for men-of-war's masts, while New Zealand had flax and hemp, for sails and ropes. (In the event, not one mast, sail or rope for a man-of-war was ever manufactured by the penal colony).

The man chosen to organise and lead the expedition was Captain Arthur Phillip RN. He was forty-eight years old, the son of an immigrant language teacher from Frankfurt who had married an English girl. He went to sea at the age of sixteen and had served in the Royal and the Portuguese navies. He was a competent but hitherto undistinguished officer who had gone on half-pay in 1784. He was living as a semi-retired naval officer and gentleman farmer at Lyndhurst in the New Forest when he had his formal commission from George III on 27 April 1787, appointing him 'Governor of our territory called New South Wales' with the rank of Vice Admiral.

In fact, Phillip proved an admirable leader, being energetic, honest and painstaking, with enough imagination to realise, while still in England, what his colony would require in Australia. In fitting out his fleet, Phillip had to deal with dishonest victuallers, corrupt gaolers, greedy shipowners and infuriatingly slow, indecisive and incompetent bureaucrats in Whitehall.

There were eleven ships in the 'First Fleet', as it became known, of which only two were warships: Phillip's flagship *HMS Sirius* and the brig-sloop *HMS Supply*. There were three store-ships and six convict ships. It was not a large fleet to carry almost one thousand five hundred people — officers, seamen, marines,

Admiral Arthur Phillip.

women, children and convicts.

The first ships assembled at the Mother Bank late in December 1786. Four ships arrived already loaded with convicts from Woolwich and Plymouth. Some convicts were brought by road from London to Portsmouth. One naval officer who escorted the first batch of convicts for Botany Bay recalled 'all the shop windows and doors of Portsmouth being closed on this occasion, and the streets lined with troops, while the waggons, I think thirty in number, passed to Point Beach, where the boats were ready to receive them; as soon as they were embarked, they gave three tremendous cheers, and were rowed off to the transport ready for their reception at Spithead.'

It is impossible now to say whether doors and windows were shut because the people of Portsmouth expected trouble, or because they had been ordered to shut them. Neither the town fathers nor the local clergy appear to have had any response to the miserable stream of convicts which passed through their town.

For years Australians believed their ancestors were mostly either murderers or prostitutes or 'political prisoners', such as rick burners and early trade unionists. In fact, there were no murderers, prostitutes or offending trades unionists in the First Fleet. All their crimes were against property. Of 733 known indictments, over four hundred were for minor theft. There were convictions for breaking and entering, highway robbery, cattle or sheep rustling and mugging, with a few convicted of grand larceny, forgery, receiving stolen goods or impersonation. The oldest convict was an eighty-two-year-old woman, the youngest a nine-year-old chimney sweep.

Considering that they were supposed to be founding a new colony on the other side of the world — the modern equivalent of an expedition to the surface of the moon — the First Fleeters were an oddly and inappropriately chosen lot. Of their known occupations, about eighty were farm labourers, with one fisherman, two bricklayers, six carpenters, five shoemakers, eight seamen, two butchers, two tailors — and a jeweller. But most of the men were small-time criminals and ne'er-do-wells, and most of the women were domestic servants.

Phillip wanted to sail before the end of 1786, but the date was postponed four times. The last big group of convicts arrived from Newgate Gaol on 3 May 1787. By then, the ill-fed and scantily-clad convicts, many of them already suffering from 'gaol fever', had been in the overcrowded and insanitary ships for months. There was an outbreak of typhus in March 1787. Seventeen convicts died on board before sailing.

Phillip intended to sail on 12 May, but there were problems to the end. The Marines, who would be responsible for guarding the prisoners on passage and in Australia, were in a state of near-riot in the convict ship *Scarborough* because they knew there was not enough alcohol on board for their daily rations. Some of the sailors in the transports refused to put to sea because they had not been paid.

At last, at dawn on 13 May 1787, the First Fleet sailed, with *HMS Hyaena* towing the convict ship *Charlotte* for some way down Channel. After a week, there was unrest in the *Scarborough*, when the convicts tried to take over the ship. The rising was suppressed and the ring-leaders flogged. After such a start, the voyage as a whole went surprisingly well, despite the distance, the difficulties and the bad weather. The First Fleet sighted the coast of mainland Australia on 19 January 1788 and anchored in Botany Bay the next morning.

Phillips had brought his eleven tiny ships safely over 15,000 miles of ocean in 252 days. Many convicts were actually fitter at the end of their voyage than when they started. Forty-eight people had died: forty convicts, five convicts' children, a marine's wife, a marine's child and one marine. Considering the length of the voyage, the diet, and the state of medical knowledge in the eighteenth century, this casualty rate of just over three per cent was minute.

The land was poor at Botany Bay and there was a shortage of fresh water. On 26 January, the ships moved nine miles northward to Port Jackson, better known as Sydney harbour, and established the first settlement at Sydney Cove, near where the Opera House now stands.

Vice Admiral Phillip accomplished one of the greatest voyages in the Navy's history. It had been mounted from Portsmouth, which became known as the 'Mother of Australia'. The assembly and sailing of convict ships became a frequent, almost a commonplace, sight at Portsmouth for the next seventy years. From 1776 to 1795, 7,999 convicts were sent to Portsmouth and Woolwich. Of these, 2,207 were transported, 790 pardoned, 1,610 discharged and 1,946 (nearly one in four of the total) died before completing their sentences. Between 1800 and 1853, about twenty-eight thousand convicts embarked at Portsmouth for transportation over the sea.

Portsmouth retained its links with Australia. In 1836, nine ships sailed from England to found 'a new Australian colony, free of convictism' — South Australia. One of the nine, *HMS Buffalo*, sailed from Portsmouth with Captain Hindmarsh, the first Governor, and 171 emigrants. The last convict vessel to leave Spithead for Australia was the 630-ton *St Vincent*, on 17 January 1853.

On 15 June 1794, Admiral Lord Howe, known as 'Black Jack', arrived at Spithead with the prizes he had taken on 'The Glorious First of June'. It was, in fact, a four-day engagement which began on 28 May when Howe, with thirty-four ships of the line, sighted the French fleet of twenty-six sail of the line under Rear Admiral Villaret-Joyeuse, some 300 miles west of Brest. After four days of tracking and skirmishing, Howe broke his enemy's line in five places, sank one French ship and captured six.

King George III and Queen Charlotte came to Portsmouth on 26 June. The Royal barge took them out to Spithead where, to salutes from ships and forts, they went on board Howe's flagship, the most appropriately named *Queen Charlotte* (100 guns).

According to Midshipman William Dillon, who was there:

To the noble and gallant Lord Howe, His Majesty presented a diamond-hilted sword of the value of 3,300 guineas; also a gold chain to be worn round the neck . . . The two next senior Admirals, Graves and Hood were created Irish peers; the four Rear Admirals, baronets. All the Flag officers received gold chains similar to that given to Lord Howe, and the Captains received medals — at least a certain number of them. Pensions were settled on all that were wounded. All the Senior Lieutenants of the ships of the Line that were in action received the rank of Commander. The Master of the *Queen Charlotte*, Mr Bowen, was made a Lieutenant.

Howe was made a Freeman of Portsmouth and continued to be one of the most popular of admirals with the lower deck. However, he was an old man and growing tired of service. A younger commander might have done even better on the First of June. The French battle fleet's objective had been to meet and escort a large convoy of grain ships

Launching the *Prince of Wales* Man of War before their Majesties in 1794, at Portsmouth.

An exact Representation of Launching the Prince of Wales Man of War; before their Majesties, at Portsmouth.

from America. The convoy escaped, and every grain ship reached France. Many said Howe should have captured the convoy too.

Two days later, on 28 June, Their Majesties witnessed the launch in Portsmouth dockyard of the *Prince of Wales* (98 guns), and then went to Spithead for another review of the fleet. Next day, Sunday 29 June, the Town Clerk Stephen Barney wrote:

their Majesties and the Royal Family heard divine service at the Dock Chapel, afterwards went on board and viewed the Prince of Wales, then in a wett dock, appeared much pleased and satisfied with the exertions of the artificers of the Dock-yard in caulking and coppering that ship, which went off the stocks at 11 o'clock on Saturday, came into the wett dock on the next tide, and was caulked and coppered complete in nine hours.

It seemed that the Navy, ashore and afloat, was in good heart. When Howe received his sword, he pointed to *Queen Charlotte*'s seamen, who had given three rousing cheers for the King, and said 'Tis not I; tis those brave fellows who have gained the victory'.

Yet, in a very short time, Howe himself was to be called upon to deal with a mutiny amongst those very same cheering sailors which threatened the security of the country.

Chapter 8

'Mutiny, sir!' exclaimed Collingwood, one of the ablest and most humane of officers, when someone mentioned the possibility. 'Mutiny on my ship! If it should come to that, it must be my fault and that of every one of my officers!'

In fact, mutiny could occur in a good ship as well as a bad one, and to a humane captain as well as to a brutal one. In the late eighteenth century Navy, the sailors' conditions of service cried out for reform. Manning the Navy in time of war relied chiefly upon the press-gang. No leave was granted because all the men who went on leave would take leave of the Navy if they possibly could. Ships returning to England from overseas could have most of their crews transferred to other outward bound ships, so the wretched sailors, who might have been years away from home, had no chance of shore leave or of seeing their families.

Sailors' pay had been unchanged for nearly one hundred and fifty years, since January 1653, when the Commonwealth raised it to nineteen shillings a month. That had been ample then, even generous, but it had long since been overtaken by the cost of living. It was a long-standing custom not to pay sailors' wages at all for six months, and only then after various deductions, such as 'slops' (clothing), which reduced it to half its already meagre nominal value.

Normally, a sailor only received his back wages when his ship paid off. In some ships which had been a long time in commission, pay could be years overdue. A sailor was paid nothing while he was sick or recovering from wounds, even wounds received in action against the enemy.

Sailors' wages were not paid in cash but in 'pay-tickets' which had to be redeemed at the port of commission or sometimes at the Pay Office on Tower Hill in London — a very long journey from Plymouth or Portsmouth in the eighteenth century. When a sailor was drafted from one ship in commission to another, he seldom saw the wages owed to him from the first ship and, if he did, it would be in the form of a ticket which he could not exchange while he was on board.

In consequence, there was tremendous traffic in pay-tickets, whereby the sailor received cash from a ticket-buyer — but only at a grotesquely large discount. Ticket-buyers, local tradesmen, bumboat women, waterfront crimps, town whores, slop-sellers, ship's pursers and, not least, but most predatory of all, Admiralty Pay Office officials, joined together to operate what was nothing less than a well-established and widespread racket to rob the common sailor of his money.

The food on board a man-of-war was basically no better or worse than a man would have had if he had stayed at home and not joined the Navy, but the difficulties of storage and preservation on board ships soon led to deterioration in quality. Quantity was reduced by such devices as the 'service' scale of measurement. A sailor's pound of salt beef weighed, not sixteen ounces, but fourteen. This was no swindle, but a legal part of the Purser's official salary. But there were other, illegal, ways of depriving the sailor of his proper ration of food.

A hard life on board ship could be made almost intolerable by the ship's officers and petty officers. Many of the best (which often meant the most humane) Captains found flogging a time-consuming and inflexible punishment, but the absolute power vested in a Captain in the days of sail lent itself to abuse. There were too many tyrannical and sadistic Captains.

'The ill-treatment which we have and do receive from the tiriant (sic) of a Captain Fraizere (Fraser),' wrote the *Shannon*'s sailors in 1796, in one of the innumerable and largely ignored petitions to the Admiralty, 'from time to time, which is more than the spirits and harts of true English Man can cleaverly bear, for we are born free, but now we are slaves.'

Some of the petitions showed a touching (and quite unrealistic) faith in the Admiralty's concern for its employees. 'The ill-usage we have on board this ship forced us to fly to your Lordships the same as a child to its father,' pleaded the sailors of the *Nassau* in 1795. 'It is almost impossible for us to pit it down in paper as cruel as it really is with flogging and abusing above humanity.'

In short, grounds for resentment leading to mutiny lay on every side, in every aspect of naval life. Mutinies took place nearly every year and often more than once a year. In April 1780, four seamen and three marines on the *Invincible* were condemned to death for refusing to put to sea when ordered. In April 1781, four men of the *Prothee* were convicted of mutiny. Three were sentenced to be flogged through the fleet at Spithead; one man was to have 400, one 500 and the third 600 lashes. The ring-leader was hanged (very probably a more merciful punishment) because he had intended to seize the ship and take her over to the enemy.

In March 1783, there was trouble in the *Janus, Ganges* and *Proselyte* over payment of wages. The crews said that if they were not paid at once they would run their ships ashore and destroy them. Lord Howe came down to Portsmouth and 'quieted their minds'. But in April, the men of the *Queen* caused a riot over pay, and lost the benefits of possibly entry to Greenwich Hospital and other rights, as punishment.

In June, men of the *Alecto* waited on Mr Lindegren, the Navy prize agent, in a riotous manner. When he refused their demands, they threatened to pull his house down. Later the same month, men of the *Raisonnable* refused to weigh anchor for Chatham, where they were told they would be paid. They demanded to be paid where they were, at Portsmouth. The Captain seized twelve mutineers, while Admiral Montagu ordered the guns of other men-of-war and of Southsea Battery to be trained on the ship. The men gave in, the twelve were convicted, seven were condemned to death and four of them were hanged on 11 August. Two men were hanged in October, after a mutiny in the *Jupiter*.

On 12 September 1792, the trial began on board the *Duke* at Portsmouth of the most famous mutineers in naval history. Some of the crew of the *Bounty* mutinied in April 1789, placing their Captain, William Bligh, and eighteen loyal men in an open launch, expecting that to be the end of them. By superlative seamanship, Bligh sailed the boat 3,600 miles to the island of Timor in the Dutch East Indies.

The frigate *Pandora* was sent to hunt the mutineers down and found fourteen of them at Tahiti. *Pandora* was wrecked on the way home but ten mutineers survived. Four were acquitted, and six condemned to death. Three were pardoned, but three were hanged at the yard-arm of the *Brunswick* in Portsmouth harbour on 29 October, 1792. Fletcher Christian and the other mutineers settled on Pitcairn Island and were never brought to justice.

There were other mutinies, notably in the *Windsor Castle* at Corsica in November 1794 and in the *Culloden* in Howe's fleet in December. Thus, by 1797, mutiny was a regrettable but familiar part of life in the Navy, but it seldom achieved its expressed objects and was almost always savagely punished. Lower deck petitions were commonplace and could be ignored, as they had always been: sailors were legendary grumblers. Their pay certainly was low and their food undeniably bad, but so they had been for years. Meanwhile, there was a war on, against revolutionary France, and the country would need every available seaman, mutinous or not.

The year had begun well, with Admiral John Jervis' famous victory over the Spanish fleet off Cape St Vincent on 14 February. Captain Horatio Nelson, commanding the *Captain* (74 guns), distinguished himself and turned the course of the battle by completely ignoring the Fighting Instructions.

The Admiralty was therefore stunned by the news, on 16 April 1797, that the Channel Fleet under Admiral Lord Bridport had mutinied at Spithead. Nor was it a case of one ship or even a few disaffected ships. Astonishingly, the whole fleet was involved: the line of battle ships *Royal George* (another first-rate, launched in 1788, and now Bridport's flagship), *Queen Charlotte, Royal Sovereign, London, Glory, Duke, Mars, Marlborough, Ramillies, Robust, Impetueux, Defence, Terrible, Pompee, Minotaur* and *Defiance*, and every frigate at Spithead, had refused to obey Lord Bridport's order to weigh anchor.

The country also could hardly credit the news. The *Navy* in mutiny! The Navy was the Nation's Bulwark. *Heart of oak are our ships, jolly tars are our men, we always are ready . . . Steady, boys, steady . . .* The Government

Alexander Hood, Viscount Bridport.

was utterly taken aback but already looking for scapegoats. The City was in a panic. Ordinary people felt the end of the normal world had come to pass. Or maybe the revolutionary spirit abroad in France was infectious and had crossed the Channel.

The British public could be excused for being amazed. The Admiralty had no excuse. They had had ample warning over a number of years. In 1795, Captain Philip Patton, the transport officer at Portsmouth who dealt with the tenders bringing in newly-pressed men, reported to Lord Spencer, the First Lord of the Admiralty, that in his opinion a general mutiny at Portsmouth was possible. Lord Spencer took no notice of the warning.

In 1795, under the pressure of the war, the pay of the private soldier was raised to one shilling a day; it was only justice that the pay of the ordinary seaman, his naval equal, should be similarly increased. The Admiralty did not do so. In December 1796, Captain the Hon. Thomas Pakenham (who had restored order on board after the *Culloden* mutiny) wrote to Lord Spencer from Portsmouth. Through the stiltedly polite wording and convoluted phrases, Pakenham's meaning was plain: seamen's pay should be increased. He suggested 'accomplished seamen' should get 30 shillings a month while the war was on, and 24 shillings 'at the peace'.

Lord Spencer replied on the same day he received the letter, in equally baroque and oblique language, that 'The other subject (i.e. pay), though undoubtedly one which we cannot but wish for a proper opportunity of giving some relief upon it, is however so very dangerous to be stirred, that I trust everyone will see the propriety of not allowing it to be agitated on any account whatever', In one word: *no*.

Lord Spencer evidently believed that, just as in the past, that would now be that, but there had recently been a small but significant change in recruiting for the Navy. The old-time sailor was like a patient beast of burden, conscious that he was being driven, abused and ill-treated, but unable to do anything to improve his state except send ineffectual petitions to Their Lordships. It had ever been thus. It had been so in their fathers' day, and in their grandfathers'. Many sailors came from sea-faring families who, literally, knew the ropes.

However, under the desperate need to man the Navy in time of war, Pitt's Government passed the so-called Quota Acts of 1795 and 1796. Under these, towns and counties were required to provide men for the Navy, according to their size. Thus, Yorkshire's quota was 1,081 and Rutland's 23; London had to provide 5,704, Newcastle 1,240, and Bristol 666.

Many of the Quota men were the uttermost sweepings of local gaols: small-time criminals, pickpockets, poachers, beggars, ne'er-do-wells and local 'hard cases', but some men enlisted voluntarily, attracted by the bounties offered. Amongst these volunteers were men of some education and professional background: discredited or bankrupted businessmen, disgraced lawyers, failed or sacked school-teachers, perhaps even men of some previous standing in their communities whose families wanted them to disappear to mitigate some scandal. Maybe there were even some young men of good family who took the bounty and joined the Navy from a sense of adventure.

It is impossible to determine precisely the part Quota men played in fostering the mutiny, the 'Breeze' at Spithead as it was called, but certainly they must have introduced new awareness, literacy and some smattering of knowledge of the law to the messdecks. For the first time there were now men ready and able to point out the wrongs done to the sailor, and ways of putting those wrongs right. In a sense, these Quota men provided a vital yeast of militancy in what could be termed the lumpen-proletariat of the lower deck.

Whoever they were, the leaders of the mutiny preserved their own anonymity. But they succeeded in involving almost every man on the lower deck, from 'old salts' to newly-pressed men, from raw ordinary seamen to senior petty officers; honest men and crooks, native Englishmen and foreigners, young and old, all took part and not one gave the game away. They made their plans and kept them secret for weeks, on messdeck after

Portsmouth 1799. 'The Spanish Dollars Make the English Sailors Merry'. The Spanish frigates *Santa Brigida* and *Thetis* were captured in October 1799; the sailors each got £180 in prize money, which they quickly spent in Portsmouth.

messdeck, where privacy was impossible, where 'narks' abounded, only too ready to relay news of disaffection to the quarterdeck, and where the least whisper of mutiny could mean the cat or the noose.

Once the mutiny had started, the leaders kept their heads when matters might have gone awry. They stuck together when indecision or internal dissent would have been fatal. They were not browbeaten or overawed by rank. They were unafraid of naval law and the terrible instruments of naval justice. They avoided antagonising public opinion; indeed, their 'public relations' throughout were excellent. They organised what was in effect a mass industrial strike superbly well, minimising bloodshed and maximising the benefits. They achieved what came near to a social revolution — and they must have organised it all during infrequent Sunday afternoons in harbour, which were the only times sailors could go from ship to ship and visit each other.

Early in 1797, the leaders prepared a 'humble' petition, soberly and respectful phrased, which addressed itself only to the particular grievances of pay. It asked for the men to be treated equally with the army and the Militia over pay, and protesting their loyalty to the Sovereign. The petitions were written out separately, but they were all clearly copies of the same original. It is likely that a common petition was drawn up and each ship was then supposed to make its own copy. However, only eleven copies were made (or survived).

By 7 March 1797, the petitions had been smuggled ashore and sent to Admiral Lord Howe, retired but still the titular Commander-in-Chief of the Channel Fleet (Bridport was his second-in-command), whom the petitioners obviously thought was their best hope.

'Black Dick' was very popular with the lower deck. They thought of him as the sailor's friend. He was known to be sympathetic to the sailors' cause. After a battle, he would come down and visit the wounded, bringing wine and sympathy, and, if the worst should happen, would write letters of commiseration to the next-of-kin. but he was now seventy-two years old and a martyr to gout. He was, in fact, at Bath, taking the waters for his affliction.

Howe noted that the petitions were 'all exact copies of each other . . . without any signature'. He decided they were 'fabricated by some malicious individual, who meant to insinuate the prevalence of a general discontent in the Fleet'. However, some small seed of doubt must have remained in Howe's mind, for he write to Lord Hugh Seymour, a Commissioner of the Admiralty, asking him whether any such discontent had been noticed at Portsmouth. Seymour made some desultory enquiries and replied that it had not.

Howe could not have been quite satisfied. When he was next able, on 22 March, he went to London and gave the petitions to Seymour, who showed them to Lord Spenser, who was loath indeed to ask Parliament for more money, or even to broach such a hoary old topic, at a time of already high taxation. Spenser was anything but a stupid man, and was certainly not an inhumane one, but, once again, he did nothing.

After a month's silence, the sailors decided 'Black Dick' must have let them down. The new plan was to send another petition directly to Parliament, and, when the ships next returned to Spithead, to refuse to put to sea again until the demands were met. By now the messdeck 'narks' were reporting that seditious meetings were being held in the ships. On 13 April, Captain Patton visited the *Queen Charlotte*, Howe's old flagship, and to his astonishment and dismay, saw sailors gathering in groups and arguing together on the foredeck. Some sailors had even trespassed on the sacred quarterdeck, with the officers doing nothing to stop them.

When Patton got ashore, he had a message sent by the newly-installed 'Semaphore' on Southsea beach, which was relayed to the Admiralty roof (in three and a half minutes) via Portsdown Hill, Telegraph Hill near Petersfield, Blackdown, Hanscomb, Cabbage Hill, Putney, and Chelsea Hospital: 'Mutiny brewing at Spithead'. Bridport himself came up to London the next day, saying that 'disagreeable combinations' were being formed, particularly in the *Queen Charlotte*.

On 15 April, Bridport, by now sure there was trouble brewing, ordered his Captains to muster their men and invite them to state their grievances. Next day, Their Lordships sent Bridport orders to prepare to put to sea and send eight ships of the line under Admiral Sir Alan Gardner down to St Helens. Bridport replied that he was convinced his crews would not sail.

Nor would they. It seems the mutiny had originally been planned for a day or two later, but evidently the men decided the moment had come and further delay might be dangerous. When the signal was hoisted to weigh anchor, nothing happened. Instead, the sailors of the *Queen Charlotte* manned the fore shrouds and gave three ringing cheers, the signal for the mutiny to begin, answered at once from every other·ship.

When Gardner tried to take his ships to sea, they also refused. Two boats, from the *Queen Charlotte* and the *Royal George*, visited every ship, to instruct their crews to allow their officers to remain on board, to obey all orders, except to weigh anchor, and to elect two 'Delegates' and send them to a meeting that evening on board the *Queen Charlotte*.

The Delegates came from all over the country (though none from Portsmouth), and included an American and four midshipmen who were not, however, the 'young gentlemen' normally associated with the rank, but senior petty officers in the eighteenth century Navy. Valentine Joyce and John Fleming, who were to play leading parts, were almost certainly Quota men, and there was also a mysterious Evans, who was reputed to have had legal training. Their ships, names, ratings and birthplaces, with their ages when they joined their ships, are:

Royal George: Valentine Joyce, Quarter Master's Mate, Jersey 25; John Morrice, A.B., Aberdeen 32

Royal Sovereign: John Richardson, A.B., Piltown 26; Joseph Green, A.B. York, 26

London: Alexander Harding, Gunner's Mate, Greenock 23; William Riley, Quarter Master, Westminster, 27; John Fleming, A.B., Glasgow, 25

Queen Charlotte: John Huddlestone, Yeoman of Sheets, Holvach, 34; Patrick Glynn, A.B., Dublin, 34

Glory: Patrick Duggan, Midshipman, Waterford, 28; John Bethell, Midshipman, London, 33

Duke: Michael Adams, Quarter Gunner, Rochester, 33; William Anderson, Quarter Master, Dublin, 33

Mars: Thomas Allen, A.B., Hartley, Northumberland, 29; James Blythe, A.B., Ashridge, Yorks, 30

Marlborough: William Screaton, A.B., London, 25; John Vassie, Yeoman of Sheets, Lanark, 27

Ramillies: Charles Berry, Midshipman, London, 33; George Clear, A.B., Angmering, 25

Robust: Charles Berry, Midshipman, London, 33; John Scrivenor, Yeomen of Sheets, North Shields, 31

Impetueux: William Porter, Quarter Master, Suffolk, 25; John Whitney, A.B., America, 24

Defence: George Gallaway, Midshipman, Coldstream, 28; James Berwick, Quarter Master, Westberry, Wilts, 30

Terrible: Mark Turner, Midshipman, Harwich, 37; George Salkeld, Yeoman of Powder Room, Walsingham, 39

La Pompee: William Potts, Quarter Master, Harthy, 24; James Melvin, Quarter Master, Sunderland, 34

Minotaur: Denis Lawler, Quarter Gunner, Kildare, 34; George Crossland, A.B., Thorn, 31

Defiance: John Saunders, A.B., Pembrokeshire, 33; John Husband, A.B., Whitby, 27

These Delegates sat daily in the Great Cabin — the Admiral's cabin — of the *Queen Charlotte*. They behaved properly and soberly at all times, enforcing discipline — one sailor of *La Pompee* was flogged at their orders for illegally bringing liquor on board — and maintaining the ship's usual routine. Captains were paid all the proper marks of respect when entering or leaving their ships. But the Delegates themselves were also paid the same respects when going over the side. Every ship gave three cheers at eight in the morning, and again at sunset, to show that all was well.

The Delegates also wanted to demonstrate to the British public that they were not wild revolutionaries but had the country's interests at heart. Their only quarrel was with the Admiralty. Normal trade must continue. Thus, on 17 April, when the crews of the *Romney* and the *Venus* wanted to stay at Spithead and see what happened instead of escorting a convoy to Newfoundland, they were prevailed upon by the Delegates to sail, which they did on the 20th.

The Delegates gained more public sympathy by publishing their petition to Parliament. It went much further than their original petition to Howe. They asked again for an increase in pay, but they also asked that the quality and quantity of their food be improved; that the sick on board should get proper medical attention; that ordinary leave be granted to the fleet in harbour; and that men wounded in action should continue to be paid while they recovered.

Lastly, but most importantly, they asked that 'if any ship has real grievances to complain of, we hope Your Lordships will readily redress them, as far as in your power, to prevent disturbances'. Flogging was not mentioned: the Delegates knew that in the eighteenth century fleet in which they served it was a necessary deterrent. What they wanted was some means of communicating and redressing grievances against brutal officers in individual ships.

The Admiralty's first reaction to news of trouble had been to give Bridport orders to sail which were so far removed from reality that even Bridport thought them ridiculous. On 18 April, Lord Spenser himself came down to Portsmouth with Lord Arden, the Civil Lord, Rear Admiral Young and the second Secretary, William Marsden. They arrived at noon, went straight to the Fountain Inn, and summoned Bridport to tell them what was going on. As a result, Admirals Gardner, Colpoys and Pole were sent back to the fleet, with the offer of a small increase of pay. But the questions of food, medical care on board and leave were ignored.

The longer the Delegates thought about this 'project', as it was called, and they considered it throughout the forenoon and afternoon of the 19th, the more irritable and impatient they became. Their answer arrived at 4.30 pm, as Their Lordships were at dinner. The Delegates repeated their previous demands, neither more nor less, except that they now specified the increase in pay; one shilling a day.

Their Lordships, who had expected acquiescence and a speedy return to normality, followed by retribution, were outraged and enraged. They still had not grasped the true nature of the problem which faced them. Spenser had just had a letter from Captain John Willet Payne, of the *Impetueux*, on the 'present unhappy posture of our fleet' in which he said that 'the character of the present mutiny is perfectly French. The singularity of it consists in the great secrecy and patience with which they waited for a thorough union before it broke out, and the immediate establishment of a *system of terror*'.

Payne was right about the secrecy and the thorough union but absurdly wrong about the 'French *system of terror*'. This was, in fact, a peculiarly English mutiny, but, labouring under such misapprehensions, and the influence of some wine with their dinners, Their Lordships hatched a plan to slip the cables of most of the ships and take them down to St Helens, leaving only the worst affected at Spithead. They summoned Bridport, the three Admirals and sixteen Captains the next day to give them their orders.

Matters looked different in the sober (in more senses than one) light of morning. Bridport and the others said the plan was quite simply impossible. Nobody would obey. Every man in the fleet was involved. Even the sick at Haslar were stringing their handkerchiefs together and flying them as banners of encouragement.

Nevertheless, it was still a very polite mutiny. On 19 April, the Prince of Wurttemburg, who was to marry the Princess Royal, came down to Portsmouth to be made a Freeman. Spencer and Bridport actually took the Prince in the commissioner's barge for a tour of the fleet. Every ship was in a state of open mutiny but the sailors manned yards and gave three cheers for His Serene Highness.

The people of Portsmouth seemed generally on the sailors' side. Certainly, the local press was sympathetic to the sailors' cause, printing their demands in full, and commenting upon their orderliness and general good conduct. National press comment, apart from *The Times*, was just as favourable. 'It is but common justice', said the *London Chronicle* on the 19th, 'to say that the seamen have conducted themselves throughout the whole business with a sobreity, steadiness, unanimity and determination, that would do honour to a better cause.'

The more sensible officers agreed. Lieutenant Philip Beaver, of the *Monarch*, wrote to his sister on 20 April, 'The seamen still continue to conduct themselves incredibly well, performing the usual duties with alacrity, and behaving towards their officers with the greatest respect. I had always great respect for an English seaman; I like the character now better than ever'.

Lord Spencer now realised he must genuinely give some ground, although he still prevaricated. He would raise the pay of ABs and ordinary seamen to what was demanded, and the pound would henceforth be 16 ounces. But on food, leave, or the redress of grievances, he was silent. Finally, as a precondition of his offer, everyone was now to return to their duty and there would be no recriminations.

Early on 21 April, the men mustered in their ships to hear the terms of the offer read out to them by their Captains who, naturally, advocated acceptance in the most persuasive terms they could muster. Some sailors were tempted to agree. They were flattered that they had brought the First Lord of the Admiralty himself down to Portsmouth. They had not won all they had asked for, but at least they had something, which was more than most mutinies had achieved. On board the *Duke*, for instance, Captain Holloway had almost persuaded his ship's company to return to duty when, at the last critical moment, a sailor at the back shouted 'Let's wait and see what the *Queen Charlotte* does!'

Admiral Gardner, flying his flag in the *Royal Sovereign*, was waiting impatiently for the Delegates of his ship to return from the *Queen Charlotte*. He had already addressed *Royal Sovereign*'s sailors on the first day, 16 April, without achieving anything. Now, he resolved to try again and had himself rowed over to *Queen Charlotte*, taking Colpoys and Pole with him.

Gardner was an eloquent speaker, although his eloquence held an underlying menace. He began to talk of 'condign punishment' if the men refused, 'the utmost vengeance of the law' and 'the forgiveness for which the Board of the Admiralty have solemnly and publicly pledged their faith'.

Like Holloway, Gardner almost succeeded. He got as far as sitting down to write a letter for submission which all the men were to sign, when four of the most influential of the Delegates, Valentine Joyce and John Morrice from the *Royal George,* and Patrick Glynn and John Huddlestone of the *Queen Charlotte*, arrived alongside by boat and joined the meeting. They had not heard Gardner's eloquence, but they had caught phrases like 'condign punishment' and 'utmost severity', and references to 'forgiveness'.

Who could trust the *Admiralty's* forgiveness? The mutineers of the *Culloden* three years earlier had thought themselves pardoned and only found out their grave mistake when it was too late to produce the evidence to save them from the noose. The Delegates were certainly not going to be trapped into the same error. The only pardon worth anything was the King's. Nothing would be agreed until that pardon was assured. At these words from the Delegates, the mood of the meeting changed, to a firm resolve once again to carry on with the mutiny.

Gardner was understandably frustrated and infuriated. He began to berate the Delegates, calling them 'a dammed mutinous blackguard set . . . who knew the French were ready for sea, but were afraid of meeting them'. He seized one by the shoulder and shook him, shouting that he would hang him and every fifth man in the fleet.

At once the Great Cabin became a scene of pandemonium, with Gardner shouting to make himself heard, while the sailors shouted back and hissed the three Admirals, who were lucky not to be assaulted. They were escorted, none too politely, to the gangway and hustled down to their boat.

Joyce and Morrice held a meeting in the *Royal George* and hoisted the red flag which the officers took as the signal for revolution. When the Captain of the *Royal George* had Bridport's flag hauled down in disgust, Bridport himself swore he would never hoist it again.

Attitudes amongst the Delegates were now hardening. Watches were set, as though the fleet were actually at sea, and expecting an enemy. Guns were run out and manned. The officers were kept confined and some of the more hated ones sent ashore. A fresh manifesto was produced which allowed no misunderstanding: their petition must be answered in full and put into effect by Act of Parliament. No verbal reply would do. The King's Pardon must be obtained for every man in the fleet.

Lord Spencer did obtain the King's Pardon, and sent a hundred printed copies of it down to Spithead. This seemed to cool the mutiny. Bridport addressed the men of the *Royal*

George, who hauled down the red flag and rehoisted his. Many ships weighed anchor and went to St Helens where they prepared to go to sea. By 24 April, most of the fleet was at St Helens and would have sailed had the wind been fair. Unfortunately for the Admiralty, the wind set foul in the east and kept the fleet in harbour.

The men, knowing nothing of bureaucracy, had expected action as rapid and dramatic as their own, but the Admiralty bureaucrats, being totally ignorant of living and working conditions in the fleet, had never made haste in their entire working lives and they did not hurry now. Any Act of Parliament took time to draft. It is unlikely that the Admiralty deliberately dragged its feet, but nobody was impressed, as they certainly ought to have been, by any sense of urgency. The days passed, while the wind stayed foul, and the men, already deeply suspicious of the Admiralty and all its works, began to suspect they had been betrayed.

On 1 May, there were rumours in the *Duke* that Captain Holloway had received some document from the Admiralty to the effect that the petition's terms were not going to be met. Whether it did or not, Holloway was alarmed enough to destroy it, or so he told the men when they insisted on seeing it. The men seized Holloway and sent a message to Bridport demanding a copy or they would either hang Holloway or give him 'a degrading punishment' — a flogging.

Bridport sent over a copy but the respite it achieved was brief. On 5 May, a boat from the *Mars* hailed the *Queen Charlotte* with the news that Parliament was not going to pass the Seamen's Bill, and threw on board a bundle of newspapers containing a report of a House of Lords debate which did appear to confirm the news.

In vain, Bridport read out his copy of the Bill as drafted. He was not believed. The men had waited a fortnight, which in their opinion was ample time to draft and pass a dozen Bills. The wind was fair on Sunday, 7 May, and the fleet could have sailed, but the men refused. The mutiny was on again, and, this time, much uglier than before.

Chapter 9

It was largely the fault of Admiral Colpoys. He had tried to stop the Delegates coming on board his flagship, the *London*, on 16 April until Bridport sensibly warned him not to resist. By 7 May, Colpoys, like all the officers, had had a difficult fortnight. Furthermore, he had just had another message from the Admiralty ordering him to be more severe on breaches of discipline. When *London*'s Captain, Edward Griffiths (actually Colpoys' nephew), told Colpoys that morning that the Delegates' boats were coming up from St Helens to visit some of the ships lying in the main anchorage at Spithead, Colpoys lost his temper and resolved he would not have these 'mutinous dogs' on board his ship again.

Colpoys ordered all *London*'s boats to be hoisted and the gun-port lids shut. He armed the officers and the marines, turned up all hands on deck and addressed them, as Gardner had done. Like Gardner, he thought they had won and the men would obey him. He ordered them below. Some obeyed and the hatches were shut on them, but some stayed on the forecastle.

When the Delegates reached the *London*, they were warned off. The men below guessed what was happening and hammered on the hatches to open them. The officers resisted them and called to Colpoys to ask if they should fire. Colpoys shouted 'Yes certainly, they must not be allowed to come up until I order them'.

The men on the forecastle, who had seen what Colpoys and the officers were doing, cast loose one of the forward guns, so as to train it aft. *London*'s First Lieutenant, Peter Bover, ordered them to stop, or he would fire. They all stopped, except one man who carried on clearing the gun. Bover fired and hit the man, mortally wounding him. With a roar of 'Blood for blood', the men on the forecastle rushed aft while the men below stormed out of the hatches. The officers fired, killing three seamen. Several men were wounded on both sides.

Colpoys and the officers had looked to the marines for support but the marines changed sides or, more probably, had never intended to act against the sailors. All except two joined the sailors or flung away their arms.

Colpoys saw that he must accept defeat. Cooler heads on both sides tried to calm the situation, which was still very tense. Bover was seized and dragged forward. A rope was rove through a block on a yard. The noose was put round Bover's neck and the hands were just about to haul him up when Valentine Joyce, *Royal George*'s Delegate, forced himself through the crush, flung his arms around Bover's neck and shouted above the uproar: 'If you hang this young man you shall hang me, for I shall never quit him!' The men on the rope hesitated. Bover was popular with the sailors, indeed one of the topmen called out at the moment that he was a 'brave boy'.

Colpoys was also a brave man and took advantage of the moment to run up and stand on the forecastle facing the sailors. There was every chance they would seize him, too. They were thoroughly roused and in such a mood they might do anything. There on the deck was the blood of their ship-mates. In front of them was the man responsible. A hoarse voice from the back growled, 'You're a damned bloody scoundrel!'

At this, a curious thing happened. While Colpoys braced himself for the rush he thought was coming, the sailors lowered their weapons, turned on the speaker and jostled him, calling out 'How dare you speak to the Admiral in that manner!'.

Evidently, the general feeling was that although there might be a mutiny in progress that was still no reason to use such disrespectful language to an admiral.

The ship's doctor, another popular personality, persuaded the men to listen to the admiral. Colpoys explained that Bover had been acting under his orders, just as he himself had been acting under 'very recent instructions' from the Admiralty.

The men pricked up their ears. What recent instructions? They demanded to see them. Colpoys was allowed to go to his cabin under escort to get them. He very wisely took as long as possible to search for the right key and find the right document, thus allowing time for tempers to cool. When he went back on deck he was relieved to see that the rope had been taken from Bover's neck, but he, Bover and Griffiths were taken to their cabins under arrest, pending court martial upon a charge of murder. The red flag flew once again at *London*'s masthead.

It might have gone hard for the accused. Many sailors still wanted 'blood for blood'. But quite unexpectedly a successful plea for clemency was made by AB John Fleming, who had replaced the *London* Delegate wounded in the fracas. He might have been a Quota man. Certainly, he was an excellent advocate. Bover was released and invited to stay in the ship. Colpoys and Griffiths were eventually put ashore (Colpoys never to serve afloat again).

A hundred other officers were put ashore, among them Admiral Gardner, James Anthony Gardner, then second lieutenant in the *Hind,* Captain Holloway and many of the officers of the *Duke,* and all the officers of the *Glory*. Portsmouth, Southsea and Gosport were suddenly filled with unemployed and homeless naval officers, their chests and their swords. 'The horror and confusion of this town are beyond description,' wrote the *London Chronicle* reporter from Portsmouth.

The Seamen's Bill was passed on 8 May. A new Royal Pardon was necessary and this was also obtained. Somebody in the Government conceived the brilliant idea of asking Lord Howe to visit the fleet on a mission of reconciliation. Howe had himself rowed to every ship and he took Lady Howe with him. Valentine Joyce, on behalf of all the Delegates, had asked for the honour of her company. Howe himself invited Joyce into the Governor's House to take a glass of wine with him, which invitation Joyce accepted 'with a manly freedom, unaccompanied by the least particle of familiarity or rudeness'.

All the Spithead Delegates' demands were granted, if not at once, then at least in principle. It was a famous victory for ordinary men who combined irresistibly to get their rights. And, apart from the trouble in *London*, it came about with very little bloodshed. No Spithead mutineer was court martialled, imprisoned, flogged, sentenced to death, or hanged. The same could not be said for the mutiny in the North Sea Fleet at the Nore, when 412 were court-martialled, twenty-nine imprisoned, nine flogged, fifty-nine sentenced to death and twenty-nine hanged, including Richard Parker, the mutiny's leader.

There were also mutinies at the Cape, in the East Indies, and at Cadiz when, later in the year, the Mediterranean Fleet was joined by 'Spithead-tainted' ships. Admiral Sir John Jervis, the Commander-in-Chief Mediterranean, was not Bridport or Lord Spenser. He was the grimmest disciplinarian in the Navy. Furthermore, he was in a difficult situation, commanding a fleet some way from home, off an enemy coast-line.

Thus, when 'Old Jarvey' dealt with a mutiny, there were no Royal Pardons, no 'Delegates', no debate, no delay at all. He hanged mutineers first and notified the Admiralty later. For instance, the court martials of four mutineers of the *St George* did not end until after dark on Saturday, 8 July 1797. All four were found guilty and condemned to death. The next day was Sunday but Jervis ordered the hangings to be carried out at half past seven the next morning, the hanging ropes to be manned by sailors from *St George* alone (and not joined, as was the usual custom in this 'painful Service', by men from other ships).

When, on that Sunday evening, Jervis' second-in-command, Vice Admiral Sir Charles Thompson, protested against the executions taking place on the Sabbath, Jervis insisted on him being removed from the Fleet immediately. But Rear Admiral Sir Horatio Nelson KB, commanding the Inshore Squadron, with his flag in the *Theseus*, fully approved.

Nelson was one of the most humanitarian of officers. More than once he himself commuted a death sentence for mutiny. When he first heard of the Spithead Delegates' petition he said: 'I am entirely with the Seamen in their first complaint. We are a neglected set'. But on this occasion he wrote to Jervis on the 9th

> In the first place, I congratulate you on the finish, as it ought, of the *St George's* business, and (if I may be permitted to say so) very much approve of its being so speedily carried into execution, even although it is Sunday. The particular situation of the service requires extraordinary measures. I hope this will end all the disorders in our Fleet; had there been the same determined spirit at home, I do not believe it would have been half so bad, not but that I think Lord Howe's sending back the first petition was wrong.

He wrote in even stronger terms to Captain Sir Robert Calder: 'Had it been Christmas Day instead of Sunday, I would have executed them.

A few weeks later, in the early hours of 25 July, Nelson's right elbow was shattered by grapeshot as he landed from a boat leading the attack on Santa Cruz, Tenerife. He was taken back to the *Theseus* where his right arm was amputated 'very high, near the shoulder' by the ship's assistant surgeon, a Royalist Frenchman, M.Ronicet.

Nelson took passage home in the *Seahorse* with her Captain, Thomas Fremantle, who had also been wounded in the arm, and Mrs Fremantle. They arrived at Spithead on 1 September. It was a gloomy day, of driving rain and wind, with a choppy sea, too rough for lady passengers, but after dinner with the Fremantles, Nelson insisted on being rowed ashore in his barge.

He stayed at the 'George' where he was welcomed by the landlord and the whole town. Nelson was now well on his way to becoming a national celebrity. 'My general reception from John Bull,' he told St Vincent, 'has been just what I wished'. On 3 September 1797, when he had received permission to haul down his flag, and the rest of his baggage had been landed, Nelson travelled to join Lady Nelson at Bath.

Nelson had a link with Portsmouth through his uncle Captain Maurice Suckling, who had first taken 'Poor Horace' to sea in the *Raisonnable* in 1771. Suckling became Comptroller of the Navy and Member of Parliament for Portsmouth. In 1776, Nelson was invited more than once to dine with his own Captain of the *Worcester* and the Mayor of Portsmouth. He was only eighteen years old and an acting lieutenant, but he was the nephew of a very important man in Portsmouth.

Nelson's visits to Portsmouth punctuated his career. In April 1777, he was appointed 2nd Lieutenant of the *Lowestoft* frigate which sailed from Spithead for Jamaica on 16 May. In December 1780, he arrived at Spithead in the *Lion*, so sick after the disastrous campaign in Nicaragua that he could only just make the coach journey to London to convalesce.

In January 1782, Nelson brought his ship the *Albemarle*, a French merchantman captured in 1780 and converted into a 28-gun frigate, to Spithead after a collision. On the 26th, the *Brilliant*, an East India store ship which was part of a convoy *Albemarle* was escorting, had been driven from her anchor in the Downs and crashed across *Albemarle*'s bows. 'All done in five minutes!' Nelson exclaimed. 'We ought to be thankful we did not founder. Such are the blessings of a sea life!'

Nelson was convinced *Albemarle*, 'poor *Albemarle*', was not worth repairing, but the country was at war and every ship was priceless. 'Mr White, the builder of Portsmouth dockyard' came on board to make a preliminary survey of the damage and declared it could be repaired by Portsmouth dockyard in three months. *Albemarle*, 'the old

Albemarle', was able to sail in April 1782 for the North American Station.

Albemarle came into Portsmouth harbour again on 26 June 1783. 'After all my tossing about into various climates,' Nelson wrote to his friend and old Captain, William Locker, for whom he had brought a fine present of rum and cigars which he hoped the Customs would overlook, 'here at last am I arrived, safe and sound. I found orders for the *Albemarle* to be paid off at this place. On Monday next I hope to be rid of her. My people I fancy will be pretty quiet, if they are not set on by some of the Ships here'.

Nelson was alluding to a spate of mutinies in ships being paid off that summer, now that war was over. Their crews insisted on being paid at Portsmouth and not at Spithead. Nelson went up to London and for three weeks was busy in affairs connected with *Albemarle*. 'My time, ever since I arrived in Town,' he wrote to Locker, apologising for not having written sooner, 'has been taken up in attempting to get the wages due to my *good fellows*, for various Ships they have served in the war. The disgust of the Seamen to the Navy is all owing to the infernal plan of turning them over from Ship to Ship, so that Men cannot be attached to their Officers or the Officers care two-pence about them'.

On 18 March 1784, Nelson commissioned the *Boreas*, another 28-gun frigate. After running aground, which Nelson blamed on the Pilot, and a 'quarrel' in the Downs 'with a Dutch Indiaman who had English aboard which we settled, after some difficulty', *Boreas* arrived at Spithead on 18 April, preparatory to sailing for the West Indies. Amongst *Boreas*' passengers for the voyage were Lady Hughes, the Commander-in-Chief West Indies' wife, who would never stop talking, and her daughter 'Rosy' who was only too clearly on the lookout for a naval husband.

Possibly to get some respite from the designing 'Rosy' and the 'infernal clack' of her mother, Nelson took another young lady for a ride on Portsea Common. Nelson's 'blackguard horse' bolted with him and carried him 'round all the Works into Portsmouth, by the London gates, through the Town out at the gate that leads to Common,

where there was a waggon in the road'. Nelson desperately flung himself off the horse 'unluckily upon hard stones' and, 'to crown all', the young lady, whose horse had also bolted, was saved 'from the destruction she could not have avoided' by a total stranger.

Boreas returned to Spithead, after three years in the West Indies during which Nelson married Fanny, on 4 July 1787. As so often, Nelson was unwell. He had been sickly on the voyage and he caught a cold on his arrival. 'It is not kind in one's Native air,' he said, 'to treat a poor wanderer as it has done me since my arrival.'

Nelson expected *Boreas* to pay off, but war with France loomed again. In September, *Boreas* was sent to the Nore to act as receiving ship for men rounded up by the press gang. The pressed men arrived by the boat-load, as many as eleven hundred in one night. But it was dispiriting and depressing duty and morale on board sagged. Unusually for one of Nelson's commands, *Boreas* became an unhappy ship. He had to order three men flogged 'for using mutinous language to their officers' and five for 'disobedience and neglect of duty'.

Nelson himself was in a low state of spirits. Fanny had arrived in England but marooned where he was 'seven miles from the land on the Impress service . . . as much separated from my wife as if I were in the East Indies'. Everybody was relieved therefore when *Boreas* finally paid off on 30 November 1787. The sailors were paid extra for the additional time spent in commission but *Boreas*' ship's company did not, as *Albemarle*'s had done, volunteer *en masse* to follow Nelson to another ship.

'Impressing' men for the Navy had existed in one form or another since the time of King John, but the press gang reached its apotheosis, as a legal and social instrument, in the French wars because of the numbers of ships in commission and the high rates of desertion. Nelson himself, in his 'Plan for Manning the Navy' written in February 1803, said that 'I know it, that whenever a large Convoy is assembled at Portsmouth, and our Fleet in Port, not less than 1,000 men desert from the Navy'.

Impressment carried the full force of the law. In March 1800, two officers of the Impress Service, Lieutenant W. Wright and Midshipman J. Salmon of the *Dromedary* (24-guns), were put on trial for the murder of a seaman called W. Jones. They had pressed him, and Jones had tried to escape. There was a scuffle in which Jones was killed.

At his trial, Wright produced his Warrant from the Admiralty Board authorising him to impress persons of Jones' description. He was immediately acquitted and discharged. After a trial of some length, Salmon was also judged not guilty by the jury.

In 1803, when the French war resumed, men were once again needed. Some recruiting was done by offering bounties. Portsmouth Corporation voted £100 to be given in addition to the State bounty to the first one hundred seamen joining at the town.

Portsmouth was, of course, a favourite stamping ground for the press gangs. On 9 March 1803, *The Hampshire Telegraph* reported:

the press continues very active in Portsmouth, large parties of seamen, about 600, were ordered on shore in separate gangs last night, and so premptory were they that they indiscriminately took out every man on board the colliers, etc. Early this morning the same bustle was repeated, and several gangs paraded Point, picked up many useful hands, and lodged them in the Guard-house on the Grand Parade.

The dockyard towns were so often scoured for men that likely lads became more and more wary and ever harder to find. Occasionally, guile was required. In March 1803 *The Hampshire Telegraph* reported again:

A very hot press commenced on Tuesday night, at this place and the neighbourhood. It was chiefly planned and conducted by Captain Bowen (of the *Dreadnought*) who pressed a great number of seamen and able watermen by the following stratagem: at ten o'clock at night he assembled a party of Marines, with as much noise and parade as possible, to march a quell a pretended riot

at Fort Monckton, on the Haslar side of the water.

As the news spread, everybody ran to the fort; and when Captain Bowen saw he had attained his object, he silently placed a party at the end of Haslar Bridge, next the Hospital, and took every man that answered his purpose as he returned from the scene of the false alarm. On the same night the boats of the *Loire*, with press warrants signed on the 7th inst., boarded all the ships in the road and harbour of Cowes, and carried away a number of able seamen.

The press gang's raids continued through the year. 'Last evening at 8 o'clock a very hot press took place at Portsmouth, Portsea, and Gosport, in the harbour, and in most places in the neighbourhood,' said *The Hampshire Telegraph* of 23 September 1803:

No protestations were listened to, and a vast number of persons of various descriptions were sent on board the different ships in the port, most of whom where this morning liberated, being master tradesmen, apprentices, and such persons; very few were detained in comparison with the number taken on board. On the whole it is not supposed the Service has acquired fifty serviceable men.'

This was the great disadvantage of the press gang system. It was grossly inefficient, producing comparatively few men for the amount of manpower required to carry it out and the degree of aggravation it caused the general population. Captain Bowen's great *coup* on the Haslar Bridge probably netted the largest number ever to be pressed in any single operation, but of those five hundred, more than half were discharged next day as being unfit or exempt.

Some captures and exemptions were bizarre. In 1807, one Portsmouth press gang under the orders of Captain Sir Robert Bromley of the *Champion* took a blind man called Madden because of his 'qualification of playing on the Irish bagpipes'. Only Madden's blindness saved him. He was discharged and the cost of his pay and victualling was deducted from Sir

Sailors carousing in the Long Room at Portsmouth. Painted for
William IV by J. C. Ibbetson in 1807. Note sailors frying their
watches.

Robert's wages, as a lesson to him to be more careful about whom his press gangs chose in future.

In 1803, Nelson had a new flagship, the *Victory*. He left London at about 4am on Wednesday, 18 May, and arrived in Portsmouth at half past noon on the 19th. He went on board and at about half past three his flag was hoisted, followed by a salute of thirteen guns fired to the flag of Admiral Lord Gardner (the same Gardner of the Spithead mutiny, now Commander-in-Chief Portsmouth) in the *Endymion* 'which was returned with an equal number'.

On Friday, 20 May, the newspapers had a story from Portsmouth:

'Such was the anxiety of Lord Nelson to embark, that yesterday, to one that spoke of his sailing, he said 'I cannot, before tomorrow, and that's an age!' This morning, about 10 o'clock, his Lordship went off, in a heavy shower of rain, and sailed with a Northerly wind.

Lady Hamilton had a letter from The George at Portsmouth, 'By Messenger':

The boat is on shore and five minutes sets me afloat. I can only pray that the great God of heaven may bless and preserve you, and that we may meet again, in peace and happiness. I have no fears.

Once on board *Victory*, he wrote again, from the Great Cabin:

You will believe that, although I am glad to leave that horrid place, Portsmouth, yet the being afloat makes me now feel that we do not tread the same element.

The publicity attending Nelson's sailing was by now not unusual. On this occasion, he sailed for the Mediterranean. For some years, Nelson's arrivals and departures from Spithead had marked the beginnings or endings of great naval events. In March 1798, he had hoisted his flag in the *Vanguard* and sailed for

87

the battle of the Nile. Early in 1801, flying his flag in the *St George* he sailed for the Baltic and Copenhagen. In August 1805, *Victory* anchored at Spithead after the 'Long Chase' to the West Indies and back.

Nelson's flag had been seen from shore. Despite the heavy showers on the evening of 19 August, the walls and every vantage point in Portsmouth were crowded, and Nelson's barge was met with loud cheers as it was rowed in. Apart from a short visit ashore at Gibraltar on the way home, this was the first time Nelson had set foot out of *Victory* for over two years.

Nelson had meant to press on with his journey, but he paused for ten minutes to take tea with the Commander-in-Chief and the Commissioner. He ordered a post-chaise and sat drinking more tea at the George while he waited for it. At 9 o'clock of a pouring wet night he set out on the London road. 'His Lordship's movements here,' someone commented, 'were in unison with his pursuit after the Combined Squadron, for he was not an hour in the town'.

On the evening of 13 September 1805 — Friday the Thirteenth — after only twenty-five days back in England, Nelson said goodbye to his house at Merton and to Emma Hamilton and his daughter Horatia for the last time. In the coach going down to Portsmouth, he wrote a prayer in his private diary, probably at a stop while horses were being changed at Guildford:

Friday night, at half-past ten, drove from dear, dear Merton, where I left all which I hold dear in this world, to go to serve my king and country. May the great God whom I adore, enable me to fulfill the expectations of my country; and if it is His good pleasure that I should return, my thanks will never cease being offered to the throne of His mercy. If it is His good Providence to cut short my days upon earth, I bow with the greatest submission, relying that He will protect those so dear to me, that I may leave behind. His will be done. Amen. Amen. Amen.

He took tea by candle light at the 'Anchor'

in Liphook and arrived once more and for the last time at the old 'George' in Portsmouth at 6 o'clock in the morning of 14 September. The Vicar of Merton, the Rev. Thomas Lancaster, was already there with his fourteen year old son who was going to start his naval career with Nelson in the *Victory*. Nelson scribbled a note to Emma:

6 o'clock, 'George Inn'. My dearest and most beloved of women, Nelson's Emma, I arrived here this moment and Mr Lancaster takes it. His coach is at the door and only waits for my line. *Victory* is at St Helens and, if possible, I shall be at sea this day. God protect you and my dear Horatia prays ever your most faithful Nelson and Bronte.

After breakfasting, Nelson went to the Dockyard to pay a call on the Commissioner, Sir Charles Saxton. He was told by the Captains of *Royal Sovereign*, *Defiance* and *Agamemnon* that their ships were at Spithead but not yet ready for sea. As he himself hoped to sail that evening, Nelson told them to follow and meet him at a secret rendezvous.

Admiral Sir Isaac Coffin and Captain John Conn accompanied Nelson back to the 'George'. His business on shore was now finished and it was time to go on board. *Victory* had moved to St Helens that morning and at 11.30am had hoisted Nelson's flag. It was now nearing noon on a Saturday and the streets of Portsmouth were crowded. The news had gone round the town that Nelson had arrived.

Nelson's barge was ordered not to wait at the Sally Port but to go to Southsea beach where the wheeled bathing machines were drawn up. To avoid the crowds, which were growing by the minute, Nelson left the 'George' by the back entrance, in Penny Street. He walked along the north side of Governor's Green, by the King's Bastion to the Spur Redoubt, and so down to the beach.

The news that Nelson was on his way to join his ship soon spread. Crowds flocked to the new route to see him. The press of people became so great that soldiers tried to clear the street in Nelson's path, but they were pushed

Lord Nelson from 'The Death of Lord Nelson' by W. Beatty M.D. London 1807.

side. An officer who ordered the soldiers to fix bayonets was no more successful. The crowd just ignored him. Nelson, elegantly dressed, as one observer commented, with 'his blue coat splendidly illuminated with stars and ribbons', pushed through the crush with great good humour, greeting people and shaking hands, saying that he wished he had two good hands so that he could shake hands with more friends.

The feelings of the people of Portsmouth for Nelson held a special quality of poignant foreboding. It seemed that many must have had some inkling that this would be the last time. There were no cheers, but a prolonged and anxious silence. People knelt by the road side as Nelson passed. Men doffed their hats. Some women were in tears. Nelson may himself have remembered a fortune teller in the West Indies years before who said she could see nothing further after the age of forty-seven — his 47th birthday was only a fortnight off.

The Death of Nelson. Cartoon of a sailor and his girl in Portsmouth.

After Nelson had embarked, men and women ran knee deep into the water as his barge was rowed out to sea. Now, there were cheers, that rolled along the beach. Nelson stood up and took off his hat and waved it to the crowds. As he sat down he said to Hardy, 'I had their huzzas before. I have their hearts now'.

The wind died that evening and *Victory* could not sail. Two politicians, Mr George Rose, the Vice President of the Board of Trade, and Mr George Canning, the Treasurer of the Navy, came on board to dine. Almost Nelson's last act that day was to take Rose aside and plead with him to approach the Prime Minister on the subject of Lady Hamilton's pension.

Victory sailed at 8am on Sunday, 15 September, with Captain Blackwood's frigate *Euryalus* in company, and by the evening was off Christchurch. A boat arrived with a letter from Merton. Nelson replied:

Off Dunnose, Sept.16th. 1805. 11 a.m. My beloved Emma, I cannot even read your letter. We have fair wind, and God will, I hope, soon grant us a happy meeting. The wind is quite fair and fresh. We go too swift for the boat. May Heaven bless you, and Horatia, with all those who hold us dear to them, for a short time, farewell, Ever yours, Nelson and Bronte.

After Trafalgar the *Victory*, much battered by her long duel with the French *Redoutable*, was taken in tow first by *Polyphemus* and then by *Neptune*, who brought her into Gibraltar on 28 October. Nelson had not been her only casualty: Nelson's Secretary John Scott, Captain Adair, Lieutenant Ram, two midshipmen, the Captain's clerk, thirty-two seamen and eighteen marines were killed, and 102 officers and men were wounded.

Nelson's body had been placed in a leaguer filled with brandy, which was put in his fore cabin and covered with a silk Royal Standard. Marines mounted guard on it by day and night. At Gibraltar, Dr Beatty the ship's surgeon had the brandy withdrawn and replaced by spirits of wine. After some refitting of her shattered masts and yards, *Victory* sailed on 3 November, accompanied by *Belleisle*.

Victory arrived at Spithead at 1.30 on the afternoon of 4 December. Her sides were battle-scarred, her decks stained and scored, her masts and yards were jury-rigged and her sails and rigging clearly improvised. The Vice Admiral's flag was at half-mast. She stayed for a week and sailed for the Medway on 10 December.

When *Victory* arrived, the walls and vantage points of Portsmouth had been packed with even more people than had seen Nelson sail in September. The town had shared the national feelings of joy and relief at the news of the great victory, which removed the threat of a French invasion, with the shock and grief of Nelson's death at the moment of victory. But Nelson had been a part of Portsmouth. He had walked its streets and knew many of its people. Portsmouth had watched his progress, from a young officer to an admiral and a national hero. In Nelson, Portsmouth felt it had lost one of its own.

Prison Ship *York* in Portsmouth Harbour, *c*. 1828. Drawn and etched by Edward Cooke.

Chapter 10

'We feel great difficulty in attempting to describe the picturesque scene which presented itself,' said *The Hampshire Telegraph*, before proceeding to do so.

> The roaring of cannon from the first-rate ships of war, the view of the thousands assembled on the shores of Southsea Common and the battlements of the town, the yards manned by British tars, and the number of vessels sailing within a distance of about four miles, amounting, upon a moderate calculation, to 700 at least, conspired together to render the whole a scene of grandeur equal to anything the mind can figure to itself.

It was 1814, the Treaty of Paris had been signed, and Great Britain, Russia and Prussia were celebrating, somewhat prematurely, a victory over Napoleon Bonaparte. The Emperor of Russia and the King of Prussia both came to England to take part in a splendid programme of entertainments. The climax was a naval review at Spithead, to show the Allied sovereigns 'the tremendous naval armaments which had swept from the ocean the fleets of France and Spain and secured to Britain the domain of the sea'.

The Prince Regent and his retinue arrived at Portsmouth on the evening of 23 June. They were met by a party of dockyard ropemakers wearing white jackets and nankeen trousers, and purple sashes across their shoulders with the Royal insignia. Five 'conductors' carried white staves, the rest white wands. The ropemakers took their place behind the cavalry and immediately in front of the Royal carriage. The whole party arrived at the Landport Gate which, according to ancient custom, was locked. The usual ceremony took place, where the keys were presented to the Royal visitor, who gave the Royal command to open the gates.

Next day, Friday, 24 June, the Royal party embarked at King's Stairs in the Dockyard. The Royal Barge flying the Royal Standard of Great Britain was accompanied by a barge flying the Imperial Standard of Russia on one side and one flying the Royal Standard of Prussia on the other. Behind them came a procession of Admirals' and Captains' barges. Gun salutes were fired as the barges pulled out to Spithead.

There were fifteen ships of the line at the Review, including the flagship *Ville de Paris*, 110 guns, and thirty frigates and sloops of war. The Royal party went on board the *Impregnable*, 98 guns, for what *The Hampshire Telegraph* called an 'elegant dejeuner . . . consisting of every delicacy and the choicest viands'. The Emperor Alexander visited one mess where eleven Marines were having their dinner and shared their meal. The King of Prussia, meanwhile, was very impressed by the *Rodney*'s barge, which had been converted for the occasion into a miniature full-rigged ship, and asked for it as a present. When the Prince Regent agreed, the King said, somewhat facetiously, 'I hope you two heads of great maritime nations will not be jealous of my Navy'.

Next day, there was a Royal inspection of the Dockyard and other naval establishments. The Royal party embarked in the *Royal Sovereign* yacht and witnessed the entire fleet weighing anchor and putting to sea for evolutions. Finally, there were the customary promotions and knighthoods and a gift of £3,000 to be distributed among the seamen and dockyard workers.

This was the last review at which only sailing vessels were present. The first steamship to visit Portsmouth arrived on her way from Greenock to London on 9 June 1815, causing such astonishment that a court martial on board the *Gladiator* broke up so that the members could go to look at the new arrival.

On 1 July 1815, fourteen men-of-war sailed from Spithead to intercept Napoleon. The news of his surrender to Captain Maitland on board the *Bellerophon* arrived in the fleet on 22 July. Next day the signal was made to cease hostilities against France. The long wars were over and the Navy suffered a rapid decline. In 1815, Britain had 214 ships of the line and 792 frigates and other minor warships. Within five years, more than 550 ships had been sold or scrapped and there were only fifty-eight ships of the line fit for service in 1835.

The first review of the long peace, and the first to mention a steam ship, was by the Duke of Clarence, later King William IV, in July 1827. William was himself a professional naval officer and the Navy remained one of his great loves.

'The Sailor Prince', newly created Lord High Admiral (an office which had been dormant for 127 years), arrived in Portsmouth on 30 July and spent more than a week inspecting the fleet at Spithead, the ships in harbour, the dockyard and a Russian squadron of nine sail of the line and eight frigates which had also arrived at Spithead. His flagship the *Royal Sovereign* was towed into Portsmouth harbour against the wind by the steam ship *Lightning* which 'brought her into the harbour in a beautiful manner amidst the cheers of thousands of most respectable

Launch of the *Neptune*, 110 guns, at Portsmouth 27th September 1832.

93

The *Lightning* Steamer bringing the *Royal Sovereign* into
Portsmouth Harbour July 31st 1827.

people assembled on the lines and beaches'.

The young Queen Victoria's first visit to Portsmouth after her accession was on Monday, 28 February 1842. Marines and soldiers lined the streets for the Royal party who were met by the Dockyard rope-makers in traditional fashion. Three triumphal arches had been erected, at Mile End, at the east end of Union Road, and at the western end of Lion Gate Road.

After the ceremony of presenting the keys of the garrison to Her Majesty, gun salutes were fired by the shore batteries and all the ships in harbour. Prince Albert was shown round the gunnery school on board HMS *Excellent* and then the Royal party visited the *St Vincent*, flagship of Admiral Sir Edward Codrington, and the *Royal George* yacht. Prince Albert went over the dockyard, inspected the blockmills, blacksmith's shop and copper foundry. He watched an anchor being forged, and a ten-inch block being made inside a matter of minutes.

Portsmouth was illuminated in the Queen's honour but spirits were damped by the weather. 'It stormed and rained all night,' the Queen wrote to Lord Melbourne, 'and rained when we set off on board the *Black Eagle* for Spithead on Tuesday morning. It however got quite fine when we got there and we went on board the *Queen* and a glorious sight it was; she is a magnificent ship, so wide and roomy, and though only just commissioned, in the best order. With Marines her crew is near upon a thousand men.'

The *Alfred* (50 guns), *Formidable* (84 guns) and the *Queen* (110 guns) were anchored at Spithead. When Her Majesty went on board the *Queen* (built at Portsmouth as the *Royal Frederick* and the first three-decker launched since her accession), she looked at the cabin, store rooms, tiers and cockpit, all brightly lit by lanthorns and a variety of lamps, repeatedly exclaiming 'This is grand! This is very fine!'.

When the Queen reached the lower deck the men at dinner there rose. She ordered them to be seated and asked to taste the grog. Captain Rich brought her a glass but she said 'No I wish to taste it as the men have it'. So a mess basin was filled from the grog-can and Rich presented it to Her Majesty on bended knee. She took one sip and then another, saying 'It is very good'. She also tasted the soup, from one of the mess iron spoons, saying 'At all events it is very hot.'

After the men gave her three rousing cheers, the Queen said, with a tear in her eye: 'I feel today that I am indeed Old Ocean's youthful Queen, and that I am indeed surrounded by those who will uphold that title in the battle and the breeze.'

On 2 March 1842, the day after Queen Victoria left Portsmouth, the Admiralty ordered that all ships were to carry full wartime complements. While the Royal Navy suffered shortages of manpower and a continuing run down of ships, the French Navy was gaining in strength especially in the number of its steam ship.

Relations between Britain and France had improved sufficiently for Queen Victoria and Prince Albert to visit France in 1843. King Louis Phillippe repaid the visit in October 1844. He should have returned to France by way of Portsmouth on 14 October but the weather was so bad he had to go to Dover.

French warships at Spithead which the King should have inspected were understandably disappointed. So Victoria and Albert, who had spent the night on board their new steam Royal yacht *Victoria and Albert*, decided to visit the French ships on their way to Osborne House on the Isle of Wight.

According to *The Times*, 'the scene at Spithead as the Royal yacht neared the fleet there anchored was one never to be erased from the memory of those who beheld it'. There were three British line-of-battleships, eight experimental gun-brigs and two small paddle steamers (the first to take part in a Spithead review) the *Volcano* and the *Comet*. The French had a line of battleship, a frigate, two sailing yachts and four steamers.

It was the four steam frigates, and especially the French flagship *Gomer*, which attracted the most attention. She had brought Louis Phillippe to England and was larger and more powerful than the largest British paddle steam frigate *Terrible*.

Although the French sailors cheered Queen Victoria, shouting 'Vive La Reine', the advent of such steamships, which could in Palmerston's famous phrase 'bridge' the English Channel, revived British paranoia about French invasion. These fears were aggravated when the Prince de Joinville, the French commander, published a pamphlet describing the defenceless state of Portsmouth and methods of destroying it.

There was therefore a less confident air at Spithead on 21 June 1845 when Queen Victoria reviewed the Experimental Squadron, formed to compare the sailing qualities of various warships and to exercise naval tactics. The Queen visited Admiral Hyde Parker's flagship the *St Vincent*, the 120-gun *Trafalgar* and the 90-gun *Albion*, a 'Symondite' i.e. designed by the controversial Sir William Symonds, and the largest two-decked sailing warship ever built for the Navy.

Great trouble was taken to adorn *Albion*, even to lining her side ropes and ladders with blue velvet. But the true state of the Navy and its shortage of men was revealed when *Albion*'s Captain, asked by the Queen if he had a good ship's company, pointedly replied that he *had* had a good one but a hundred of his best men had just been taken away from him.

Another sign of the times at Spithead in June 1845 was the presence of the screw steamer *Rattler*. At Portsmouth on 3 April that year she had won her celebrated 'tug of war'. Lashed stern to stern with the paddle steamer *Alecto*, she had towed *Alecto* backwards at 2.7 knots with both vessel's engines working at full speed.

After the review on Saturday there was to have been a display by the ships on the Monday. Huge crowds gathered to witness it. 'The beach of Southsea Common, from the King's Rooms to Southsea Castle,' said *The Morning Herald*, 'was literally covered with a dense mass of people and every steam boat was in requisition, and made a good day's work by taking people out at 2S. per head to Spithead.'

The crowds were disappointed when only one ship, the 80-gun 'Symondite' *Superb*, actually put to sea. The rest gave a display of making and furling sail at anchor. The Royal Yacht and hundreds of others followed *Superb* to sea. Victoria herself was very impressed and made a sketch of the scene. She returned on 15 July, with several members of Euro-

Launch of the *Dauntless*. wooden steam frigate at Portsmouth,
5th January 1847.

pean royalty, to see the whole Experimental Squadron sail.

As the nineteenth century progressed, naval reviews marked the beginnings and endings of great events. They were symbols of empire. They served a political purpose, to impress friends and foes. They showed off new technologies, in the Navy and in the country. The coming of the railways, for instance, enabled many more people than before to attend the 'Grand Naval Review' on 11 August 1853, held before the start of the Crimean War.

This was the first Review to which Members of Parliament and the Press were invited. It was the first for which ships were fitted with semaphores, fitted on the taffrails of the steam-ships, to assist them in keeping station. Above all, it was the first Review of a predominantly steam-driven Navy (the man from *Punch* complained he could not see the ships for their smoke). Of the twenty-five Channel Squadron warships present, ranging from the Commander-in-Chief Sir Thomas Cochrane's flagship, the 131-gun screw line of battleship *Duke of Wellington*, down to the 6-gun paddle gunboat *Barracouta*, only three, *Queen* (113 guns), *Prince Regent* (90 guns) and *London* (90 guns), were sailing warships.

The Royal family attended, with foreign royalty, members of both Houses of Parliament, naval and army officers, diplomats and distinguished visitors. An estimated one hundred thousand people came to Portsmouth for the day; there was not a spare bed to be had anywhere. The Royal Yacht *Victoria and Albert* and the Admiralty steam yacht *Black Eagle* were followed by hundreds of private steamers, yachts and boats. The sailors manned the yards and cheered, and one marine in *Queen* removed the fore-royal-mast lighting conductor and, with folded arms, balanced *on his head* on the truck.

The climax was a set-piece 'sham battle' in which Spithead was threatened by the sailing warships, under Admiral Fanshawe, and defended by the steam ships. The steam ships sortied to the east, fought a twelve-minute 'battle' with the sailing ships, ending with a spirited boat attack. It was all intended to demonstrate, as it did, the Navy's ability to take care of any sudden invasion, and the superiority of the screw warships over the sailing ships and indeed over the paddle-steamers. Certainly, the sailing ships were still beating laboriously back to harbour long after the steamships had secured for the day.

All went well. 'The gigantic ships of war, among them the *Duke of Wellington* with 131 guns,' wrote Prince Albert, 'went without sails, and propelled only by the screw, *eleven miles an hour*, and this against wind and tide! This is the greatest revolution effected in the conduct of naval warfare which has yet been known'.

In March the following year, *The Times* recorded:

All the world seems moving again towards Portsmouth in anticipation of a grand spectacle taking place at Spithead . . . already is every hotel full, every house occupied, and provisions rising to famine prices . . . Not a bed or a sofa is to be obtained even in the most unwelcome of localities, but at a price which few would think of paying.

On Saturday, 10 March 1854, Queen Victoria reviewed the advance squadron of ships for the Baltic which Admiral Napier ('Baltic Charley', as the ballads called him) had managed to scrape together. It consisted of eight screw ships of the line, four screw frigates and three paddle sloops, manned by scratch crews whose only skilled seamen were reluctant coastguardsmen, but, next day, the Queen herself in the yacht *Fairy* led the ships to sea as far as St Helen's, where she wished them God speed. Her Majesty, the Prince Consort and members of the Royal family, curiously all wearing kilts, could be seen waving from the *Fairy's* deck as the cheering ships passed.

With the Channel Fleet on its way to the Baltic and the Mediterranean Fleet on its way to the Crimea, the people of England confidently expected one, if not two, Trafalgars. But there was little seaborne opposition in either theatre and the only active service many sailors saw, albeit very dangerous and arduous, was with the Naval Brigade ashore. Soon, there was general disappointment at home. 'What is the difference between the Baltic Fleet and the Black Sea Fleet?' asked *Punch*. 'The Baltic Fleet was expected to do everything and did nothing. The Black Sea Fleet was expected to do nothing and did it'.

For the people of Portsmouth, the Russian war brought mixed emotions. There was the gratification of seeing the first Russian prizes, seized in the Channel, brought into the harbour, the patriotic thrill of watching soldiers marching through the streets to join the troopships, and the victory celebrations — the Alma was marked with peals of church bells, ships dressed overall and Royal gun salutes.

But there was another, darker side. On 2 January 1854, the *Himalaya* arrived with 136 men, wounded, sick or frostbitten, 225 women, many widowed, and 300 mostly fatherless children. Soon Portsmouth was cheering away ships packed with healthy fighting men and receiving, by the same tide, other ships crammed with invalids, cripples, widows and orphans. During 1855, eighty ships landed 9,728 sick and wounded.

Portsmouth was the main port of arrival and departure throughout the war. Total embarkations, including women and children, were 63,749 in 151 ships; arrivals were 86,344 from 280 ships.

In March 1855, a second Baltic Fleet had assembled under Admiral Dundas, who was sixteen years younger than Napier. Queen Victoria came down again, reviewed the ships in the *Fairy* on 20 March, accompanied them to the Nab and signalled 'Success-Farewell'.

But this review, and all previous ones, were eclipsed by the 'Great Peace Review', held at Spithead on 23 April 1856 to celebrate the end of the Russian War. An estimated six hundred thousand people converged upon Portsmouth. One visitor was reported to have paid £15 for a room. 'Perhaps they permitted that tenant to take his bed and bedding away with him in the morning', commented *The Hampshire Telegraph*.

The record number of 254 ships attended the Review, manned by over fifty thousand men, and carrying 1,132 guns. There were twenty-two line-of-battleships, sixteen screw frigates and sloops, twenty-six paddle frigates and sloops, nine Royal yachts and tenders, seven screw mortar vessels and floating batteries, six troop ships, seven sailing vessels and 188 gunboats, including three small armoured vessels.

The Queen arrived at about noon and embarked in the new Royal yacht *Victoria and Albert II*. The line of battleships, in two squadrons, led by the C-in-C Sir George Seymour in the *Royal George*, steamed in turn past the Royal yacht, while the crews manned the sides and yards and cheered ship.

There were mishaps. A train bringing hundreds of guests broke down at Woking. The troopship *Transit*, carrying the House of Lords, also broke down because the Engineer was drunk. The Admiralty yacht *Black Eagle* belched out dense clouds of noisome black smoke, being the only vessel at the Review not to obey the Admiralty's own orders to use Anthracite coal. The news that the fleet was to be illuminated that night was not made public. Many visitors had left and never saw it.

Worst of all, the Review was held to be dull and dreary, with the ships anchored in two unimaginative lines five or six miles long; 'even the little gunboats,' said *Blackwood's Edinburgh Magazine*, 'which clearly have no place in the line of battle, and are as like each other as peas in a pod, were drawn out in endless succession'. Even the evolutions were cut short because the Lieutenant Governor of Portsmouth thought he would have to pay for the ammunition.

Peace was commemorated in Portsmouth by a general holiday on 29 May 1856, with a review of the garrison troops on the Common, the firing of a *feu-de-joie* and a Royal salute. Finally, on 16 September, a specially-built pavilion was erected on the Governor's Green and 2,500 sailors, soldiers and Marines who had served in the war were entertained to a sumptuous banquet surrounded by the most handsome decorations of masses of red, white and blue flowers sent by Florence Nightingale.

The latter half of the nineteenth century was the heyday for Spithead Reviews. On 29 August 1865, there was a review for the visit of a French squadron of nine ironclads and three wooden sloops. French officers and men were feted in Portsmouth which was illuminated in the visitors' honour. For the first time at a Review, every ship present flew the White Ensign, the old Red, White and Blue Squadrons having been abolished in August 1864.

On 17 July 1867, eight wooden line of battleships, eight wooden frigates, two wooden sloops, fifteen iron or ironclad frigates and sloops, sixteen gunboats, five Royal yachts, and eighteen troopships and tenders turned out to welcome the Sultan of Turkey. Torrential rain fell during the day and there was very little for the sodden and bitterly disappointed crowds to see.

On 23 June 1873, the visitor was the Shah of Persia. The fleet consisted of forty-four ships, of which twenty-one were gunboats. This time there were criticisms that the Royal Navy was not sufficiently strongly represented and was beginning to be compared unfavourably with foreign navies. An admonishing letter from an admiral in *The Times* pointed out that 'boasting was not power'.

On 13 August 1878, Queen Victoria reviewed the Particular Service Squadron under Admiral Sir Geoffrey Phipps Hornby at Spithead. The Squadron had been formed because of a 'Russian Scare', with the possibility of war against Russia, earlier that year. In fact the 'Scare' had subsided by the time of the Review and the Squadron was disbanded shortly afterwards.

In 1884, there was another 'panic', this time about the Navy itself and its capabilities, or lack of them. It was largely a one-man campaign by W.T.Stead, editor of the *Pall Mall Gazette*, on 'the truth about the Navy by one who knows the facts'. In 1885, the Poet Laureate Lord Tennyson published his celebrated accusatory poem 'The Fleet' addressed to the Sea Lords who were failing in their duty. Rear Admiral Lord Charles Beresford, a Tory MP and a serving naval officer who became Fourth Sea Lord in 1886, consciously sought out the help of the press to reform the Navy and especially to reduce the large numbers of obsolete warships.

For Beresford, the Naval Review for Queen Victoria's Golden Jubilee in 1887 was a heaven-sent chance to interest public opinion in the Navy and also to show intelligent and influential people in what a poor state the Navy really was. Beresford worked tirelessly towards these ends, showing parties of MPs round Portsmouth dockyard to brief them on the state of the fleet, seeing to it that guests

Right & below: H.M.S. *Warrior* 1860. The relative luxury of the Captain's living accommodation compared to those of the seamen is evidenced by these scenes from the superbly restored quarters aboard the latest addition to the Naval Heritage area at Portsmouth.
(Warrior Preservation Trust Ltd.)

Right: H.M.S. *Warrior* 1860. William Armstrong, the Tyneside engineer designed this revolutionary rifled, breech-loading gun for the Admiralty; *Warrior* carried ten of these 110-pounders. In addition she was also armed with 26 smooth bore, muzzle-loading 68-pounders.
(Warrior Preservation Trust Ltd.)

Left: H.M.S. *Warrior* 1860. The officers' accommodation on the main deck included this well appointed Wardroom. Their cabins measured 6 feet by 10 feet and for the first time on a British warship there was full headroom in most of the crew accommodation.
(Warrior Preservation Trust Ltd.)

Right: H.M.S. *Warrior* 1860. On her four-day passage from Hartlepool an encounter with H.M.S. *London,* the Royal Navy's newest warship, resulted in the following signal from her Captain, ''Navy's newest ironclad in company with its oldest . . . I hope we look as good at your age.'' This photograph shows *Warrior* returning to Portsmouth on the 16th of June 1987, accompanied by the Alexandra tugs *Powerful* and *Bustler,* fifty-eight years after she had left Portsmouth as a decaying relic.

(W. Sartori.)

were allowed on board the ships (there had been an order forbidding them) and that the press had all the passes for the Review they wanted (to say nothing of food and drink).

But the Review as a whole, which was not Beresford's responsibility, was not particularly well organised. For instance, the tides on the chosen day, 23 July, meant that big ships could not come into Portsmouth harbour until 9pm. Spectators who wanted to land before that would have to be ferried ashore at some expense. This was not discovered until it was too late to change the date.

Nor were the preliminary omens good. On 13 July, the *Victoria and Albert*, with the Crown Prince and Princess of Germany on board, embarrassingly collided with the troopship *Orontes*. A few days later, *Black Prince* ran into *Agincourt* and on the 19th, two first-class ironclads of the Steam Reserve Squadron, the *Devastation* and the admittedly notoriously unhandy *Ajax*, collided, again with the Crown Prince of Germany a witness. 'Foreign visitors', commented the *Daily News* sourly, 'ought to be kept out of the way until our bumping races of ironclads have come to an end'.

There were 128 ships in the Review, with some foreign visitors from France, Germany and the Netherlands, drawn up in three review squadrons and five flotillas: twenty-six armoured ships, including the new battleship *Inflexible*, and nine unarmoured ships, three torpedo cruisers, one torpedo gunboat, one gun and torpedo vessel, thirty-eight first-class torpedo boats, thirty-eight gunboats, twelve troopships, a paddle frigate and six training brigs. All were from the Home Fleet (Reserve, Training and Channel Squadrons). Not one ship was brought from abroad.

They made a brave show, except to the expert eye. Rear Admiral Eardley-Wilmot called them a 'motley collection of ancient constructions'. The French naval attaché was unimpressed; this was nothing more than a spectacle for the general public, he reported, of no professional interest (although he did take notes of several ships). *The Times*, in an article on the eve of the Review, pointed out that almost all the 128 ships had faults in design, armour and weaponry. Many ships

still had muzzle-loading guns which Beresford called 'absolutely useless'.

Sir Edward Reed, the famous naval architect, told MPs that only six or seven of the warships in the Review were fit to go to war. Admiral Hewett, who had won a Victoria Cross in the Crimea, said that 'Most of what you see is mere ullage'. On the day of the Review, a gun on the gunboat *Kite* exploded, killing one man and injuring several others. In the post-Review exercises, more than half of the torpedo-boats broke down and in nineteen of them, internal mishaps caused casualties amongst their crews. Very few commented upon a tiny war-vessel, the submarine *Nordenfelt*, with its hull almost awash, on the fringes of the Review.

But, on the day, the sun shone and it was perfect 'Queen's weather'. The crowds enjoyed themselves and the press reaction was, for Beresford, gratifyingly enthusiastic. 'The people love their Navy and believe in it,' said *The Daily Telegraph* .

There was a Review in honour of the Kaiser on 5 August 1889, when His Majesty described the eighty-one ships including thirty-three ironclads, displacing 243,000 tons, carrying 596 guns and manned by twenty thousand men, all drawn up in his honour, as 'the finest fleet in the world'. There were further Reviews, for another French Squadron on 19 August 1891, and for an Italian Fleet on 9 July 1895. But the last and greatest Review of the century was for Queen Victoria's Diamond Jubilee at Spithead on 26 June 1897.

This time there was no 'ullage'. The Naval Defence Act of 1889 had brought in a new era of naval shipbuilding. This was a show of real strength and once again, as in 1887, not one ship came from abroad. All were from the Channel, Reserve and Training Squadrons, with a few ships specially commissioned.

There were 165 warships, moored in five lines, the longest line extending over seven miles. The included twenty-one battleships, eleven first-class cruisers, twenty-seven second-class cruisers, five third-class cruisers, twenty torpedo-gunboats, five gunboats and gun vessels, thirty torpedo-boat destroyers, twenty torpedo-boats, eighteen training ships and brigs, and eight special service vessels, all under the command of Admiral Sir Nowell Salmon VC GCB, the Commander-in-Chief, flying his flag in the battleship *Renown*. There were also warships from France, Germany, Austria, Russia, Spain, Italy, the United States, Portugal, the Netherlands, Norway, Denmark and Japan. All the major steamship companies sent representative ships and there were, of course, thousands of private steamers, yachts and craft.

The Queen was too old and frail to attend and was represented by the Prince of Wales, later Edward VII. It was once again perfect 'Queen's weather' when the *Victoria and Albert* left Portsmouth at two o'clock that afternoon, to thunderous Royal gun salutes. She was preceded by the Trinity House yacht *Irene*, and followed by the P & O liner *Carthage*, with Royal guests for whom there was no room in the Royal yacht, another Royal yacht the *Alberta*, the yacht *Enchantress*, with the Lords of the Admiralty and their guests, the *Danube*, with members of the House of Lords, the yacht *Wildfire*, with the Colonial Prime Ministers and their suites and the Rt. Hon. Joseph Chamberlain, Secretary of State for the Colonies, the Cunard liner *Campania*, carrying the House of Commons,

ss *El Dorado*, with the foreign Ambassadors, the yacht *Elfin*, with distinguished guests, and the Commander-in-Chief's yacht *Fire Queen* bringing up the rear.

This procession steamed up and down the lines, with every ship cheering as the Royal yacht passed. There was a reception for the admirals on board the *Victoria and Albert* before the Royal yacht returned to harbour, just in time to avoid a violent thunderstorm which broke over the Solent. However, the weather cleared that evening when the fleet was illuminated.

Victoria's Diamond Jubilee is not now chiefly remembered for its imposing lines of warships. There was one unscheduled, unofficial appearance, by the tiny *Turbinia*, in which the Hon. Charles Parsons had for some years been carrying out privately-financed trials on steam turbine propelling machinery. *Turbinia* raced up and down the Review lines at reported speeds of 34.5 knots, far higher than anything the Navy's torpedo boats could achieve. In that elusive will-o'-the-wisp silhouette, as in the humped back of the *Nordenfelt* ten years earlier, there was the authentic shape of the twentieth century which was just about to open.

Chapter 11

After the great French war, as after every great war, there was a rapid reduction of the Navy, which drastically affected Portsmouth and its dockyard. From the frantic activity of wartime, when unskilled labour and unseasoned wood were both pressed into service, there were suddenly redundancy and idleness. In September 1813, 3,582 men were employed in Portsmouth yard, of whom 1,330 were shipwrights. There were eighty-eight vessels in the harbour including powder ships, prison ships and medical depots, and 165 small vessels in Yard service.

But in March 1816, over fifty labourers were discharged, and three hundred 'mechanics' i.e. skilled men with a trade were also turned adrift with one week's pay. Two months later ninety of the oldest mechanics, some of whom had fifty years' service in the yard, were superannuated on bounties ranging from £14 to £24 a year. In February 1817, wages were lowered to the lowest peace time level and working hours were reduced. Four years later, more men were paid off on bounties, rates of pay were cut again and working days reduced from six days a week to five.

In 1822, when numbers of officers and seamen were being reduced, many ancient offices in Portsmouth Dockyard were abolished, including the Clerk of the Survey and the Clerk of the Rope Yard, the Master Mast Maker, Master Boat Builder, Master Carpenter and Master Joiner. Workmen were paid off in weekly batches until their number fell below two thousand two hundred.

There was no longer any hurry to build ships. For instance, the *Indus*, 80 guns, laid down at Portsmouth in 1819, was not launched until 16 March 1839, having been twenty years on the building slip. Also launched at Portsmouth that year was the *Queen*, 3,104 tons and 110 guns, one of the most celebrated of all the 'Symondite' ships. The last sailing ship of the line, she was 'razeed' i.e. had decks removed and fitted with engines in 1859.

The year 1830 was the nadir, when dockyard employment and pay were at their very lowest, but the advent of steam propulsion and iron construction brought Portsmouth dockyard to full and profitable life again. The first paddle steamer to be built at Portsmouth was the *Hermes*, 6 guns, 712 tons, designed by Sir William Symonds, with 220 horse-power engines by Maudslay and Field, launched on 26 June 1836. Portsmouth's first screw warship, launched on 10 August 1846, was the wooden steam gun vessel *Rifleman*, 8 guns, 484 tons, designed by John Fincham, with 100 horse-power engines by Miller and Ravenhill.

Throughout the 1840s new ships were launched at Portsmouth at the rate of about two a year, an increasing proportion of them wooden steam ships. The last sailing warship to be built at Portsmouth was the fourth-rate *Leander*, 50 guns, 1,987 tons, designed by Richard Blake when he was Master Shipwright of the Dockyard. Laid down in 1845 and launched on 8 March 1848, she was converted into a screw frigate in 1861.

A new era demanded new docks, buildings and facilities. There had been considerable expansion during the Napoleonic Wars. General Samuel Bentham, made Inspector General of Naval Works in 1796, had inspected Portsmouth a year earlier and reported that its working practices were inefficient and open to abuse. He proposed an extension of the Great Basin, to allow twelve ships of the line to be berthed for repairs afloat, and new docks opening off it. Much of the work was done by convicts.

The enlarged Basin was finished on 12 June 1801, when *HMS Britannia* sailed through its entrance which was closed by a caisson. Great crowds gathered on the opening day, expecting the caisson, the first in England, to collapse, but they were disappointed. The first of Bentham's dry docks, No. 2 (where *HMS Victory* has been since 1922) was begun in 1799 and completed in 1801. The second, No. 3 Dock, was finished in 1803, and now houses the *Mary Rose*.

Under Samuel Bentham, saw mills were erected in the dockyard and a steam engine installed for pumping out some of the docks. Bentham was impressed by new inventions for making pulley blocks. Between 1802 and 1806, he had forty-five machines, designed by Marc Isambard Brunel and built by Henry Maudslay, installed in what became the first steam-powered factory in a Royal Dockyard. It was also the world's first example of the use of metal machines for mass production. Ten men could do the work of one hundred and ten craftsmen and produce one hundred and forty thousand pulley blocks a year. Some of this machinery was still in use until the 1960s.

Paddle wheels did not make for efficient warships. The paddles obstructed the positioning of gunports and were themselves vulnerable to gunfire. But the development of the screw propeller by Francis Pettit Smith in 1836 and the decisive victory of the screw-driven *Rattler* over the paddle steamer *Alecto* in 1845 opened the way for new technology. In 1843, an ambitious programme was approved for Portsmouth dockyard, including a steam basin, four docks and several new buildings. Work on the seven-acre Steam Basin began on 29 May 1843 and was finished four days ahead of schedule on 25 May 1848. Its cost of £242,000 was kept down by using one thousand two hundred convicts from hulks moored in the Harbour, although one thousand and forty paid labourers were also employed.

The entrance had a metal caisson, built by the firm of Fairbairn for £5,260 but the entrance was found to be inadequate and was replaced by another in the north-east wall in 1876. The original caisson was simply walled in and was rediscovered during road surface repairs in 1984. Two docks led from the Basin: No 7, opened in 1849, and South Inlet, or No 8, 42 fleet longer then No 7, in 1850. The Basin was formally opened by Queen Victoria with great celebrations on 25 May 1848.

Portsmouth dockyard built over one hundred and fifty warships during the nineteenth century, accurately reflecting the tremendous technological changes in warship construction, propulsion and armament which took place during the century. HMS *Warrior* was the first ocean-going, iron-hulled 'battle-ship' in the modern sense of the word.

She was built on the Thames, but many of her successors, almost as revolutionary in their day, were built at Portsmouth. By the end of the century, it was customary for Portsmouth to build the first of every new class of warship.

The first rate *Royal Sovereign*, 130 guns, was laid down at Portsmouth on 17 December 1849 and launched on 25 April 1857, but in January 1855, while she was still on the slip, work had begun to turn her into a screw line of battleship. On 4 April 1862, when she was newly completed, the Admiralty ordered an even more radical conversion which took two years.

She was cut down to the lower deck, giving her a freeboard of about 7 feet. Her oak hull was sheathed with 5.5-inch thick iron plate. She was rearmed with five 10.5 inch 300-pounder, 12.5-ton muzzle loading guns, in three single and one double centre-line turrets. She was the first first rate in the Royal Navy to dispense with sails for propulsion, having three stumpy pole-masts with jib sails, to steady her roll at sea. Her two-cylinder 2,460 horse-power Maudslay engines gave her a speed of 11 knots. Her final displacement was 5,080 tons.

First commissioned at Portsmouth on 7 July 1864, *Royal Sovereign* was the first turret ironclad in the Royal Navy, and the first British capital ship to carry her main armament outside her hull.

H.M.S. Swallow at Portsmouth with covers of Nos 3 & 4 dry docks in background. 1869.

Leaving Portsmouth for the Baltic Fleet. *Illustrated London News* 14th April 1854.

Launch of *H.M.S. Victoria* at Portsmouth. *Illustrated London News* 12th November 1859.

Launch of *Royal Sovereign* at Portsmouth. *Illustrated London News* 2nd May 1857.

In November 1869, another epoch-making ship was laid down at Portsmouth. She was HMS *Devastation*, the Navy's first true sea-going mastless capital ship, the first iron capital ship built at Portsmouth and the first of over 9,300 tons. In 1860, the largest naval guns had been 68-pounder smooth bores weighing five tons, but only ten years later *Devastation* was armed with four 35-ton rifled muzzle loaders, firing a 714 pound shell. The twin turrets had armour plate 14 inches thick, a diameter of 31 feet, and twenty-two man crews, and could be trained through 280 degree arcs. The guns were the heaviest ever to be hand-worked but the turrets were steam-trained.

Devastation was launched in July 1871 and first commissioned at the end of 1872. Her complement was four hundred officers and men, and her two-to-one ration of combatants to engine room staff was the highest of any capital ship before or since. She had two propellers, with a top speed on trials of 13 knots. Her coal capacity of about 21,800 tons gave her a range of about 4,500 miles at 10 knots.

Conservatives criticised every aspect of *Devastation*. Never did a ship first leave harbour under denser clouds of pessimism and gloomier forecasts of impending doom. But she proved an excellent sea boat and a steady gun platform and was rightly described at the time as 'an impregnable piece of Vauban fortification with bastions mounted upon a fighting coal mine'.

Some nineteenth century Portsmouth-built ships were famous in their day. The wooden steam frigate *Shannon*, launched at Portsmouth in November 1855, achieved immortal fame during the Indian Mutiny in 1857-58 when her Naval Brigade, under Captain Sir William Peel VC, won five Victoria Crosses in action at Lucknow.

The iron steam frigate HMS *Shah*, laid down at Portsmouth in 1873 as *Blonde* and renamed in honour of the Shah of Persia, fought the rebel ironclad *Huascar* off the coast of Peru on 29 May 1877 and fired the first Whitehead torpedo in action (it missed).

The battleship HMS *Inflexible* was an extraordinary colossus. Laid down in 1874, she was named and launched in April 1876 by Princess Louise, Queen Victoria's fifth daughter and later Duchess of Argyll, who also opened seven basins and docks in another huge extension of Portsmouth dockyard.

At nearly 12,000 tons, *Inflexible* was the largest ship yet built in Portsmouth. She had four giant 80-ton muzzle loading rifled guns in twin 750-ton turrets mounted in echelon, with the port side turret forward of the starboard, and she was the first ship to have submerged torpedo tubes.

Inflexible's 24-inch side armour was the thickest of any ship before or since. She had electric light, then a novelty, anti-roll tanks, a primitive form of stabiliser, and compartmentation so complicated that men got lost in her. Her first Captain, 'Jackie' Fisher, who commissioned the ship in 1881, devised an ingenious code of coloured symbols painted on bulkheads and doors to restore order out of chaos.

A Portsmouth ship made the world's headlines in March 1889 when the corvette HMS *Calliope* escaped from the harbour of Apia in Samoa in the teeth of a hurricane. Three American and three German warships in the harbour were sunk or driven ashore.

There were, of course, disasters as well as triumphs. In September 1870, a sad little card was being sold, price 2d, on the streets of Portsmouth to help the dependents of the crew of HMS *Captain*. *Captain*, with a name redolent of Nelson himself, was a turret ship designed by Captain Cowper Coles and built, with public money but at a private yard, Cammell Lairds at Birkenhead.

The notions of ships having low freeboards and their guns in turrets were sound enough, but *Captain* herself was a case of invention outrunning discretion. Everything, from her designer's over-confidence to the operational requirements of the Admiralty, conspired to make her cranky and top-heavy. The Navy's constructors were deeply suspicious of her.

Their suspicions were well-founded. *Captain* commissioned under Captain Hugh Burgoyne VC at Portsmouth on 30 April 1870. Lower deck legend had it that the signalman hoisted her ensign upside down that day. She joined the Channel Fleet in August for cruise down to the Mediterranean, but on the night of 7 September she capsized in a sudden squall in the Bay of Biscay, with the loss of 472 lives including her Captain and Cowper Coles who was on board as an observer. Only the Gunner and eighteen sailors got ashore in a pinnace the next day.

Over a decade later, a Portsmouth built

H.M.S. Devastation, the first mastless capital ship, 1873.

107

battleship, HMS *Camperdown*, collided with the Mediterranean Fleet flagship HMS *Victoria* in manoeuvres off the Lebanese port of Tripoli on 22 June 1893. *Victoria*. sank with the loss of some three hundred and sixty officers and men, including the Commander-in-Chief himself, Admiral Sir George Tryon, whose error of judgement had led to the catastrophe. A national subscription was launched to raise a large sum of money for *Victoria*'s widows and orphans, most of whom belonged to Portsmouth.

These disasters were serious enough, but the naval disaster of the nineteenth century which touched the nation's core most deeply, so that people ever afterwards remembered where they were and what they were doing when they heard the news, was the loss of the sail training ship HMS *Eurydice*. She was what was known as a 'Jackass' frigate, launched as a sixth rate, 24 guns, at Portsmouth in May 1843. She commissioned under Captain

Marcus Hare in February 1877 and in November went on a cruise to the West Indies. She left Bermuda for Portsmouth on 6 March 1878 with over three hundred people on board including her fifteen officers, over two hundred seamen under training, and some passengers, amongst them court-martialled prisoners being sent home to serve their sentences.

By noon on 24 March, after a quick passage, *Eurydice* was off the Isle of Wight, and everybody expected to anchor at Spithead that evening. She was carrying all plain sail, with studding sails, and making about seven knots against an ebb tide. Hare was cutting corners, sailing as close to the land as he could. The Isle of Wight's steep cliffs and deep chines running down to the sea, are notorious for sudden squalls, but *Eurydice* had a large crew, superbly trained and fit, and Hare was confident they could have everything off her in time.

Launch of *H.M.S. Inflexible* at Portsmouth. *Illustrated London News* 6th May 1876.

H.M.S. Eurydice sinking, 24th March 1878.

At about 3.30pm the ship was struck by a snow squall. Hare ordered men aloft to shorten sail but evidently he then decided there was not time before the squall arrived and ordered the men down again. Sheets and halliards were cut but *Eurydice* was overwhelmed and pushed over onto her starboard beam ends. Her main deck flooded through the open gun ports and she sank, righting herself as she went down, in seven fathoms. When the snow cleared, her royals could be seen, flapping above the water.

The schooner *Emma* picked up five men — the First Lieutenant, an army captain, a petty officer and two sailors. The first three died. The sailors, Ordinary Seaman Sydney Fletcher and Able Seaman Cuddiford, were the only survivors. When the ship was raised in September, one prisoner was found still in his cell.

A large granite memorial to *Eurydice*, surmounted by one of the anchors recovered from the ship, was erected in Haslar Cemetery, and Dr Arthur Conan Doyle, who had a practice in Southsea in the 1880s, wrote some banal commemorative verses.

Eurydice's best memorial, and probably the most durable, came from an improbable direction. A young Jesuit priest, Gerard Manley Hopkins, read of the tragedy in *The Times* and wrote a poetic masterpiece, a parable which compared this naval disaster, in which so many men had drowned with no chance of absolution, to what he considered the much greater spiritual disaster of the abandonment by the British nation of the Roman Catholic religion.

Two years later, an eerily similar accident befell the training ship *Atalanta*. Formerly the 26-gun frigate *Juno*, she served for many years as a hulk for the water police in Portsmouth until she was refitted, renamed and commissioned as a sail training ship in 1878. She sailed from Bermuda for home on 1 February 1880 and was never heard of again. She was lost, probably in a hurricane, with all 113 officers and men and 170 seamen under training on board. Both ships, *Eurydice* and *Atalanta*, were commemorated by a stained glass window in St Ann's, the Portsmouth dockyard church.

The change from sail to steam inevitably

Ordinary Seaman Sydney Fletcher (left) and Able Seaman Cuddiford, the only two survivors of *H.M.S. Eurydice*.

Portsmouth Dockyard, New Docks and Basin. *Illustrated London News* 13th May 1876.

caused periodical casualties. In January 1868, one thousand five hundred men were discharged from the Dockyard. In May, the famous Ropery was closed. However, in the 1870s there was the 'Great Extension', opened by Princess Louise. With later extensions, the Dockyard covered an area of about 300 acres by the end of the century.

Most of the spoil from the excavations was transported by train and used to reclaim about 90 acres of mud north of the Dockyard. The work was done by convicts, most of them 'lifers'. There were usually some four hundred of them at a time, working in gangs of twenty-five. This island of mud, known as Whale Island, was to become famous as the site of the Portsmouth gunnery school.

In spite of Trafalgar and the Royal Navy's towering reputation during the French Wars, the American War of 1812 had shown that the Navy's gunnery was not all it should be. The larger, better armed and better fought American ships had been too much for the British, with the splendid exception of the *Shannon*.

British Captains could train their guns' crews much as they liked. There was no common gunnery doctrine. Broke of the

Shannon had trained his guns' crews hard and well, but in many ships the handling of the guns was left entirely to individual gun captains who fired whenever they liked and at whatever they saw through the smoke.

In June 1830, the Admiralty recognised the hard truth about naval gunnery and authorised the establishment of a gunnery school at Portsmouth. The ship chosen was the *Excellent*, 74 guns, Collingwood's ship at St Vincent. She was moored with her port broadside pointing out over the harbour, so that her guns could be fired without endangering anybody.

The Admiralty prospectus for *Excellent*, full of key words and phrases, was one of the most revolutionary documents in the Navy's history. There was to be a *permanent corps* of seamen to act as Captains of Guns, and a Depot for the instruction of officers and seamen. There was to be a *uniform system* of naval gunnery. Young and active seamen were to be engaged for *five or seven years* — *renewable*, with pay *increased* at each reengagement. There was *extra pay* for a gunnery qualification, and advancement *according to merit* and the degree of attention paid to duty.

Here, without anybody quite realising it, was the first basic framework of a permanent professional career for the seaman in the Royal Navy.

On board *Excellent*, officers and men were taught the theory and practice of gunnery in a systematic manner for the first time. They drilled on the kinds of guns they would have on board their own ship when they commissioned her. A red flag was hoisted to show that firing was about to start — never until the mudbanks were uncovered by the ebbing tide. Shot was recovered by 'mudlarks', many from the splendidly-named local family of Grub, who used to 'ski' about the mud with wooden boards strapped to their feet and had special 'mud-groping' instruments for extracting the shot which they then sold back to the Navy.

Despite diehard criticism from conservative officers, one or two of whom actually suggested *Excellent* be paid off, the new system was very successful. The expertise and the extra money were popular with the sailors. The 'Excellent men' were comparatively few in any ship's company but their training and marksmanship made them stand out from the rest.

Excellent rapidly grew in influence and in size. Accommodation hulks, first *Illustrious* and then *Calcutta*, were moored ahead of her. The first *Excellent* was broken up in 1834 and replaced by the *Boyne* which was renamed *Excellent*. She too was replaced in 1859 by the *Queen Charlotte*, also renamed *Excellent*, who stayed until the gunnery school moved ashore to Whale Island in 1891.

The first building on the island, 'The Excellent House that Jack Built', was erected in 1864. From 1891, more buildings, roads, barracks, batteries, lecture rooms, proof butts, firing ranges, parade grounds, pitches for cricket and football, a chapel dedicated to St Barbara (patron saint of artillerists), gar-

H.M.S. Excellent and *H.M.S. Calcutta* c. 1860.

4.7" Gun Drill at *H.M.S. Excellent*.

dens, an aviary, and even a zoo, followed in the years to come. For years there was no bridge to the mainland: access was by boat, or by railway from the dockyard.

In 1867, a special section of *Excellent* was formed to study the new science of torpedo warfare and the application of electrics to gunnery. In 1872, the hulk *Vernon*, a Symondite frigate launched at Woolwich in 1832, was moved to Portsmouth and moored close to the Dockyard wall in Fountain Lake, where she became a tender to *Excellent* and a floating classroom for instruction in torpedoes, electrics and mining. Two other hulks were added: the *Ariadne*, for officers' accommodation, connected to the *Vernon* by a bridge, and the old sixth rate, *Actaeon*, as a workshop.

Vernon's first commanding officer, the newly-promoted Commander 'Jackie' Fisher, realised the importance of torpedo work and proposed that *Vernon* should become a separate command. *Vernon* was commissioned as an independent establishment, the Portsmouth Torpedo School, under Captain W. Arthur, on 26 April 1876.

As time went on, other hulks became part of *Vernon*: the screw line of battleship *Donegal* (*Vernon I*), built in 1858, replaced *Actaeon* in 1885; the screw line of battleship *Marlborough* (*Vernon II*), launched at Portsmouth in 1855, replaced *Ariadne* in 1903; and the epoch-making *Warrior*, now reduced to a hulk, was attached as *Vernon III*, a floating workshop and wireless telegraphy (W/T) instructional ship, in 1904. *Vernon* and its hulks removed to Portchester Creek in 1895. The whole establishment moved ashore to the Gunwharf, south of the Dockyard and on the other side of the main railway, in 1923.

Before she became one of *Excellent*'s hulks, *Illustrious* herself had been part of another revolutionary change in the Navy. Traditionally, the Navy had always had difficulties in obtaining enough men, especially in times of crisis and rapid mobilisation, as at the start of the Crimean War. From 1 July 1853, in an attempt to solve this seemingly perennial problem of manning, all new boy entrants engaged for ten year's continuous service, their 'time' to start from the age of eighteen.

The new boys, know as 'Jemmy Graham's Novices' after Sir James Graham, the First Lord, went to the old two-decker *Illustrious*, moored off Haslar, where they underwent a year's course of seamanship instruction, with some general education, instituted by *Illustrious*' Captain, Robert Harris, a very able officer. The boys were issued with a standard uniform (which they had to pay for out of their wages) and had a varied syllabus, from knots and splices to cutlass drill, and from

113

marching and rifle drill to 'boxing' the compass and heaving the lead. After six months the boys went for a cruise in the brig *Sealark* to learn sail drill at sea.

The scheme began in 1854 and, as was to be expected, the older 'shellbacks' sneered at the 'Novices'. But the scheme was a success, so much so that Captain Harris had his own son do the same course. Young Robert Harris joined in January 1856 and he was followed by the first batch of twenty-three Naval Cadets (a title which replaced the old First Class Volunteer in 1843) in August 1857.

This was, in fact, the start of formal officer training afloat. The young gentlemen were taught seamanship, drill and navigation, with cruises in the *Sealark*, and recreation on a field ashore at Haslar, but it was soon clear that cadets' and seamen's training did not go well together. It was also clear that a larger ship was required. On 1 January, 1859, Captain Harris shifted his pennant to the three-decker *Britannia* (the fourth of the name, which had been Dundas' flagship in the Crimea).

Portsmouth was considered unsuitable for the training of cadets. *Britannia* moved in February 1862 to Portland and then finally to Dartmouth in September 1863. In the same year, the 120-gun ship *St Vincent*, for several years the receiving ship in Portsmouth Harbour, was converted into a training ship for boys. She was moored off the entrance to Haslar Creek where she remained until the boys transferred to a shore establishment in Gosport towards the end of the century.

It seemed that in the second half of the nineteenth century that sailors' behaviour ashore was as riotous as ever. The scenes which so terrified Henry Capper as a young child in the 1850s continued in the 1860s and, indeed, could have taken place at any time in the previous century. He particularly remembered the 'exploits' of one ship's company paid off at Portsmouth in 1864.

They engaged every available cab in the town and formed these up in procession on Common Hard. With each man was his 'long-haired chum' — generally a woman of the town. The cabs were decorated with flags and pennants, each box seat holding one or more men and women, a similar number being mounted on the roof. A few men were astride horses, and two of these to show their independence sat facing the tails of their beasts, which were towed in the procession by lines to the horse or cab next ahead. This procession went, accompanied by the tooting of horns and the strains of chanties sung to fiddle accompaniments, to some of the villages surrounding Portsmouth, Fareham or Botley where unreportable orgies took place.

Capper correctly put the cause of such behaviour down to the Admiralty's stupid system of withholding men's pay during long commissions and then suddenly releasing the men ashore with their pockets full of money, but there were already signs of reform. Capper joined *St Vincent* as a boy in 1869, the 'bottom of the ladder' as he called it, and himself witnessed 'the continuous rising of the men in self-respect, self-reverence and mental efficiency, from the lowest dregs of the community to a relatively high social position'. By the end of the nineteenth century, there had indeed been a dramatic improvement in the public's perception and approval of the Navy and the sailor. The 'common sailors', who rioted whenever they got ashore, became the 'Handymen', with songs and verse written in their honour.

Much of the improvement in the sailor's self-respect was due to the work of a barrister's daughter, born in London in 1840, called Agnes Weston. 'Aggie' Weston had her critics, in and out of the Navy, but in her own way and in her own field she was one of the great reforming figures of the nineteenth century Navy.

Whilst staying with friends at Devonport in 1872, Aggie saw every Sunday hundreds of sailors strolling aimlessly about with nowhere to go. She held prayer meetings, with hymn singing and Bible Readings, and tea, in her friend's kitchen. She worked tirelessly for the temperance cause in the Navy and was present at the inaugural meeting of the Royal Naval Temperance Society at Devonport in April 1873.

Several sailors had told Aggie they wished

Portsmouth Sailors' Home.

they had 'a public house without the drink'. Aggie and her indefatigable friend Miss Sophia Wintz found a house in Fore Street, Devonport, and with money raised through the temperance movement converted it into a restaurant and kitchen, with a reading room. What became internationally famous as Aggie Weston's Sailors Rest opened in May 1876.

Aggie started branches of the Royal Naval Temperance Society on many ships, including *Eurydice*. She had visited the ship shortly before she sailed. 'I can almost see those hundreds of bright, young faces now,' she said. The pledge book and membership cards went down with the ship but Aggie got them back when the ship was raised. Aggie could read the names, but the paper crumbled to dust after a little exposure.

Aggie made many visits to Portsmouth and wanted to open a Sailor's Rest there. She had her eye on Commercial Road, one of the busiest streets in England, but property was expensive and rarely changed hands. So Aggie rented a Music Hall with two small houses and a shop attached. She fitted it out with a brightly-decorated coffee bar and a reading room. Aggie paid particular attention to the decor of her Sailors' Rests. As she shrewdly said, 'I was competing against public houses.'

There were no bedrooms in the Music Hall and barely room for a manager and his wife, but the place was a success from the first day. The coffee bar and reading room were usually full. The entertainments given on stage every Saturday night, with a band and a pianist, songs by the bluejackets and musical friends, recitations, feats of agility and strength, were always packed to the door.

Some time later, Aggie heard of a good site in a splendid position. The owner was willing to sell privately if he had a good enough offer. The sum of £1000 was needed to buy the site. £1050 was raised at one meeting which Aggie addressed at the house of a friend. The Portsmouth Sailors' Rest opened on 13 June 1881.

At that time, 'Aggies' had little competition from the Sailors Home opened in Portsea in 1852. It had begun with the best intentions but it was badly managed, uncomfortable, ill-furnished, and out of date and, according to Capper, who became involved in it, 'the attendants acted as though they were ships' police afloat'. Capper was one of a committee which brought about changes, including the resignation of the superintendent. The Home was eventually run as a Club by the sailors themselves.

By contrast, Aggie's Sailors' Rests were, for nineteenth century sailors, a revelation:

To men accustomed to eat from tables covered with tarpaulin cloths (wrote Henry Capper), their own knives and never even a two-pronged fork in the mess, and only basins and plates when these were purchased by themselves, the change was startling indeed. Many of the waitresses were unpaid volunteer ladies, and the rule enforced was to avoid all familiarity, so that whereas in their own haunts they were called 'Jack', 'Tom' or 'Bill', here each customer was 'Mr ---', and 'Yes, sir', and 'No, sir', the method of reply. What wonder that a new atmosphere created new desires, and that in some measure what they had experienced on shore began to be the rule afloat.

Chapter 12

The Old Queen died at her favourite Osborne House, on the Isle of Wight, with many of her children and grand-children around her, at about 6.30 on the evening of 22 January 1901. On 1 February, bluejackets drew the gun carriage bearing the Queen's coffin through the streets of Cowes to Trinity Pier and carried the coffin on board the Royal Yacht *Alberta* lying alongside. Offshore lay the guard ship, the cruiser *Australia*, firing eighty-one minute guns, one for each year of the Queen's life.

Alberta sailed at three o'clock for the eight-mile passage across to Portsmouth. It was a perfect winter's afternoon, of brilliant sunshine and no wind. The Solent lay like glittering glass and the ripples of passing ships' wakes travelled for miles. The sun hung in the west like a great golden ball, its slanting light throwing long shadows of ships across the water. To the east lay the grey shapes of a vast array of warships which included four German battleships, the French battleship *Dupuy de Lome*, the Japanese *Hatsuse* and the Portuguese *Dom Carlos I*.

Preceded by an escort of eight destroyers and followed by *Victoria and Albert*, with the new King Edward VII and the Royal Family embarked, the yacht *Osborne*, the German Emperor's huge white yacht *Hohenzollern*, the Admiralty yachts *Enchantress* and *Elfin*, *Alberta* steamed at six knots between the lines of warships. *Alexandra*, the first battleship to port, fired one warning gun which was answered by *Majestic* five miles away. The whole fleet fired minute guns, and manned their sides, masts and yards with hundreds of sailors as *Alberta* passed them. Huge crowds stood bare-headed and in silence on the Portsmouth side, listening to the thudding of the guns.

After the arrival of the coffin at Clarence Yard, the Navy's scheduled part was over, but there was an unexpected sequel. When the

Naval Review at Spithead for Queen Victoria's Diamond Jubilee. 26th June 1897.

Royal party arrived at Windsor GWR Station, the horses drawing the gun carriage had grown restive through waiting too long and, because of a misunderstanding, never got the order to move off.

The result was that only two horses tried to drag the gun-carriage, and finding it unusually heavy, they began to kick and plunge. While the gun-carriage was stalled, the leading portion of the procession, unaware that anything was wrong, marched on and round a corner and out of sight. Soon the whole solemn ceremony was in confusion.

At the suggestion of Prince Louis of Battenberg, implemented with the King's agreement by the late Queen's equerry Sir Frederick ('Fritz') Ponsonby, the horses were replaced by the bluejackets in the Guard of Honour. The horses were unharnessed and led away. The sailors piled their arms and, to the fury of the Artillery, took up the traces and easily drew carriage and coffin to the Chapel of St George. Thus was a naval tradition for future Royal funerals established.

Anchor Lane, Portsmouth Dockyard 1899.

In the late 1890s, Portsmouth Dockyard laid down at least one battleship and sometimes two every year. All had a main armament of 12-inch guns, and most had some innovation in their construction or their history: in 1895, *Majestic* was the name ship of nine 'Majestic' Class battleships, the epitome of the Victorian battleship and the most numerous battleship class ever built; in 1897,

Canopus, was the name ship of a class of six, the first Royal Navy battleship class to have water-tube boilers; a year later, *Formidable*, the first of her class of three, was the first battleship to cost more than £1 million; and in 1899, *London* led a class of five 'Londons' and, in 1912, was one of the first battleships to have aircraft launched from her fore gun turret.

The battleship *Royal Sovereign*, launched by the Queen at Portsmouth in 1891, was commissioned in May 1892, four months ahead of schedule and only two years and eight months after her keel was laid. This was achieved by the daemonic drive and energy of the Admiral Superintendent of Portsmouth Dockyard, 'Jackie' Fisher. On 21 October, Trafalgar Day, 1904, Fisher became First Sea Lord and with the same urgency began to press forward the design of a new battleship, who was to lend her name to all similar battleships and indeed to a whole new naval era.

HMS Dreadnought was laid down at Portsmouth on 2 October 1905 and built at a frantic pace. Portsmouth Dockyard was the only place in the world at that time where such a ship could be built at such speed (the US Navy had already designed their 'Dreadnought', the *USS Michigan*, but she was completed years after *Dreadnought*).

Improvements and enlargements to Portsmouth Dockyard continued to the end of the nineteenth century and into the twentieth century — including a Gun Mounting Shop, Torpedo Store, Armour Plate Workshop, Steam Factory, larger cranes and bigger docks, a railway extension into the Dockyard from the Harbour Station. The largest workshop ever built in Portsmouth Dockyard, called simply the Factory, was completed in 1905 while *Dreadnought* was building.

For *Dreadnought*, time was saved by obtaining ample supplies of material well in advance of the work and by ordering large numbers of plates of standard size and thickness so as to avoid the usual trouble and time of cutting and sorting plates of different sizes. More time was saved by appropriating the 12-inch guns and spares for *Lord Nelson* and *Agamemnon*. As a result, *Dreadnought* was launched

H.M.S. Dreadnought building at Portsmouth. 1906.

after only 130 days on the building slip.

The launching ceremony was carried out by King Edward VII on Saturday, 10 February 1906. His Majesty arrived the night before and went on board *Victoria and Albert* at South Railway Jetty. In the morning he boarded a train which took him through the yard to the launching platform. He named the ship, broke a bottle of Australian wine over her bows, and then launched her by tapping a chisel which cut the cord holding the weights on the dogshoes.

Celebrations were muted because the Court was in full mourning after the death of the King of Denmark. Guards were paraded, but no bands. The route was decorated, but HM Ships and buildings were not dressed overall or illuminated. Nevertheless, it was still a great occasion as befitted the opening of a new naval epoch. Vast and enthusiastic crowds were present to cheer *Dreadnought* as she took the water.

Dreadnought displaced 18,110 tons, was armed with ten 12-inch guns, and cost £1,793,883. She commissioned in the Reserve for trials on 1 September 1906 and sailed for trials on 3 October 1906, an astonishing year and a day after she was laid down.

She was the first 'all big gun' battleship to do 21 knots (21.6 knots on trials), and the first to have four shafts and twin rudders. Furthermore, she was a handsome and striking ship. She actually looked the part of the most powerful warship of her time, superior in fire power and speed to any other capital ship then afloat.

Dreadnought and Fisher had their critics, especially among those who argued that by building a ship which made all her contemporaries obsolete at a stroke, which *Dreadnought* certainly did, the Royal Navy had wilfully sacrificed its advantages over other navies. The 'Dreadnought Controversy' as it was called, rumbled on for years, but the sincerest tribute to *Dreadnought* was paid by those other navies who began furiously to build their own Dreadnoughts.

Thus *Dreadnought* lent fresh impetus to the Arms Race, but Britain was able to outstrip the rest and built thirty Dreadnoughts in the eight years between the launch of the first and the outbreak of World War One. There were some very famous names amongst them, including *Bellerophon, St Vincent, Neptune, Orion, King George V* and *Iron Duke*, all built at Portsmouth.

The excitement over *Dreadnought* in October 1906 had hardly subsided before there was uproar of quite a different kind in the Royal Naval Barracks, Portsmouth, over what became known as the 'On the Knee Mutiny'. The Barracks themselves were comparatively new. A barracks for four thousand men at Portsmouth seems to have been suggested as early as 1862, but there were to be almost forty years of enquiries, counter proposals, financial stringencies and postponements when extensions to the Dockyard took priority.

'Rotten Row'. *Royal George* (r) and *Pitt.* 1899.

Meanwhile, hulks continued to provide the space for the administrative life of the Port and accommodation for officers and men, as they had done in Nelson's day. In 1899, when Mr Lovatt of Wolverhampton submitted the winning tender to build the Barracks and work began, the 'Royal Navy Depot' at Portsmouth consisted of five main hulks: the *Victory*, which was the Signal School and receiving ship for Boys 1st Class; the *Duke of Wellington*, the receiving ship for seamen,

stokers, artisan ratings (ship's company) and domestics; the *Marlborough*, for Wardroom and Gunroom officers, and stokers second class; the *Hannibal*, for Marines, new entries and all other artisan ratings; and the *Asia*, for Warrant officers, Engine Room artificers, Chief Stokers and Chief Carpenter's Mates.

A Draft for China 1900.

The Barracks were built on the sites of the Anglesey Barracks and the Military Prison, and the old convict prison and the warder's quarters, with land purchased from the Corporation, and a drill hall which had formerly belonged to the Hampshire Regiment. Holy Trinity became the Barracks church.

Royal Naval Barracks, Battalion at Drill.

Some four thousand officers and men marched from the *Duke of Wellington* into their new quarters in the Barracks on 30 September 1903. *The Hampshire Telegraph* described it as having 'something like the appearance of a triumphal procession. Immense crowds lined the route from the Dockyard to the main gates in Edinburgh Road and the Bluejackets were cheered loudly as they passed.'

Nobody regretted the passing of the hulks which were, in *The Hampshire Telegraph's*

Terrible back from Boer War 19th September 1902.

words, 'vacated with no ceremony or regret as they were unpleasant and miserable quarters'. 'It is remarkable', said the *Portsmouth Evening News*, 'that so many hundreds of men should have been compelled to live in undesirable quarters for so long'. 'As compared with the old *Duke* and the *Marlborough*,' continued *The Hampshire Telegraph*, 'the quarters are a perfect palace with electric light, lavatories on each floor and water taps in every room, which are lofty and well lighted.'

Victory cap ribbons were issued in December 1903 but not until April 1905 were all hands transferred from the books of the Commander-in-Chief's yacht *Firequeen* to the *Victory*'s books and the move from hulks to Royal Naval Barracks was finally complete.

King Edward VII visited the Barracks in February 1904 and inspected everything thoroughly. He dismissed a parade in his honour early because it was raining heavily. The Officer of the Day on Sunday, 4 November 1906 was not so considerate.

At about four o'clock that afternoon, the duty watch of seamen, signalmen and stokers were mustering for evening quarters when heavy rain began to fall. After his inspection the Officer of the Day, Lt. B. St. George Collard, gave the order to dismiss. The duty watch, already somewhat resentful that they had had to fall in on the open parade ground when there was ample space under cover in the gymnasium nearby, began to disperse in some disorder. The stokers were particularly noisy and unruly.

Collard, a Gunnery Officer, called the men back and ordered them to fall in again in the gymnasium. The sailors and signalmen he dismissed almost at once, but he intended to reprimand the stokers for their behaviour and gave the preliminary order 'On the Knee'. This order, whereby the front row of men knelt on one knee, was usually given only in a gunnery drill context. Collard later claimed that he gave it only because he was of short stature and he wanted the rear ranks to see and hear him. A more sensitive man might have paused to consider whether this order was appropriate.

Whatever Collard's intention, the effect was to make the stokers believe they were being insulted. There were shouts of 'Don't obey!'. Collard repeated the order. At last, with a show of open reluctance, the front row knelt and the stokers were reprimanded and dismissed.

Collard later reported the incident to the Commodore of the Barracks, the Hon. W. G. Stopford, by telephone. He assured him that although it had been a serious incident of insubordination all was now well.

All might have been well, but for a remark in the Canteen that evening. In fairness to Collard, it should be said that there was already unrest in the Stoker Branch of the Navy over their pay and conditions of service. Probably, if it had not been 'On the Knee', it would have been something else.

In the Canteen that evening, the seamen treated the whole incident as a huge joke, laughing and chaffing about it, but the stokers were convinced that the officer had been trying to humiliate them. Some three hundred of them sat drinking their beer in sullen groups. However, they were behaving in a comparatively quiet and orderly manner. All might still have been well, except that at about 9.30 when the Canteen was being cleared up before closing, somebody — possibly a seaman — came into the Canteen and mischievously shouted 'On your knees!'.

At this, the stokers' feelings of anger and frustration boiled over and they began smashing tables, glasses, windows and anything else they could lay hands on. Some of the wilder spirits ran out of the Canteen and rushed for the Main Gate, possibly with the idea of going across the road to the Wardroom and demanding an apology, but the Duty Petty Officer in the Canteen managed to warn the Guardhouse. The Main Gate was locked and the full guard turned out to restore order.

Meanwhile, the rest of the stokers poured out on to the parade ground and by the time the Commodore arrived he was confronted by an angry mob. He tried to address them but was booed and shouted down. Three stokers had already been arrested and the rest demanded their release before they would listen. The Commodore said that they must be quiet before he would even consider it.

This seemed to give the stokers the impression they had struck some form of bargain with the Commodore. They broke up into smaller groups and dispersed. When all was quiet again, the three stokers were released, but the Main Gate remained locked. Returning libertymen were sent away to find a night's lodging in the town.

On the next day, Monday, all was quiet. Daily routine carried on as normal. Libertymen went ashore in the evening. The Commodore, convinced that the trouble was over, went to a Ball. That evening, a Duty Warrant Officer went over to the Canteen to check that all was quiet.

He could see very few men drinking in the Canteen, most having already gone to turn in, but near the door sat a group of about twenty men, audibly discussing the disturbance the night before. At closing time, a Petty Officer called out to them 'Come along, you men, clear out'. As the men got up, one of them accidentally or on purpose knocked over a small table. Its marble top shattered on the floor. At once, somebody swept half a dozen glasses off another table close by.

At the sound of breaking glass, everyone in the Canteen except the group causing the disturbance made a rush for the door and left as quickly as they could. The Warrant Officer sent a Petty Officer to summon the guard from the Main Gate. As soon as they arrived, the order was given to fix bayonets. The unruly group was detained in the Canteen corridor and the doors were shut. The Warrant Officer sent a message to the Commander to tell him what had happened.

At that time, the parade ground was deserted and the Barracks was quiet. Had the men from the Canteen been marched over to the Guardhouse and placed under arrest, all might still have been well. But Commander Drury-Lowe either misunderstood the message, or it was wrongly delivered to him. When he reached the Main Gate he gave the order to sound the 'Assembly'. Ship's police and duty petty officers ran from building to building ordering the men to turn out. Soon the whole place was in noisy turmoil, with shouted orders to 'Come on come on, turn out and fall in' while men still half asleep were asking each other 'What's up?'

The party of stokers was still in the Canteen corridor. The Warrant Officer sent another message to the Commander asking what he was to do with them. Misunderstanding again, Drury-Lowe told the Warrant Officer to let them fall in with the rest and to send the guard over to him. The troublemakers thus joined the main body.

When all the buildings had been reported clear, Drury-Lowe began to address the crowd — it was not orderly enough to be called a parade. He told them that what they were doing was damaging the good name of the Barracks and the Navy. He urged them to go back quietly and turn in and not make fools of themselves. He ordered the bugler to sound the 'Disperse'.

To men who had just been turned out of their hammocks by order of authority the Commander's words were incomprehensible, not to say laughable. Indeed some men began to jeer and cat-call. There was scuffling and horse-play in the ranks.

At this moment Commodore Stopford himself arrived. The scene must have seemed to him barely credible. The parade ground was packed with excited men, milling about in the darkness, with Drury-Lowe's voice trying to rise above derisive laughter and shouting. It appeared to Stopford that the whole Barracks was in or very near a state of mutiny. He ordered the Main Gates shut, and nobody to be allowed in or out.

Stopford also addressed the crowd, with no more success than Drury-Lowe. At last he said 'Will someone who knows what the matter is and what the men want come out front and let me know?'. This was a very, very dangerous thing for any sailor to do, as they all knew full well. Finally, an officer who knew a Stoker named Moody called to him saying 'You seem to know what these fellows want, come and tell the Commodore'. Moody came to the front and said

something about the stokers wanting 'an apologisation' which, needless to say, was not given.

Shutting the Main Gates had prevented libertymen coming back into the Barracks. Soon a large crowd, of sailors and civilians, had gathered outside. By mischance the road was under repair. Granite chippings made excellent ammunition. Somebody picked up a stone and threw it at the Wardroom. Others followed suit and a hail of missiles began to rattle against the walls and smash the glass in the windows.

The men inside the Barracks could hear the angry yells and hoots and breaking glass, and could see the crowd's gestures, encouraging them to go on with their riot. Both sides, the large hostile crowd outside and the hundreds of sailors inside, egged each other on. Some stokers tried to storm the guardhouse and overpower the guard. Others went in to their blocks and tore up bedding and broke up furniture. A few climbed over the railings into the road.

The City police were called out in some numbers but by midnight the situation had become so serious that armed parties were landed from ships in harbour, with two companies of Royal Marine Artillery from Eastney. They formed lines across the road and gradually forced the crowd, which had risen to over a thousand, to retreat down Queen Street. Groups of thirty or forty rioters charged, but were driven back. By three in the morning the mob had almost completely dispersed, with a dozen arrests.

Eleven stokers, including Moody, were tried by court martial on board *Victory* and received heavy sentences — Moody was given five years' penal servitude. Collard was also court-martialled, on 26 November. It transpired that he had given the same 'On the knee' order to a stoker called Albert Acton in November 1905 and he was charged with giving Acton unauthorised punishment and abusive language. He was also charged with improper use of the order 'On the knee, you dirty dog, and learn some manners'. (This was so widely believed it appeared upon postcards of the time). But Acton deserted in April 1906. Other evidence was contradic-

"On The Knee": Postcard of 1906 lampooning Lt. Collard, who is said to have called Stoker Acton a 'dog'.

tory. Collard defended himself with vigour. He was found guilty of giving Acton unauthorised punishment on the first charge and reprimanded, but acquitted of the second charge.

Moody's sentence was reduced to three years, but Stopford was relieved of his command, and Drury-Lowe and a third officer were given other appointments. It was laid down that the order 'On the knee' was only to be used for drill purposes.

Metal sheeting was put up along the Edinburgh Road railings, to stop the public staring in. It stayed until 1956 when Commodore J. Y. Thompson obtained the Commander-in-Chief's approval to remove it, saying, 'Nothing occurs on the parade ground of which I am ashamed and there is plenty going on of which I am proud'.

Collard complained at his trial that he had been attacked by the 'mercenary halfpenny press throughout the Kingdom'. He sued *The Daily Mail* for defamation and obtained £5,000, with which he bought a country house and got married. The *Mail* columnist responsible for the attacks, Edgar Wallace, became rich and famous as a novelist.

On 26 August 1902, the Royal Navy's first two submarines arrived in Portsmouth. Known as *Holland I* and *Holland II*, after their American designer John Patrick Holland, they had been built under licence by Vickers at Barrow in Furness, whence they had an eventful passage, escorted by their first depot ship, the gunboat *HMS Hazard*.

At first, the submarines berthed alongside *Hazard* in Portsmouth Harbour. They were regarded with some suspicion. When *A1*, the first of a new and larger class arrived, she had to berth alongside *HMS Latona* in a remote northerly part of the harbour, so that this 'dangerous craft' would do as little damage as possible if she should blow up.

However, in 1904, the submarines moved to their permanent base at Fort Blockhouse on the Gosport side. The place had been fortified since the Middle Ages, extensively rebuilt in 1813, and taken over by the Royal Engineers, who were in charge of submarine mining, in 1873. The Army added to the Fort's buildings and facilities, and extended the Fort's activities to the area which was to become 'Petrol Pier', where the early submarines were berthed.

The takeover was done without ceremony. One day in 1904, one of the first submarine officers Sub Lieutenant Charles Little (a future admiral), who happened to be duty officer in *Hazard*, was told to mount a Naval Guard in the Fort. He exchanged formalities with a party of Army Mining Engineers, mounted the guard and returned to *Hazard*.

The first officer, a Torpedo Gunner, was appointed to Fort Blockhouse in May 1905 and the first Commanding Officer, Commander F.L. Attenborough, in November 1906. That year, the old composite screw sloop *Dolphin* was towed to Blockhouse from Portland. She had been built in 1882 and served in the Egyptian and Sudan campaigns of the 1880s. She was to stay at Fort Block-house, leaking but still afloat, until replaced by *Pandora* in 1923.

Fort Blockhouse proved an admirable choice as a submarine base. Haslar Creek was deep enough for submarines, and the Block-house peninsula had enough room for expansion, and it became the United Kingdom's premier submarine base. It was near enough to Portsmouth Dockyard to make use of its repair facilities but distanced enough from the Commander-in-Chief officers to remain a separate, and idiosyncratic, entity.

Submariners were regarded by the rest of the Navy as 'scruffy little men in scruffy little boats'. Submarine warfare was looked upon as being unfair, 'below the belt', 'unworthy of officers and gentlemen', 'damned un-English'. It was suggested that in time of war captured submarine crew should be hung as pirates.

Scruffy, uncomfortable and mechanically unreliable though these first primitive submarines were, they soon had their successes in naval exercises. The 'Holland' and 'A' Classes were quickly followed by larger, faster and more efficient 'B', 'C' and 'D' Classes. Sixty submarines had been built for the Royal Navy by 1910.

With the successes came the penalties. In Haslar Cemetery a stone obelisk stands in memory of Lieutenant Loftus Mansergh and his crew, who lost their lives when *A1* was sunk in collision with the *ss Berwick Castle* while carrying out a dived attack on *HMS Juno* off the Nab Light Vessel on 18 March 1904. It was not long before the other sides of the obelisk were also inscribed: to Lieutenant Frederick Skinner and five of his crew, killed by an explosion on board *A5* at Queenstown on 16 February 1905; to Sub Lieutenant Fletcher and fourteen men of *A8*, which foundered off Plymouth on 6 June 1905; and to four officers and ten ship's company of *A3*, sunk after a collision with *HMS Hazard* off the Isle of Wight on 2 February 1912. These were only some of the first of what was to become a long and melancholy tale of submarine losses.

Submarines attracted Royal interest from

Submarines A5 and A10 alongside torpedo boat.

Jetty at *H.M.S. Dolphin*, Portsmouth Submarine Base, with submarines alongside, *c.* 1911.

their earliest days. Queen Alexandra and Princess Victoria thoroughly inspected *A3* at Portsmouth in March 1905. The Prince of Wales, later King George V, himself a professional naval officer, went to sea and dived in an A-boat. The first British submarine to attend a Royal Review was *D1*, with seven other boats, at King George V's Coronation Review in 1911.

Reviews were even more common in the Edwardian Navy than they had been in the Victorian Navy, although not all were full formal Royal occasions. King Edward VII's Review was held at Spithead on Saturday, 16 August 1902. It was the last at which ships wore what was already beginning to seem an archaic appearance: black hulls, red or green boot-topping, yellow and white superstructure, buff masts and funnels, and elaborate gilt 'gingerbread' ornamentation on bow and stern.

There were 114 ships present, including twenty-one first-class battleships, seventeen torpedo gunboats and thirty-two destroyers. The Commander-in-Chief Portsmouth,

Admiral Sir Charles Hotham, flew his flag in the Navy's newest battleship, *HMS London*. There were foreign warships from every country with a Navy worthy of the name.

British and French sailors, Whale Island 1905.

More reviews followed, one almost every other year. French warships, including six battleships and five armoured cruisers, under their Commander-in-Chief, Admiral Caillard, arrived at Spithead in August 1905 for what was known as the 'Entente Cordiale'

Review. In 1907, there were two reviews: in May for the Colonial Premiers who had attended the Imperial Conference, and in August for 'Our Sailor King's Review', when Edward VII reviewed a huge concourse of 181 warships which, it was claimed, did not include a single obsolete ship. The King went to sea in *Dreadnought* and witnessed twelve rounds being fired from the big guns in three minutes; the range was 2,600 yards and 'there was only one miss'.

In 1909, there were two reviews in two months. On 12 June, 144 ships of the Home and Atlantic Fleets assembled at Spithead for a visit by delegates of the Empire Press. The Navy went to some trouble to put on a show. Fisher himself accompanied the party on a special train from Victoria. The visitors were shown over *Dreadnought*, witnessed a mock attack on her by destroyers, and landing manoeuvres at Whale Island.

On 31 July, the King held a Review at Spithead, which was attended by many Members of Parliament and was the first to include the new Dreadnoughts, the battle-cruisers, represented by *Indomitable* which had recently made a record run to Canada and back with the Prince of Wales on board.

Landing the Duke of Connaught's elephant at Portsmouth, 1908.

Coronation Review at Spithead, 24th June 1911.

Edward VII died on 6 May 1910. King George V and Queen Alexandra were crowned on 22 June 1911 and their Coronation Review took place at Spithead two days later. There were 170 ships: thirty-two battleships, eight of them Dreadnoughts, twenty-five armoured cruisers, including four Dreadnought battle-cruisers, nine cruisers, twelve depot ships, seventy-two destroyers, twelve torpedo boats and eight submarines. This was nothing like the nation's whole naval strength. The ships were nearly all provided from the Home and Atlantic Fleets, being only the 'home guard', in fact. There were also eighteen foreign warships.

As the years ran out before the start of World War One, the Naval Reviews increased in size, almost as though it were hoped that the overwhelming numbers of warships and the sheer weight of their armaments might somehow overawe and avert Amrageddon. On 9 July 1912, Members of both Houses of Parliaments attended a Review of 223 warships and 106 destroyers. Aircraft took part for the first time — one took off from *HMS London*, and submarines made mimic attacks on the Dreadnoughts.

Even this assembly was totally eclipsed by the Grand Fleet Review of 16 July 1914, a

H.M.S. Iron Duke 12th October 1912.

fortnight before the outbreak of war. It was held ostensibly because the Admiralty wished to test the efficiency of the system for mobilising the fleet and calling up reservists, but it was as much a response to the deepening political crisis.

Described by *The Times* as 'an incomparable armada', 648 ships were drawn up in eleven lines forty miles long. There were twenty Dreadnoughts and forty pre-Dreadnoughts, nine battle-cruisers, forty-six cruisers, sixty-two light cruisers, 215 destroyers, 106 torpedo boats and seventy-six submarines.

There was also an aircraft carrier (the old converted cruiser *Hermes*) and seaplanes (who also rode to their own anchors). The Royal Naval Air Service had begun its official existence on 1 July 1914, when it had fifty-two seaplanes, thirty-nine aeroplanes and seven airships.

The King was to have spent the weekend with the fleet but the political situation prevented him arriving until Saturday evening. On Sunday morning, the King cruised up and down the lines of ships in *Victoria and Albert*. He visited *Iron Duke, King George V, Bacchante, Queen Mary* and *Collingwood*, and held an Investiture and a banquet on board the Royal Yacht.

On Monday morning, *Victoria and Albert* anchored off Nab End Buoy and the King took the salute as his fleet passed in review, ship after ship. This, said Winston Churchill, First Lord of the Admiralty, 'constituted incomparably the greatest assemblage of naval power ever witnessed in the history of the world'. It took hours before the last ship had steamed, and the last seaplane had flown, past His Majesty. The aeroplanes flew in a large 'V' in the first public exhibition of formation flying.

The fleets were to have dispersed after exercises that week, but Churchill placed the Navy on a 'preparatory and precautionary basis' on 28 July. Next day, the First Fleet left Portland and on the night of 29/30 July passed, at high speed and with lights out, through the Straits of Dover, heading up the North Sea to Scapa Flow. As Churchill said, 'the King's ships were at sea'.

Chapter 13

The outbreak of war on 4 August 1914 was greeted with general acclamation by the whole country. Mr Herbert Asquith, the Prime Minister, was cheered when he rose in the House of Commons to give Members the details of the ultimatum calling upon Germany to respect the neutrality of Belgium, guaranteed by Great Britain, France and Germany in a treaty of 1839, but already dismissed by the Kaiser as a 'scrap of paper'. Huge and excited crowds surged through the streets of London and other towns and cities, gathering to cheer and sing the National Anthem in Downing Street, outside Buckingham Palace and town halls throughout the land.

Amongst the cheering crowds in Portsmouth was a group of puzzled contractors. They had been supplying food to the ships in the Review. But suddenly, the ships had vanished, and nobody would tell the contractors where they had gone.

At that early stage of the war, nobody would tell anybody anything. In Portsmouth, as everywhere else, there was a severe outbreak of 'spy scares'. Armed sentries were posted at the Royal Naval Barracks gates. Extra Metropolitan police were drafted in to guard the Dockyard, and for a time were accommodated in the Barracks.

In such an atmosphere, spies were seen on every street corner. There were all manner of false alarms: motor car headlights on the Portsdown Hill road were reported more than once as aircraft just about to attack Portsmouth. Suspicion turned on people, shops and business with foreign names, especially German-sounding names. The First Sea Lord, Admiral H. S. H. Prince Louis of Battenberg, was forced to resign on 29 October 1914 through the pressure of totally unfounded slurs about his loyalty to the Nation and the Navy, because of his German name and family.

The 'White Feather' was already abroad in the land, presented to young men who were thought, rightly or wrongly, to be shirking by not joining up. Fred T. Jane, writing in *The Hampshire Telegraph* in August 1914, remarked on what he called the 'White Feather Brigade' and reproved these 'young knuts' for riding about the place on motor bikes with girls in the sidecars.

At the same time and in the same newspaper, Harold Begbie, the author of the original verses which gave the nineteenth century sailor the nickname 'The Handy Man', was writing:

How will you fare, Sonny, how will you fare
  In the far-off winter night,
When you sit by the fire in an old man's
    chair
  And your neighbours talk of the fight?
Will you shrink away, as it were from a
    blow,
  Your old head shamed and bent,
Or say: I was not with the first to go
  But I went, thank God, I went?

These were curious comments to make at that particular time, because men were actually coming forward in their thousands to join the Colours. Portsmouth in particular was shortly to be overflowing with men.

In July 1911, the Kaiser had sent the gunboat *Panther* to the Moroccan port of Agadir, seriously alarming the British and French governments as to German intentions and awakening them to the likelihood of a war with Germany. After that crisis, the Admiralty had begun to overhaul and bring up to date the administrative machinery for placing the fleet on a war footing. A special mobilisation exercise in July 1914 had seemed to show everything would work smoothly.

However, under the pressure of events in a real war, the system became strained and almost broke down. The plan was to allocate men in advance to the ships and vessels they would join when war broke out, but when war did break out, some ships required manning urgently, irrespective of their priority in the peace time list. Other ships were not immediately available to receive their full complements and the men had to be sent elsewhere.

Some manning problems had not been foreseen. Ships building for other navies in British yards were simply taken over and extra men were needed to man them. The two Turkish battleships *Sultan Osman I* at Elswick, and *Rechad V* at Vickers, Barrow, for example, were renamed *Agincourt* and *Erin* respectively and commissioned with officers and men from the Royal Yacht, the Royal Naval Colleges at Dartmouth and Osborne and other sources.

At Whale Island, a new Commander had just joined when war was declared. The first bugle call he ordered was 'Mobilize'. It had an amazing effect. Within days, the Island was virtually deserted. The Captain, the staff, the Officers' Long Gunnery Course, 146 sublieutenants and every active service rating in the establishment had all gone to sea.

After this first exodus, there was an even greater inflow as thousands of officers and men of the Royal Naval Reserve and Royal Fleet Reserve obeyed the Royal Proclamation and joined their depots. All drafting vacancies were filled and still more men arrived, hundreds of them by every train. The Barracks blocks were full to over-crowding with every corner and every hammock space occupied. Eventually, late-comers had to be turned away at the Barracks gates and told to go back home on leave and wait until their services were needed.

The Barracks' offices were open day and night, with the Depot staff working until they were exhausted. One contemporary account recorded, with some feeling:

> 'It is a pyramid of difficulties and troubles; the dust of the Parade ground, unnumerable signals, toil and lack of sleep, and the burning sun of August, 1914, which must be placed in the foreground of any picture representing life as it was lived within the iron palings of the Naval Barracks during the first few weeks of the Great War'.

Men had to be accommodated where possible in other establishments. Whale Island received several hundred Scottish fishermen from the Western Isles. They had no papers or identification and many of them had only the Gaelic. All were clamouring to get to sea and have a go at the Huns before the war ended. When the name 'Campbell' was called at the first pay parade, seventy men stepped forward. Fifty of them had the same single christian name, Donald. Soon the Island, too, was overflowing, with every available building in use. The drill shed, half of which was used as a mess for three hundred men, became known as 'the Bulgarian Camp'.

While the sailors were waiting to be sent on draft, they were kept busy by boxing matches — every man had to box a few rounds every morning and afternoon — and playing football on the Depot and United Services grounds. There were cinema shows, concerts and sing-songs. Actors and actresses gave their professional services for nothing.

The Southsea Salvation Army band visited the Barracks one Sunday evening that August. Amid what *The Hampshire Telegraph* called 'a scene of almost unprecedented enthusiasm' they played for two hours, ending with the English and French National Anthems which were cheered to the echo by the thousands of bluejackets present. An impromptu collection also realised £7 2s 8d.

Very quickly there was much grimmer news in the papers. On the afternoon of 5 September 1914, the light cruiser *HMS Path-finder* was patrolling off the Firth of Forth when she was torpedoed by *U-21*. The torpedo detonated in the forward magazine and 259 of *Pathfinder*'s people were lost. She was the first warship in naval history to be sunk by a self-propelled torpedo fired from a genuine submarine in the open sea. She had her obituary notice in *The Hampshire Telegraph*, written by Mr Charles Marriott who believed, as did everyone at the time, she had struck a mine:

> In open sea, careless of all that came
> On peaceful quest, they laid the mine.
>   She found
> The path to Britain's glory, and their
>   shame.

Pathfinder was actually a Chatham-manned ship but it was not long before there were Portsmouth ships in the news: the cruiser *Hawke*, sunk by a submarine in the North Sea on 14 October with the loss of nearly five hundred lives; the battleship *Audacious* mined and sunk off the north coast of Ireland on 27 October; the cruiser *Good Hope*, sunk with all hands, over nine hundred officers and men, by *Scharnhorst* and *Gneisenau* at Coronel on 1 November; and the battleship *Bulwark*, which blew up whilst embarking ammunition off Sheerness on 26 November, with only twelve survivors from a complement of over seven hundred and fifty.

The newspapers were full of lists of names, of casualties, and of survivors; in October 1914, there were lists of the Portsmouth men interned with the Naval Brigade in Holland. Looking through the casualty lists in the newspapers became almost a way of life for Portsmouth people, an accepted part of their daily and weekly existence.

The battle of Jutland on 31 May 1916 was a private disaster for Portsmouth. Of the six thousand officers and men lost, the majority came from the town. The Admiralty's maladroit handling of the first announcements aggravated public alarm. Initially, it appeared that Jutland had been a German victory. Dockyard workers were reluctant to take returning ships' lines and Beatty's flagship, the battered battle-cruiser *Lion*, was booed back into harbour at Rosyth.

The official Admiralty statement on Jutland, released on 3 June, appeared to be a catalogue of Portsmouth ships lost:

On the afternoon of Wednesday, May 31st, a naval engagement took place off the coast of Jutland. The British ships on which the brunt of the fighting fell were the Battle-cruiser Fleet and some cruisers and light-cruisers supported by four fast battleships. Among these the losses were heavy. The German battle fleet, aided by low visibility, avoided prolonged action with our main forces, and soon after these appeared on the scene the enemy returned to port, though not before receiving severe damage from our battleships. The battle-cruisers 'Queen Mary' (Portsmouth), 'Indefatigable', 'Invincible' (Portsmouth) and the cruisers 'Defence' and 'Black Prince' (Portsmouth) were sunk. The 'Warrior' was disabled and after being towed for some time, had to be abandoned by her crew. It is also known that the destroyers 'Tipperary' (Portsmouth), 'Turbulent', 'Fortune', 'Sparrowhawk' (Portsmouth), and 'Ardent' (Portsmouth) were lost and six others are not yet accounted for (including another Portsmouth destroyer, 'Shark', whose Commanding Officer, Commander Loftus Jones, won a posthumous Victoria Cross. No British battleships or light cruisers were sunk. The enemy's losses are serious. At least one battle-cruiser was destroyed; one battleship reported sunk by our destroyers during a night attack; two light cruisers were disabled and probably sunk. The exact number of enemy destroyers disposed of during the action cannot be ascertained with any certainty, but it must have been large'.

As this news flashed round the town, a great communal cry of grief rose from the houses and streets of Portsmouth. Men rushed outside, as though to stare at a comet in the sky. Women wept quite openly outside their homes. Some fainted. Rumour increased the losses tenfold. It was firmly believed that the Admiralty statement had put matters in the best possible light. Actual losses must be much greater.

The gloom of grief and sorrow, which was

to hang like a pall over the town for weeks, deepened only two days later, when the cruiser *Hampshire*, yet another Portsmouth ship, was mined and sunk off the Orkneys on her way to Russia on 5 June 1916. All but twelve of those on board were killed or missing, and amongst those lost were Lord Kitchener and his staff. The lists of names in *The Hampshire Telegraph* on 9 and 16 June ran to nearly fourteen columns.

At times it was hard to pick out some good news from the bad in Portsmouth, but early in 1915 the people of Portsmouth were invited to subscribe to a fund to commemorate deeds of daring by men belonging to or attached to the port. They did so enthusiastically, and the first recipient was Lieutenant Norman Holbrook.

In December 1914, Holbrook had made a daring penetration of the Dardanelles in his small and obsolete submarine *B.11* and had sunk the Turkish battleship *Messudiyeh*. He was awarded the Victoria Cross on 22 December 1914, the first to be gazetted in the war and the first ever won by a submariner. He was presented with his Cross by King George V at an Investiture in Buckingham Palace on 5 October 1915.

Holbrook was born in Southsea on 9 July 1888 and went to Portsmouth Grammar School before joining the *Britannia* as a cadet in 1903. He was one of a famous naval and military family whom the newspapers called — somewhat to the family's embarrassment — 'The Fighting Holbrooks'. His father was Colonel Sir Arthur Holbrook KBE, and he had four sisters and five brothers, four of whom served in the Navy or the Army.

It was one of Holbrook's sisters who said in a letter to the Portsmouth *Evening News* that the crew of the submarine were in need of warm clothing. At once a tidal wave of woollen garments, 'enough to sink half a dozen submarines the size of *B.11*', began to flow into Portsmouth. Eventually, the *Evening News* arranged for the garments to be distributed to other submarines and, when the supply still seemed inexhaustible, 'enormous parcels' were sent to the battleships in the Grand Fleet.

On 16 November 1916, the Mayor of Portsmouth presented a scroll of honour in a beautiful casket to express the town's cordial congratulations to another local hero, Commander Edward Unwin, who was born at Forest Lodge, Fawley. Unwin won a Victoria Cross in command of the landing ship *River Clyde* which put troops, including men of the Hampshire Regiment, ashore under a murderous Turkish fire at 'V' Beach on the Gallipoli peninsula on 25 April 1915. Unwin's was one of five VCs won by the officers and men of *River Clyde* that day. 'Every one of those men did far more than I did,' Unwin told the Mayor, 'but my show was rather well staged, and therefore I got it'

The first Portsmouth-born winner of the Victoria Cross was Seaman Thomas Reeves, one of three sailors from *HMS Albion* serving with the Naval Brigade who won VCs for an incident during the battle of Inkerman, in the Crimea in November 1854. Reeves received his Cross from Queen Victoria herself at the first Investiture of VCs in Hyde Park on 26 June 1857. He died in 1862 and was buried in Portsea Island General Cemetery (now Mile End Gardens).

There was a Victoria Cross Investiture on Southsea Common on 22 September 1865, when Admiral Sir Michael Seymour, Commander-in-Chief, presented their VCs to Midshipman Duncan Boyes, Captain of the After Guard Thomas Pride, and Seaman Henry Seeley, all of *HMS Euryalus*, for great gallantry while carrying the Queen's Colour into action against the Japanese at Shimonoseki in September 1864. Seeley was actually an American citizen, the first to win a VC.

The next Victoria Cross Investiture on the Common was on 6 June 1884, when Admiral Sir Geoffrey Pipps Hornby, accompanied by HRH the Duke of Edinburgh and witnessed by a vast crowd, presented the VC to Captain (later Admiral of the Fleet Sir) Arthur Knyvet Wilson. 'Tug' Wilson won his VC in hand-to-hand combat with Sudanese tribesmen when the British square broke at El Teb on 29 February 1884. He was then in command of *HMS Hecla* but had walked up to the front to see what was happening. Never one to waste words, Wilson wrote in his diary: '6th June. Docked ship. Received VC'.

Israel Harding was a Portsmouth man, born to the sea, being the son of a Queen's Pilot and grandson of a King's Pilot. He went to the Bethel School, Bath Square, in Portsmouth and joined the Navy in 1849 when he was sixteen. He qualified in gunnery at *Excellent* and by 1882 was Gunner of the battleship *Alexandra* when she took part in the bombardment of Alexandria in July that year. During the action a 10-inch shell from a shore battery penetrated the ship's side and lodged just above a magazine. Harding picked it up and plunged it into a tub of water, for which cool thought and brave act he was awarded the VC.

Harding retired from the Navy as a Chief Gunner in 1885 but rejoined in 1914. Though over eighty, he served in minesweepers and broke his left leg when a mine exploded under his ship. He died in May 1917 and was buried in Highland Road Cemetery, Portsmouth.

Portsmouth had its first and last air raid of the Great War on 25 September 1916. The sirens sounded just after 11 pm. About thirty minutes later the long black cigar shape of a Zeppelin was sighted over the harbour, illuminated in the glare of searchlights, first from *Vernon* and then from all round the port.

The Zeppelin dropped two bombs, one near *Victory* in the harbour and the other near *Renown* in dock. Anti-aircraft guns in the port and at Whale Island opened fire but did no damage. Most of them could not bear on the target. There was a 6-inch gun mounted on the pierhead at Whale Island but it was never fired, for fear of injuring people in the Dockyard.

There was also an elementary form of ARP on the Island: protection for the main services, fresh-water tanks on the Quarterdeck and a stand-by wooden bridge in case the foot-bridge were destroyed by bombs, but none of these precautions was ever needed. In the Barracks, men were ordered to take shelter behind the railway embankment in the event of a bombardment or an air raid. It was curious that history was thus repeating itself: the railway embankment actually replaced the old defensive ramparts, built to protect Portsea in the eighteenth century.

The best defence against aerial attack was by aircraft. The Royal Flying Corps was established on 13 April 1912 with a Naval and a Military Wing. The Naval Wing became the Royal Naval Air Service on 1 July 1914, entrusted at first with reconnaissance for the fleet and coastal patrols, to which was added in 1914 the air defence of Great Britain.

A seaplane station at Calshot on the Solent, where the Admiralty already owned the Castle, was established on 29 March 1913. Seaplane bases and landing grounds were also established pre-war at Lee-on-Solent, the Isle of Grain in Kent, Felixstowe in Suffolk, Hawkscraig in Fife and at Yarmouth in Norfolk, with an airship base at Kingsnorth in Kent.

From its beginnings, with a few primitive aircraft and a handful of pilots, the RNAS grew with astonishing rapidity. By the time it was absorbed into the RFC when the new Royal Air Force was formed on 1 April 1918, the RNAS had more than a hundred stations, from the Orkneys to Cornwall, some fifty-five thousand officers and men, and over two thousand five hundred aircraft and had flown operationally across the continent of Europe from the North Sea to the Dardanelles.

On 28 May 1916, King George V inspected the Royal Navy Barracks, and Haslar Camp where some two thousand men were awaiting draft to the Grand Fleet. Haslar had originally been intended to house only eight hundred men but it grew until at its peak in 1918 there were two thousand five hundred officers and men living in tents, with wooden huts as mess rooms. There was a second camp nearby for another eight hundred men serving in the Coastal Motor Boats.

By September 1918, when there was another Royal visit, by His Royal Highness the Duke of Connaught with his daughter, Princess Patricia, the Rear Admiral commanding the General Depot, Portsmouth, had several ships and establishments under his command: not just the Barracks and the Haslar Camp, but also the Navigation School, the Signal School, the accommodation ships *Terrible* and *Diadem*, and the *Redoutable* Group (the old battleships *Prince of Wales* and *Revenge*), and the Port Escort Flotilla, totalling some twenty-two thousand officers and men.

Accommodation was so short that the Physical Training School in Pitt Street became a convalescent hospital for 120 beds, with another thirty-six beds when the Roman Catholic Club was acquired as an annex. The Lion Hotel was also taken over for additional offices.

The Lion also housed the cookery demonstration room and living quarters for the Women's Royal Naval Service. With the slogan 'Release a man for sea service', the WRNS had been officially formed, to substitute women for men in certain shore jobs, by direction of an Admiralty Memorandum of 29 November 1917 (narrowly escaping being called the Women's Auxiliary Naval Corps, or WANCs). Not everyone in the Navy approved of Wrens. Some looked on them as a monstrous regiment of women. 'Of all the 'orrible things this 'orrible war 'as done,' said one Chief Cook, 'these 'orrible women are the 'orriblest!'.

When the first Director of the WRNS, Dame Katherine Furse, came to Whale Island late in 1917 to look into the possibilities of her Wrens being employed as cooks and waitresses in the overflowing officers' messes, the Captain and the Commander both regarded her visit with gloomy scepticism. Knowing the sailors' activities ashore in foreign ports and the evening proclivities of some of their junior officers much closer to home, they feared that Sex was about to Rear its Ugly Head.

However, Dame Katherine was very enthusiastic about everything she saw, saying that the place 'was just like a big London Club' (many of which, she said, she had provided with waitresses). The first (slightly reluctant) Wrens in Portsmouth were recruited from women already working in offices and the dockyard, and the Division formed on 22 January 1918.

First, those with the Royal Marine Artillery at Eastney were enrolled. Wren units were quickly formed in the Barracks, at Whale Island, at *HMS Dolphin*, the Mining School, the Paravane Department, Forton Barracks and the Signal School. The first Portsmouth Divisional Director was Miss Johnstone-Douglas, who was in charge of all Wrens in the Port, as well as those at Southampton, Portland and Weymouth.

Miss Johnstone-Douglas and five of her officers moved into their local headquarters at 18 Lion Street towards the end of February 1918. Every morning a working party brought their rations across from the Barracks on a hand-cart. Every day the new WRNS became more 'naval' in its behaviour and outlook. WRNS ranks and ratings addressed superiors as 'Ma'am'. All complaints were treated in the proper Service manner and forwarded through the usual Service channels.

Saluting was a source of embarrassment until everybody grew used to it. The rule was that WRNS ranks and ratings saluted their own officers but naval ratings were not to salute WRNS officers, although many of them often did. WRNS officers were not to salute naval officers but an Admiralty Fleet Order laid down that they were to bow and smile if they were saluted by naval officers!

In February 1918, training of Wren cooks and stewards started in the Barracks, supervised by the Barracks messman, Mr J. F. Marshall. Their numbers grew so rapidly that the Lion Commercial Hotel was taken over in June and converted into the Lion Hostel, including the WRNS Cookery School, under Miss Stevens, who was qualified in domestic training. By June 1918, there were 782 Wrens in the Port, with numbers still growing, so that in July the Miller's Hotel in Hampshire Terrace was taken over and converted into another hostel, which in time became the largest mess for WRNS officers in the Portsmouth Division.

By Armistice Day, after which no more Wrens were enrolled, there were 1,148 working in the Port, not just as cooks and stewards, but as clerks and typists in the Pay Offices and Drafting Office, and in the Signal School as clerks, store-women, packers, sorters and valve testers. From August to November 1918, there were courses in coding and decoding in the Signal School for WRNS officers.

The Wrens were drilled on the parade ground by a Chief Petty Officer, but later

WRNS officers drilled their own companies and ran the Saturday morning inspections. Once a month the Wrens were inspected by the Rear Admiral of the Royal Naval Barracks. During the Duke of Connaught's visit in September 1918, Princess Patricia inspected the Wrens assembled in the Gymnasium and commented upon the smartness of their marching. This smartness was achieved by extra drill under a PT Instructor. 'Not enjoyed by any of us,' said one who endured it, 'who did not take kindly to marching.'

There was no doubt that the Wrens were a great success. The number of 'sexual' incidents was minute. One couple early on were discovered embracing in the rose garden at Whale Island; the girl was publicly reprimanded while the sailor was awarded fourteen days stoppage of leave and extra drill.

Successful though the Wrens were, to their intense disappointment they were disbanded by order of Their Lordships on 1 October 1919, having had a peak strength of 438 officers and 5,054 ratings, but they had won the respect and affection of the Navy. 'Now that we are losing your refining influence', the Commodore of Portsmouth Barracks told a demobilisation parade of Wrens in October 1919, 'I hope we shall not drift back again into our previous barbarism'.

Miss Davies, Chief Section Leader, who had been the first Wren enrolled by Miss Johnstone-Douglas in 1918, was the last to be demobilised and she finally turned the key in the door of the WRNS headquarters at 18 Lion Street, on Trafalgar Day 1919.

In Portsmouth Dockyard, the battleship *Royal Sovereign* was launched on 29 April 1915. She was the third ship of the name to be built at Portsmouth, the last battleship to be built there and, with *Queen Elizabeth* (completed December 1914), the largest. That year Portsmouth Dockyard turned to building submarines. The first two, *J1* and *J2*, were laid down in the same dry dock and were launched together, on 6 November 1915, by flooding the dock. They were large boats, of 1,210 tons, designed to operate with the fleet, and with diesel engines giving them 20 knots on the surface, they were the fastest submarines of their day in the Navy.

They were followed by *K1, K2* and *K5*, all launched at Portsmouth in 1916 and completed in 1917. They were also designed to operate with the main fleet. The 'K' Class were larger (1780 tons) and, with boilers and steam turbines, even faster, at 25 knots, than the 'J' boats. But they were unwieldy, unlucky and unpopular submarines. Of the seventeen 'K' Class which were completed many had mishaps and fatal accidents.

K1 suffered an explosion and fire on her first diving trials. Her trials, in both senses of the word, eventually lasted from January to May 1917. She collided with *K4* in flotilla exercises off the Danish coast on 17 November 1917, and had to be sunk after her crew had been taken off. *K2* also had defects and design faults on her trials, but survived to be scrapped in 1926. *K4* herself was sunk on 31 January 1918 after a collision with *K6*. *K5* failed to surface during fleet exercises off the Scillies on 20 January 1921 and was lost with all hands: six officers and fifty-one men,

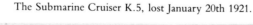

The Submarine Cruiser K.5, lost January 20th 1921.

many of them Portsmouth ratings.

Five months later, on the evening of 25 June, *K15* (built at Scotts' on the Clyde) was alongside the cruiser *Canterbury* in the tidal basin in Portsmouth Dockyard when leaking main ballast tank vents caused her to sink to the bottom of the basin. She was raised and beached, but was scrapped in 1923.

Shipbuilding may have decreased in Portsmouth Dockyard during the war but the work-load undertaken was still enormous and the number of personnel employed rose to twenty-three thousand. Apart from the two battleships and five submarines built, the light cruiser *Effingham* was laid down; 2,410 vessels were refitted; 1,784 ships docked or slipped; and thirteen large and innumerable small ships were fitted out; major repairs, due to battle damage, mines, torpedoes and collision, were carried out on sixteen large ships and numerous small craft.

Portsmouth Dockyard also fitted out special service 'Q' boats, tugs, mine-layers, paddle steamers, yachts and trawlers; armed hundreds of merchant vessels; and landed, armed and prepared for commissioning six hundred motor launches from America. The Dockyard also manufactured platforms for anti-aircraft defences, sweep gear, gun pedestals, four thousand two hundred floats and kites, and fittings for submarines and air stations.

Portsmouth celebrated the signing of the Treaty of Peace in 1919 with a salute of 101 guns. On 22 September, the Lower Deck of the Fleet entertained Admiral Beatty and other distinguished officers to a banquet at the Guildhall. Everybody celebrated the ending of the war to end all wars.

On 15 October 1924, HRH The Duke of York unveiled the Royal Naval War Memorial on the Esplanade at Southsea. On one panel is carved:

In honour of the Navy and to the abiding memory of those Ranks and Ratings of this Port who laid down their lives in the defence of the Empire, and have no other grave than the sea. 1914-1918.

The number of names upon the Memorial was 9,279.

Dockyard Gate 19th July 1919.

Chapter 14

On 26 July 1924, the first postwar Review of the fleet, the first for ten years, took place at Spithead. This was a very different Navy. There were more than two hundred ships present, from the Atlantic Fleet and vessels in reserve at Portsmouth, Devonport, Chatham and Portland, but only a few of them had been at the 'Mobilisation' Review in 1914. The battleships had dropped from fifty-five in 1914 to ten. The battle-cruisers were down from four to one, the cruisers from fifty-five to nine — although *Hood, Repulse* and the First Light Cruiser Squadron were still away on a nine-month Empire cruise. But there was an aircraft carrier, the number of destroyers rose from forty-six to eighty-eight and there were more submarines. There were large numbers of minesweepers for the first time.

Inside the harbour, Nelson's *Victory* had been swinging to the tide for over a century and was showing her age. Large parts of her hull were rotten. Her decks and rigging, as well as the hull, had had alterations and anachronisms added over the years. There were always dangers in a busy harbour; *Victory* had a large hole knocked in her side in 1903 when the old battleship *Neptune* broke adrift whilst under tow to the breakers' yard and collided with her.

In 1921, the Society for Nautical Research began what amounted to a crusade to save *Victory*. As a result, *Victory* was moved into No. 2 Dock, Portsmouth, the oldest surviving dry dock in the world, on 12 January 1922. A 'Save the *Victory*' appeal was launched by the Society's President, Admiral of the Fleet Sir Doveton Sturdee, to raise the funds to restore *Victory* to her Trafalgar appearance, inside and out.

The appeal opened on Trafalgar Day 1922 and although somewhat overshadowed by a General Election campaign, it raised enough money in two years at least to start the work — which, in fact, has been going on ever since. Repairs began on the 'Glorious First of June' 1923, appropriately inaugurated by Lord Howe.

Victory floated for the last time on 8 April 1925, so that her waterline was level with the edge of the dock. The dock was then emptied, leaving *Victory* resting under a special stone, concrete and iron base cradle, which gave the impression that she was still floating, if not on water, then in air. King George V visited the ship on 17 July 1928 to declare the ship officially open to the public and to unveil a commemorative tablet.

A week earlier, on 10 July, the King had conferred upon the Mayor of Portsmouth, as Chief Magistrate, the honour and dignity of the title of Lord Mayor. Portsmouth town had been raised to the position of a city on 21 April 1926.

The 1920s and early 1930s were a curiously lethargic time, of disarmament and pacifism. Under the League of Nations, war seemed so far away as to be impossible. Indeed, treaties were signed agreeing that nobody was allowed to go to war for at least ten years.

In Portsmouth, many men were laid off in the Dockyard. In 1921, the Admiralty ordered a reduction in the working week of seven hours, so that more than one thousand of the men discharged could be re-employed. The cruiser *Effingham*, laid down in 1917, was finally launched on 8 June 1921 (and unkindly called *HMS Methuselah* in Parliament). After *Effingham* there was to be nothing more on the stocks at Portsmouth until the cruisers

Suffolk and *London*, launched in 1926 and 1927.

In 1923, the Royal Marine Light Infantry (the Blue Marines) left their barracks at Forton in Gosport (which were reported to be falling down) and amalgamated with the Royal Marine Artillery (the Red Marines) to become 'Royal Marines', with their permanent home at Eastney Barracks. Portsmouth has had links with the Marines since their formation in 1664 when Charles II had ordered the raising of a special regiment for sea service called 'The Duke of York and Albany's Maritime Regiment of Foot'; the Duke of York, later James II, was Governor of Portsmouth at the time. In 1755, when there was yet another war with France and Spain, an Order in Council of 5 April authorised the raising of fifty companies of Marines, twelve companies at Chatham, eighteen at Plymouth and twenty in Portsmouth. These three divisions of marines, known as 'The Grand Divisions', were to be the official fixed establishment and permanent framework of the Marines for the next two centuries.

The Portsmouth Division was originally

Marine parade for presentation of new colours, Eastney 1904.

stationed at Hilsea. On 25 May 1755, some one thousand Marine officers and men moved into billets in Portsmouth, to 'relieve them of the inconvenience and hardship to which they were exposed in quarters'. In 1783, when the Marines began to do garrison duty in the Dockyard, they moved into the King's Cooperage and Brewery buildings in St

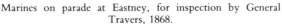

Marines on parade at Eastney, for inspection by General Travers, 1868.

Practice drill 12″ gun turret for the Marines at Eastney.

Nicholas Street. First erected in 1513, they were converted into Barracks. They were called Clarence Barracks, after the Duke of Clarence who presented the Regiment with new colours on Southsea Common on 27 October 1827.

In 1802, Lord St. Vincent, who was First Sea Lord, recommended to King George III that the Regiment should be given the style of 'Royal'. The King agreed and the regiment became the Royal Marine Light Infantry. Two years later, one division was formed into the Royal Marine Artillery.

While the Royal Marine Light Infantry moved from Portsmouth across to Forton Barracks in March 1848, the Artillerymen led a somewhat nomadic existence. In 1824, their officers took over 'the premises of the late W. Turner Esq. in the High Street and St Thomas's Street'. The Marines were divided between the Victualling Store on the Gunwharf and Fort Cumberland. Later in the nineteenth century, they all moved to Fort Cumberland, but it was a leisurely process. The Royal Marine Artillery was formed into a separate three-thousand strong Division on 1 November 1859. A new Barracks was built for them at Eastney, which finally opened in 1867. But as late as 1879 RMA officers were still going to and fro between the Gunwharf and the Fort — taking with them their shotguns, in the hope of a shot at a snipe on the Craneswater.

The Dockyard underwent a programme of modernisation in the first twelve years after the end of the Great War. The process took some time, because it had to contend with the British Admiralty and the British Workman, two of the most conservative bodies in British history. Jetties were rebuilt, workshops improved, some new machinery installed, and electric power and light fitted in many parts of the Dockyard for the first time. Syrens replaced the old muster bell which had stood on a post outside the Main Gate on the Hard since 1791. In July 1930, a new Semaphore Tower and Sail Loft, built on the original eighteenth century foundations and incorporating the old Lion Gate, was opened to replace the Tower destroyed by fire in December 1913.

Portsmouth Dockyard was still the premier

naval yard in the Kingdom, covering nearly 300 acres, with fifteen dry docks, a floating dock, sixty acres of enclosed basins, 18,400 feet of wharfage and some ten miles of railway. It employed over twelve thousand people, over ten thousand of them in ship-building, repairs and maintenance, with about one thousand three hundred men in the Works Department, and four hundred in the Torpedo Depot.

In 1929, a scheme was introduced whereby dockyard workmen were given six days' leave with pay. From 1930, this leave was taken during the first week in August. While the Yard was closed, Navy Weeks were held, when thousands of visitors paid a small entrance fee, devoted to Naval, Marine and Metropolitan Police charities, to look round the ships and side shows open to the public.

These Navy Weeks, the forerunners of the Navy Days still held on Bank Holiday weekends in major naval ports today, became more and more sophisticated and attracted many thousands of visitors. Navy Week of 1935 was publicised beforehand by a pla-carded lorry touring the streets of Ports-mouth towing a trailer with a large model of the battle cruiser *Repulse*.

Navy Week that year was formally opened by Rear Admiral HRH The Duke of York. Visitors could go on board various ships, from *Hood* to 'L' Class submarines. There was tea in the upper hangar of the aircraft carrier *Courageous*, *Iron Duke* cheered ship, and a model of *Victory* flew Nelson's Trafal-gar signal 'England Expects' in No 2 Basin. In the following year, an added attraction was a 'mock battle' in No 3 Basin between a 'Mystery' Q-ship and a submarine, playing the part of a U-boat.

Establishments had their own celebrations. Whale Island held a Tattoo in July 1930 to mark its 150th anniversary. There were guards of honour and marching bands and 'Sunset' and historical scenes re-enacting the evolution of naval gunnery, from archers and crossbow men, Drake's swivel guns and muzzle loaders, the matchlock drill of the Marines of 1664, Nelson's seamen, the Boer War, with the 4.7-inch 'Long Tom' gun from Ladysmith, ending with the 6-inch gun crews

of a modern battleship. These were followed by scenes showing the Press Gang, King George's visit with Queen Charlotte to the *Charlotte* at Spithead, and the battle of the Glorious First of June.

On 21 October that year, the first Trafalgar Day dinner was held in Nelson's cabin on board *Victory*. Admiral of the Fleet Sir Roger Keyes, Commander-in-Chief Portsmouth, took Nelson's chair. The guests were Vice Admiral Sir Henry Buller, commanding the Royal Yachts; Vice Admiral L. A. B. Donald-son, Admiral Superintendent of the Dock-yard; Vice Admiral F. Larken, commanding the Reserve Fleet; Rear Admiral Dunbar-Nasmith, VC, commanding the Submarine Service; Surgeon Rear Admiral H. C. White-side, Haslar Hospital; Engineer Rear Admiral H. S. Garside; and Lieutenant P. V. Organ, Lieutenant in charge of the *Victory*. The courses for the dinner were cooked in *Vic-tory*'s galley and the pudding was a chocolate ice for each guest moulded into the shape of the old ship herself.

The year 1931 was the mid-point of the inter-war period for the Navy. Until that year, the Great War seemed very close and very recent in everyone's memories. From that year onwards, the apparition of the next war lay just on the horizon. It was a mixed year, for the Navy and for Portsmouth. On 17 May, a memorial to the Unknown Sailor was unveiled in St Ann's Church in the Dockyard by Sir Roger Keyes.

He was actually an unknown stoker, killed in HMS *Vindictive* during the raid on Ostend harbour on 9–10 May 1918, after which two officers and a number of men from *Vindictive* were unaccounted for. When Ostend was captured on 17 October, the graves of the missing men were found in the German military cemetery. The unknown stoker's grave was marked by a wooden cross with the inscription 'Ein. Unbek Engl Heizer Kreuzer Vindictive'. When the wooden cros-ses were replaced by stone, the Admiralty directed that this cross should be placed in St Ann's, where it was embedded in stone and led into the pavement on the south side of the pulpit.

Early on Saturday, 19 September, in a

H.M.S. Nelson entering Portsmouth 1931.

misty dawn, the battle-cruiser *Hood* and the battleship *Nelson* entered Portsmouth harbour with very little ceremony, considering that *Nelson* was the flagship. The ships of the Atlantic Fleet were returning to their home ports after the Mutiny at Invergordon when over twelve thousand sailors had simply refused to obey orders.

It was a time of financial stringency, not to say crisis, and the government of Ramsay Macdonald had proposed swingeing pay cuts for the public service including the Navy. There were already two basic rates of pay in the Navy depending upon whether a man joined before or after 1925. The pre-1925 men were most affected by the cuts, which bore particularly hardly on the lowest rates, of able and ordinary seamen. In those days very few sailors owned their own houses. Most paid rent and bought their furniture on hire purchase. For many of these, the new rates meant great financial hardship for their wives and families.

There was at that time no means of expressing, let alone redressing, sailors' grievances. A great gulf, social and mental, had widened between the wardroom and the lower deck. Junior officers believed they could do nothing to help the sailor. So they did nothing. First lieutenants and commanders tended to look upon any man who put in a request to make a complaint as little better than a mutineer; thenceforward, he would certainly be a 'marked man'. Ship's Captains were only too ready to threaten the direst penalties of the clause in the King's Regulations and Admiralty Instructions proscribing lower deck assemblies. Commodores of drafting barracks connived at, where they did not personally arrange, 'pierhead jumps' to remote stations abroad out of draft turn for 'trouble makers'.

A potentially explosive situation was exacerbated by the appallingly maladroit manner in which the Board of Admiralty handled the announcements of the new pay codes. The Board appeared both unfeeling and feckless. Due to incompetence, wrongly addressed letters and a measure of bad luck, the sailors first heard of the swingeing cuts in their pay through rumours and press reports, days before any official information was available. After some disorder in the canteen ashore in Invergordon, some ship's companies refused to take their ships to sea for exercises on Tuesday, 15 September.

It was a very polite mutiny, which lasted for two days. There was never any ill-feeling between officers and men. 'Strike' would be a better description. The men simply downed tools until they got their demands (while maintaining essential fire-fighting and watch-keeping duties to ensure their ships' safety). The mutineers kept up their communal spirits and communicated with each other by a system of concerted cheering from ship to ship, which suggests a measure of pre-planning and the presence of ring leaders, but it seems there was none. Some of the more intelligent and eloquent amongst the sailors took advantage of the moment.

Hood and *Nelson*, both Portsmouth-manned ships, were deeply implicated in the mutiny. While there was a furore in the country and abroad, which resulted in Great Britain being forced off the Gold Standard on 20 September, the atmosphere in Portsmouth was not so much one of condemnation as of reserving judgement. There was hardly a household in the city not affected by naval rates of pay. Captain W. G. Hall, one of the Members for Portsmouth, raised the matter in Parliament. On 21 September the Prime Minister announced that the pay cuts would be limited to ten per cent, as opposed to twenty-seven per cent in some cases under the first proposals.

The Communist Party of Great Britain attempted to make political capital out of Invergordon, without much success. Special Branch and M15 agents also visited Portsmouth and Plymouth to try to identify ring-leaders, again with little result. In Devonport — whose ratings were generally more involved in the mutiny than those from Portsmouth — some sailors were subjected to a

H.M.S. Seahorse, Portsmouth 1933.

The Fleet Review from Southsea Common July 1935.

course of 'training' in the Barracks which amounted to harsh and illegal punishment, before being discharged from the Service.

The Board of Admiralty, who were themselves the real culprits, tried to save their own faces by making a scapegoat of Vice Admiral Tomkinson, the senior officer present at Invergordon in the absence of the Commander-in-Chief due to sickness.

Nelson was somewhat accident-prone. In January 1934 she ran aground on Hamilton Bank while steaming out of Portsmouth harbour, leading the fleet on a visit to Vigo. She lay aground opposite Southsea Pier for some hours, while efforts were made to refloat her. At one point, most of the ship's company mustered on the quarterdeck carrying their hammocks, to shift weight aft, and then jumped up and down in unison by order, while the engines went astern. But *Nelson* had to stay where she was for another tide, when she was finally got off and berthed alongside.

The newspapers understandably made much of the fact that *Nelson* was aground on 'Hamilton' Bank. One Army wag in Clarence Barracks sent the ship the message: 'Colonel and Officers hope you will consider yourselves honorary members of the Mess during your stay'. Luckily, the ship came off with no damage except to the sense of humour of her Captain, P. Macnamara.

The mid-1930s were marked by two Royal Reviews at Spithead. In July 1935, King George V inspected ships from the Home, Mediterranean and Reserve Fleets for his Silver Jubilee. The Review ended with a fly past of the Fleet Air Arm, and the King himself led the Battle Fleet to sea. In May 1937, the ships assembled again at Spithead for King George VI's Coronation Review.

Between those two Reviews there was another Royal event at Portsmouth. On 2 May 1907, Cadet HRH Prince Edward had embarked in a ferry at the Railway Jetty to

143

cross to the Isle of Wight to join the Royal Naval College, Osborne. On the night of 11/12 December 1936 he embarked at Portsmouth again, in very different circumstances.

Earlier that evening he had broadcast to the nation, announcing his Abdication as King Edward VIII. Ironically, the King had visited Portsmouth to inspect the Barracks (in rain so heavy the inspection had to be held in the Drill Hall) in June and had inspected his fleet only the previous September. The streets of Portsmouth had been lined with cheering crowds. The Fleet had spliced the main brace and fired Royal Salute. But on that December night, HRH The Duke of Windsor, as he now was, arrived in Portsmouth in darkness and drove through deserted streets to the Dockyard.

It was a curiously informal almost haphazard affair, after such a major constitutional crisis. The Duke arrived very much later than expected. The Commander-in-Chief, Admiral Sir William Wordsworth Fisher, and a naval guard of honour waited for an hour and a half, whilst all sense of impending drama

wore off, to be replaced by a feeling of anti-climax. Some telephoning established that the King had left Windsor late.

At 12.20 am, a saloon car and two shooting brakes crossed the Guildhall Square, drove down the High Street and Broad Street, to reach the Portsmouth-Gosport ferry. One driver got out and asked another motorist, who seemed to have followed this cavalcade out of curiosity, the way to the Unicorn Gate. The three cars entered the Dockyard through the Gate and drove alongside the destroyer *Fury*.

Shortly after 1.30 am another single saloon car entered the Dockyard by the Main Gate instead of, as expected, the Unicorn Gate. Admiral Fisher himself drove after the car to intercept it and direct the chauffeur to where *Fury* was lying. Admiral Fisher, who had come to say the Navy's farewells, had tears in his eyes. But the Duke himself, accompanied by his friend and adviser Walter Monckton, appeared in very good spirits, seemingly quite unaffected by the occasion. He walked up *Fury*'s gangway, to be greeted by the

Navy Days 1935: Visitors going on board *H.M.S. Hood*.

Navy Days 1935: H.R.H. Duke of York opening the day with C. in C. Admiral Sir John Kelly.

H.M.S. *Repulse* Portsmouth 1936, sunk by Japanese aircraft off Malaya 10th December 1941.

Captain. Within half an hour *Fury* sailed, to anchor in St Helen's Roads, where she was joined by another destroyer, *Wolfhound*, from Portland. Both sailed in time to reach France in the morning.

The Spithead Coronation Review of 20 May 1937 could be said to be the last true peacetime naval event of the 1930s. There were 141 ships from the Home, Mediterranean and Reserve Fleets, including nine battleships, led by *Nelson, Rodney* and *Queen Elizabeth*, the battle-cruisers *Hood* and *Repulse*, five aircraft carriers, twenty-two submarines, with a Royal Indian Navy sloop and two Royal Canadian Navy destroyers.

There were also seventeen foreign warships present and the Portsmouth shore establishments acted as hosts: the Royal Naval Barracks to the Japanese cruiser *Asigara* and the Roumanian destroyer *Regina Maria; Vernon* to the US battleship *New York* and the Portuguese escort vessel *Bartolomea Dias; Excellent* to the Argentine battleship *Moreno; Dolphin* to the Estonian submarine *Kalev;* and the Navigation School to the Cuban escort vessel *Cuba* and the Turkish destroyer *Kocatepe.* Some of the ships also played host to the foreign visitors: *Queen Elizabeth* to the French battleship *Dunkerque; Barham* to the Russian battleship *Marat;* and *Revenge* to the German pocket battleship *Admiral Graf Spee.*

The big foreign ships attracted much attention. *Graf Spee* was considered to be 'right on the top line' in every respect, and her sailors ashore seemed eager to fraternize with the British.

The Russians, on the other hand, did not get ashore much but distinguished themselves by the cheer they gave the Royal Yacht *Victoria and Albert*: 'more like the sustained roar of a football crowd rather than the organised cheering of a normal ship's company'.

The Japanese in *Asigara*, with her 'switchback' upper deck, were hospitable but very circumspect. Everything of interest in the ship was hidden in canvas sheeting, and even the most innocent question was met with cries of 'Never mind about that, let's have some more sake'. Japanese sailors ashore surprised everybody by marching two abreast along the most crowded pavements.

On the day after the Review, the King inspected four flagships: *Nelson* (Home Fleet), *Queen Elizabeth* (Mediterranean), the cruiser *Dunedin* (Reserve Fleet), and the new cruiser *Southampton*, flagship of the 2nd Cruiser Squadron, flying the flag of Rear Admiral T. F. P. Calvert. The signal 'Splice the Mainbrace' was made. A Coronation Ball for one thousand five hundred guests was given by Their Lordships in the Gymnasium of the Barracks. Next day, the ships began to disperse, not to meet again.

From now on, there was a sombre undercurrent to events. During that summer of 1937, Civil Defence training began in the Portsmouth naval area, as part of a general coastal defence exercise. From the Mediterranean, where the Spanish Civil War was in progress, came the news that the destroyer *Hunter* had been mined off Almeria, with eight of her crew killed and twenty-four injured, and reports that the Italians supporting Franco had begun a submarine campaign which was nothing less than piracy.

In August, the Japanese bombed Shanghai and two thousand British women and children were evacuated in the P&O liner *Rajputana*. In December, the Japanese attacked British ships on the Yangtse, and one sailor was killed in HMS *Ladybird* at Wuhu. Parliament voted in favour of air raid shelters in most cities and towns. Trials were held of different types of shelter, whilst Labour councillors protested that it would mean big rises in the rates. It was announced that all children were to be issued with gas-masks. A law was passed making children's gas-mask drill compulsory. Cities such as Leicester carried out mock wartime 'Black-out' exercises.

In April 1938, Britain and the United States of America abandoned the London Treaty, limiting the building of battleships. The naval bases at Cobh and Berehaven in County Cork and Lough Swilly in County Donegal were handed over to the Irish government, with all their buildings, ammunition and armaments, but with no agreement that the Royal Navy could use them in war.

In September 1938, during the 'Munich Crisis', Portsmouth Barracks had a full-scale rehearsal for war. Royal Proclamations were issued, mobilising the Royal Navy and Royal Marine Reserves. Men began to converge upon Portsmouth from all over the country and there were soon crowd scenes in the Barracks and in Queen Street reminiscent of the earlier war. But Mr Chamberlain returned from his meeting with Hitler on 30 September saying about the agreement they had signed, 'I believe it is peace for our time'. The Reserves in the Barracks went home again, for the time being.

In December 1938, the Government unveiled plans for a 'National Register', laying down what everybody would do in time of war. In April 1939, conscription for military service was approved for men of twenty. Farmers were urged to dig for victory, by ploughing up grazing land to increase food production, and were paid £2 an acre to do so. The Government announced plans for the immediate evacuation of two and a half million children from cities and towns should hostilities begin. The Health Minister revealed that 279,435 shelters had been delivered, providing cover for one and a half million people, and eighty thousand more shelters were being made very week.

With every month events seemed to gather fresh impetus towards war. The scenes of successive crises shifted news attention around the world: Austria, the Sudetenland, Prague, the Danzig Corridor, Albania and Madrid, finally entered by Franco's troops in March 1939. In April, an Anglo-French-Polish military alliance was signed: Britain and France pledged to assist Poland if she were attacked. Italy and Germany signed a Pact of Steel in May 1939. In August, Germany and Soviet Russia signed a Non-Aggression Pact, which made war virtually inevitable. It was duly declared on 3 September, three days after Germany invaded Poland.

The Mobilisation of 1938 now proved its worth. After the Royal Proclamation was posted, hundreds of reserves and pensioners began to pour into Portsmouth Barracks. In the words of Admiral Sir William James, who was appointed Commander-in-Chief Portsmouth in June 1939, the mobilisation

. . . went like clockwork; I have seldom seen anything better done. The Reservists were shepherded first to the doctors, then to the dentists, then to the oculists; they drew their kit and some advance pay and were then directed to lorries marked with the names of their ships . . . One man, who had been celebrating his call-up arrived with a carpet-bag and a hot-water bottle and asked to be called next morning at seven with a cup of tea! I wish I had been able to follow his career; I feel sure he commanded a ship before the war was over.'

As in the previous war, the earliest days were occupied in convoying the British Expeditionary Force to France. The soldiers embarked in troopships in Southampton and the convoy escorts sailed from Portsmouth, as they had done since the Middle Ages. On 24 September, one of Admiral James' staff reported to him 'We've been weaned, sir', meaning that the last of the convoys to Brest had arrived safely: the Army and its equipment was established in France.

Other matters did not go so well. A test 'black-out' imposed on Portsmouth on 5 September was officially described as 'not good enough'. Police and ARP wardens redoubled their efforts to get people to 'put that light out'. As the black-out deepened, road casualties rocketed. By late 1943, when it was estimated that thirty thousand had been killed on the roads since the outbreak of war, the Ministry of War Transport was eventually forced to admit that during the winter the black-out was killing more people than the air raids.

By 3 September 1939, more than twelve thousand children had been evacuated from Portsmouth and district to billets all across southern England, from the Isle of Wight to Salisbury. As the days went by and no air raids took place parents became less and less willing to be parted from their children. By 12 September, the Lord Mayor was complaining about the number of children still in Portsmouth. Some children had even started to drift back, to the consternation of council officials. Likewise, cinemas and theatres, peremptorily closed for the public's own good by officialdom when war broke out, were reopened in response to public demand.

On 12 September, the Duke of Windsor returned to Portsmouth with the Duchess in the destroyer *Kelly* which had gone to Cherbourg to collect them, their mountain of luggage of cardboard boxes and their three dogs. It was well after 9 pm and dark when they arrived but Churchill had ordered that the Duke was to be received with all honours. Thus, almost unprecedentedly (guards are not paraded after sunset), the Duke was met by a guard, wearing tin hats and carrying gas-masks, and a band playing 'God Save the King'. By coincidence, the jetty was the same from which the Duke had embarked in *Fury*, but there were also red carpets and the blackout, both of which had been absent in 1936.

The Duke and Duchess were accompanied by Randolph Churchill, wearing the uniform of a lieutenant in the 4th Hussars (with his spurs on upside down), and were met by Walter Monckton and Lady Metcalfe. But

Sailors 'doing their bit' by touring Portsmouth during a War Weapons Week.

there was no member of the Royal Family, nor any message. The Duke and Duchess had had a difficult and tiring journey across France. They had not been treated as privileged persons. The Duke had no valet and no secretary and was concerned about his car. Walter Monckton telephoned the Palace to ask for a car but the request was refused.

Admiral Sir William James put the Windsors up for the night at Admiralty House.

As in earlier wars, it was not long before bad news began to arrive from sea. Captain W. T. Makeig-Jones was to have relieved Rear Admiral W. E. C. Tait in command of the Barracks at Portsmouth in September 1939 but, being unemployed when the fleet mobilised in the summer, he was given command of the aircraft carrier *Courageous*. On 17 September 1939, *Courageous* became the first British warship lost to enemy action in the war. She was torpedoed by *U-29* west of Ireland when, ironically, she was hunting for U-boats. She sank in fifteen minutes with 519 of her people, including Makeig-Jones who reputedly stayed on his bridge, saluting the flag, as his ship went down.

A month later, in the early hours of 14 October, Kapitan Lieutenant Gunther Prien in *U-47* carried out one of the most daring exploits in all naval history by penetrating the Home Fleet anchorage at Scapa Flow on the surface and torpedoing the battleship *Royal Oak*. Her captain, W. H. Benn, was blown over the side and survived; as the Board of Enquiry found, he 'remained in his ship until the last possible moment, until in fact the ship left him'. But Rear Admiral H. A. C. Blagrove, flying his flag in *Royal Oak*, and 785 others were lost with the ship. *Royal Oak* had only recommissioned at Portsmouth in June 1939.

On 19 December 1939, King George VI made the first of his war-time visits to Portsmouth, spending some seven hours in the port area, inspecting naval and dockyard personnel. It was a very cold day but His Majesty set a hot pace. He visited the anti-submarine and torpedo school, *Vernon*, where he decorated the officers and men who had stripped down the first magnetic mine on the mudflats of Shoeburyness in November and revealed its secrets; there were Distinguished Service Orders for Lieutenant Commander John Ouvry and Lieutenant Commander Roger Lewis, and Distinguished Service Medals for Chief Petty Officer Baldwin and Able Seaman Vearncombe.

In the afternoon, the King visited the Barracks. His Majesty was received by Rear

A survivor from the battleship *Royal Oak*. October 1939.

Admiral Tait and together they mounted the platform in one corner of the parade ground. But the parade ground was empty, with not an officer or rating to be seen. There was a short dramatic silence. Suddenly, a bugle sounded and the loud-speakers blared the order 'Clear the trenches!'

Officers and men swarmed out of the air-raid shelters beneath the parade ground and within two minutes some six thousand men had fallen in on their markers for the King's inspection. As the King walked round, Admiral Sir William James said to him: 'I have something to show you, sir, that you have never seen before — twelve dentists standing shoulder to shoulder!'

Besides dentists, the King inspected survivors from the battleship *Royal Oak*, fishermen from Newfoundland, Reservists of all kinds, and the Wrens, commenting that many of them were not wearing uniform. He went round the Barracks galleys, and told the sailors' wives and daughters who worked there he thought the work was too rough for them.

It was so bitterly cold — the winter of 1939/40 was to be the coldest for many years — and the wind off the sea so cutting at the Royal Marine Barracks, Eastney, that the programme was shortened and the King went early into the officers' mess. He was asked to sign his name in the visitors' book, but the ink-well was empty. 'The Marine officers' faces would have delighted H. M. Bateman', said Admiral James, delightedly.

The King had tea at Whale Island and came back to Admiralty House, where Lady James had a Christmas tree and a party for wives and children. The King went into the drawing room to join in the games and the fun. It was some time before the other guests realised who had joined them.

By the end of 1939, some schools in Portsmouth were reopening. Food rationing began on 8 January 1940. By February, Portsmouth housewives were complaining about the scarcity and cost of meat and bacon, and the shortage of fresh vegetables, their cost and their poor quality. But people were slowly becoming accustomed to a regime of black-out and bureaucracy, to new regulations by the score, to a world where air-raid drills were a part of daily life. In the Barracks, for example, there was air-raid drill every forenoon, with everyone rushing to the shelters and staying there until the 'All Clear' was sounded. But it was not long before the drills became reality.

Chapter 15

The first offensive act of the Royal Air Force in the war was a bombing raid on the German naval port of Wilhelmshaven on 4 September 1939. The people of Portsmouth, the British equivalent of Wilhelmshaven, expected early retaliation. But nothing happened. The 'Phoney War' went on, from weeks into months, and still nothing happened.

A major ARP exercise was held in Portsmouth on 14 February 1940. It was not a success. As a result of the over-zealous enforcement of rules and regulations, compounded by the overweening arrogance of council bureaucrats enjoying their new-found powers, the people of Portsmouth were beginning to show a hostile and scornful attitude towards Civil Defence in general and ARP Wardens in particular. The exercise was regarded with an indifference approaching contempt.

But still the bombers did not come. The main preoccupations of the ordinary citizen were the bitterly cold weather and the acute shortage of coal. It was not the *Luftwaffe* that concerned everybody but how to keep warm and out of the easterly wind.

The war spread to Norway, to the Low Countries and to France. For ten frenzied days at the end of May and the beginning of June 1940, Portsmouth was wrapped up in the drama of Dunkirk. The harbour was cleared of every possible type of ship and craft. Officers and men said goodbye to their wives one morning and then simply disappeared for days. When they came back they did not talk much about where they had been or what they had seen, but the newspapers were full of the tremendous events taking place in France.

Admiral Sir William James had received what he called 'some disturbing signals' about the Army's preparations for a withdrawal from France on 21 May. He had a rapid survey made of all the small ships in Portsmouth Command. The code-word *Dynamo* was signalled on 26 May. On that day of national prayer, several thousand people attended a service in Guildhall Square. On the 29th an extraordinary armada of assorted shipping set off from Portsmouth and other harbours on the south and east coasts of England.

Portsmouth's contribution to the Dunkirk armada included destroyers, minesweepers and motor torpedo boats; Hayling Island ferries and Pickford's fleet of small coasters; trawlers and motor fishing vessels; private yachts and harbour defence vessels; the Solent passenger paddle steamer *Whippingham* requisitioned as a minesweeper; the Captain of *Nelson*'s barge and a launch from *Dolphin*; the *Lady Southborough* which, belonging to the Tilbury Dredging Company, had been peacefully dredging in Portsmouth harbour; Admiral James' own barge and '*Vernon*'s Private Navy' of a pinnace and a 16-foot torpedo recovery vessel; and five wooden drifters requisitioned for the campaign against the magnetic mine.

Many ships were lost, amongst them the Red Funnel Line Isle of Wight ferry *Gracie Fields*, bombed and sunk off La Panne, but the bulk of the British Expeditionary Force and many French soldiers, an estimated three hundred and forty thousand troops in all, were brought off. As Admiral James wrote to a friend: 'The future is undoubtedly very black. Thank God we live in an island, and thank God for that miracle at Dunkerque.'

After the fall of France an extraordinary

H.M. King George VI taking the salute at a review of coastal
forces ships.

feeling, almost of defiant relief and exhilaration, swept through the Navy and the country as a whole. Great Britain had no allies now. On the other hand, there was no one to let the British down either. A poem by Dorothy L. Sayers in *The Times Literary Supplement*, 'Praise God, now, for an English war' caught the mood of the time exactly.

There were doubts about what precisely the French would do, as indeed, there were to be such doubts about the French all over Europe and North Africa throughout the war. After the fall of France, Admiral Darlan refused to sail the French Navy to British or French colonial ports, but some French warships escaped to Plymouth and Portsmouth.

At Spithead were the French battleship *Courbet*, the large destroyer *Leopard* and several escorts and minesweepers. Admiral James had no ships powerful enough to seize the battleship, so he told the French Admiral Muselier that his ships must clear Spithead for important trials. When the French ships came up harbour, Commodore 'Hookey' Walker of the Barracks with one thousand sailors, five hundred marines and an infantry battalion boarded them at daybreak on 2 July.

There was no trouble, except from Admiral Muselier, who was so abusive Admiral James was glad to see him off to London, and the Gunnery Officer of *Courbet*. Asked for the keys of magazines, he said 'I throw zem overboard. In five minutes se ship go pouf.' In the event, the magazines were declared safe.

As Dorothy Sayers' poem also made clear, the *Wehrmacht*, like the armies of Napoleon and the Duke of Parma, was now only a few miles away across the Channel. The south of England braced itself for invasion. People began to look out for suspicious characters on the streets, mysterious flashing lights which could be Morse code, and parachutists descending disguised as nuns. An unusually thick 'peach-coloured' sea fog which rolled in one day over Portsmouth and Southsea was thought to be a German secret weapon.

Regular troops were so few that Portsmouth was to be defended on land by three naval battalions, named 'Cornwallis', 'Benbow' and 'Anson', raised from shore establishments in the port area, two companies from *HMS Excellent*, and the Home Guard.

The Home Guard was known until August 1940 as Local Defence Volunteers. Local firms such as Airspeed and Vospers formed their own LDV companies (known unkindly as 'Look, Duck and Vanish'). The Volunteers were given LDV arm-bands and (a few) guns which were mostly museum-pieces. Portsmouth Dockyard had its own Dockyard Defence volunteers who, at first, literally did drill with 'pikes' made of conduit pipes with bayonets stuck in their ends. Naval volunteers were issued with long Lee Enfield rifles, believed to be relics from the Boer War. Perhaps fortunately, little or no ammunition was issued.

In Portsmouth, as in other ports, there was a rhythm of expectation. The tension rose throughout that summer and autumn whenever the critical period of moon and tide made conditions for invasion most favourable to the enemy. In those hot summer afternoons and evenings, it was as though the whole countryside of England lay listening, waiting for the peal of church bells to break the silence and give the prearranged signal, with the chosen code-word 'CROMWELL', that the invaders had arrived.

But it was left to the *Luftwaffe* to prepare the way. German aircraft appeared off Portsmouth before Dunkirk. They dropped mines off Bembridge, Isle of Wight, on 26 May. Single German aircraft began to fly over on most nights, for reconnaissance or mine-laying.

The first daylight air raid on Portsmouth was on the evening of 11 July 1940. It was a fine warm evening, one of many in that wonderful summer. Twelve Heinkel He 111s escorted by twelve Messerschmitt Me 110 fighters dropped bombs in the Kingston Cross district, destroyed the Blue Anchor Hotel, blew a hole in the gas-holder at Rudmore and scored a direct hit on an ARP First Aid Post in Drayton Road School. The French escort vessel *Savorgnan De Brazza*, in Fountain Lake, suffered damage from near-misses and three barges were sunk near Priddy's Hard.

The twenty bombs dropped killed nineteen people, eleven of them in the First Aid Post, and injured eighty, twenty-six of them seriously. The casualties and the damage aroused a great surge of public anger in Portsmouth. indifference and hostility towards Civil Defence vanished, literally overnight. The *Evening News* launched an appeal to raise £6,000 to 'buy a Spitfire'. That sum was subscribed in only ten days and the fund eventually reached £12,365 19s 1d.

Not all the casualties were human. When Joy Packer arrived as the 'Captain's Wife' at Whale Island in 1941 she saw a sad little memorial:

ARP
SHOT ON 27th May 1940
In Memory of

Lionesses	Lorna and Topsy
Polar Bears	Nicholas and Barbara
Sun Bears	Henry and Alice

These animals were put down 27th May 1940 in preparation for German Air Raids
Their loss was keenly felt by the whole Whale Island community

The Luftwaffe had fixed on 13 August as 'Adler Tag' ('Eagle Day'), the start of a massed air attack on Britain. Portsmouth had its second raid the day before. The main target was the Dockyard. A floating crane alongside the battleship *Queen Elizabeth*, undergoing major reconstruction and refit, in No 3 Basin was badly damaged.

A stick of bombs straddled the south-east corner of the Barracks parade ground, missed the sailors' shelters by only a few yards, but damaged the Bandstand. One bomb in Edinburgh Road knocked down part of the wall of the Barracks, so that the parade ground was visible for the first time since the 'On the Knee' affair. Another bomb damaged the back of the Wardroom and destroyed the staircase leading down into the garden. Blast lifted the Mess ceiling but luckily it fell back into place.

One 500lb bomb fell down a Wardroom chimney and, without exploding, came to rest on the bed in the cabin of a lieutenant commander who returned after the 'All Clear', had one look and took to his heels.

Many bombs fell short of the Dockyard, in Old Portsmouth. The Harbour Station had a direct hit, caught fire and was destroyed.

The third raid, on the afternoon of 24 August, was one of the heaviest. Over fifty Junkers Ju 88s dropped some sixty-five bombs, some with delayed-action fuses, over a wide area of Portsmouth and Southsea, causing casualties of 117 killed and 100 badly injured. The old George Hotel in the High Street, where Nelson frequently stayed and spent his last hours in England, was largely destroyed. The Princes Theatre in Lake Road was hit during a children's film matinee and only speedy evacuation limited casualties to eight killed and seventeen injured.

Buildings were damaged in *Vernon*, and the destroyer *Acheron*, alongside in the Dockyard, was badly damaged by a direct hit. Another direct hit on an underground vault being used as air raid shelter between the Block Mills and the Central Estimating Office killed twenty-five and injured forty

Dockyard workers. The cruiser *Manchester* in dry dock put up a spirited defence with her anti-aircraft guns.

Blast sometimes had odd effects. The corpses in that Dockyard shelter were found sitting in a row, apparently untouched; they were all dead, without a mark on them. There were some bizarre incidents in the blitz. Able Seaman Golding (Sir William Golding, Nobel Prize winner for Literature) saw from his slit trench shelter in the Barracks a petty officer trying to calm two sailors who had joined the Navy that day. To prove his point, that they need not be scared, the petty officer stood up saying 'Look, you can even stand up in an air raid' and was instantly blown in two.

There were two more air raids on Portsmouth in August, five in September and a total of thirty by the end of 1940. The New Year of 1941 began with a devastating raid on the evening of 10 January. On a fine bright moonlit night, an estimated three hundred bombers dropped high explosive bombs and

'Twice Nightly – once is enough!' Sailors clearing up outside the Hippodrome, Commercial Road, 10th January 1941.

153

land mines and twenty-five thousand incendiaries.

Three clusters of incendiaries set the Guildhall alight and a large bomb hit the roof, which collapsed. The Lord Mayor and the ARP personnel barely escaped from the building in time. The 200-foot tower blazed through that night and for the next three days, with flames actually spouting from the top, and the copper dome glowing in the sky until the plates of the cupola fell away.

Sailors from the dockyard and ships joined Civil Defence workers, firemen, police and civilians to try to fight fires, rescue survivors and clear away rubble. A large naval working party doubled through the streets to report to the Guildhall for any services they might be required to render. Numbers of sailors went out in small detachments, known as Friendly Aid Parties.

As somebody recalled, the sailors came by 'just to see what you wanted done. You were standing by your front door, looking and feeling rather lost, and the Friendly Aid Party would help you to patch up your windows, or move your sick wife, or take the broken glass out of the larder. These things were the small change of after-raid work, but they are the very stuff of memory'.

When the sun rose after that terrible January night, people who had lived in Portsmouth all their lives could hardly recognise it. It seemed the whole city was a mass of flame, smoke and wrecked buildings.

At one time there were twenty-eight major fires burning in the city, with no water to fight them because the mains were fractured. Besides the Guild Hall, six churches, the Eye and Ear Hospital, part of the Royal Hospital, Clarence Pier, the Hippodrome and three cinemas, the Dockyard School, Connaught Drill Hall, the Central Hotel, Aggie Weston's Royal Sailor's Rest were destroyed, and the main shopping centres of Palmerston Road, King's Road and Commercial Road were wrecked, as well as row upon row of private houses. There were 2,314 fires, 171 people were killed, and 430 injured, and some three thousand were made homeless.

Another heavy raid lasting four hours began on the night of 9 March, followed by one of six hours on the next night, and a third on 11th. Total casualties were 120 killed and over three hundred injured; among the buildings lost were the Keppel's Head Hotel, and the Sailors Club. Admiralty House was hit twice by large bombs, which fortunately did not explode, but was finally wrecked by one that did explode on 17 April. Admiral James moved his headquarters on board *HMS Victory* who herself survived a bomb which exploded in the dry dock under her bows.

Portsmouth's spirit never wavered. 'We are bruised but we are not daunted,' wrote the Lord Mayor, Sir Denis Daley, in the *Evening News* after the January 1941 raids, 'and we are still as determined as ever to stand side by side with other cities who have felt the blast of the enemy'.

Wartime Portsmouth was well described by Joy Packer.

Portsmouth, fanning out in interminable terraces of little semi-detached brick houses and undistinguished buildings between Cosham Bridge and the dignified purlieus of the Dockyard, seemed infinitely dreary to me. Several thousand bicycles, ridden to and from the Dockyard by 'mateys' in threadbare overcoats, dominated the traffic four times a day, the sky was grey and lowering and the air raw. The women, with their string shopping bags, were far from picturesque, and outside the grocer's and the butcher's stood shabby prams in which apoplectic infants strove like bulls to burst their harnesses, rocking their vehicles furiously and yelling lustily till their mothers appeared and shook them impatiently. 'Put a sock in it, Alfy, or I'll dot you one!' Only the sailors were engaging, with their square collars, taut behinds and bell-bottoms. How expressive are the backs of sailors — jaunty or dejected in the manner of small boys!

Only one thing angered Portsmouth: the constant references on the BBC News to London, and Coventry, and other cities, and 'a south coast town', being bombed: 'They'd never say it was Portsmouth'.

However, Portsmouth's ordeal was officially recognised by a visit from the Prime Minister, Mr Churchill, who toured the bombed areas on 31 January with President Roosevelt's special envoy, Mr Harry Hopkins. He was cheered through the Dockyard and presented a half-smoked cigar to a workman who asked for souvenir of the visit.

On 6 February, the King and Queen visited Portsmouth. They too walked through the devastated streets, to tremendous cheers from an enormous crowd. Repeated shouts of 'Are We Downhearted?' were greeted with thunderous replies of 'NO!' The Royal party toured side streets as well as main roads, stopping frequently to shake hands and chat with people on their own doorsteps.

Captain Andre Jubelin of the Free French Navy, who arrived in Portsmouth on 16 February 1941 to take command of the battleship *Courbet*, wrote vividly of his first sight of

. . . a devastated city. Whole streets were down, leaving nothing but the pavements. With praiseworthy attention to order, the bricks of the houses that had collapsed during the night were collected in pink rows every morning. Elsewhere blackened sections of walls remained in position. Portsmouth has been half annihilated. Some ruins have been smoking ever since the 10th January, when there was a raid that killed eight hundred people (sic). The ferry boat station, with its steel girders twisted and its rails bent in all directions, is a nightmare.

According to figures published by the Portsmouth *Evening News* at the end of the war, there were sixty-seven German air raids on Portsmouth between 11 July 1940 and the end of May 1944, in which 1,320 high explosive bombs, approximately thirty-eight thousand incendiaries and thirty-eight parachute bombs or landmines fell on the city. There were 1,581 'alerts'; 930 civilians were killed, 1,216 admitted to hospital, and 1,621 slightly injured; thirty churches and mission halls were destroyed or very badly damaged; eight schools were destroyed, nine seriously and eleven slightly damaged; sixty-one public

houses, forty-nine beer houses and forty off licences ceased to trade because of destruction of bomb damage; 6,625 premises were totally destroyed, 6,549 seriously and 68,886 slightly damaged.

In March 1941, Admiral James decided that training establishments must be moved from Portsmouth. Men could not be expected to learn in classrooms during the day after firefighting for most of the night. The Navigation School and Signal School moved into the country, *Vernon* to Roedean School, the Tactical School to a fort on Portsdown Hill.

Rear Admiral (Submarines) moved from Port Blockhouse to Aberdour, near Rosyth, in 1939, but this proved unsatisfactory. From April 1940 until September 1945, RA (S) and his staff occupied 'Northways', a block of flats in north London. Meanwhile, *HMS Dolphin*, Fort Blockhouse, remained the home of the 5th Submarine Flotilla, carrying out patrols in the Channel and the Bay of Biscay, and the base for submarine training. A submarine returning from patrol was always welcomed by 'Clear Lower Deck', with the entire ship's company of the Fort lining the walls to 'Cheer ship'.

In May 1940, fourteen Dutch 'O' Class submarines arrived in *Dolphin* and, in July, several French submarines. Of twenty French officers and two hundred ratings, only one officer and ten sailors chose to return to France. Polish and Norwegian submarines were also welcomed to Blockhouse, and, in 1942, a Russian submarine.

The local defences of Fort Blockhouse had to be improvised with submariners' traditional ingenuity. In 1939 there two 12-pounders manned by the Royal Artillery on the ramparts. Later a Bofors gun and two twin Low Angle 6-pounders were added. A 4-inch submarine gun, originally used for training, was mounted on the sea wall, guarding the squash courts. The Fort Engineers converted two saluting guns to discharge an old-fashioned 'langridge' mixture of nuts, bolts and any old iron, and provided intrepid stokers' guns crews to fire them.

There were also: a 20 mm Pom-Pom recovered from some scrap heap in the Dockyard; a French machine gun of unknown antecedents; a supply of rifles stowed around the Fort perimeter (although there was a shortage of men to fire them); light guns manned by Royal Marines on the tops of buildings in the Fort; twenty-five Home Guard pikes; and an awe-inspiring fowling-piece called a 'Jones-wise anti-tank gun' made from a section of metal drain-pipe and fired by striking a hammer against a .22 cartridge stuck in the vent. The Blockhouse Pom-Pom claimed a hit on the tail of a German aircraft on 16 August 1940 which crashed on the Isle of Wight.

The road near the main entrance was mined with two tons of TNT, which fortunately were never needed. The wardroom lawn was covered with concrete slabs, as a site for 'Dolly Dolphin', the barrage balloon. In 1943, the Wrens manned a searchlight.

Some two hundred incendiaries fell inside the Fort in the January 1941 raids. Luckily, the high explosive bombs fell in the water but in the raid on 10 March the Floating Dock was sunk by a direct hit. Haslar Bridge was destroyed in June. As a result of the raids, Fort Blockhouse was closed as a submarine base in 1941. The operational submarines moved to Dundee and later to Rosyth, while the training classes went to Blyth in Northumberland.

When the submarines left, Fort Blockhouse continued to run specialist courses, for submarine coxswains, for the preliminary part of the Submarine Commanding Officers' Qualifying Course (always known as the 'Perisher') and for higher instruction in radar, torpedoes and anti-submarine warfare.

The Fort also housed the Royal Naval Physiological Laboratory, which carried out experiments in physiology, bio-chemistry, histology and haematology. Further, the Fort became in effect a base for Coastal Forces, in conjunction with *HMS Hornet* nearby in Haslar Creek. Some forty Motor Launches and Motor Torpedo Boats were administered from the Fort. All submarine trophies, pictures and photographs had been removed from the walls and in the absence of these mementoes Coastal Forces officers came to look upon the Fort as their own. As one Temporary Acting Sub-Lieutenant RNVR was heard to say, 'This wouldn't half be a bad job if we could only get rid of those perishing submariners'.

Most of the naval establishments on the Gosport side had their own Home Guard units, and all had their 'blitz' stories. At Haslar Hospital, the large eighteenth century buildings' basement made excellent air raid shelters for patients and staff, but the hospital lost £80,000 worth of medical stores and equipment, and its library and museum, to bomb damage in 1941.

A priceless collection of specimens collected by naval doctors from all over the world was destroyed but fortunately most of the more valuable books, including the hospital's minute books and numerous manuscript journals, were rescued. A German pilot explained why the Hospital was not more severely damaged by bombing; Haslar water tower was an invaluable navigation aid for the *Luftwaffe* and it was important it should not be knocked down.

Bombs destroyed over 200,000 square feet of storage space and millions of pounds worth of stores at the Royal Clarence Yard. Staff and stores had to be dispersed over a wide area: to an isolation hospital in Guildford, a paper mill at Thatcham, a chair factory at Peasmarsh, a clothing factory in Swindon and a tannery in Godalming.

Every establishment had problems with vast increases in staff, most of the extra personnel being unskilled and untrained. By 1944, the numbers working in the Royal Naval Armament Depot at Priddy's Hard, for example, had risen to three thousand seven hundred, nearly treble the pre-war complement. The Yard also suffered several bomb hits.

The Royal Naval Aircraft Yard at Fleetlands was still being built when war broke out. By the end of 1942, it employed well over a thousand people, many of them actually under training. The situation was resolved by starting training schemes for women, eight hundred of whom eventually worked in the Yard, and the Ministry of Labour used wartime regulations to direct labour to Gosport from other parts of the country.

Portsmouth Dockyard, of course, was the one establishment which could not be moved and whose staff could not be evacuated, although some facilities were dispersed to other areas. The Dockyard was badly damaged in the raids of January and March 1941. Many buildings, including the homes of Dockyard workmen, were destroyed, but the Dockyard resumed work after every raid very quickly. A huge programme of repairs and conversions continued throughout the war, to convert destroyers into anti-submarine escort vessels, to fit ships with radar, anti-submarine detection equipment and weapons, degaussing gear to counter the magnetic mine, new developments in W/T and Direction Finding equipment, armour protection for exposed upper deck positions, and gear for refuelling at sea.

Queen Elizabeth steamed to Rosyth with Dockyard officers and men on board in November 1940 to finish her modernisation, which was completed in three months. Thereafter, large warships rarely visited the Dockyard until late in 1944, when the enemy had been cleared from northern France. Work continued on smaller ships, however. The Dutch light cruiser *Heemskerk*, which had arrived unfinished, was partially redesigned and completed. The cruiser *Sirius* whose construction had been delayed (once by a direct hit) was finished in May 1942. Two submarines, *Tireless* and *Token* and two destroyer floating docks were built. Two more submarines, *Thor* and *Tiara*, were launched but cancelled before completion. Several liners and merchant ships were converted as fleet repair ships.

Another establishment which never closed was *HMS Excellent*. The Experimental Department went to Bordean House, near Petersfield. Full calibre and sub-calibre firings at sea were carried out in the cruiser *Cardiff* in the Clyde, but *Excellent* itself carried on gunnery training for as many as one thousand five hundred men, British and Allied, at a time. Additional training ranges were set up at Bembridge (*HMS Blazer*), on Bognor Regis Pier (*HMS St Barbara*) and at Southport Lido, Ainsdale-on-Sea, in Lancashire (*HMS Queen Charlotte*).

Whale Island's ship's company included many Wrens. As in 1914-18, the Wrens made a major contribution to the war, in Portsmouth and elsewhere, at home and abroad. In June 1939, there were no Wrens. By the peak time of September 1944, there were well over seventy-four thousand, in ninety categories and fifty branches. The Superintendent WRNS in Portsmouth was Miss Amy Curtis. Admiral James thought very highly of her — 'a very remarkable woman', he said. 'She had all the gifts to control the Wrens, whose numbers rapidly increased until there were over 8,000 in the (Portsmouth) Command'.

In October 1942, Admiral Sir William James was relieved as Commander-in-Chief Portsmouth by Admiral Sir Charles Little, but he kept his links with Portsmouth, being elected as Nationalist MP for North Portsmouth, and was later Chief of Naval Information. King George VI came down to Portsmouth — his fourth wartime visit to the City — on Admiral James' last day. Admiral James arranged a full day's programme for His Majesty, including a 'steam-past of 25 coastal craft of six different types'. He 'also presented the Wren dispatch riders who had done magnificent work at the time of the Dieppe Raid (in August 1942), and on board the *Victory* I had drawn up for his inspection the bluejacket cadets from the Gunnery School and the barracks'.

On 15 September 1942, Admiral Sir William James became a Freeman of the City of Portsmouth, the first naval officer to receive the honour since Admiral Collingwood. His speech at the ceremony, made at the height of the war, perfectly expressed the complex relationship between Portsmouth and the Royal Navy, in peace and in war:

Portsmouth and the Royal Navy have been linked together ever since the first king's ship took the water. Generation after generation of sturdy Portsmouth lads have sought adventure and a man's life in the deep seas. The Royal Dockyard has hammered into shape a thousand vessels to carry the White Ensign to the four corners of the globe. But this war, which has heralded a new era of greatly intensified air attack, has inevitably strengthened the bonds between those that I have the honour to command and those who live and work in this city. A unity of purpose stayed us all during the long-drawn attack from the air. If ever there was a dividing wall between the city and the Royal Navy it was blown away on a certain 10th of January and is now in the rubble heap.

I have often had the honour to speak in Portsmouth and, as you all know, it is to me irresistible to link the Portsmouth of today with the Portsmouth of the past. Perhaps it is because I walk daily on decks that once echoed to the roar of the broad-sides and to the tramp of Portsmouth men clothing the great ship with a mighty spread of canvas, and look daily on stone setts laid truly by Tudor masons who lived in the little waterside streets; but more likely it is because all Portsmouth is re-dolent with great history and because it requires little imagination to recapture the past.

Look over the Common of an evening and give imagination play. The huts, the guns and the men and women in khaki and blue will soon transform into rows of tents pegged down against the Channel breeze, to gay-coloured banners and pennons flying aloft and to Tudor men in brown and green testing their skill. When the tide serves they will embark for France. Horse and Foot to France! How often since then has Portsmouth filled the ranks, fashioned the weapons, supplied the needs for Horse and Foot to France. To-day, there is no revelry and no gay bunting when Horse and Foot embark. The only colour is a blue light on the jetty, the only music the tramp of marching men in darkened streets. But three years ago the low throb of engines and the measured beat of screws, stealing over the water on quiet nights, told Ports-mouth that once again Horse and Foot were on their way to France. And that will not be the last time; in the final crossings Portsmouth will play its old historic part.

Horse and Foot to France! Admiral Sir William James' vision was still nearly two years in the future, but it did come to pass and, just as he said, Portsmouth was indeed to play its old historic part.

158

Chapter 16

It was obvious, from Portsmouth's geographical position and its harbour and Dockyard, that it would be the hub of any invasion of the Continent. In fact, for almost a year before D-Day the City and the surrounding area had virtually become an armed camp, subjected to tighter and tighter security, with ever more barriers to entry and restrictions on movement, all shrouded in deeper and deeper secrecy.

For instance, as a security measure to keep preparations for invasion away from prying eyes, the whole sea front from Southsea to Eastney was declared a 'Restricted Zone' as early as 17 August 1943. Entry was forbidden to anyone without authorisation. People still living there were simply cleared out. The beaches at Southsea, Eastney and Stokes Bay were covered in barbed wire and concrete tank traps.

Restrictions were extended to most of the British Isles in the winter of 1943. Large areas

Build-up to D-Day: North-west corner, No. 3 Basin, 25th May 1944.

of the country, especially near the coasts, were put off bounds. Travel was not permitted except by those who had special passes. A complete coastal ban, affecting a belt 10 miles deep from the Wash to Land's End, came into effect on 1 April 1944. Members of the armed forces on duty, MPs and government servants on government business were exempted from the restriction order, but anyone else who was not living in the restricted area on that date could not enter it after that date.

The ban was fully enforced on 10 April with security checks at all railway stations. There were frequent security checks on public transport and in public places, such as hotels, boarding houses, restaurants and theatres. The police knew the number of season ticket holders travelling between Portsmouth and London (actually it was forty-four) and could arrest anybody on a train who was not a regular traveller. The Isle of Wight was out of bounds virtually to everybody. Islanders could not visit the mainland and mainlanders could not visit the island unless they could provide a convincing reason for their journeys. Anybody found anywhere without an identity card was liable to arrest.

Naval preparations for the training, berthing and accommodation of the armada of ships and craft which were to take part in the invasion — the actual number was over seven thousand — began as early as March 1942. New naval establishments, occupying former holiday camps, hotels, yacht clubs, guesthouses and other exotic situations, sprang up all over the Solent area.

Combined Operations Headquarters was set up in Forth Southwick on Portsdown Hill. The Landing Craft Base Headquarters was *HMS Porcupine* — actually the remaining two-thirds of the hull of the destroyer torpedoed by a U-boat in the Mediterranean in December 1942 and towed to the United Kingdom. The Nautical College at Warsash became *HMS Tormentor*, the School of Raiding, for training special parties carrying out raids and landing clandestine agents on the coasts of France, Holland and Norway.

Hayling Island, including the Island Sailing Club club-house, was taken over for the training of Combined Operations Pilotage Parties, in *HMS Northney, I, II, III* and *IV*. A collection of bathing huts in Langstone Harbour became the maintenance base *HMS Dragonfly*. *HMS Seaserpent* was at Birdham and Bracklesham Bay. *HMS Squid* was a shore base at Elmfield Court in Millbrook with a subsidiary unit at Hythe. At Exbury was *HMS Mastodon*, the base for a flotilla of tank landing craft (LCTs).

Other landing craft bases were on the Isle of Wight, at Yarmouth (*HMS Manatee*), Cowes (*HMS Vectis*) and the Puckpool Holiday Camp at Ryde (*HMS Medina*), which became the training base for Thames bargees whose barges were used in the invasion.

At Woolston, the bombed-out Vickers-Supermarine factory became *HMS Abatos*, the HQ Depot for *PLUTO* (Pipe Line Under The Ocean) for refuelling the invasion fleet off the Normandy beaches. *Abatos* was the base for training those who worked on *PLUTO* and for servicing the motley assembly of vessels commandeered to put it into effect.

Two systems of piping were adopted: 'Hais', a flexible hollow cable laid on the sea floor like a telephone cable, and 'Hamel', lengths of 3-inch diameter steel pipe welded together and coiled on to 30-foot diameter drums, known as Conums and given the cover name *HMS Conundrum*. The first laying tests of Hamel pipe were carried out from a

Coding Room, Combined Operations H.Q. Southwick, 31st January 1945.

drum mounted on a converted Thames lighter — *HMS Persephone*.

Not all the names proposed were happily chosen. In September 1942 Admiral Sir William James protested to the Admiralty about *HMS Polyp*:

It is appreciated that a Polyp is an aquatic animal of the radiate kind with many arms, but to the personnel of the establishment its more usual application will be better known i.e. a tumour growing in the nose (see *Chambers Dictionary*).

Allied planners knew that the invasion of France, codenamed Operation *OVERLORD*, the air and naval operations and the assault phase being codenamed Operation *NEPTUNE*, would require the early capture of a major port through which the Allied armies could be supplied. The raid on Dieppe in August 1942, which had been a failure, had shown that adequate support from heavy guns was essential for the success of any opposed amphibious assault, but such an assault would almost certainly destroy or badly damage the very docks and facilities for which the port was being captured.

Some other solution had to be found. On 30 May 1942, Mr Churchill minuted to Lord Louis Mountbatten, Chief of Combined Operations:

Piers for beaches. They must float up and down with the tide. The anchor problem must be mastered. Let me have the best solution worked out. The difficulties will answer for themselves.

In 1942, lengthy and detailed model tests on various forms of floating breakwater began at the Admiralty Experimental Laboratory at Haslar. The earliest models were made of inflatable rubber. When a prototype was tested in Portsmouth Dockyard it was found, not surprisingly, to be vulnerable to shrapnel.

Between May and November 1943, sixteen different artificial breakwaters were tested in the large No 2 Ship Tank at Haslar. The two harbours which, after many trials and changes of plan and studies of wind and tide and weather conditions off the Normandy coast, eventually evolved were codenamed *MULBERRY 'A'*, capable of handling 5,000 tons of supplies a day, for the Americans at St Laurent, and *MULBERRY 'B'*, handling 7,500 tons a day, for the British at Arromanches. The British *MULBERRY* was to have berthing within the breakwaters for seven deep draught ships, twenty coasters, four hundred tugs and auxiliary vessels, and a thousand small craft.

Each harbour was to have an outer main breakwater of floating cruciform-shaped steel structures, codenamed *BOMBARDON*, and an inner main breakwater of hollow cement caissons, 200-foot long and displacing between 2,000 and 6,000 tons, codenamed *PHOENIX*. There were also to be five shelters, codenamed *GOOSEBERRY*, provided by sunken blockships, codenamed *CORNCOBS*: fifty-five elderly merchantmen (twenty-three of them American) and four obsolete warships, including the old battleship *Centurion,* the cruiser *Durban,* and the French battleship *Courbet* which had been lying in Hardway Creek since the fall of France.

Inside the caissons were nine 'spud' pontoon pierheads in the British harbour, six in the American, codenamed *WHALE*, with flexible bridges and roads on pontoons, codenamed *BEETLE,* connecting the pierheads to the shore. The harbours were to be robust enough to withstand a strong Force 6 wind and to remain useable for ninety days.

The War Office was responsible for designing the caissons, the piers and pierheads, and their laying-up in British waters until they were required to be towed across the Channel. The Admiralty was responsible for the towing, for the choice of harbour sites, the placing of the breakwaters and blockships and for marking out navigational channels.

Work began in December 1943, with a tight completion deadline of seven months. A total of 212 caissons was built, mostly in yards along the Thames Estuary, at Southampton and Portsmouth, with some being built on beaches at Langstone, Stone Point near Fawley and Stokes Bay and launched down slipways.

Build-up to D-Day: North-west corner of No. 2 Basin, taken
from travelling crane, 26th May 1944.

Portsmouth Dockyard had already been working at full capacity, and was still being subjected to air raids, though not now with quite the frequency and ferocity of 1941. Apart from the usual continuing repairs and conversions to ships, the Dockyard was also preparing nearly a thousand assault craft for D-Day. Personnel-carrying landing craft were being modified to carry rocket launchers. Two landing ships, HMS *Bulolo* and *Largs*, were being converted with over £1 million of radio and radar equipment for their new functions as Headquarters Ships. But, in spite of this existing workload and with additions to the workforce, the Dockyard took on the work of building twenty PHOENIX caissons, twelve in 'C' Dock, and eight in the Floating Dock.

The *MULBERRY* building programme was beset by problems. The winter weather was consistently bad, and there were severe shortages of steel and cement, but the main problem was shortage of manpower, especially skilled labour, such as welders and fitters. In the end, the *MULBERRY* labour force rose to about forty-five thousand men, many of them brought over from Ireland, adding to the difficulties of security.

Fourteen PHOENIX caissons were built at Stokes Bay by some one thousand six hundred men — scaffolders, carpenters, fitters, steelworkers and Irish labourers. Launching these huge grotesque structures — each 60 feet high and as big as three normal houses — required a series of complicated manoeuvres, involving colossal weights. When the first caisson was launched at Stokes Bay it toppled, crushing and killing three men.

The caissons were built in echelon, one behind the other, on keel block walls about 20 feet in height and then transferred to eighteen ball carriages using special wedges and clamps. They were hauled forward one by one with winches and tackles until they lay over a track running parallel to the foreshore and drawn along until they were positioned lying broadside on to a specially constructed and strengthened slipway, down which they were launched. After that first accident, the fire brigade cleared the slipways of sand and shingle with high pressure hoses before a launch.

Once launched, the caissons were towed away to deep-water 'parking' berths where flood valves were opened and the caissons were submerged. They would lie underwater until they were raised when needed for D-Day. They were towed across by ocean-going tugs, assembled for the purpose — 132 tugs in all, 108 tugs to tow the *PHOENIXES*, the other twenty-four to tow the various types of barges.

Such an unprecedented number of rugs (in fact, 160 were involved in *OVERLORD*), many not equipped with radio, needed its own operational command. Allied Operational Tug Control Headquarters was accommodated at Lee-on-Solent Tower. CO-TUG, it was reported, kept in touch with many of their charges by loud-hailer.

Strengthened embarkation beaches, made of concrete blocks able to withstand the weight of tanks and armoured vehicles, were constructed at Beach Street and Hardway in Gosport. The Gosport firm of Camper & Nicholson designed and made their own contribution to D-Day — *SLUG*, or Surf Landing Under Glider. It was a 20-foot shallow draught twin-engined motor boat specially adapted to pass under the floating bridge units carrying the linking and mooring shuttle equipment for joining up sections of the *MULBERRY* harbour.

As the New Year of 1944 advanced and D-Day came nearer, Portsmouth and other cities, towns and villages in the south found themselves swamped with men. In Portsmouth alone accommodation had to be found for twenty-nine thousand extra personnel, excluding the troops to be embarked for *OVERLORD*. Hotels and boarding houses were requisitioned by the street. Local schools whose staff and pupils had been evacuated were taken over. Church halls, garages and cinemas, some of them partly blitzed, were temporarily commandeered. Hostels for those made homeless in the air raids were used for *MULBERRY* workers. Eight tented camps, each for five hundred men, were set up at different sites on Portsea Island. Every naval establishment was crammed to capacity.

Many public houses ran out of beer and 'No Beer' signs were commonplace as would-be drinkers went from pub to pub in search of a pint. The shortage was almost certainly due to the sheer number of extra throats in the area, but there were dark suspicions that it was all a plot by the authorities, who wanted to keep the troops and civilians sober at such a critical time by rationing supplies of beer.

With the spring of 1944 the troops arrived — thousands of them, British, Canadian, American and French. As one Gosport schoolboy recalled in later years:

1944 was a schoolboy's dream of heaven. One long procession of tanks, guns, lorries, jeeps, DUKWs, vehicles of every kind practising for D-Day. Kids used to climb over and inside these and run errands for the troops and scrounge badges which we got our mothers to sew on old jackets . . . some of them were real works of art.

Barriers were placed across many roads which then became gigantic vehicle parks for lorries, cars and jeeps. The London Road from the George Inn to Horndean was an almost solid mass of vehicles, parked nose to tail. One carriage-way of the Winchester By Pass was closed to traffic and became a tank and armoured car park several miles long. There were tanks and armoured cars, painted green and brown and camouflaged with small branches, in every wood and copse accessible from the roads. There was even a squadron of bull-dozers parked at Cowplain, with large tents and a field kitchen set up for their crews in the meadow nearby.

For civilians, travel became even more difficult. People living in Portsmouth could not go beyond Cosham without a pass. When a bus reached the George at the top of Portsdown Hill it was met by an inspector

Build-up to D-Day: loading the DUKWs on the Hardway at
Gosport, 1944.

who demanded to see every passenger's pass
and identify card and to know their destination. Those who did not satisfy the Inspector
were turned off the bus. The war was a dream
of heaven, not just for schoolboys but for
busybodies, snoopers, petty officials, jacks-
in-office and all those who delighted in
ordering their fellow citizens about.

There were Canadians at Horndean, and
Americans seemingly everywhere. With their
smart uniforms, ample pay, lavish food, and
apparently limitless supplies of stores, vehicles and equipment, their chocolate, chewing
gum and nylon stockings, the GIs were like a
vision from another world to the people of
wartime Britain.

From December 1943, Priddy's Hard had
greatly increased the number of shells, anti-
aircraft rockets and mines manufactured for
OVERLORD. Twenty thousand tons of
ammunition was manufactured for the bombarding forces, from 16-inch and 15-inch
calibre downwards, with fifty thousand

rockets for the Landing Craft Rocket (LCRs)
armed with multi-barrel rocket launchers,
and thousands of mines for the minelayers
and minelaying aircraft. The one thousand
seven hundred women employed at Priddy's
Hard were working a twelve hour day. Such
was the spirit of the time that even though
public transport was very restricted, the
black-out continued and passes and identity
cards were required everywhere, some of the
women were travelling in to work at Gosport
every day from as far away as Fareham,
Portchester and Paulsgrove.

The Royal Clarence Yard and its subsidiary
depots dispersed around the country, originally in case the main Yard was incapacitated
by bombing, worked day and night as the
invasion armada began to assemble at Spithead and in the Solent. The Yard's own fleet
of victualling ships was increased by seven
ex-Motor Fishing Vessels to carry stores,
seven more small water tankers, and three
10,000-gallon water tankers converted from

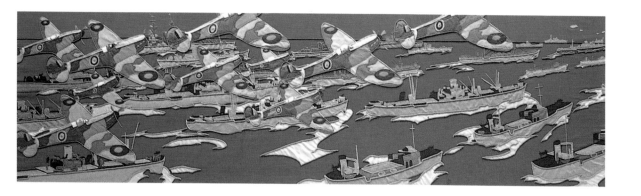

The Overlord Embroidery. Much of this famous embroidery depicts the events of May and June 1944 in 'vignette' fashion with each panel illustrating a specific event or activity. The three panels shown here depart from this style to create an impression of the vast scale and might of the Allied Naval forces as they set out on Operation Neptune. The right-hand side of the last panel depicts the role played by the 300 minesweepers that preceded the five assault flotillas and cleared the sea lane or 'spout' down which the estimated 7000 vessels proceeded on their way to the Normandy beaches.

(Portsmouth Museum Services.)

H.M.S. *Bristol* returning from the Falklands in September 1982. This type 82 destroyer arrived back in Portsmouth with H.M.S. *Invincible*.
(Wright and Logan.)

oil tankers with their tanks cleaned out.

'The invasion fleet was so tightly packed', said one Stores Assistant from Clarence Yard, 'we could practically walk across to the Isle of Wight on dry land. We used to go alongside each boat and tap on the hull, calling out, "Any bread today?" or "Any milk?". It seems hard to imagine but that's how it was as the ships assembled for the "off" just outside Portsmouth Harbour.'

Every day the little ships from Clarence Yard plied to and fro between the shore and the ships at anchor, carrying 20,000 tons of fresh water for drinking and washing every day, and 400 tons of potatoes, 100 tons of meat and 50 tons of fresh vegetables every week. The Mobile Bakery baked an extra 20,000 pounds of bread daily, in addition to the 13,000 pounds per day already supplied by commercial bakeries.

Like everybody else, the Victualling Yards were hard-pressed for manpower. Their regular staff were joined by men from the New Barracks, and some quite unexpected victualling recruits — dairymen, company directors, retired Admirals and Baronets.

Gosport, like Portsmouth, became a community under arms prior to D-Day. Streets were lined with parked armour and vehicles. Beach Road and the whole area near the ferry was sealed off from the public. Residents needed passes to get through a maze of road barriers and into streets teeming with Military Police. Hotels, guest-houses and larger houses in Alverstoke were requisitioned. A D-Day signalling station was set up at Stokes Bay, near the present site of the Sailing Club.

Haslar Hospital prepared for the reception of wounded, of both sides. The Principal Medical Officer was responsible for the planning and coordinating of all naval, army and civil arrangements for receiving casualties who arrived in the Dockyard. Haslar and local EMS hospitals would take all serious cases, until Ambulance trains arrived.

There were Advance Dressing Stations in Clarence Barracks and the Queen Alexandra Hospital, Cosham, and a naval sick bay in Portsmouth Grammar School. A Blood Bank was organised at Haslar and, as Haslar Bridge had been bombed in 1941, local people made the long journey round by road to give blood. An emergency medical marquee was put up on the Putting Green in Gosport.

HMS Hornet, the Coastal Forces base in Haslar Creek, had so many Motor Torpedo Boats (MTBs), Motor Launches (MLs) and Harbour Defence MLs as D-Day approached that they overflowed, not just down the Creek to *HMS Dolphin* as they had done for some time, but across the river to *HMS Vernon*. At times, the Creek was packed as full as ships, gunwhale to gunwhale, as the Solent.

Coastal Forces made scores of sorties across the Channel and along the French coast to attack enemy shipping, land clandestine agents, and to lay defensive minefields off the invasion beaches. The 13th and 14th MTB Flotillas, joined by the 64th Flotilla of 'D' Class MTBs from Harwich, laid a total of 562 mines, most of them in two minefields off Le Havre and Cherbourg.

General Dwight D. Eisenhower, the Supreme Allied Commander, approved the final plan for *NEPTUNE* on 1 February 1944. On 8 May, he decided that D-Day would be Y plus 4 (Y-Day was 1 June). The tides would be right on Y + 4, 5, 6 and 7 and the moon was full. On 17 May, Eisenhower decided upon 5 June. Exact H-Hour would depend upon the tides at individual beaches but the general plan was to land the assault troops as soon as possible after dawn, on a three-quarters tide.

The British troops were to land on the three eastern-most beaches. Assault forces were allocated for each beach: Force *S*, SWORD Beach (3rd Infantry Division); Force *J*, JUNO Beach (3rd Canadian Infantry Division); and Force *G*, GOLD Beach (50th Infantry Division). Force *S* Headquarters were in Commercial Buildings in Portsmouth, Force J HQ in Cowes Castle, home of the Royal Yacht Squadron, and Force G HQ in the South-Western Hotel.

Each Force was supported by a Bombarding Force: Force S by Force D, whose HQ ship was the cruiser *Mauritius*; Force J by Force E, whose HQ ship was the cruiser *Belfast*; and Force G by Force K, whose HQ ship was the cruiser *Argonaut*. Heavy gun support, on D-Day and subsequent days, was to be provided by the battleships *Warspite, Rodney, Nelson* and *Ramillies* and the monitors *Erebus* and *Roberts*.

The whole British force, designated the Eastern Naval Task Force, was commanded by Rear Admiral Philip Vian, flying his flag in the light cruiser *Scylla*. The Western Naval Task Force, covering the American landings on *UTAH* and *OMAHA* Beaches, was commanded by Rear Admiral Alan G. Kirk *USN*, flying his flag in the cruiser *USS Augusta*. The total number of warships allocated to both Task Forces for the Assault Phase was 1,213. The total number of Landing Ships and Craft allocated was 4,126.

Portsmouth was the command headquarters for the Navy and Army, and the communications nerve centre for *OVERLORD*. Admiral Sir Bertram Ramsay, the Allied Naval Expeditionary Force Commander, moved with his staff into his headquarters in Southwick House, on the other side of Portsdown Hill from Portsmouth, on 26 April.

General Montgomery's Headquarters moved to Southwick House on 28 April. His campaign caravan, with his Tac HQ (Tactical Headquarters), was parked in the grounds. The General himself was soon in residence; but, to assist in confusing the enemy, Montgomery's signals went by landline to Kent and were transmitted from there. General Eisenhower established a Forward *SHAEF* (Supreme Headquarters Allied Expeditionary Force) in the 3.5-ton trailer, nicknamed the 'Citrus Wagon', in a hazel copse about a mile from Southwick House and arrived himself shortly before D-Day.

Final rehearsals for *NEPTUNE* took place late in April and early in May. Exercise *Tiger*, to rehearse the American assault on *UTAH* with a practise landing on Slapton Sands, met disaster in Lyme Bay. In the early hours of 28 April, the landing force was attacked by nine German E-boats after their escorting destroyer *HMS Scimitar* had had to return to Plymouth with collision damage. *LSTs 507* and *531* were torpedoed and sunk, and *LST 289* damaged and towed to Brixham. The casualties were so heavy, 197 sailors and 441

soldiers killed (ironically, more than the invasion force actually suffered on *UTAH* on D-Day) that for a time Allied Intelligence believed the encounter had not been fortuitous and the enemy might have had forewarning of the invasion.

Exercise *Fabius*, which began on 3 May, was more successful. Forces G, J and S, who were to assault *GOLD, JUNO* and *SWORD* beaches, were landed on Hayling Island, Bracklesham Bay and Littlehampton respectively. Lessons were learned and incorporated into the design for *NEPTUNE* until, on 5 May, Admiral Ramsay ordered that no more changes were to be made to the *NEPTUNE* plan.

On 26 May, a security curtain descended on the South Coast. The camps, depots and vehicle parks were sealed off from the outside world. All leave was stopped. There was no more movement, in or out. For the waiting troops there was now no other destination but the ships and the French coast. On 28 May, the day the actual date of the invasion was promulgated to those taking part, a similar security clamp was imposed on the ships. Ship's companies were 'sealed' into their ships. Their leave was also stopped. Mail was impounded and the use of cables and telephones was forbidden.

The authorities were almost paranoiac about security. There were several 'scares'. *Daily Telegraph* crosswords, compiled by men who certainly were not in the D-Day secret, unwittingly contained solutions with several D-Day code-words. Much more reprehensibly, senior officers talked indiscreetly in their cups — and were speedily sacked. Mail went astray, and secret documents and charts were delivered to unauthorised, and unsuspecting, persons. A careless telegraphist, almost 'doodling' on the air, broadcast the news of the invasion prematurely and it was flashed round the world before being denied.

But, by what now seems a miracle, the secret of D-Day was kept and thus, astonishingly, the *Luftwaffe* seemingly ignored the greatest mass of shipping ever assembled in the Solent. There were air raids over the Solent, Portsmouth and Southampton in April and May. Damage was done and disruption to D-Day preparations was caused, but it was nothing like the aerial assault which might have been and which some Allied planners had feared. The formidable fighter defences of the United Kingdom, and the elaborate deception schemes designed (successfully) to convince Hitler that the Allies would land in the Pas de Calais area, ensured that the juiciest maritime target ever offered to an air force escaped virtually unscathed.

Late in May, King George VI — who was only dissuaded with difficulty from taking part in the D-Day invasion by Mr Churchill, who himself was only dissuaded with even greater difficulty from taking part by the Chiefs of Staff and by the King — came down to Portsmouth. He visited *HMS Scylla* to wish Godspeed to Admiral Vian and the officers and men of the Eastern Naval Task Force.

His Majesty embarked from *Scylla* in the *Rescue ML 529* to review the ships had landing craft who were to take part in *NEPTUNE*. 'The D-Day Review is a great memory of a lovely man', said Lieutenant Ted Wilkes *RNVR, RML 529*'s First Lieutenant.

Throughout the whole day he talked to every man in the crew. Admiral Vian (as well as quite a few more top brass) was much in evidence and questioned my navigation twice. The third time, the King took Vian aside and said 'Leave him alone Vian, he seems to me to know what he's doing'. No more interference, but I could feel his gaze on the back of my neck. We put the King ashore in Southampton after a long day of passing up and down the cheering ships, which stretched from the Nab Tower to Southampton as far as the eye could see (and beyond). I shall never forget it. He thanked the assembled ship's company and we received a signal from Buckingham Palace that evening and also

H.M. King George VI embarked in *R.M.L. 529* (wearing the Royal Standard) reviewing the Invasion Fleet in the Solent.

one from the C-in-C Home Fleet. We were well pleased.

At noon on 1 June, from his headquarters at Southwick House, Admiral Ramsay assumed operational command of the *NEPTUNE* forces and general control over all movements in the Channel. On the evening of Friday, 2 June, the first ships of the bombarding forces sailed from the Clyde.

At 9.30 pm on the same evening, two X-craft 'midget' submarines of the Twelfth Submarine Flotilla, *X-20* (Lieutenant K. R. Hudspeth, *RANVR*) and *X-23* (Lieutenant G. B. Honour *RNVR*) left *Dolphin*. They passed through the harbour boom and were met outside by the trawlers who were to tow them halfway across to the French coast. Since their arrival from Scotland, *X-20* in January and *X-23* some weeks later, the two X-craft had been acting as discreet survey vessels, ferrying to and from close inshore on the French coast members of the Combined Operations Pilotage Parties *(COPPs)*, in what the Commander-in-Chief Portsmouth described as 'a sustained and impudent reconnaissance under the very nose of the enemy'.

The COPPs' task was to survey and if possible photograph the shape and contours of the enemy coastline, measure distances, depths of water, tidal strengths and directions, and determine the gradients, textures and lengths of likely beaches, so as to provide, by means of a kind of clandestine Ordnance Survey, the essential hydrographic and topographic information for the assault landing forces.

But this time, the two X-craft were sailing for Operation *GAMBIT*, to act themselves as navigation beacons off the invasion beaches. They were precisely on their stations, about a mile offshore, *X-20* off Courseulles on *JUNO* Beach, and *X-23* off Ouistreham near the mouth of the River Orne, on *SWORD* Beach, by dawn on Sunday, 4 June, which was Day D-1. Each X-craft had on board its CO, First Lieutenant, Engine Room Artificer and two COPP members. They were the first D-Day naval personnel to arrive off the French coast.

On 3 June, Mr Churchill arrived, his special train shunted into the siding at Droxford Station. Thwarted of his wish to go over with the assault troops, he spent the afternoon at Southampton Docks with General Smuts and Ernest Bevin, watching the troops embark.

Mr Churchill was eager for the invasion to start. The X-craft were on station. The troops were embarking. The ships were ready to sail, indeed some had already sailed. But there was a delay. The weather throughout May 1944 had been calm, clear and sunny — jolly jumping weather, perfect for an invasion. But on 1 June the good weather began to fade. The winds strengthened, the clouds gathered, and it was soon obvious that the landings were threatened. After taking advice from his Chief Meteorological Advisor, Group Captain J. M. Stagg, Eisenhower decided on 4 June, in one of the hardest decisions taken by any military commander in history, to postpone D-Day by twenty-four hours, to 6 June.

On 5 June, Eisenhower himself went down to South Parade Pier to visit British troops embarking. Southsea beach was packed, for the last time, with lines of troops, bent under their weapons and equipment, waiting to board their landing craft from specially constructed piers made of scaffolding.

That day the convoys began to sail in their prearranged order, from Southampton and Southsea, from hards and beaches around the Solent, from Portland and the West Country, all heading out to Area *Z* or 'Piccadilly', as the assembly point south of the Isle of Wight was nicknamed, and thence down the 'Spout', the marked, swept, buoyed and guarded seaway which led across the Channel to France. Lieutenant Commander Denis Glover *RNZNVR*, commanding *LCI(S) 516* in a convoy taking Lord Lovat's Commando Brigade to assault Ouistreham, recalled the scene vividly:

The flotilla made a grand sight, streaming down to the open sea, threading its way in line ahead through the massed transports crowded with men and vehicles that lay at anchor in the landlocked roadstead. In the grey evening could be smelt and felt the fresh tang of the Channel in one of its boisterous, threatening moods. The Commandos on deck looked round at the unfamiliar scene, at the waters they had exercised in so often. They were cheerful but restrained. There was the island, there the spit. The mainland lay on the quarter, misty, indistinct, in the smoky setting sun. For many it would be the last sight of England.

'There was a most peculiar feeling of quietness for about six weeks before D-Day', said one Portsmouth resident, 'and of course there were vast amounts of American troops in Portsmouth as well as British. Suddenly they all disappeared . . . '

People in Portsmouth woke up that morning to the roar of aircraft overhead. But there were no air raid sirens. These were Allied transport aircraft, towing gliders. On the ground everything was uncannily quiet. Fields which had been packed with vehicles were now completely cleared. Roads which had been lined with tanks and armoured cars were open again for normal traffic. There were only tyre tracks and ruts and scattered branches in the empty woods. The Winchester By Pass was deserted. The only signs of all that had so recently happened were the messages written in large chalk letters on the roads 'Thank You Waterlooville', and 'Thank You Cowplain'.

Portsmouth Harbour was emptier than at any time in the war. There were actually buses running along Southsea Front, for what seemed the first time in years. But for those left behind in Portsmouth, D-Day was still almost an anti-climax. They heard the news on the radio and half-expected immediate German retaliation from the air, followed by fleets of ambulances racing around the streets. But nothing happened.

However, later that day, the first casualties arrived and the ambulances were soon busy enough.

A liaison officer in St James's Hospital recalled: as the convoys came in on the first day, June 6th, those that had landed on the beaches were back in hospital terribly burnt the same day, mostly Canadians. My job was to talk to them when possible and get their addresses of next of kin and write to them and tell them that they were safely back in England, and make light of their injuries. There were terrible injuries — mostly I could only see their mouths. They were nearly all black. Some were only boys and very shy. I would ask them whether they had a sweetheart, and whether they would like me to write to her.

Amongst the public rejoicing over D-Day, there were very soon to be private griefs. 'Two of my friends lost brothers in the landings in Normandy on D-Day,' wrote one Portsmuthian. 'One friend had two brothers. One was killed in the Spanish Civil War, which was very sad. And the other was killed in the Normandy landings'.

Chapter 17

On VE Day, May 1945, there were parties and dancing in the streets in Portsmouth and Gosport, and community singing, and bonfires. Houses were decked with Union Jacks and flags of the Allies and coloured bunting. Hitler was burned in effigy many times. Tables and trestles were set out in the open and, by virtue of a superhuman effort by the women, the children enjoyed cakes and jellies and such treats virtually unknown in wartime Britain.

In the evening a vast crowd, estimated at over twenty-five thousand, gathered in Guildhall Square to listen to the King's speech relayed over loudspeakers. Somebody produced an accordion, somebody else a banjo. Sailors danced with housewives, GIs with Wrens, Marines with ATS. Somebody lit a newspaper, others followed and very soon air raid notice boards, seats from Victoria Park, the wooden gates of the Corporation yard, a giant indicator board showing the War Savings 'score', and anything combustible the crowd could lay their hands on all went to make an enormous bonfire.

The general happy delirium was repeated for victory over Japan. The police and naval patrols were kept at full stretch, not to arrest drunks, for there was a critical shortage of beer, but to extinguish unofficial bonfires. After the official announcement at midnight on 14 August, Portsmouth erupted with hooters, sirens, and rockets, and more singing and dancing. Another huge crowd filled the Guildhall Square and danced into the small hours. Sailors climbed the scorched and shattered Guildhall tower to ring out the 'Pompey chimes' for the first time in five years. In Southsea what seemed like the whole population took to the streets to march arm in arm to the Common singing 'Rule Britannia'.

Next night there were official bonfires on Southsea Common, Portsdown Hill and Great Salterns and scores of smaller unofficial bonfires on waste land and bombed sites — of which there were plenty. It had been a long and hard war and in many ways the last year of it had been one of the hardest to bear, especially as the last winter was as bitterly cold as the first, with blocks of ice floating in Portsmouth harbour, the moat and Baffins Pond frozen, and another shortage of coal.

There had been news of success for Allied arms on the Continent, but at home the *Luftwaffe*'s raids had been replaced by the V-1 flying bomb or 'Doodle Bug'. From 15 June 1944 and at intervals for the next nine months, they came over London and towns in southern England at a speed faster than many fighters could achieve.

The V-1s had an unmistakeable metallic engine noise — which suddenly cut out. There was silence, while everybody who could took cover, followed by a thunderous detonation. It was a particularly unnerving form of weapon for a civil population who had already endured years of raids and who had hoped that D-Day would bring the end of attacks from the air.

King George VI did achieve his heart's desire of a trip over to the Normandy beaches. He left Portsmouth in the light cruiser *Arethusa*, with the Royal Standard flying at the main, at 8am on 16 June 1944. They passed outgoing and incoming convoys on the way, and saw the minesweepers at work. The King noticed *Nelson* and *Ramillies* and watched the cruiser *Hawkins* bombarding the shore as *Arethusa* came in.

The King transferred to an ML and then to a DUKW and was met by General Montgomery at Courcelles beach. After lunch at Montgomery's Tactical Headquarters (Tac HQ), the King held an investiture. He returned to Portsmouth in *Arethusa* at 9pm that night, after what he called a long and very interesting day. He was most encouraged that it had been possible for him to land on the beaches only ten days after D-Day.

In September 1944, the black-out was lifted from all except certain coastal areas — including Portsmouth — and many Home Guard units held their last 'standing down' parades before disbanding.

The WRNS, too, had passed the peak of their war contribution by the end of 1944. In the months immediately before and after D-Day the WRNS had made the most prolonged, intense and concerted effort of any women's service in history.

There were Wren ship mechanics, Wren chart-correctors, Wren confidential book officers, Wren boarding officers, Wren meteorologists, Wren parachute packers, Wren signallers, and Wren coding officers. Wren dispatch riders and motor transport drivers commonly worked forty-eight-hour shifts. Wrens in Fleet Mail offices and Wren censors dealt with millions of items of mail, and Wrens crewed the boats taking the mail sacks out to the ships.

Wren supply assistants issued food, clothing, and stores in prodigious numbers; at *HMS Vectis* at Cowes, for example, they dealt with over one hundred ships every day. There was a large Wren contingent in *HMS Marshal Soult*, the Depot Ship for the minesweepers and trawlers in the Portsmouth Command and, during the invasion period, the supply ship for many of the landing craft and Motor Fishing Vessels (MFVs).

WRNS and WAAFs worked together on the D-Day Plot in Combined Headquarters at Portsmouth, plotting top secret information from both sides of the Channel and from ships at sea. There were three wardrooms in the HQ, one of them underground, in each of which Wrens served eight hundred meals every twenty-four hours. In the WRNS mess some one thousand two hundred meals a day

were cooked and served, and there was also a mid-morning canteen. Two-course supper was provided below ground, in five shifts from 8.30 to 11pm. Wrens made up hundreds of beds and changed and laundered hundreds of sheets every day. In the Commander-in-Chief Portsmouth's Signal Distribution Office, some of the Wrens described by their Director WRNS as 'immobiles of a certain age' worked until they were literally crying with tiredness, but carried on without making mistakes.

Release of married Wren officers and Wrens in high priority groups began in March 1945. Some categories of Wrens were declared redundant and others obsolescent in July, and recruiting for them stopped. The WRNS was not disbanded as in 1919 but was retained as a permanent and professional women's service.

There were sixteen thousand five hundred officers and men on the books of the Barracks serving in establishments all over the Portsmouth area. Over two hundred and fifty officers used the Wardroom. Many were too old for active service. At one time there were only five active service Royal Navy officers in the Barracks. The lieutenant commander in charge of Parade Training was seventy-two. The average age of section commanding officers, all ex-warrant officers, was sixty-three.

Whale Island was an empire on its own. In September 1945, there were 150 officers and 215 Gunnery Instructors in the Gunnery School, fifty officers in the Experimental Department, and fifteen WRNS officers and 750 Wren ratings, with a total of some three hundred officers, two out of three of them Reserve officers, and six thousand ratings, many of them under training.

As well as the ranges at Eastney and Fraser Battery, there was a High Speed Target Service, to train gunners to shoot against E-boats, and the Navy's first helicopter station, on the football pitch, with a Sikorsky helicopter running a taxi service to any of the Island's outlying establishments, or to Larkhill on Salisbury Plain, or to *Vernon* in Roedean School.

Demobilisation began on 18 June 1945. The

first three hundred went through the dispersal centre at Stamshaw Camp, where their service documents were brought up to date, and then on to the Portsdown Motor Garage at Cosham which had been converted into a giant warehouse for issuing civilian clothes. The Centre claimed to be able to deal with forty men an hour and to kit out every man with everything from raincoat to collar studs and cuff-links in fifteen minutes.

The ships began to come home. The battleship *Nelson* returned from the Far East to South Railway Jetty in November 1945. Fort Blockhouse's piers were filled with submarines returned from the East Indies and the South Pacific. Captured E-boats came up Haslar Creek to *HMS Hornet*, and one of them was put on show.

Many ships' operational days were done, and most of them were laid up after the war. Within months, the furthest reaches and creeks of Portsmouth and Fareham, and many other harbours and river estuaries around the country, began to receive, in Captain Roskill's words:

groups of salt-rimed, rust-stained little ships — corvettes and destroyers, sloops, minesweepers and frigates. Their fragile and valuable equipment removed or protected by sealed 'cocoons', funnel covers laced on, and gun tampions driven hard home. Moored bow and stern they could not even swing to the tides they had known so well, but as the ripples ebbed and flowed could only gently nudge each other, and pass through the group the mumbling mutters of their memories.

After being flagship of the Commander-in-Chief Home Fleet, *Nelson* went with the battleships *Anson* and *Howe* to Portland for training purposes. They were followed there by the carriers *Indefatigable* and *Implacable*, but the carrier *Formidable* swung to a buoy at Spithead for years, until she was towed away to be broken up in 1953.

However, there was one more glimpse of

Demobilisation Clothing Centre, Cosham, June 1945, which claimed to be able to fit a man out with everything from raincoat to collar studs in fifteen minutes.

the glory that had been. On 1 February 1947 the King and Queen, with the two Princesses, sailed from Portsmouth in the new battleship *Vanguard* for the Royal Tour of South Africa. They were met in the Channel by *King George V*, the Commander-in-Chief Home Fleet's flagship, *Nelson*, flagship of the Training Battle Squadron (the nineteenth and last admiral's flag she wore in her lifetime), *Anson* and *Howe*. This was probably the very last occasion when five British battleships manoeuvred together in the open sea.

The aircraft carrier *Victorious* replaced *Nelson* at Portland before going in 1950 to Portsmouth Dockyard for modernisation and refit which was to last until 1958. The Dockyard, like the Navy, faced a rapidly changing postwar world. The first priority was to repair the worst of the bomb damage. Very few ships were built. The first postwar ship built at Portsmouth, the all-welded frigate *Leopard*, was launched in May 1955. She was followed by the frigates *Rhyl*, *Nubian* and *Sirius*, launched in March and September 1959, and September 1964. The frigate *Andromeda*, the three hundredth (approximately) and last warship built at Portsmouth, was launched in May 1967 and completed in 1968.

Besides *Victorious*, the Dockyard carried out major repairs or modernisations to other carriers, cruisers, destroyers and submarines, and converted five destroyers to frigates. The Dockyard's task became ever more complex, requiring up to eight times more labour effort for some installation work than prewar. The Navy's postwar ships were generally smaller but much more complicated than their predecessors, with much more equipment fitted in them. They had more electrical generating capacity, more radar and electronic equipment, and better living conditions for the ship's company. Their designs, specifications and layouts were changed more frequently than in the past (such changes were partly responsible for *Victorious*'s long stay in the Yard).

In December 1949, there was a naval occasion which would today be regarded as an act of pure vandalism against the nation's heritage. The old 'Wooden wall' HMS *Implacable* was taken out to sea from Portsmouth and sunk off the Owers light-vessel.

On 4 November 1805, some 260 miles west of Rochefort, Captain Sir Richard Strachan in the *Caesar*, with the *Hero*, *Namur* and *Courageux*, captured the French *Formidable*, *Scipion*, *Mont Blanc* and *Duguay-Trouin*. These were the first survivors of Trafalgar to be captured. In his despatch Strachan wrote 'We were delighted' and was known ever afterwards as 'delighted Sir Dicky'. *Duguay-Trouin*, a splendid 74-gun ship, was taken into the Royal Navy and renamed *Implacable*.

After service in the Baltic in 1808-9 and in Syria in 1840, *Implacable* became a boys' training ship at Devonport in 1855. When the *Lion* arrived in 1871, *Implacable* became part of the training establishment, named *Lion*. She was for sale in 1908 but was saved for restoration and repair and in 1932 she was towed to Portsmouth where *Foudroyant* joined her.

In the next seven years, until the outbreak of war, the two ships were dedicated by the Society for Nautical Research for holiday training, and to keep alive the traditions of the Sea services. Some ten thousand young people learned elementary seamanship and practical boatwork on board. *Implacable* was docked in Portsmouth in February 1943, converted as a training ship and commissioned in June. She finally paid off in January 1947.

Implacable's hull had deteriorated during the war. It was proposed to restore and re-rig her and put her in a dry dock near the Royal Naval College Greenwich on the site of the blitzed Ship Tavern, where she would be 'London's Trafalgar Ship', but the Society for Nautical Research could see no prospect of raising the necessary money or, in a time of postwar Austerity, of obtaining the labour and timber. It was, as they said, 'simply a matter of mathematics'.

Implacable was taken by tugs out of the Tidal Basin on 1 December 1949 and towed out of harbour, exchanging compliments on the way with *Foudroyant*, moored between Gosport and Fort Blockhouse. She was secured to a buoy at Spithead for the night, attended by two tugs, *Alligator* and *Excluder*.

At 8 am on 2 December, the cortege set off:

the frigate *Redpole*, entrusted with the navigation; *Alligator* towing *Implacable*, who flew the White and French Ensigns at her stern; *ML 6002*, from which the explosive charges would be fired; and *Excluder*. They were joined later by *Boxer* (an ex-LST converted into a navigating and electrical officers' training ship) with specially invited guests, and the destroyer *Finisterre* wearing the flag of the Commander-in-Chief Portsmouth, Admiral of the Fleet Sir Algernon Willis.

The ships arrived at the rendezvous, some 10 miles south-east of the Owers light-vessel at 1.30 pm. Colours were half-masted in the ships, ship's companies had fallen in by divisions and a Marine bugler sounded the Last Post. The four charges were fired at 1.45. There was a cloud of black smoke and debris. *Implacable* began to sink at once, but then seemed to hesitate, with her top deck awash, as though reluctant to go. It was supposed that her upper-works had become detached and

H.M.S. Implacable being towed out of Portsmouth Harbour by the tug Alligator to be scuttled by demolition charges ten miles S.E. of the Owers Light Vessel, 2nd December 1949.

were still floating. Thus the two Ensigns still flew proudly, almost symbolically, from her stern, long after the ships had turned for home and the spectators had gone. The remains were reported to have disintegrated later that evening.

Such a scene would be unthinkable today, when there is such popular interest in the Navy's past, and the Society for Nautical Research has an unofficial motto, which in a sense represents the Society's philosophy, 'Never Again *Implacable*'.

On 15 June 1953 there was a much happier occasion, the Review of the Fleet at Spithead to celebrate the Coronation of Her Majesty Queen Elizabeth II. It was the first Review since the war and, like its predecessors, it showed a changing Navy.

The lines of ships which the Queen inspected from *HMS Surprise*, the despatch vessel converted from the 'Bay' Class frigate *Gerrans Bay* and acting as Royal Yacht for the day, had only one battleship, *Vanguard*, but nine aircraft carriers including the new *Eagle*, 38,000 tons, at that time the largest carrier built for the Navy.

Some ships were still in the Far East, serving in the last months of the Korean War, but over two hundred ships were on view including 'Flower' Class corvettes, which had borne much of the heat and burden of the day in the battle of the Atlantic, the new 'Daring' Class destroyers, which were the size of pre-war light cruisers, modern submarines with streamlined casings and conning towers, and landing craft of various shapes and sizes, many of which had taken part in wartime amphibious landings.

For the first time at a Royal Review, there were ships with gas turbines and aircraft with jet engines. The fly-past of some three hundred aircraft from British, Canadian and Australian squadrons also included Whirlwind helicopters, the first ever to take part in a Royal Review.

The Italian Navy sent their striking sail training-ship *Amerigo Vespucci*, which looked like an old 'wooden wall' but was in fact built in 1930. Also present were the American cruiser *USS Baltimore*, the Brazilian cruiser *Almirante Barroso*, the Swedish cruiser *Gota*

Lejon and the new Russian cruiser *Sverdlov*.

The Queen and the Duke of Edinburgh dined on board *Vanguard* and the Queen gave the signal for illuminating the fleet by pressing a single gold Morse key. The illuminations were followed by fire-works, with a final salvo of over two thousand five hundred rockets.

In the following year, 1954, the *Portsmouth Navy News* was first published. It was the brainchild of Captain I. L. M. McGeoch *DSO DSC RN*, who commanded the Royal Naval Barracks, the Rev. W. J. E. Tregenna-Piggott, and Mr John Mason of Gale & Polden, the publishers. It cost three old pence, plus one penny postage, and soon had a circulation of seven thousand. In 1959, when the circulation had nearly trebled and the paper had become accepted as the official 'organ' of the Fleet Air Arm, the Chatham Port Division and the Royal Naval Association, the name was changed to *The Navy News* and could fairly claim to be the Royal Navy's own newspaper (although Devonport Port Division published *The Sailor*, previously the *Guzz Gazette*).

In 1955, there was a 'thaw' in East-West relations, after a Four Power Summit conference was held in Geneva in July with the aim of ending the 'Cold War'. In October, the light fleet carrier *Triumph*, wearing the flag of the Commander-in-Chief Home Fleet, Admiral Sir Michael Denny, with the minelayer *Apollo* and four destroyers, visited Leningrad and were warmly welcomed by the local population.

The same month a Soviet naval squadron of two *Sverdlov* cruisers and four destroyers, under the command of the Commander-in-Chief of the Russian Baltic Fleet, Admiral Golovko, visited Portsmouth. It was the first such visit by Russian ships since World War One and the Russian sailors were as warmly received as the British had been in Russia.

It seemed that a genuine 'thaw' was possible, but the atmosphere of good will was soured the following year, when the *Sverdlov* Class cruiser *Ordzhonikidze*, escorted by two destroyers, arrived in Portsmouth on 16 April bringing the Russian Prime Minister, Marshal Bulganin, and the First Secretary of the

Cdr. Lionel Crabb, during diving operations at Tobermory, *c*.1950.

Communist Party, Mr Khrushchev, for an official visit to Britain.

The ten-day visit itself went off very well, with everybody behaving with the utmost cordiality to everybody else, and it ended in a flurry of goodwill signals from both sides. But, on 30 April, the Admiralty unexpectedly released an official statement that Commander Lionel Crabb RN was 'missing, presumed dead after failing to return from underwater trial. He did not return from a test dive which took place in connection with trials of certain underwater apparatus in Stokes Bay, in the Portsmouth area, about a week ago (on 19 April)'.

The press immediately, and understandably, jumped to the conclusion that Commander Crabb had met with a fatal accident whilst diving under the hull of the Russian cruiser, to obtain information about her underwater hull shape, propellers and sonar equipment. Speculation was fuelled by a statement on 4 May by the Russian Assistant Naval Attache in London that a frogman had been seen to surface near *Ordzhonikidze* while she was in Portsmouth.

Lionel Kenneth Philip Crabb, known as 'Buster', was a celebrity in his profession. As a skilled and brave wartime 'frogman' in the RNVR he had won the George Medal and had been awarded an OBE for his exploits in disarming underwater explosive devices. He had operated in Gibraltar harbour in 1942, and in northern Italy in 1943. After the Italian surrender in September 1943, he persuaded Italian frogmen to help clear Leghorn harbour of German mines.

After the war, Crabb carried out 'antifrogmen' work in Haifa harbour before the founding of the state of Israel. He was at the Admiralty Research station at Teddington when the submarine *Truculent* sank after a collision in the Thames in January 1950. Crabb went down to her with another frogman and was the first to reach the conning tower and report no sign of life. He was involved in the development and technique for using the underwater television camera which located the sunken submarine *Affray* near the Hurd Deep in the Channel in 1951. For some time up to 1954 he worked for the Duke of Argyll on a sunken Armada galleon at Tobermory. He was recalled for duty in the Royal Navy in April 1955.

On 9 May, the Prime Minister, Sir Anthony Eden, was questioned about Crabb in the Commons but said it would not be in the public interest to disclose the circumstances of his presumed death, and made it clear that what had been done, if it had been done, was done without authority, and disciplinary steps were being taken.

The controversy swelled by the day. A remark by Mr Khrushchev while he was in London had seemed to hint that the Russians knew the British had spied on their ships during the previous visit in 1955. The Russian press began to accuse the British of 'shameful underwater espionage'.

Admiral Kotov, who had commanded the Russian squadron, told *Isvestia* that he had questioned the Chief of Staff to the Commander-in-Chief Portsmouth about a frogman near his ships, and had been told he could not have been a naval diver, and the frogman's gear as described by him must have been a civilian, not naval, pattern. On 11 May, Moscow Radio gave the texts of a Russian Note asking for an explanation for the appearance of a frogman near a Russian cruiser, and the Foreign Office reply which explained that the frogman's presence was unauthorised and expressed regret.

In July 1956, the *News* gave Crabb's date of death as 19 April, his age forty-six, and his estate as £1,205. In June 1957, Mr John Randall and Mr Ted Gilby in their six-tonner *Red Goose* found the headless body of a man in frogman's uniform at the mouth of Chichester harbour. At the inquest later in the month, the Chichester Coroner was convinced that the body was Crabb and returned an open verdict.

At Crabb's funeral service in Portsmouth Roman Catholic Cathedral, an observer noted 'the almost complete absence of naval uniforms'. He is buried in Milton Cemetery with a modest headstone inscribed 'In Loving Memory Of My Son Commander Lionel Crabb R.N.V.R. G.M. O.B.E. At Rest At Last 1956'. The 'Crabb Affair' faded out of the headlines, but continues to flare up from time to time to this day.

In 1958, *Victorious* recommissioned at Portsmouth after the most extensive (and at £20 million, one of the most expensive) refits and modernisations ever undertaken by a Royal Dockyard. The ship had been rebuilt from the hangar deck up. The flight deck had been lengthened by some 30 feet, lifted by four feet to increase hangar head-room below, strengthened to take heavier aircraft such as the Buccaneer, angled out to port to 8.3/4 degrees, and fitted with two steam catapults, two hydro-pneumatic centre-line aircraft lifts twice the size of the original lifts, and mirror deck landing sights. The flight deck overhang caused by the angled deck was so large a travelling dockyard crane had to be rerouted before the ship could be moved out of dock.

There was, as always, a procession of new and modernised ships passing through Portsmouth. *HMS Bulwark*, the first British 'Commando' carrier, commissioned at Portsmouth in January 1960. Helicopter-borne troops had done well at Suez in November 1956 and the 'Commando' carrier was an extension and refinement of the idea of having a highly mobile amphibious force embarked and ready to go anywhere at short notice.

Bulwark was to be based at Singapore and operate 'east of Suez'. She carried a complete Royal Marine Commando of six hundred officers and men, with all their weapons and equipment, and four landing craft (assault) on special gantries. The arrester wires and catapult had been removed thus converting her into an all-helicopter troop carrier, with sixteen Westland Whirlwinds, (later replaced by Westland Wessex).

In March 1960, Lady Carrington, wife of the First Lord, 'launched' Admiralty Floating Dock No 59 at Portsmouth. The 400-foot long AFD 59 was constructed in dry dock and floated out after the ceremony. It was capable of docking destroyers, frigates and the latest submarines, and was to be used initially for the fitting-out of the new nuclear submarine *Dreadnought*.

But, as the new faces arrived, the old departed. In August 1960, tugs took charge of *Vanguard* to tow her to the breaker's yard. She could have been preserved, as the US Navy preserved their 'Iowa' Class battleships, and might have been of incalculable value, in the Falklands conflict, for instance. She had never seen an enemy, nor fired a shot in anger but, like a curiously large number of warships throughout naval history, she seemed to

H.M.S. Vanguard aground on Portsmouth Point on her way to the breakers' yard 4th August 1960.

resent and even tried to resist her ignominious fate by running aground. She was aground on Portsmouth Point for an hour before she could be pulled off.

After a love-hate relationship between Service and City which had lasted nearly a thousand years, the Honorary Freedom of the City was conferred upon the Portsmouth Command of the Royal Navy on 7 May 1965 — the date specially chosen as the two hundredth anniversary of the keel laying of *HMS Victory* at Chatham.

Just before 8am, the Lord Mayor of Portsmouth, Alderman J. A. Nye, was welcomed on board *Victory* by the Commander-in-Chief, Admiral Sir Wilfrid Woods, and a distinguished assembly of naval officers, to witness the ceremony of Colours and the hoisting of flags to dress the ship overall. Alderman Nye planted a commemorative tree on the dockside on behalf of the City.

On Southsea Common, which had seen so many parades and ceremonies over the years, there was a parade of over a thousand naval personnel, with the Royal Marine Band of the Portsmouth Command. The Lord Mayor inspected the parade, presented the Freedom Scroll to the Commander-in-Chief and, witnessed by the Town Clerk, Mr John Haslegrave, both then signed the Freedom Roll. The Naval Command marched past the Guildhall with bayonets fixed, as was now their privilege as Freemen, where the Lord Mayor took the salute from the Guildhall steps. The Lord Mayor then gave a splendid lunch and the Naval Command presented the city with a magnificent silver model of the *Victory*.

Gosport, too, had its civic ceremonies. The Freedom of the Borough was granted to the Submarine Command at a parade of four hundred serving submariners on 7 July 1961. The Mayor, Councillor J. F. Fairhall JP, presented the Scroll of Freedom to Rear Admiral A. R. Hezlet, Flag Officer Submarines, the Commanders-in-Chief Home Fleet and Portsmouth, senior naval army and RAF officers, submarine holders of the Victoria Cross and many families.

Afterwards, the four hundred submariners marched with bayonets fixed through the streets of Gosport. On parade for the first time was the Queen's Colour, presented to the Submarine Branch by Her Majesty the Queen in 1959.

Gosport airfield at Grange, which had links with the Navy going back to the Royal Naval Air Service in 1914, closed in 1955 and eventually became the engineering training establishment *HMS Sultan*. The Borough presented its Honorary Freedom to the Fleet Air Arm on 20 May 1966. The parade formed up in Clarence Yard and marched to St George's Barracks for the ceremony at which the Mayor, Councillor H. W. Cooley JP, presented the Casket and Scroll to Vice Admiral D. C. E. F. Gibson, the Flag Officer Naval Air Command. Afterwards, there was a fly-past of twenty-eight aircraft, representing all marques currently in service, and led by the last flying Fairey Swordfish.

There was probably more turmoil and upheaval amongst naval establishments, more closures and amalgamations, due to changes in the Navy's geographical and technological needs, in the mid-twentieth century than at any time in the Navy's history. Many stores and depots, and obsolescent camps and stations, were closed under the 'Way Ahead' programme of the 1950s and 1960s. In Gosport, *Sultan* waxed in size and importance, but *St Vincent*, the boys' training establishment closed in 1969.

Some of the most far-reaching changes arrived in the wake of 'Plan Opstrain' in 1973, under which the training of all seamen officers and men became centred at *HMS Dryad* at Southwick. The Operations Branch for ratings was introduced on 1 January 1975, and over the years the training functions of *Excellent*, *Vernon* and some parts of *Mercury*, the signal school, were concentrated at the School of Maritime Operations at *Dryad*.

Dryad, which grew year by year into one of the largest and most influential establishments in the Navy, also houses the Maritime Tactical School. The Gunnery Branch as such was abolished. In October 1974, the unthinkable came to pass; *Excellent* closed as a Gunnery Schoool, although it retained some training functions, as it still does today, albeit as a satellite of *HMS Nelson*, the Naval Base.

The most spectacular naval occasion of the 1970s was another Review — for Queen Elizabeth II's Silver Jubilee, at Spithead on 28 June 1977. there were 180 ships, of eighteen nations, anchored in ten lines, seven miles long. Nuclear submarines were present at a Review for the first time. It was also the first time that the most powerful warships in the Navy, the Polaris submarines, were absent from a Review; it was decided that to have one present would, in the Commander-in-Chief Fleet's words, 'degrade the deterrent'.

The American cruiser USS California was the first nuclear-powered surface warship to attend a Review. There were two hovercraft from the Naval Hovercraft Trials Unit, also making their Review debut. The largest vessel present was the 136,601 ton BP tanker British Respect, the largest warship the aircraft carrier Ark Royal, and the fastest the 57-knot missile attack craft Pahlawan of the Royal Brunei Malay Regiment.

The reviewing convoy was led by the Trinity House vessel Patricia, with the Elder Brethren embarked, exercising their ancient privilege to lead the Sovereign who, with other members of the Royal Family and the First Sea Lord, Admiral Sir Terence Lewin, was in the Royal Yacht Britannia, flying the Admiralty flag at the fore, the Royal Standard at the main, and the Union flag at the mizzen.

Then came the new Type 42 destroyer Birmingham, with the Board of Admiralty embarked; the RFA helicopter support ship Engadine, with more than three hundred and fifty pressmen and photographers from all over the world; and three more RFAs, Lyness, Sir Geraint, and Sir Tristram, which had sailed from Southampton that morning, with Ministers, MPs, ambassadors, defence attachés, well-known figures from public life, representatives of industry, the trade unions and ex-Servicemen's associations, and naval holders of the Victoria Cross and George Cross.

The weather was poor and as the day went on it turned colder, the wind brisker and the rain heavier. The thirty thousand sailors who had lined the upper decks for two hours were glad to get below. A fly-past of fixed-wing Phantoms, Buccaneers and Gannets was cancelled and the number of helicopters reduced from 110 to about seventy.

There was some disappointment in Portsmouth. The weather, full television coverage, and the threat of massive traffic jams kept the number of visitors down from the expected million to only about two hundred thousand. Instead of thousands of small craft out in the Solent, there were only hundreds. Visibility was poor that evening for the fleet illuminations and the fireworks.

However, the Queen ordered the traditional signal 'Splice the Mainbrace' which, as the tot of rum had been abolished in 1970, was celebrated by three pub measures of commercial brand spirits per man. Two hundred sailors went to a reception given for them by the Queen in Ark Royal. Later, according to tradition, the Queen dined with her Admirals and Captains in the upper hangar of Ark Royal. The Palace had asked that there should be no expense to the public purse, so the diners all paid £15 each for their dinners — but were allowed to keep their dinner plates.

Chapter 18

H.M.S. Invincible sailing for the Falklands.

'I suppose the Spanish Armada enjoyed a send-off like this,' said one of *Hermes*' Sea King helicopter pilots, with a certain degree of foreboding. It was Monday morning, 5 April 1982, and the aircraft carrier *Hermes* was at sea, heading for the South Atlantic and having just witnessed an astonishing sight.

Of all the naval farewells in Portsmouth's history, that morning's had been one of the least expected — a spectacle of leave-taking which few in Portsmouth, or in England, had ever thought they would see again in their lifetimes.

The walls, the roads and jetties, every

building and every vantage point in Portsmouth and Gosport were black with people, bands played, banners and flags waved to bid farewell and Godspeed to the 'Task Force', which was to grow into the largest fleet to sail from the shores of Britain since World War Two.

'As we leave the Dockyard,' said a watcher in *Invincible*, the second carrier who sailed with *Hermes* that day, 'we become aware that many of the people who have worked so hard to get us on our way have turned out to see us off, but we are quite unprepared for the amazing scenes of patriotic fervour as we leave the harbour. There are thousands of people cramming every inch of sea wall and beach to give us a send off the like of which we have never seen before. It is certainly a highly emotional experience and one which none of us will ever forget. Our confidential time of departure must have been the year's worst kept secret!' (The occasion was altogether too much for the officer on the ceremonial broadcast who piped 'Attention to Port! Commander-in-Chief Sink Nav Home!'). *Hermes'* account of the departure from Portsmouth was much less emotional. Her deck log recorded 'large crowds wave ship off.'

The Argentine invasion force had arrived off the Falkland Islands after nightfall on 1 April. The first landings began at 9.15 pm. After a spirited resistance by the tiny Royal Marine garrison, the islands were surrendered on 2 April. The first Argentine air force C-130 Hercules landed on Port Stanley airfield at 8.30 AM. South Georgia surrendered on 3 April.

Only two days later, Task Group 317.8, as it was to be designated, but known irradicably to the British public as the 'Task Force', was steaming south to begin the recapture of the Falkland Islands, in an Operation code-named *CORPORATE*.

The impression given at the time of a powerful 'Task Force' of many large and formidable warships heading steadily, inexorably and irresistably southwards. In fact, TG 317.8 began with only six ships, with others joining and leaving during the passage south. Ships stopped more than once, turned round and retraced their tracks for political or other reasons.

The first ships to sail were the two aircraft carriers, *Hermes* and *Invincible*, which were to form the nucleus and main striking force of the Task Force. They were joined by the Royal Fleet Auxiliary (RFA) tanker *Olmeda* and the frigates *Alacrity* and *Antelope* from Devonport. The RFA tanker *Pearleaf* sailed from Portsmouth and the RFA AEFS (Ammunitiion, Explosives, Food and Stores ship) *Resource* from Rosyth.

These sailings were only made possible by the prodigious efforts of thousands of people, in particular the men and women of the RN Supply & Transport Service (RNSTS), in dockyards, workshops, stores, garages and depots, not just in and around Portsmouth but all over the UK. (One RNSTS stores officer was visiting *Victory* with his family on the first Sunday when he saw the activity in the Yard. He handed his camera to his wife, joined a working party, and got home at 2 am next day).

On Friday, 2 April, *Invincible* was alongside Pitch House Jetty, at forty-eight hours notice for sea, her ship's company on Easter leave. No 801 Squadron Sea Harriers were disembarked to RNAS Yeovilton. No 820 Squadron were also on leave but their Sea Kings were on board. In the early hours of 2 April, the Duty Lieutenant Commander received a signal ordering the ship to four hours' notice for sea. All hands were recalled from leave at 6 am. With some remarkable assistance from the Dockyard telephone exchange over five hundred members of the ship's company were contracted and told to report back on board. The squadrons had their own recall procedures.

By noon, the first stores had begun to arrive in what was to be a never-ending stream over the whole weekend. The last items were passed over literally as the brows were taken in before sailing. *Invincible* had been due to spend two months in the Mediterranean from the middle of April, so stores demands were already in at Royal Clarence Yard and with NAAFI. These were called forward by two weeks.

That afternoon, a basin trail of three

engines was successfully carried out. By mid-afternoon there was an ammunition lighter alongside and a traffic jam had built up on shore, with long queues of lorries, vans and tankers bringing food, stores, clothing, extra damage control and firefighting equipment, an enlarged medical outfit which appeared 'as if by magic' from Haslar, and liquid oxygen.

So much more ammunition was embarked than the normal peacetime outfit that Director General Ships' reassurance was sought that magazine decks would take the extra load! All wardroom trophies and silverware were returned to *HMS Nelson* — except a toast-rack which had been battered and bent when a German shell blew it into the wardroom piano of the battle-cruiser *Invincible* during the previous battle off the Falklands in 1914.

The drafting authorities at *HMS Centurion* exerted themselves to ensure that *Invincible* and other ships had their full complements. The squadrons were 'enhanced' with extra aircraft, requiring more aircrew. Even so, there was a shortage of hands to shift the stores and packages, in *Invincible* and in every ship. Ship's companies and dockyard stores men were joined by a large working party from *HMS Nelson* and other shore establishments, with such unexpected additions as the RN Display Team, the Field Guns Crew from Whale Island, and inmates of Naval Detention Quarters.

Hermes was in the second week of a six-week DAMP (Dockyard Assisted Maintenance Period). Her island superstructure was shrouded in scaffolding and much of her main machinery and her main systems were opened up or stripped down for maintenance or repair. The scaffolding had to be removed and everything below buttoned up by Monday morning. Storing *Hermes* went on with the same intensity as in *Invincible*, with the added commitment that, having the most up-to-date communications outfit, she was to be the Task Force flagship.

Eight Sea Harriers of No 800 Squadron flew on board *Hermes* on 2 April, and three more on the 4th, Palm Sunday, when *Invincible*'s eight Sea Harriers also arrived, shattering the peace of a calm, bright Portsmouth Sunday but providing a grandstand spectacle for passengers on the Gosport ferry.

The assault ship *Fearless*, the Dartmouth Training Ship, had disembarked her 'young gentlemen' to go back to the College and was one week into a Maintenance Period in Portsmouth Dockyard. She had one 'sick' boiler with brickwork defects and many of her systems opened for repair. Then, in the ship's own account, 'miracles started to occur'. The Dockyard and Fleet Maintenance Group put everything back together and rebricked the boiler by 5 April.

Fearless sailed next day, 6 April, with the 'sick' boiler's brickwork being slowly dried out, having embarked vehicles and heavy equipment for 3 Commando Brigade, Scout helicopters of the Brigade Air Squadron, three Sea Kings, and Commodore Michael Clapp, Commodore Amphibious Warfare, and his staff. Having docked down to retrieve her four LCU landing craft at sea, she headed for Ascension. *Fearless*'s sister ship, *Intrepid*, was also at Portsmouth, but had been paid off towards reserve and an uncertain future. Her Engineer Officer was on leave in the United States. The major and complex tasks of refitting, recommissioning, and restoring *Intrepid* and working her up to operational efficiency were accomplished by Portsmouth Dockyard and Portland Naval base in the astounding time of twenty-two days.

On 7 April, four Landing Ships Logistic (LSLs) sailed, *RFAs Sir Galahad* and *Sir Geraint* from Devonport and *Sir Percivale* and *Sir Lancelot* from Marchwood, near Southampton, each with over four hundred Naval, Marines, Army and RAF personnel on board, stores, weapons and ammunition, and three Scout and nine Gazelle helicopters of 3 Commando Brigade Air Squadron. The LSLs sailed south on 7 April and were joined four days later by *RFA Stromness*, who had also sailed from Portsmouth.

The fast replenishment ship *RFA Stromness* had been due to be withdrawn from RFA service and was being destored. She was in fact almost empty when it was realised there was a shortage of troop lifting capacity. On 2 April, it was decided to bring her back into service as a combined replenishment ship and assault troop carrier for four hundred Marines of 45 Commando. Sailing date was 6 April — only four days hence.

Stromness was in C Lock at Portsmouth and could be loaded by cranes from both sides of the ship. It was just as well. Stores began to arrrive from local victualling yards in Portsmouth, from the RAF in Stafford, from specialist stores all over the UK, from NAAFI and from the Marines' own base at Arbroath. Amongst other things *Stromness* embarked military rations for seven thousand five hundred men for a month and 'Airport 82' — a portable airstrip of some ten thousand interlocking runway sheets.

Portsmouth Dockyard converted the top deck of No 4 Hold, normally used for NAAFI stores and dry provisions, into a messdeck for three hundred Marines, complete with three-tier bunk beds, shaving points, mirrors, heaters and a central recreation area with dart board and video (a whip-round amongst the Naval Stores staff produced £90 to buy TV and other games for the Marines). The galley was enlarged and two banks of tea-urns installed in a space known as 'Tea Urn Square'. The work was finished in three days.

Nobody was more appreciative of Portsmouth Dockyard's efforts than *Stromness'* officers. 'Dockyard workers as a rule are much maligned by seagoing people,' wrote Chief Officer RFA Peter Moore, a Commander RN (Retd). 'On this occasion the dockyard men worked like demons, cheerfully and unselfishly. We were indeed handsomely served and no praise is too high for Portsmouth Dockyard. Nothing was too much trouble and considering a good proportion of workers had received redundancy notices a week earlier the efforts were remarkable'.

Stromness' sailing was put back twenty-four hours. She left in the gathering dusk of 7 April, with 429 Marines lining her rails, to another emotional farewell, of blasting sirens, waving crowds and the distant notes of a bugle from *HMS Victory*.

After this first 'wave' had sailed, the Dockyard began to prepare the next group of warships and RFAs. But there was still a shortage of ships. On 3 April, the necessary Statutory Instruments were signed permitting the Navy Department to take up ships from trade.

The largest Ships Taken Up From Trade (STUFTs, to use the usual acronym) were taken in hand at Devonport and Southampton, but Portsmouth converted more STUFTs than any other yard — twenty-one in all. From early April to early July, the yard always had one and sometimes as many as five merchant vessels at a time in hand. They included ten tankers, which were fitted with Replenishment At Sea (RAS) gear for passing fuel across to RFAs, storage for lubricating oils, commercial satellite communications and, in some cases, extra accommodation.

Conversions were carried out in addition to normal warship work, including designing and fitting the modifications which became necessary as the result of war experience 'down south'. The steelwork for the various extra installations was designed by the Royal Corps of Naval Constructors (celebrating their centenary that year) and prefabricated in Portsmouth Dockyard workshops.

The largest ship converted at Portsmouth was the 12,988 ton P&O 'Ro-Ro' ferry *Norland*. The Dockyard had only twenty-eight hours' notice from the first enquiry to the ship's arrival on 22 April. She was in hand for only eighty-two hours (three and a half days) in which three hundred and twenty man-weeks of work were carried out to finish off a conversion begun in Hull; the manufacture and fitting of two helipads, fresh water distillation plant, extra communications and accommodation. All this was done while the ship swarmed with men loading stores and eight hundred men of 2 Para were embarking. She sailed on 26 April for Ascension.

The 6,061-ton Multi-Purpose Diving and Surface Support Vessel *Stena Seaspread* was on station in the North Sea Thistle Alpha Field when she was requisitioned on 10 April and still had a diver in her recompression chamber when she arrived at Portsmouth on 12 April. Containers and temporary bulkheads were used to give her storerooms (she had never before been more than two hours' helicopter flight from land) and living quarters for the extra one hundred and seventy strong naval party including divers embarked. She had a mobile retail store, used for *Hermes*'s refit, welded to her upper deck and was also fitted with another heavy machine shop, naval and satellite communications, and another crane, before sailing on 16 April.

Portsmouth also converted three United Towing tugs, *Salvageman*, *Irishman* and *Yorkshireman*, and two Townsend Thoresen ferries, *Baltic Ferry* and *Nordic Ferry*, and at a time of a Papal visit, converted a saint — seven hundred and twenty-five man-weeks' work was done in seventeen days to transform the Royal Mail ship *St Helena* into a Mine Counter Measures Vessel support ship, with RAS gear, fresh-water distilling plant, helipad (formerly the circular swimming pool), satcom, four Oerlikon guns and extra fuel stowage.

Meanwhile, the Royal Naval Armament Depot at Gosport not only loaded ships with ammunition but dispatched tons of explosives by air freight. The firing range at Elson, where small arms were proved and zeroed, was in use every daylight hour, seven days a week. The Depot also commissioned, warheaded and tested sixteen Stingray torpedoes in six days, brought 112 Sea Dart missiles to A1 State in fourteen days, and in the same period warheaded and tested sixty Sea Skua missiles (although at that time the missile was so new that only one Sea Skua had ever been successfully warheaded and tested).

With this furious activity continuing at home, the Task Force steamed south. Diplomatic moves crossed and recrossed the Atlantic. In an era of naval cuts, the Portsmouth *News* took advantage of popular and local feeling to start a 'Keep the Fleet' campaign, which eventually gained over one hundred thousand signatures. But the Falklands tended to drop out of the news until the almost bloodless recovery of South Georgia at the end of April, which seemed a good omen. The sinking of the Argentine cruiser *General Belgrano* on 2 May was like the thunder of a distant gun. Then, two days later, came news that stunned the country and the Navy and was a personal body blow to the people of Portsmouth.

The *News* headlines on successive days were 'CITY OF ANGUISH', 'WARSHIP TOLL 87', 'IN THE HUSH OF MOURNING'. Just after 2 pm on Tuesday, 4 May, an Argentine Super Etendard fired an Exocet missile which hit the Type 42 destroyer *HMS Sheffield*, at sea with the Task Force off the Falklands. The missile hit the ship on the starboard side amid ships some six feet above the water-line. Twenty of *Sheffield's* people were lost. The ship herself rolled over and sank while under tow on 11 May.

Sheffield was a Pompey ship, although she had not been in her home port since she sailed for a patrol in the Persian Gulf the previous November. She had been within two days of returning home when the Falklands crisis began. In many homes in and around Portsmouth, parties had been planned, families had prepared their welcomes, wives had cleaned the house, bought new clothes for themselves and the children, and presents for the fathers who were coming home. Then *Sheffield* joined the Task Force.

Pubs and clubs were quiet that Tuesday night. Some people thought back to World War Two, to the news of the losses of *Royal Oak*, and *Hood*, and *Prince of Wales*. This was the dark side of Portsmouth's history, the reverse of the cheering crowds and the bands and banners, the knowledge that with glory went grief.

The special switchboards of the Naval Families Service were soon jammed with enquiries. Naval chaplains and social workers, who had been on twenty-four-hour call for just such an emergency in the previous four weeks, set off to meet and console the families of the dead.

But, after the first shock, the feeling in the city as a whole was one of determination, that this terrible news made it all the more necessary for the business in the Falklands to be pursued with vigour and brought to a victorious conclusion as quickly as possible. As the Lord Mayor, Councillor John Fisher, said, 'Portsmouth is a naval city. We have suffered shocks like this before and we will again. We must just get on with it.'

However, there was also an impatience,

amounting almost to contempt, with the media, and especially the 'impartiality' of BBC television news editors and broadcasters who clearly had as much sympathy for the *General Belgrano* as for *Sheffield*.

There were further losses and more casualties. The destroyer *Coventry*, bombed and sunk on 25 May with the loss of nineteen lives, was a Portsmouth ship. So too was the destroyer *Glamorgan* who suffered a last Parthian shot from an Exocet on 11 June which cost another thirteen lives.

At home, some wives became upset and emotional whenever the Falklands was mentioned. Others said that crying would not make their husbands any safer or bring them back any sooner. Some refused to switch on the television. Others kept the set on all day. Some spent the nights at each others' houses, trying to keep their spirits up with endless cups of tea or coffee. Others preferred their own company and threw themselves into activity, any activity, such as spring-cleaning the house several times, to calm their fears. Some welcomed offers of company and counsel. Others resented it and refused to have anything to do with 'friendly wives' or any other association.

In some ways it was as though the Falklands put Portsmouth and the surrounding area into a kind of social limbo. Family plans, for holidays, weddings and christenings, were held over. House sales flagged and then almost dried up with so many house-owners away in the South Atlantic. Letters in the local paper commented upon the much greater scales of pensions to be paid to Falklands widows, compared with those paid to war widows of World War Two.

At last, on 14 June, not a moment too soon for the battered ships down south or for those who had followed events from home, the white flags were flying over Port Stanley and it was all over. The ships began to come home, to rapturous receptions, but with tears as well as cheers. *Hermes*, claimed damaged and even sunk by the Argentine air force, was salt and rust-stained but not war-damaged when she returned on 21 July. *Glamorgan*, however, showed the evidence of her Exocet hit.

By the time *Invincible* returned on 17 September, to be met by HM The Queen, HRH The Duke of Edinburgh and HRH The Princess Anne, she had spent 166 days at sea, a world record for continuous carrier operations.

By July, although not all the ships had returned, there was a strong desire in Portsmouth to pay a corporate tribute. A Falkland Islands Service was held on the evening of Thursday, 29 July, in Guildhall Square. Prayers were led by the Chaplain to the City Council, the Very Rev. Michael Nott. Silence was kept for one minute. Trumpeters sounded the Last Post and Reveille. To the music of the Royal Marine Band, and led by the Hampshire Constabulary Male Voice Choir, the congregation of several thousands sang 'Eternal Father, Strong to Save', 'Praise My Soul The King of Heaven', 'Abide with me', 'Now Thank We All Our God' and the National Anthem.

The press and others had often commented that the workmen who worked so hard and well during the Falklands conflict did so with redundancy notices in their back pockets. It was true enough. Portsmouth Dockyard closed in March 1984, after nearly a millenium in existence. Portsmouth remained a major naval base and port. Much work was still done in the yard. But the Royal Dockyard, which had been the City's major employer and which for so long had given the City its personality as well as its prosperity, vanished. It was left to the Portsmouth Royal Dockyard Historical Society to pick up the pieces, in some cases literally, and to record, preserve, interpret and exhibit the artefacts and documents of an industrial world that had gone.

At a time when a steadily shrinking Royal Navy and the closure of the Dockyard made the future seem uncertain for Portsmouth, it was the City's naval history which offered a new opportunity. Nelson's *Victory* remained, as almost a permanent symbol of the Navy's historical presence in Portsmouth. But she was to be joined by others.

In 1965, amateur divers led by the naval historian Alexander McKee began to search for traces of Henry VIII's *Mary Rose*, both

H.M.S. Intrepid returning from the Falklands.

ashore in the archives, on the seabed of the Solent, and below the seabed with side-scan and sub-bottom sonar equipment. They formed the *Mary Rose* (1967) Committee which obtained a lease of the area where the ship lay. From 1971, whenever weather and holidays permitted, over six hundred volunteer divers, scientists and archaeologists carried out a sustained programme of exploration and survey.

Ship's frames, planking and deck beams were identified and some excavation was done inside the ship to see how much had survived. In 1978, a trench across the bow showed that two decks had survived *in situ* at that point. It was decided that the ship should be totally excavated, and its contents and structure recorded.

The *Mary Rose* Trust was formed in 1979 with HRH The Prince of Wales as President. A full-time staff was appointed to manage the work of excavating and recovering the ship and her contents. By September 1982, decks,

cabins, bulkheads and companionways had been surveyed, dismantled and brought ashore to be conserved, studied and displayed.

The work of lifting the entire ship began in 1982. In June, a steel frame was positioned above the wreck, with lifting wires fastened to the hull. In September, a steel cradle cushioned with airbags and shaped to conform to *Mary Rose*'s hull (she was lying at an angle of sixty degrees to the vertical) was placed to the west of the wreck. On 9 October, the lifting frame was raised by the crane *Tog Mor* and the hull, hanging from the frame, was moved underwater until it was over the cradle and lowered into it.

Two days later, cradle and hull (weighing 580 tons in total) were lifted by crane into the air and placed on a barge. The whole was towed ashore where *Mary Rose* came to rest at last, 437 years after she sank, in No 3 Dry Dock in Portsmouth (completed in 1799 and itself a scheduled monument). The cradle with the hull was turned upright in 1985. Treatment of the water-logged hull, the replacement of the three thousand timbers removed, and other restoration work, will continue for many years. Meanwhile, the ship is on view to the public.

In December the same year, another survivor from the past surfaced for the first time in sixty-nine years, when water was pumped out of a dock in Devonport to reveal the hull of *Holland 1*, the Royal Navy's first submarine, built in 1901. She was located in 1981 in 30 fathoms of water near the Eddystone Lighthouse, where she sank whilst on tow to the breakers yard in 1913. Salvaged, she was taken by road to the Royal Navy Submarine Museum at Gosport where she joined the 1940s design submarine *Alliance* on show to the public.

The historic warships are matched by the buildings. A *Mary Rose* Exhibition is housed in Boathouse No 5, dating from 1882. The Royal Naval Museum with the *Victory* Shop and Buffet extends over four buildings: the *Victory* Gallery built in 1938, the Present Use Storehouse No 11 (1763), Middle Store No 10 (1776), and South Store No 9, (1782).

Elsewhere in what is now rightly called the 'Naval Heritage' area of Portsmouth are the Great Double Ropehouse (1770-1776); Admiralty House, built as the Commissioner's House by Samuel Wyatt in the 1780s, and now the residence of the Commander-in-Chief Naval Home Command; the Naval Academy (1729-32), now used as the Portsmouth Staff Officers' Mess; and the Lion Gate of 1770, formerly part of the old Portsea fortifications, dismantled in 1871, and embodied in the building of the new Semaphore Tower in 1929.

To this Naval Heritage came in 1987 one of the most striking warships of all time. Arriving in Portsmouth she still looked as Charles Dickens described her, 'A black vicious ugly customer as ever I saw. Whalelike in size, and with as terrible a row of incisor teeth as ever closed on a French frigate.'

When she was first commissioned in August 1861, *HMS Warrior* was the largest, fastest, most powerful warship of her time. The first ocean-going, iron-hulled battleship, in the modern sense of the word, she made all her predecessors obsolete at a stroke. But, when she anchored at Spithead on 11 May 1883, after her last sea passage under her own power, *Warrior* had long been obsolete herself.

In 1902, *Warrior* commissioned as Stationary Depot Ship for Destroyers and Torpedo Boats, wearing the pennant of the Captain, Portsmouth Flotilla. In 1904, she paid off again and recommissioned as Torpedo School Ship, *HMS Vernon*. After *Vernon* moved ashore in 1923, *Warrior* paid off again the following year. In 1927, she was taken in hand for conversion to an oil fuel pontoon hulk and in 1929 she was towed to Pembroke Dock, South Wales.

In August 1942, *Warrior*'s name was required for a new aircraft carrier and she was designated Oil Fuel Hulk C.77. For a time during the war she acted as a depot ship for coastal forces. Finally, in 1979, she was scheduled for scrapping, and would have been, had not one far-sighted man, Sir John Smith, realised that here by some miracle of chance was the intact hull, still sound after being regularly docked over the years, of the Royal Navy's first battleship.

Warrior was taken over by the Maritime Trust and towed to Hartlepool. With Sir John's inspiration, and gift for raising money, she was restored, inside and out, with masts and rigging, guns, decks, and ship's fittings, as she was in 1861. She left Hartlepool under tow on 12 June 1987, arrived in Portsmouth to go alongside a specially designed and constructed berth near the Victory Gate on the 16th. When *Warrior* was first opened to visitors on 27 July, she looked as though her original Victorian ship's company had only just gone ashore.

The concept of a Naval Heritage has latterly been expanded to embrace the 'Defence of the Realm', and to include, not just Portsmouth, but also Hampshire and the Isle of Wight. But the contribution of Portsmouth and its surrounding district is still paramount, with the Royal Navy, Royal Navy Submarine, Royal Marine and D-Day Museums; the fortifications of Old Portsmouth, the Round Tower and the Square

Tower, Southsea Castle, Spitbank Fort, Portchester Castle and the 'Palmerston's Follies', Fort Nelson and Fort Widley, on Portsdown Hill.

Signs of Portsmouth's naval history are everywhere in the City. The Domus Dei or Garrison Church has memorials to the Crimea and, outside, the stone effigy of one of the Napier brothers, while the Welshman Foley, who led the line at the Battle of the Nile and was flag-captain to Nelson at Copenhagen, also lies there. Cornwallis is mentioned, as Commander-in-Chief Portsmouth soon after Trafalgar.

In the Cathedral hang the banners of Admiral Brock, Chief of Staff to Beatty, and Madden, Chief of Staff to Jellicoe, both Commanders-in-Chief Portsmouth. The pulpit's panels are constructed from the wood of *Queen Charlotte*, *Tremendous*, *Actaeon* and *Chesapeake*. The original gilded copper ship weather vane, made in 1710 but blown down in a gale in 1954, is in the north nave aisle; it is supposed to be a miniature of the *Royal George*, so named after Queen Anne's husband, Prince George of Denmark, who was First Lord of the Admiralty during the War of the Spanish Succession.

The stained glass windows in the south transept show D-Day scenes in memory of Admiral Sir Bertram Ramsay. The notice board of the Guild of Friends of Portsmouth Cathedral is made of teak from *HMS Defiance*. An alms box is made of wood from *HMS Tremendous*, Howe's flagship at 'The Glorious First of June'; an inscription notes that *Tremendous* was later cut down to serve as a 50-gun frigate, renamed *Grampus*, and was in service as a powder hulk until broken up in 1897. Oak from the *Victory* frames a scrap of the White Ensign worn by *Victory*. It was carried in Lord Nelson's funeral procession and afterward torn into shreds by the sailors to keep for souvenirs.

Garrison Church, Portsmouth.

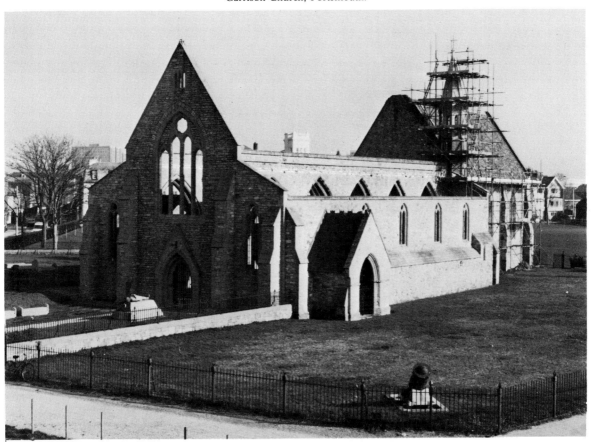

191

On the east wall there is a monument to Admiral Sir John Kempthorne, and nearby a model of his *Mary Rose*, wearing his flag, in which he defeated seven Algerine pirates in 1669, with a wooden tablet showing all the famous naval engagements in which ships called *Mary Rose* took part, from 1509 to 1917. The altar cross in the Baptistry is of wood from the Tudor *Mary Rose*, brought up by divers in 1836, and set in silver. The Cathedral also has the tomb of an unknown sailor of *Mary Rose*.

Many of the churches of Portsea and Southsea contain naval memorials. Milton and Highland Road Cemeteries have scores of naval graves. Near the Square Tower, only a few yards from King Charles' bust in its wall-

niche, are a memorial to the sailing of the First Fleet in 1787, and a wall tablet to commemorate the Falklands in 1982.

In a row on Southsea front, beside the pavement oposite the Naval Memorial itself, are obelisks to the dead and wounded of Sebastol, Alma, Inkerman, Balaclava, Sweaborg and Kertsch in the Russian war of 1854-5; to '48 officers and men who died of yellow fever on board *HMS Aboukir* in 1873-4'; to '44 officers and men of *HMS Trident* who died of yellow fever in the short space of six weeks in the epidemic at Sierra Leone in 1859'; marble pillars commemorating *HMS Chesapeake's* commission of 1857-61 in India, Arabia and China, and the *Shannon's* Naval Brigade in the Indian Mutiny; and, at the

Navy Days, 28th August 1988.

H.M.S. Illustrious Navy Days, Portsmouth 28th August 1988.

westward end of the row, *HMS Victory*'s anchor.

In Victoria Park are more obelisks and pillars and memorials, all mute relics of the City's naval history: to the men of *HMS Shah* who died in the commission in the Pacific and in the Zulu War (1876-9); to those who lost their lives in *HMS Victoria*'s collision with *HMS Camperdown* in 1893; to those of *HMS Powerful* killed in the Boer War; to the dead of *HMS Active* killed in the Kaffir War of 1877 and the Zulu War of 1879; to those killed in a gun accident on board *HMS Royal Sovereign* off Plataea in 1901; to Admiral Napier (1786-1860), paid for by the Lower deck; to the dead of *HMS Centurion* in North China in 1900; and a pagoda with an oriental bell in memory of *HMS Orlando*'s China commission, 1899-1902.

But Portsmouth's naval past is best represented and displayed in one superb building — the church of St Ann, in the Naval Base. The original church was built in 1704 with voluntary subscriptions from officers and men of the Royal Navy, and endowed by men of the Dockyard who agreed to have 2d. a month deducted from their wages to help support the minister.

In 1785, the site was required for the Commissioner's house (now Admiralty House) and another church, a classical gem of glowing red brick by Marquand, was built on the present site. It cost £1,850 and was opened on 4 February 1786. A plan dated 1793 shows that the church then had 'horse-box' pews, graded by seniority and status for various dignitaries and workers in the Yard, and a huge pulpit standing in front of the chancel.

The church was originally 16 feet longer, but the north-west corner was hit by a bomb in April 1941 and again by another a fortnight later. The bell cupola and two bells were destroyed, and the east windows, memorials to the two sail training ships *HMS Eurydice* and *Atalanta*, lost in 1878 and 1880, were smashed. The church was reconstructed by A. E. Cogswell & Sons in 1955-56 from original drawings of 1785. The beautiful ceiling rose, and the magnificent pewter chandelier hanging from it, made in 1704 for the original church, still survive today.

Another survivor of the Blitz is a splendid Georgian Royal Arms from the Commissioner's barge, sumptuously carved in wood by Dockyard craftsmen.

The memorial to *Eurydice* and *Atalanta* was replaced in 1948 by a window, designed by Lieutenant Commander Hugh Easton *RNVR*, of Christ Ascendant over a panorama of the Dockyard. The marble font was carved by convicts working in the Yard and presented to St Ann's in 1856. Another font with matching candle stands was presented by the *Royal Oak* Association as a memorial to those lost in the ship. The pulpit was given in memory of Vice Admiral Sir Henry Barry KCVO, Admiral Superintendent, 1905 to 1906. The lectern, a High Victorian Butterfield-style 'Eagle', made of brass but gleaming like silver, was made by Dockyard apprentices in 1882.

Naval references and resonances lie on every side. The marble monument beneath the Good Samaritan window on the south side of the chancel is a half-length niched figure of Rear Admiral Sir Frederick Maitland. A beautiful carved stone tablet to Admiral Sir John Kelly, who died in 1936, is by Eric Gill. The bust above the font is of Admiral Sir Leopold McLintock, one of the great Arctic explorers of the nineteenth Century.

A Book of Remembrance contains the names of all those whose ashes have been committed to the deep off Spithead since 1972. Two cased ensigns, above the balcony on the west wall, were flown at the surrender of the German fleet in 1919, and at the Allied Naval Commander Expeditionary Force's Headquarters at St Germain-en-Laye when the German Armed Forces surrendered unconditionally on 17 May 1945.

There are many memorials, amongst them tablets to Admiral Sir John Commerell VC; two relatives of Jane Austen, Rear Admiral Charles John Austen, and Henry Austen, Captain in HM 73rd Regiment, killed by a fall; the officers and men of HM Submarine *M1*, lost in a collision with a merchantman off Start Point, on 12 November 1925; and Lieutenant Percy Borough O'Brien RN, lost in Submarine *B2* off Dover on 4 October 1912.

Navy Days 28th August 1988.

With its graceful proportions, its sunlit interior and airy high ceilings, its naval memories and memorials, and its position in the very heart of the Naval Base, St Ann's is the perfect spiritual and architectural symbol of the Royal Navy's close links with the City of Portsmouth. The visitor is irresistibly reminded of Robert Browning's 'Home Thoughts from the Sea':

'Here and here did England help me: how can I help England?' — say,
    Whoso turns as I, this evening, turn to God to praise and pray . . .

APPENDIX 1: ROYAL REVIEWS

1346   10 July. King Edward III's review of his fleet before sailing for France.

1415   11 August. King Henry V reviewed his fleet of 1,400 ships at Portchester before the campaign leading to Agincourt.

1512   2 August. King Henry VIII reviewed twenty-five ships at Portsmouth before they sailed to the French War of 1512-13.

1552   King Edward VI reviewed the fleet during a visit to Portsmouth.

1582   Queen Elizabeth I reviewed a squadron at Spithead, when yards were manned and gun salutes fired for the first time.

1627   11 June. King Charles I reviewed the fleet before the expedition to Rochelle.

1662   May. King Charles II inspected his fleet at Portsmouth.

1712   Prince George of Denmark reviewed the fleet.

1773   22 June. King George III reviewed the fleet at Spithead.

1778   2 May. King George III and Queen Charlotte reviewed the fleet at Spithead.

1794   26 June. King George III and Queen Charlotte visited Spithead and went on board *Queen Charlotte*, the flagship, after Howe's victory on the Glorious First of June.

1803   13 September. Prince of Wales inspected the fleet at Spithead.

1814   24 June. The Prince Regent, with the Emperor of Russia and the King of Prussia, reviewed the fleet at Spithead. Last review to contain only sailing ships.

1827   August. The Duke of Clarence's (later King William IV) review of the British and Russian fleets at Spithead. First mention of a steam ship.

1842   1 March. Queen Victoria's first review of the fleet at Spithead, and visit to *Queen*.

1844   October. Visit of King Louis Philippe. Queen Victoria inspected British ships and a French squadron at Spithead.

1844   21 June. Queen Victoria reviewed the Experimental Squadron.

1853   11 August. 'Grand Naval Review' at Spithead.

1854   10 March. Queen Victoria reviewed Admiral Napier's Baltic Fleet.

1855   20 March. Queen Victoria reviewed Admiral Dundas' Baltic Fleet.

1856   23 April. Great Peace Review. Queen Victoria reviewed fleet after the end of the Russian War.

1865   29 August. Review for the visit of a French fleet of nine ironclads and three wooden sloops.

1867   17 July. Review for the visit of the Sultan of Turkey.

1873   23 June. Review for the visit of the Shah of Persia.

1878   13 August. Queen Victoria reviewed the Particular Service Squadron.

1886   Review for colonial visitors to the Indian and Colonial Exhibition.

1887   23 July. Queen Victoria's Golden Jubilee Review.

1889   5 August. Review in honour of the Kaiser.

1891   19 August. Review for visit of the French Fleet.

1895   9 July. Review for visit of the Italian Fleet.

1897 26 June. Queen Victoria's Diamond Jubilee Review.

1899 5 August. Inspection of the Mobilised Fleet by the Kaiser.

1901 1 February. Naval Homage on the Passing of the Great Queen.

1902 16 August. King Edward VII's Coronation Review.

1905 August. Entente Cordiale Review.

1907 May. Colonial Premier's Review.
August. 'Our Sailor King's Review'.

1909 12 June. Empire Press Review.
31 July. King and Parliament Review.

1911 22 June. King George V's Coronation Review. First to include submarines.

1912 9 July. Inspection of Fleet by Members of Parliament.

1913 24 June. Review for visit of French President, M. Poincare.

1914 16 July. 'Mobilisation' Review before the outbreak of the Great War

1924 26 July. Royal Review.

1935 16 July. King George V's Silver Jubilee Review.

1937 20 May. King George VI's Coronation Review.

1944 May. Review by King George VI of ships and craft taking part in OVERLORD.

1953 15 June. Queen Elizabeth II's Coronation Review.

1977 28 June. Queen Elizabeth II's Silver Jubilee Review. First to include nuclear-powered ships and submarines.

Above: H.M.S. *Churchill* at the Silver Jubilee Fleet review.

Below: H.M.S. *Britannia* at the Silver Jubilee Fleet review on the 28th June 1977.

H.M.S. *Victory*. Today she rests on tailor-made cradles, designed so that her water-line is parallel with the top of the dock.
(Pitkin Ltd.)

APPENDIX 2: OFFICERS IN COMMAND AT PORTSMOUTH

Captain Wishart	1695
Captain Sir Isaac Townshend	1714-1730
Captain Richard Hughes	1730-1744
Rear-Admiral Sir Edward Hawke, KB	1748-1750
Admiral H. Osborn	1755-1756
Admiral Hon. E. Boscawen	1756
Admiral H. Osborn	1756-1757
Vice-Admiral Sir Edward Hawke, KB	1757
Captain Philip Durrell	1757
Admiral Thomas Brodrick	1758
Rear-Admiral Sir Francis Holburne	1758
Vice-Admiral Sir Edward Hawke, KB	1758
Rear-Admiral Sir Francis Holburne	1758
Rear-Admiral Philip Durrell	1758
Rear-Admiral Lord Rodney	1759
Rear-Admiral Philip Durrell	1759-1760
Vice-Admiral Sir Francis Holburne	1761-1766
Rear-Admiral Sir John Moore, Bart.	1766-1770
Vice-Admiral Francis Geary	1770-1771
Vice-Admiral Thomas Pye	1771-1774
Vice-Admiral Sir James Douglas	1774-1777
Vice-Admiral Sir Thomas Pye	1777-1778
Vice-Admiral John Montague	1778-1786
Rear-Admiral Lord Hood, KB	1786-1789
Vice-Admiral Robert Roddam	1789-1792
Vice-Admiral Lord Hood, KB	1792-1793
Admiral Sir Peter Parker	1793-1799
Admiral M. Milbanke	1799-1803
Admiral Lord Gardner, KB	1803
Admiral George Montague	1803-1809
Admiral Sir Roger Curtis, Bart.	1809-1812
Admiral Sir R. Bickerton, Bart.	1812-1815
Admiral Sir Edward Thornborough, KCB	1815-1818
Admiral Sir George Campbell, GCB	1818-1821
Admiral Sir James Hawkins Whitshed, KCB	1821-1824
Admiral Sir George Martin, GCB	1824-1827
Admiral Hon. Sir Robert Stopford, KCB	1827-1830
Admiral Sir Thomas Foley, GCB	1830-1833
Admiral Sir Thomas Williams, GCB	1833-1836
Admiral Sir Philip Charles Calderwood Henderson Durham, GCB	1836-1839
Admiral Hon. Charles Elphinstone Fleeming	1839
Admiral Sir Edward Codrington, GCB, GCMG	1839-1842
Admiral Sir Charles Rowley, Bart., GCB, GCH	1842-1845
Admiral Sir Charles Ogle, Bart.	1845-1848
Admiral Hon. Sir Thomas Bladen Capel, KCB	1848-1851
Admiral Sir Thomas Briggs, GCMG	1851-1852
Vice-Admiral Sir Thomas John Cochrane, KCB	1852-1856
Vice-Admiral Sir George Francis Seymour, KCB, GCH	1856-1859
Admiral William Bowles, CB	1859-1860
Vice-Admiral Sir Henry William Bruce KCB	1860-1863
Vice-Admiral Sir Michael Seymour, Bart., GCB	1863-1866
Admiral Sir Thomas Sabine Pasley, Bart.	1866-1869
Admiral Sir James Hope, GCB	1869-1872

Admiral Sir George Rodney Mundy, KCB	1872-1875
Admiral Sir George Elliott, KCB	1875-1878
Admiral Edward Gennys Fanshawe, CB	1878-1879
Admiral Alfred Phillipps Ryder	1879-1882
Admiral Sir Geoffrey Thomas Phipps Hornby, KCB	1882-1885
Admiral Sir George Ommanney Willes, KCB	1885-1888
Admiral Sir John Edmund Commerell, VC, GCB	1888-1891
Admiral Rt. Hon. Earl of Clanwilliam, KCB, KCMG	1891-1894
Admiral Sir Nowell Salmon, VC, KCB	1894-1897
Admiral Sir Michael Culme-Seymour, Bart., GCB	1897-1900
Admiral Sir Charles Frederick Hotham, GCB, GCVO	1900-1903
Admiral Sir John Arbuthnot Fisher, GCB	1903-1904
Admiral Sir Archibald L. Douglas, GCVO, KCB	1904-1907
Admiral Sir Day H. Bosanquet, GCVO, KCB	1907-1908
Admiral Sir Arthur D. Fanshawe, GCVO, KCB	1908-1910
Admiral Hon. Sir Assheton Gore Curzon-Howe, GCVO, KCB, CMG	1910-1911
Admiral Sir Arthur Moore, GCB, GCVO, CMG	1911-1912
Admiral of the Fleet Hon. Sir Hedworth Meux, GCB, KCVO	1912-1916
Admiral Hon. Sir Stanley Colville, GCVO, KCB	1916-1919
Admiral Sir Cecil Burney, Bart., GCB, GCMG	1919-1920
Admiral Hon. Sir Arthur Gough-Calthorpe, GCB, GCMG,CVO	1920-1923
Admiral Sir Sidney Robert Fremantle, KCB, MVO	1923-1926
Admiral Sir Osmond De Beauvoir Brock, GCB, KCMG, KCVO	1926-1929
Admiral of the Fleet Sir Roger Keyes, Bart., KCB, KCVO, CMG, DSO, LLD, DCL	1929-1931
Admiral Sir Arthur K. Waistell, KCB	1931-1933
Admiral of the Fleet Sir John Kelly, GCB, GCVO	1933-1936
Admiral Sir William Wordsworth Fisher, GCB, GCVO	1936-1937
Admiral of the Fleet The Earl of Cork and Orrery, GCB, GCVO	1937-1939
Admiral Sir William Millais James, KCB	1939-1942
Admiral Sir Charles Little, GCB, GBE	1942-1945
Admiral Sir Geoffrey Layton, GBE, KCB, KCMG, DSO	1945-1947
Admiral Lord Fraser of North Cape,GCB, KBE, DCL	1947-1948
Admiral of the Fleet Sir Algernon Willis, GCB, KBE, DSO	1948-1950
Admiral of the Fleet Sir Arthur John Power, GCB, GBE, CVO	1950-1952
Admiral Sir John H. Edelsten, GCB, GCVO, CBE	1952-1954
Admiral of the Fleet Sir George E. Creasy, GCB, CBE, DSO, MVO	1954-1957
Admiral Sir Guy Grantham, GCB, CBE, DSO	1957-1959
Admiral Sir Manley L. Power, KCB, CBE, DSO★	1959-1961
Admiral Sir Alexander N. C. Bingley, GCB, OBE	1961-1963
Admiral Sir Wilfrid Woods, GBE, KCB, DSO	1963-1965
Admiral Sir Varyl C. Begg, GCB, DSO, DSC	1965-1966
Admiral Sir Frank E. Hopkins, KCB, DSO, DSC	1966-1967
Admiral Sir John B. Frewen, GCB	1967-1970
Admiral Sir Horace R. Law, GCB, OBE, DSC	1970-1972
Admiral Sir Andrew M. Lewis, KCB	1972-1974
Admiral Sir Derek Empson, GBE, KCB	1974-1975
Admiral Sir Terence Lewin, GCB, MVO, DSC	1975-1977
Admiral Sir David Williams, GCB	1977-1979
Admiral Sir Richard Clayton, GCB	1979-1981
Admiral Sir James Eberle, GCB	1981-1982
Admiral Sir Desmond Cassidi, GCB	1982-1985
Admiral Sir Peter Stanford, GCB, LVO	1985-1987
Admiral Sir John Woodward, KCB	1987-1989
Admiral Sir Jeremy Black KCB, DSO, MBE	1989-

APPENDIX 3: PORTSMOUTH-BUILT WARSHIPS

1497 *Sweepstake*. Ship. 80 tons. 70 men. 80 oars. Rebuilt 1511. Renamed *Katherine Pomegranate* under Henry VIII.
Mary Fortune. Ship. 60 oars.

1509 *Mary Rose*. Ship. 60 guns. 500 tons. 200 soldiers, 180 sailors, 20 gunners. Rebuilt 1536. Capsized in Solent, 19 July 1545.

1510 *Peter Pomegranate*. Ship. 60 guns. 450 tons. 150 soldiers, 130 sailors, 20 gunners. Rebuilt 1536, renamed *Peter*.

1539 *Jennet*. Ship. 41 guns. 180 tons. 100 × 29 × 13ft. Rebuilt 1558.

1649 *Portsmouth*. Ship, 4th Rate, 46 guns. 463 tons. 100 × 29 × 14ft. 220 men. Built by Thomas Eastwood. Dover 1652, Gabbard and Schevingen 1653, Lowestoft 1665, The Four Days Battle 1666, Orfordness 1666, Texel 1673. Captured by the French ship *Marquis,* 9 August 1689 and blown up.

1651 *Laurel*. Ship, 4th Rate, 38 guns. 600 tons. 103×30×15ft. Portland 1653. Lost on Newarp Sands, 1657.

1652 *Martin*. Ship, 6th Rate, 14 guns. 124 tons. 64×19×7ft. Built by Sir John Tippetts, Lowestoft 1665. Sold 1667.
Sussex. Ship, 4th Rate, 46 guns. 600 tons. Destroyed in accidental explosion 1653.

1653 *Bristol*. 4th Rate, 48 guns. 534 tons. 104 × 31 × 15ft. 230 men. Built by Sir John Tippetts. Santa Cruz 1657, Lowestoft 1665, The Four Days Battle 1666, Orfordness 1666, Solebay 1672, Texel 1673, Guadeloupe 1690. Rebuilt 1693. Captured by French 12 April 1709, recaptured, and finally sunk by French.
Marigold. Hoy, 3 guns. 42 tons. 32 × 14 × 9ft. Dockyard tender. Broken up 1712.

1654 *Lyme*. Ship, 4th Rate, 52 guns. 764 tons. 145 × 35 × 18ft. Renamed *Montagu,* 1660. Lowestoft 1665, Orfordness 1666, Solebay 1672. Rebuilt Chatham 1675, again Woolwich 1698, to 905 tons. Gibraltar and Velez Malaga 1704, Gaspe 1711. Again rebuilt Portsmouth, 1,025 tons. Cape Passare 1718, Cartagena 1741. Broken up Portsmouth, 1749.

1655 *Dartmouth*. Ship, 6th Rate, 22 guns. 265 tons. 80 × 25 × 10ft. 130 men. Converted to fireship 1668. Wrecked Isle of Mull, 9 October 1690.
Wakefield. Ship, 6th Rate, 26 guns. 313 tons. 90 × 25 × 11ft. Renamed *Richmond* 1660, converted to fireship 1688. Sold 30 August 1698.

1656 *Chestnut*. Ketch, 8 guns. 110 tons. 45 × 18 × 8ft. Wrecked 1665.

1661 *Monck*. Ship, 3rd Rate, 52 guns. 703 tons. 136 × 35 × 16ft. 280 men. Lowestoft 1665, Orfordness 1666, Solebay 1672, Schooneveld and Texel 1673. Rebuilt Rotherhithe 1702. Recommissioned as 4th Rate 800 tons. Velez Malaga and Gibraltar 1704. Wrecked Yarmouth Roads 24 November 1720.

1664 *Royal Oak*. Ship, 2nd Rate, 76 guns. 1,021 tons. 121 × 40 × 17ft. 462 men. Lowestoft 1665, Orfordness 1666. Burned by the Dutch in the Medway 13 June 1667.

1665 *Portsmouth*. Ketch, 14 guns. 90 tons. 48 × 18 × 9ft. Fought in every battle against the Dutch from 1666. Captured at the Texel 1673.

1667 *Portsmouth*. Sloop, 6 guns. 43 tons. 40 × 14ft. Captured by the Dutch 1672.

1668 *Nonsuch*. Ship, 4th Rate, 42 guns. 368 tons. 88 × 28 × 10ft. 180 men. Built by Sir Anthony Deane. Texel 1673. Captured by French privateer *Le Francais* 23 February 1695.

1669 *St Michael*. Ship, 2nd Rate, 90 guns. 1,101 tons. 155 × 42 × 20ft. 600 men. Rebuilt 1706, renamed *Marlborough,* 96 guns. Toulon 1744. Reduced to 68 guns, 1752. Foundered in the Atlantic, 29 November 1762.

1670 *Saudadoes*. Sloop, 10 guns. 83 tons. Rebuilt Deptford 1673, 180 tons. Captured by the French 23 February 1696.

1671 *Cleveland*. Royal Yacht, 8 guns. 107 tons. 53 × 19 × 9ft. 30 men. Built by Sir Anthony Dean. Sold 1716.
Phoenix. Ship, 5th Rate, 42 guns. 389 tons. 90 × 28 × 11ft. 180 men. Built by Sir Anthony Deane. First warship to have lead-sheathed bottom as protection against ship-worm. Solebay 1672. Set on fire and burned off Malaga 1692 to prevent capture by French.
Royal James. Ship. 1st Rate, 100 guns. 1,426 tons. Sunk by Dutch, Solebay, 28 May 1672.

203

1672 *Greyhound*. Ship, 6th Rate, 16 guns. 184 tons. 93 × 22ft. 75 men. Built by Sir Anthony Deane. Barfleur 1692. Sold 1698.

Prevention. Sloop, 4 guns. 46 tons. Sold 1683.

1673 *Cutter*. Ketch, 2 guns. 46 tons. Wrecked in Channel 1673.

Hunter. Sloop, 4 guns. 46 tons. Sold 1683.

Invention. Sloop, 4 guns. 28 tons. Sold 1683.

Isle of Wight. Yacht, 4 guns. 31 tons. Rebuilt 1701, 38 tons. Sold 1712.

Navy. Yacht, 8 guns. 74 tons. Sold 1698.

Royal Charles. Ship. 1st Rate, 100 guns. 1,443 tons. Renamed *Queen* 1693, rebuilt at Woolwich, 1,658 tons. Renamed and rebuilt as *Royal George* at Woolwich, 1,810 tons. Renamed *Royal Anne* 1756. Broken up 1767.

1675 *Royal James*. Ship. 1st Rate, 100 guns. 1,486 tons. 163 × 46ft. 780 men. Built by Sir Anthony Deane. Renamed *Victory* 1691. Rebuilt Chatham 1695. Renamed *Royal George* 1714. Reverted to *Victory* 1715. Accidentally burned 1721, and scrapped.

1678 *Vanguard*. Ship, 2nd Rate, 90 guns. 1,357 tons. 660 men. Built by Daniel Furzer. Sank in the Medway, Great Storm, 26 November 1703. Raised 1704, rebuilt Chatham, 1,511 tons. Rebuilt 1739, 1,625 tons. Renamed *Duke*. Broken up 1769.

1679 *Eagle*. Ship, 3rd Rate, 70 guns. 1,053 tons. 152 × 41ft. 460 men. Built by Daniel Furzer. Barfleur 1692. Rebuilt Chatham 1699, 1,099 tons. Gibraltar 1704. Wrecked off Scilly Is. 22 October 1707.

Expedition. Ship, 3rd Rate, 70 guns. 1,116 tons. 152 × 41ft. 460 men. Built by Daniel Furzer. Beachy Head 1690, Barfleur 1692. Rebuilt Chatham 1699, 1,111 tons. Renamed *Prince Frederick* 1715. Cartagena 1741, Finisterre 1747. Sold 1784.

1682 *Ossory*. Ship, 2nd Rate, 90 guns. 1,682 tons. 161 × 45ft. 560 men. Built by Daniel Furzer. Barfleur 1692. Rebuilt Deptford 1711, 1,570 tons. Renamed *Princess* 1716. Renamed *Princess Royal* 1728. Broken up 1773.

1685 *Coronation*. Ship, 2nd Rate, 90 guns. 1,427 tons. 161 × 45ft. 660 men. Built by Isaac Betts. Beachy Head 1690. Went ashore in a storm off Rame Head 3 September 1691, total loss.

1686 *Nonsuch*. Hoy, 5 guns. 95 tons. Sold 1714.

1690 *Portsmouth*. Ship, 5th Rate, 32 guns. 412 tons. 107 × 30ft. Barfleur 1692. Captured by French in Channel 1 October 1696.

1691 *Norwich*. Ship, 4th Rate, 48 guns. 616 tons. 156 × 42ft. Wrecked West Indies 6 October 1692.

1692 *Russell*. Ship, 2nd Rate, 80 guns. 1,177 tons. 156 × 42ft. 490 men. Built by Stiggatt. Rebuilt Deptford 1735. Cartagena 1741. Sunk as breakwater Sheerness 1762.

1693 *Forester*. Hoy, 7 guns, 125 tons. 63 × 21ft. Wrecked 1752.

Weymouth. Ship, 4th Rate, 48 guns. 673 tons. 133 × 35ft. 236 men. Built by Stiggatt. Rebuilt Woolwich 1718, 715 tons. Broken up Portsmouth 1732.

1694 *Fly*. Advice boat, 6 guns. 73 tons. 62 × 16ft. Wrecked 22 August 1695.

Mercury. Advice boat, 6 guns. 78 tons. 62 × 16ft. Captured by French privateer off Ushant, 19 June 1697.

Newport. Ship, 6th Rate, 24 guns. 253 tons. 95 × 25ft. 245 men. Built by Stiggatt. Captured by French, Bay of Fundy, 5 July 1696.

Scout. Advice boat, 6 guns. 38 tons. 39 × 14ft. Sold 1703.

1695 *Lichfield*. Ship, 4th Rate, 48 guns. 682 tons. 62 × 16ft. Built by Stiggatt. Velez Malaga 1704, Cartagena 1741. Rebuilt Plymouth 1730, 754 tons. Broken up 1744.

Express. Advice boat, 6 guns. 77 tons. 66 × 16ft. Sold 1712.

Postboy. Advice boat, 4 guns. 77 tons. 66 × 16ft. Captured by French off Plymouth 3 July 1695.

Shrewsbury. Ship, 2nd Rate, 80 guns. 1,257 tons. 158 × 43ft. 776 men. Built by Stiggatt. Velez Malaga 1704, Cape Passaro 1718. Rebuilt Deptford 1713, 1,314 tons. Broken up, Portsmouth 1749.

1696 *Fly*. Ketch, 4 guns. 70 tons. 62 × 20ft. Sold 1712.

1697 *Association.* Ship, 2nd Rate, 90 guns. 1,459 tons. 165 × 46ft. Vigo 1702. Wrecked on Scilly Is. 22 October 1707.

Exeter. Ship, 4th Rate, 60 guns. 949 tons. 148 × 38 × 16ft. Built by W. Bagwell. Rebuilt Plymouth 1744, 1,068 tons. Broken up Portsmouth, 1763.

Looe. Ship, 5th Rate, 32 guns. 390 tons. 108 × 29ft. Wrecked Scratchwell Bay, I. of Wight, 12 December 1705.

Seaford. Ship, 6th Rate, 24 guns. 248 tons. 93 × 25ft. 160 men. Rebuilt Deptford 1724, 375 tons. Broken up 1740.

1699 *Nassau.* Ship, 3rd Rate, 80 guns. 1,080 tons. 151 × 40ft. Gibraltar, Velez Malaga 1704. Wrecked Kent coast 30 October 1706.

Swift. Sloop, 4 guns. 65 tons. 48 × 16ft. Captured by French 18 August 1702.

Woolf. Sloop, 2 guns. 65 tons. 48 × 16ft. Captured by French 1704, recaptured 1708. Captured again 19 June 1708, retaken three days later. Sold 1712.

1703 *Portsmouth.* Royal Yacht, 6 guns. 50 tons. 52 × 15ft. Rebuilt Portsmouth 1772, renamed *Medina.* Broken up Portsmouth 1832.

Squirrel. Ship, 6th Rate, 20 guns. 258 tons. 93 × 25ft. Captured by French 1703.

1704 *Roebuck.* Ship 5th Rate, 42 guns. 494 tons. 115 × 32ft. Velez Malaga 1704. Rebuilt Woolwich 19733. Sunk Sheerness breakwater 1743.

Squirrel. Ship 6th Rate, 20 guns. 260 tons 94 × 25ft. Captured by French 1706, renamed *Ecureil.* Retaken 1708 but foundered.

1706 *Nassau.* Ship, 3rd Rate, 70 guns. 1,104 tons. 151 × 41ft. Rebuilt Chatham 1740 as 64 gun, 3rd Rate. Toulon 1741. Sold 1770.

1707 *Hastings.* Ship, 5th Rate, 44 guns. 533 tons. 118 × 32ft. Hulked 1739. Sold 1745.

Truelove. Hoy, 76 tons. 67 × 18ft. Rebuilt Portsmouth 1720, renamed *Old Truelove.*

1708 *Sapphire.* Ship, 4th Rate, 44 guns. 686 tons. 118 × 33ft. Hulked 1739. Sold 1745.

1709 *Bolton.* Yacht, 6 guns. 42 tons. 53 × 15ft. 12 men. Broken up Portsmouth 1817.

Fowey. Ship, 5th Rate, 44 guns. 528 tons. 118 × 32ft. Renamed *Queenborough* 1744. Sold 1746.

1711 *Launceston.* Ship, 5th Rate, 42 guns. 528 tons. 118 × 32ft. Rebuilt 1728, 603 tons, and renamed *Princess Louisa.* Wrecked Dutch coast 29 December 1736.

Seahorse. Ship, 6th Rate, 20 guns. 282 tons. 95 × 26ft. Rebuilt Deptford 1727. Sold 1748.

Solebay. Ship, 6th Rate, 20 guns. 272 tons. 95 × 26ft. Fireship 1727, hospital ship 1742. Sold 1748.

1712 *Success.* Ship, 6th Rate, 20 guns. 275 tons. 95 × 26ft. Fireship 1739. Sold 1743.

1721 *Spy.* Sloop, 8 guns. 103 tons. 62 × 20ft. Sold 1731.

1729 *Hayling.* Hoy, 126 tons. Storeship Portsmouth. Rerigged as Sloop 1759, 10 guns, renamed *Goree.* Broken up 1763.

1732 *Centurion.* Ship, 4th Rate, 60 guns, 1,005 tons. 114 × 40ft. 400 men. Anson's flagship for circum-navigation of the world 1740-44. Finisterre 1747. Siege of Louisburg 1758. Broken up 1769.

Shark. Sloop, 14 guns. 201 tons. 80 × 25ft. Sold 1755.

Worcester. Ship, 4th Rate, 60 guns. 1,061 tons. 144 × 42ft. Porto Bello 1739, Cartagena 1741. Broken up 1765.

1737 *Victory.* Ship, 1st Rate, 100 guns. 1,921 tons. 175 × 51 × 21ft. Wrecked on the Casquets, 5 October 1744.

1742 *Portsmouth.* Royal Yacht, 6 guns, 83 tons. 60 × 19ft. Rebuilt Portsmouth 1794, 102 tons. Broken up Portsmouth 1869.

1745 *Tilbury.* Ship, 4th Rate, 58 guns. 1,130 tons. 147 × 42ft. 420 men. Foundered in hurricane off Louisburg 24 September 1757.

1749 *Hazard.* Sloop, 8 guns. 140 tons. 77 × 21ft. Sold 1783.

Wasp. Sloop, 8 guns. 140 tons. 74 × 21ft. 80 men. Sold 1781.

1750 *Grafton.* Ship, 3rd Rate, 70 guns. 1,414 tons. 160 × 45ft. 520 men. Porto Novo 1759, Manila 1761. Sold 1767.

Newcastle. Ship, 4th Rate, 50 guns. 1,053 tons. 144 × 41ft. 350 men. Sadras and Negapatam 1758, Porto Novo 1759. Foundered with *Sunderland* in cyclone off Pondicherry 1 January 1761.

1752 *Fly.* Sloop, 8 guns. 140 tons. 75 × 21ft. 80 men. Belleisle 1761. Sold 1772.

1753 *Chichester*. Ship, 3rd Rate, 74 guns. 1,401 tons. 160 × 45ft. 520 men. Quiberon Bay 1759, Belleisle 1761. Broken up 1803.

1754 *Gibraltar*. Ship, 6th Rate, 20 guns. 430 tons. 108 × 31ft. 160 men. Lagos 1759. Broken up Portsmouth 1773.

1757 *Dorsetshire*. Ship, 3rd Rate, 70 guns. 1,436 tons. 162 × 45ft. 520 men. Quiberon Bay 1759. Broken up 1775.

Neptune. Ship, 2nd Rate, 90 guns. 1,798 tons. 171 × 49ft. 750 men. Converted as sheer hulk in Portsmouth Dockyard 1784. Broken up Portsmouth 1816.

1758 *Chatham*. Ship, 4th Rate, 50 guns. 1,052 tons. 147 × 41ft. 350 men. Quiberon Bay 1759, Rhode Island 1776. Harbour service Chatham 1793. Powder hulk 1805. Renamed *Tilbury* 1810. Broken up 1814.

1762 *Britannia*. Ship, 1st Rate, 100 guns. 2,116 tons. 178 × 52ft. 850 men. Flagship Vice Admiral William Hotham, Toulon 1793, flagship Vice Admiral Charles Thompson, St Vincent 1797, flagship Vice Admiral The Earl of Northesk, Trafalgar 1805. Renamed *Princess Royal* and then *St George* 1812. Hospital ship. Renamed *Barfleur* 1819. Broken up 1825.

1764 *Asia*. Ship, 3rd Rate, 64 guns. 1,364 tons. 158 × 45ft. 500 men. Martinique 1794. Broken up 1804.

1767 *Ajax*. Ship, 3rd Rate, 74 guns. 1,615 tons. 168 × 48ft. 600 men. St Vincent and Martinique 1780. Chesapeake Bay 1781 and 1782, The Saintes 1782. Sold 1785.

Warwick. Ship, 4th Rate, 50 guns. 1,073 tons. 151 × 40ft. 350 men. Receiving ship Portsmouth 1783. Store and accommodation ship. Sold 1802.

1769 *Elizabeth*. Ship, 3rd Rate, 74 guns. 1,617 tons. 168 × 47ft. 600 men. Ushant 1778, Grenada 1779, Martinique 1780. Broken up 1797.

Worcester. Ship, 3rd Rate, 64 guns. 1,380 tons. 159 × 45ft. 500 men. Ushant 1778, Sadras 1782, Providien 1782, Negapatam 1782, Trincomalee 1782, Cuddalore 1783. Store hulk Deptford 1788. Broken up 1816.

1771 *Falcon*. Sloop, 14 guns. 302 tons. 95 × 27ft. 125 men. Sunk as block ship Narragansett Bay, Rhode Island, August 1788. Salved but foundered September 1779.

1773 *Princess Royal*. Ship, 2nd Rate, 90 guns. 1,973 tons. 178 × 51ft. 750 men. Grenada 1779, Martinique 1780, Toulon 1793. Flagship Vice Admiral Sam Cranst Goodall, Genoa 1795. Reduced 74 guns 1800. Broken up Portsmouth 1811.

1775 *Berwick*. Ship, 3rd Rate, 74 guns. 1,623 tons. 169 × 47ft. 600 men. Captured by three French frigates off Leghorn 7 March 1795, recaptured at Trafalgar 1805. Wrecked off San Lucar, 28 October 1805.

Sphinx. Ship, 6th Rate, 20 guns. 431 tons. 108 × 30 × 10ft. 160 men. Captured by French in the West Indies 1778, recaptured same year. Cape of Good Hope 1795, Madagascar 1796. Broken up Portsmouth 1811.

1776 *Cygnet*. Sloop, 14 guns. 301 tons. 97 × 27ft. 125 men. Sold 1802.

1777 *Lion*. Ship, 3rd Rate, 64 guns. 1,378 tons. 159 × 45ft. 500 men. Java 1811. Hulk Chatham 1816. Broken up 1837.

Swift. Sloop, 14 guns. 303 tons. 97 × 27ft. 125 men. Caught fire and wrecked off Cape Henry, Virginia, November 1778.

1781 *Crocodile*. Ship, 6th Rate, 24 guns. 519 tons. 114 × 32ft. 160 men. Lost off Start Point coming home from the East Indies, 1784.

Eurydice. Ship, 6th Rate, 24 guns. 521 tons. 115 × 32ft. 160 men. Martinique 1809. Broken up 1834.

Warrior. Ship, 3rd Rate, 74 guns. 1,642 tons. 169 × 48ft. 600 men. The Saintes 1782, Copenhagen 1801, Calder's Action 1805. Receiving ship 1818. Prison ship 1840. Broken up 1875.

1785 *St George*. Ship, 2nd Rate, 98 guns. 1,950 tons. 178 × 50ft. 750 men. Genoa 1795, Copenhagen 1801. Wrecked with *Defiance* on west coast of Jutland, Christmas Eve, 1811, over 500 lives lost.

1790 *Fury*. Sloop, 16 guns, 323 tons. 100 × 27ft. Toulon 1793, St Lucia 1796. Converted to bomb vessel 1798. Egypt 1801. Broken up 1811.

1793 *Swift*. Sloop, 16 guns. 329 tons. Foundered with all hands in China Sea April 1797.

1794 *Prince of Wales*. Ship, 2nd Rate. 90 guns. 2,010 tons. 182 ×51ft. 750 men. Groix 1795. Flagship Vice Admiral Sir Robert Calder in action off Ferrol 1805, Baltic 1807. Broken up Portsmouth 1822.

1801 *Dreadnought*. Ship, 2nd Rate, 98 guns. 2,110 tons. 185 × 51ft. Designed by Sir John Henslow. Trafalgar 1805. Seamen's Hospital Ship, Greenwich 1827. Broken up 1857.

1802 *Grampus*. Ship, 4th Rate, 50 guns. 1,115 tons. 151 × 42ft. Harbour service 1820. Sold 1832.

1806 *Alexandria*. Ship, 5th Rate, 32 guns. 663 tons. 127 × 34ft. Built of fir, last frigate of her class. Broken up 1819.

1807 *Bulwark*. Ship, 3rd Rate, 74 guns. 1,940 tons. 183 × 49ft. Laid down as *Scipio*. Designed by Sir W. Rule. Broken up Portsmouth 1826.

1808 *Brazen*. Ship, 6th Rate, 26 guns. 422 tons. 110 × 30ft. Designed by Sir John Henslow. Became floating church on Thames 1827. Broken up 1848.
Podargus. Brig, 14 guns. 252 tons. 99 × 26ft. Designed by Surveyors of the Navy and built by Dockyard apprentices. Action against Danes off Norwegian coast 1812. Receiving hulk Portsmouth 1822. Broken up 1833.

1809 *Zephyr*. Brig, 16 guns. 252 tons. 92 × 26ft. Designed by Surveyors of the Navy and built by Dockyard apprentices. Sold 1818.

1810 *Boyne*. Ship, 2nd Rate, 98 guns. 2,155 tons. 186 × 52ft. Gunnery training ship 1834, renamed *Excellent*. Hulk as *Queen Charlotte* 1859. Broken up Portsmouth 1861.
Pyramus. Ship, 5th Rate, 35 guns. 920 tons. 141 × 39ft. Designed after *Belle Poule*. Accommodation ship Portsmouth 1832. Receiving hulk, Halifax N.S. 1833. Broken up 1879.
Primrose. Brig. 'Cruizer' Class, 18 guns. 383 tons. 101 × 31ft. Designed by Sir W. Rule and built by apprentices. Broken up 1832.

1811 *Hermes*. Ship, 6th Rate, 20 guns. 512 tons. 120 × 31ft. Designed after *Bonne Citoyenne* and built by apprentices. Grounded, caught fire and lost, attacking shore batterey Mobile, Alabama, 15 September 1814.

1812 *Childers*. Brig 'Cruizer' Class. Action with *Hermes* off Mobile 1814. Broken up 1822.
Lacedaemonian. Ship 5th Rate, 38 guns. 1,073 tons. 151 × 40ft. Broken up Portsmouth 1822.

1813 *Grasshopper*. Brig. 'Cruizer' Class. Sold 1832.
Vindictive. Ship, 3rd Rate, 74 guns. 1,758 tons. 176 × 49ft. Razeed (reduced) to 50 guns Portsmouth 1832. Depot hulk Fernando Po 1861. Sank there November 1871. Wreck sold for £20.

1814 *Icarus*. Brig. 'Cherokee' Class, 10 guns. 234 tons. 90 × 25ft. Designed by School of Naval Architecture and built by apprentices. Coastguard vessel Beaulieu 1838. Broken up 1863.

1816 *Pallas*. Ship, 5th Rate, 36 guns. 951 tons. 146 × 39ft. Designed by Sir W. Rule. Laid down at Northam as *Guillaum*, frames to Portsmouth 1811. Coal depot Plymouth 1836. Sold 1862.
Pitt. Ship, 3rd Rate, 74 guns. 1,751 tons 176 × 49ft. Never at sea. Coal depot Portsmouth 1853. Broken up there 1877.

1818 *Waterloo*. Ship, 3rd Rate, 80 guns. 2,056 tons, 90 × 25ft. Designed by Sir Henry Peake. Laid down as *Talavera*, built as *Waterloo*, renamed *Bellerophon* 1824. Harbour training ship Portsmouth 1848. Sold 1892.

1819 *Delight*. Brig. 'Cherokee' Class, 10 guns. 237 tons. 90 × 25ft. Designed by Sir H. Peake. Wrecked 23 February 1824, off Mauritius.

1820 *Britomart*. Brig. 'Cherokee' Class. Sold 1834.
Jasper. Brig. 'Cherokee' Class. Wrecked on Isle of Santa Maura, 'Mediterranean, 13 October 1828.
Minerva. Ship, 5th Rate, 46 guns. 1,082 tons. 152 × 41ft. First round sterned frigate built in England. Never went to sea. Sheer hulk and store ship Portsmouth 1861. Sold 1895.
Prince Regent. Yacht. 282 tons. 96 × 26ft. Given to Imaum of Muscat 1836.
Ranger. Ship, 6th Rate, 28 guns. 502 tons. Sold 1832.

1821 *Ferret*. Brig. 'Cherokee' Class. Sold 1837.

Plover. Brig. 'Cherokee' Class. Became a Falmouth packet, converted into a lazarette 1836. Sold 1841.

Martin. Sloop, 18 guns. 461 tons. 109 × 29ft. Designed by Sir Robert Seppings. Foundered off Cape of Good Hope with all hands, February 1826.

Rose. Sloop. 18 guns. 397 tons. 105 × 30ft. Navarino 1827. Broken up 1851.

1823 *Arrow*. Cutter, 10 guns. 157 tons. 64 × 25ft. Designed by Admiral Hayes. Broken up at Portsmouth 1852.

Carnatic. Ship, 3rd Rate, 72 guns. 1,790 tons. 177 × 49ft. Built of teak. Never went to sea. Coal hulk at Portsmouth 1860. Loaned to Army 1866-91 and used as powder store. Sold 1914.

Philomel. Brig. 'Cherokee' Class. Navarino 1827. Sold 1833.

Royalist. Brig. 'Cherokee' Class. Sold 1838.

Tweed. Ship, 6th Rate, 28 guns. 500 tons. 114 × 32ft. Designed by Admiral Hayes. Razeed Portsmouth 1831. Broken up 1852.

1824 *Champion*. Sloop, 18 guns. 456 tons. 110 × 31ft. Designed by Admiral Hayes. Burma 1824-26. Water police ship Portsmouth 1860. Moored in Solent as target. Broken up 1867.

Orestes. Sloop, 18 guns. 460 tons. 110 × 31ft. Famous sailer but became coal hulk *C28* Portsmouth 1852. Sold 1905.

1825 *Leveret*. Brig. 'Cherokee' Class. Sold 1843.

Musquito. Brig. 'Cherokee' Class. Navarino 1827. Sold 1843.

Myrtle. Brig. 'Cherokee' Class. Wrecked of Nova Scotia, 3 April 1829.

Princess Charlotte. Ship, 1st Rate, 104 guns. 2,443 tons. 199 × 54ft. Designed as lengthened 'Victory'. Biggest ship yet built at Portsmouth. Depot ship at Hong Kong 1857. Sold 1875.

Volage. Ship, 5th Rate, 28 guns. 516 tons. Aden 1839, China 1839-42. Survey ship 1847. Baltic 1855. Powder hulk for Army 1864. Broken up 1877.

1826 *Challenger*. Ship, 6th Rate, 28 guns. 603 tons. Designed by Admiral Hayes. Wrecked off Moquilla, Chile, 19 May 1835.

Columbine. Sloop, 18 guns. 492 tons. 105 × 34ft. First vessel designed by Sir William Symonds. China 1841-42. Coal depot Sheerness 1854. Sold 1892.

Wolf. Sloop, 18 guns. 454 tons. 114 × 31ft. Coal hulk Queenstown 1848, Devonport 1859. Broken up 1878.

1827 *Sapphire*. Ship, 6th Rate, 28 guns. 604 tons. 119 × 34ft. China 1839-42. Converted to troopship. Hulk Trincomalee. Sold 1865.

Sylvia. Cutter, 6 guns. 70 tons. 53 × 18ft. Symondsite. Survey vessel 1842. Sold 1859.

1829 *Favourite*. Sloop, 18 guns. 429 tons. 110 × 31ft. Coal hulk Devonport 1859, *C3* later *C77*. Sold 1905.

Fox. Ship, 5th Rate, 46 guns, 1,063 tons. 151 × 41ft. Designed after French *Leda*. Burma 1852-53. Converted into screw steamship 1856. Store ship 1862. Broken up 1882.

President. Ship, 4th Rate, 52 guns. 1,537 tons. 174 × 45ft. Designed after American *President*. Became RNR drill-ship, Thames 1862. Sold 1903.

Rapid. Brig. 'Cherokee' Class. Wrecked off Cape Bon, 12 April 1838.

Recruit. Brig. 'Cherokee' Class. Foundered off Bermuda with all hands 1832.

1830 *Seaflower*. Cutter, 4 guns. 116 tons. 60 × 22ft. Designed by Admiral Hayes. Sold 1866.

1831 *Actaeon*. Ship, 6th Rate, 26 guns. 620 tons. 122 × 35ft. Survey ship 1856. Lent Cork Harbour Board as hulk 1870. Sold 1889.

Admiralty. Yacht. 136 tons. 69 × 22ft.

Charybdis. Brig. 'Cherokee' Class. Sold 1843.

Fanny. Yacht. 136 tons. 60 × 22ft. C-in-C's yacht. Coastguard 1862. Sold 1863.

1832 *Neptune*. Ship, 1st Rate, 120 guns. 2,694 tons. 206 × 56ft. Biggest ship yet built at Portsmouth. Razeed and made a screw ship, 72 guns, Portsmouth 1859. Sold 1875.

1833 *Lynx*. Brigantine, 3 guns. 232 tons. 90 × 25ft. Broken up 1845.

Racer. Brig, 16 guns. 431 tons. 101 × 33ft. Designed by Symonds. Sold 1852.

1834 *Buzzard.* Brigantine, 3 guns. 231 tons. 90 × 25ft. Sold 1843.

Drake. Dockyard lighter. 109 tons. 60 × 21ft. Converted to Mortar Vessel at Portsmouth 1854, renamed *MV1*. Reverted dockyard lighter 1856, renamed *Sheppey*. Became *YC1* at Pembroke 1860. Broken up 1867.

1835 *Hermes.* Paddle steamer, first built at Portsmouth, 6 guns. 712 tons. 150 × 33ft. 220hp (Maudsley & Field). Rebuilt Chatham 1842, 830 tons. Burma 1852, China 1853. Sold 1866.

1836 *Inconstant.* Ship, 5th Rate, 36 guns. 1,422 tons. 160 × 45ft. Hospital ship Queenstown. Sold 1862.

Volcano. Wooden paddle steamer, 2 guns, 720 tons. 151 × 33ft. Designed by Symonds. Floating factory at Portsmouth 1854. Sold 1894.

1837 *Electra.* Sloop, 18 guns. 462 tons. 114 × 31ft. Sold 1862.

Hazard. Sloop, 18 guns, 431 tons. 111 × 31ft. Symonds. China 1839-42, Syria 1840, New Zealand 1845-47. Broken up 1866.

1838 *Termagant.* Brigantine, 3 guns. 231 tons. 90 × 25ft. Symonds. Broken up 1844.

1839 *Indus.* Ship, 2nd Rate, 80 guns. 2,098 tons. 189 × 51ft. Guardship Devonport 1860. Sold 1898.

Queen. Ship, 1st Rate, 110 guns. 3,104 tons. 204 × 60 × 24ft. Laid down 1833. First three-decker designed by Symonds. Launched as *Royal Frederick,* renamed *Queen*. Black sea 1854-55. Razeed (cut down to two decks) and made a screw ship 1859. Sold 1871.

Stromboli. Wooden steam paddle sloop. 6 guns. 967 tons. 180 × 35ft. 280hp. Designed by Symonds. Syria 1840, Baltic 1854, Black Sea 1854-55. Sold 1866.

1840 *Bittern.* Brig. 12 guns. 484 tons. 105 × 34ft. Symonds. Burma 1853, China 1856-60. Broken up 1860.

Rapid. Brig, 8 guns. 319 tons. 90 × 30ft, Symonds. Sold 1856.

Driver. Wooden steam paddle sloop, 6 guns, 1,054 tons. 180 × 36ft. 280 hp. Symonds. New Zealand 1845-47, Baltic 1854-55. Wrecked 3 August 1861 on Bahama Bank.

1842 *Thunderbolt.* Wooden steam paddle sloop, 6 guns. 1,058 tons. 180 × 36ft. 280 hp (Napier). Symonds, Wrecked 3 February 1847, Algoa Bay.

Albatross. Brig, 16 guns. 484 tons. 105 × 33ft. Symonds. Broken up 1860.

Frolic. Sloop, 16 guns. 511 tons. 105 × 34ft. Designed by Captain Hendry. Sold 1864.

Firebrand. Wooden steam paddle frigate, 6 guns. 1,190 tons. 190 × 38ft. Laid down as *Beelzebub*. 410 hp (Seward & Capel). Symonds. Sold 1865.

1843 *Eurydice.* Ship, 6th Rate, 24 guns. 908 tons. 141 × 39ft. Designed by Admiral Elliott. Sail training ship 1861. Foundered off I of Wight 24 March 1878, with 318 lost. Raised and scrapped 1879.

Sealark. Brig, 8 guns. 319 tons. 90 × 30ft. Symonds. Training ship for boys Portsmouth 1875. Sold 1898.

1844 *Daring.* Brig, 12 guns. 426 tons. 104 × 32ft. Designed by White of Cowes. Sold 1865.

Osprey. Brig, 12 guns. 425 tons. 102 × 32ft. Designed by R. Blake. Wrecked off Hokianga, New Zealand, 11 April 1846.

Scourge. Wooden steam paddle sloop, 6 guns, 1,059 tons. 190 × 36ft. 420 hp (Maudslay). Symonds. Crimea 1855. Broken up 1865.

1845 *Centaur.* Wooden steam paddle frigate, 11 guns. 1,269 tons. 200 × 38ft. 540 hp (Boulton & Wall). Symonds. Baltic 1855. Pei-Ho Forts 1859. Broken up 1864.

1846 *Rifleman.* Wooden steam screw gun vessel, 8 guns. 486 tons. 150 × 27ft. 100 hp (Miller & Ravenhill). Designed by John Fincham. Sold 1870

1847 *Dauntless.* Wooden screw steam frigate, 26 guns. 1,575 tons. 210 × 40ft. 580 hp (Napier). Designed by Fincham. Baltic 1854, Black Sea 1855. Sold 1885.

1848 *Leander.* Ship, 4th Rate, 50 guns. 1,987 tons. 181 × 51 × 16ft. Designed by R. Blake. Black Sea 1854-55. Converted to screw frigate Sheerness 1861, 51 guns, 400 hp. Sold 1867. Last sailing vessel built at Portsmouth.

Arrogant. Wooden screw steam frigate, 46 guns. 1,872 tons. 200 × 46ft. 360 hp (Penn). Designed by Fincham. Baltic 1854-55. Sold 1867.

Plumper. Wooden steam sloop, 9 guns. 490 tons. 140 × 28ft. 30 hp (Miller & Ravenhill). Designed by Fincham. Sold 1856.

1849 *Argus.* Wooden steam paddle sloop, 6 guns. 981 tons. 190 × 33ft. 300 hp. Ashantee 1873-74. Broken up 1880.

1850 *Furious*. Wooden steam paddle frigate, 16 guns. 1,286 tons. 210 × 36ft. 400 hp. Black Sea 1854-55, China 1856-60. Coal hulk Portsmouth 1866. Sold 1884.

1853 *Princess Royal*. Ship-rigged wooden steam screw, 2nd Rate, 91 guns. 3,129 tons. 217 × 58ft. Designed by the Committee of Reference. Launched as *Prince Albert*, converted to screw during building. Baltic 1854, Crimea 1855. Sold 1872.

1855 *Marlborough*. Wooden steam screw, 1st Rate, 121 guns. 4,000 tons. 245 × 61ft. 800 hp. Largest ship built at Portsmouth to date. Converted during building. Harbour training ship 1878, renamed *Vernon II* 1904. Sold 1924, capsized and sank on tow to breakers.
Shannon. Wooden steam frigate, 51 guns. 2,667 tons. 235 × 50ft. 600 hp (Penn). China 1856-57, Indian Mutiny 1857-58. Sold 1871.

1857 *Royal Sovereign*. Wooden steam screw, 1st Rate, 121 guns. 3,765 tons. 241 × 62ft. Rebuilt Portsmouth 1864 as RN's first turret ship. Tender *Excellent*. Rearmed 1867. Sold 1885.

1859 *Bacchante*. Wooden steam frigate, 51 guns. 2,667 tons. 235 × 50ft. Broken up 1869.
Victoria. Wooden screw, 1st Rate, 121 guns. 4,127 tons. 1,000 hp (Maudslay). Sold 1892.
Duncan. Wooden screw, 1st Rate, 101 guns. 3,727 tons. 252 × 58ft. 800 hp (Penn). Disarmed 1889 renamed *Pembroke*, flagship Chatham. renamed *Tenedos II* 1905. Sold 1910.

1860 *Frederick William*. Wooden screw, 1st Rate, 110 guns. 3,241 tons. 204 × 60ft. Laid down as *Royal Frederick*. 1876 training ship in Thames renamed *Worcester*. Sold 1948.
Prince of Wales. Wooden screw, 1st Rate, 121 guns. 3,994 tons. 800 hp (Penn). 252 × 60ft. Symonds. Training ship for cadets 1869, name changed to *Britannia*. Hulked in 1909. Sold 1916.
Rinaldo. Wooden steam sloop, 17 guns. 951 tons. 185 × 35ft. Sold 1884.

1861 *Chanticleer*. Wooden steam sloop, 17 guns. 950 tons. 185 × 33ft. Sold 1875.
Glasgow. Wooden steam frigate, 39 guns. 3,037tons. 250 × 52ft. 600 hp. Designed by Sir B. Walker. Sold 1884.

1864 *Royal Alfred*. Wooden ironclad steam ship. Laid down 1859 as two-decker, 90 guns. Converted to ironclad on stocks. 18 guns. 4,068 tons. 273 × 58 × 27ft. Last timber-hulled capital ship to be built at Portsmouth. Sold 1885.

1865 *Helicon*. Paddle dispatch vessel, 2 guns. 837 tons. 220 × 28ft. Designed by Sir Edward Reed. Renamed *Enchantress* 1888. Sold 1905.
Minstrel. Wooden steam gunboat. 2 guns. 330 tons. 120 × 26 × 8ft. Coal hulk Bermuda 1874.

1866 *Netley*. Wooden steam gunboat, 2 guns. 268 tons. 120 × 22 × 8ft. 9 knots. Sold 1885.
Orwell. Wooden steam gunboat, 2 guns. 330 tons. 120 × 22 × 8ft. 40 men. 260 hp. 9 knots. Broken up 1891.

1867 *Avon*. Steam gun vessel, 4 guns. 467 tons. 155 × 25 × 9ft. 10 knots. Sold 1890.
Cracker. Steam gun vessel, 4 guns. 467 tons. 155 × 25 × 9ft. Designed by Reed. Broken up Portsmouth 1889.
Danae. 'Eclipse' Class wooden steam ram bow corvette. Two 7in, four 64-pdr guns. 1,287 tons. 212 × 36 × 16ft. Barque-rigged. 350 hp. 11 knots under sail, 13 knots under steam. Designed by Sir E. Reed. Hulked 1886 lent to War Department in the Mersey. Sold 1906.
Ringdove. Wooden steam gun vessel, 3 guns. 666 tons. 155 × 25 × 9ft. 160 hp. Designed by Sir E. Reed. Sold 1883.

1868 *Elk*. Steam gun vessel, 4 guns. 465 tons. 155 × 25 × 9ft. 120 hp. (Penn). Designed by Sir E. Reed. Tug 1890. Sold 1905 as dredger Manchester Ship Canal. Laid up 1930.
Magpie and *Swallow*. Wooden steam gun vessels, 3 guns. 665 tons. 170 × 29 × 10ft. *Magpie* converted to survey vessel 1878. Both sold 1885.
Sirius. 'Eclipse' Class corvette. Sold 1885.

1869 *Dido*. 'Eclipse' Class corvette. Zulu war 1881. Hulked and renamed *Actaeon* 1906. Sold 1922.

1870 *Blazer* and *Comet*. 'Ant' Class iron steam gunboats. One 10-in gun. 254 tons. 85 × 26 × 7ft. 9 knots. *Blazer* seagoing tender for testing guns 1904. *Comet* sold 1908, *Blazer* 1919.
Plucky. Prototype 'Ant' Class. 196 tons. 80 × 25 × 6ft. Renamed *Banterer* 1916. sold 1928. Broken up 1969.

1871 *Devastation*. Iron turret ship. Four 12-in in two turrets. 9,330 tons. 285 × 62 × 27ft. First RN capital ship to mount guns on top of instead of inside hull. 13 knots. 1,600 tons of coal. Home and Mediterranean Fleets. Guardship Queensferry 1885, Devonport 1893, Bantry Bay 1898. Sold 1908.

1873 *Shah.* Iron steam frigate, 26 guns. 6,250 tons. 334 × 52 × 25ft. Laid down as *Blonde* but renamed after Shah's visit. Fought action with Peruvian ironclad *Huascar*, off Ho, Peru, 29 May 1877. Hulked in 1904 and used as coal store, renamed *C470*. Sold 1919, coal store in Bermuda. Wrecked 1926.

1875 *Boadicea.* 'Bacchante' Class iron screw corvette. 14 7in, two 64-pdr guns. 3,913 tons. 280 × 45 × 24ft. Sold 1905.

1876 *Bacchante.* 4,103 tons. Sold 1897.

Inflexible. Battleship. Four 16-in guns in twin turrets. 11,880 tons. 320 × 75 × 26ft. Biggest ship yet built at Portsmouth. TT (Torpedo tubes). 14 knots. Mediterranean Fleet. Bombardment of Alexandria July 1882. Guard ship Portsmouth 1893-4. Sold 1903.

1881 *Canada* and *Cordelia.* 'Comus' Class corvettes. Ten 6-in guns. 2,380 tons. 225 × 25 × 19ft. 13 knots. *Canada* sold 1897, *Cordelia* 1904.

1882 *Colossus.* Battleship. Four 12-in, five 6-in breech loading guns. 9,150 tons. 325 × 68 × 26ft. 16 knots. Home and Mediterranean fleets. Guard ship Holyhead 1893. Tender to *Excellent* 1904. Sold 1906.

1883 *Imperieuse.* Armoured Cruiser. Four 9.2-in, ten 6-in breechloaders and four 6-pdr 8,500 tons. 315 × 62 × 27ft. China Station 1889-94, Pacific 1896-99. Recommissioned 1905 as *Sapphire II*, Destroyer Depot ship Portland. Sold 1913.

1884 *Calliope.* Corvette. Four 6-in and 12 5-in guns. 2,770 tons. 235 × 44 × 20ft. Barque-rigged. 14 knots under steam. Escaped from hurricane at Samoa, March 1889. Tender to training ship *Northampton* 1897. RNVR Drill ship Tyne 1906. Renamed *Helicon* 1915. Resumed *Calliope* 1932. Broken up 1951.

1885 *Camperdown.* Battleship. Four 13.5-in, six 6-in and 12 6-pdr guns. Five TT. 10,600 tons. 330 × 69 × 28ft. 17 knots. Flagship Med. Fleet 1889-92. Survived collision with *Victoria* 22 June 1893. Guardship Lough Swilley 1900. Submarine Depot Ship Harwich 1908-11. Sold 1911.

1887 *Trafalgar.* Battleship. Four 13.5-in, six 4.7-in guns. Eight TT. 12,590 tons. 345 × 73 × 29ft. 17 knots. Flagship Med. Fleet 1890-7. Guardship Portsmouth 1897-1902. Gunnery drill ship Sheerness 1907. Sold 1911.

1888 *Nymphe.* Composite screw sloop. Eight 5-in guns. 1,140 tons. 195 × 28 × 12ft. 14 knots. Base ship 1906, renamed *Wildfire* at Sheerness, *Gannet* 1916, *Pembroke* at Chatham 1917. Sold 1920.

Melpomene. 2nd Class Cruiser, 16 guns. 2,950 tons. 265 × 42 × 16ft. 19 knots. Sold 1905.

1889 *Barham.* 3rd Class Cruiser. Six 4.7-in, four 3-pdr guns. 1,803 tons. 280 × 35 × 13ft. Sold 1914.

Barrosa. 3rd Class Cruiser. Six 4.7-in, four 3-pdr guns. Two TT. 1,580 tons. 233 × 35 × 15ft. 16 knots. Home and Med. Fleets. Sold 1905

Beagle. Sloop. Eight 5-in guns. 1,170 tons. 195 × 28 × 12ft. 14.5 knots. Sold 1905.

Vulcan. Torpedo boat carrier. Eight 4.7-in, 12 3-pdr guns. Carried six 2nd Class torpedo boats on deck. 6,600 tons. 372 × 58 × 22ft. Submarine depot ship, 7th Flotilla, Leith, 1914-16. Later Humber, Berehaven and Blyth. Depot ship Portland. Renamed *Defiance III* 1931, torpedo school ship Plymouth. Sold 1955.

1890 *Pallas.* 3rd Class Cruiser. Eight 4.7-in, eight 3-pdr guns. Two TT. 2,575 tons. 278 × 41 × 15ft. 19 knots. Served in West Indies. Sold 1906.

1891 *Royal Arthur.* 1st Class Armoured Cruiser. One 9.2-in, 12 6-in, 12 6-pdr and five 3-pdr guns. Four TT. 7,700 tons. 388 × 60 × 24ft. 20 knots. Flagship Pacific 1893. Returned Portsmouth 1912. Training ship Queenstown 1913. 10th Cruiser Sq North Atlantic 1914. Submarine depot ship Rosyth 1915. Sold 1921.

Royal Sovereign. Battleship. Four 13.5-in and 28 secondary armament guns. Seven TT. 15,585 tons. Made of steel. Biggest ship yet built at Portsmouth. 380 × 75 × 28ft. 712 crew. Sold 1913.

1892 *Centurion.* 2nd Class Battleship. Four 10-in, 30 secondary armament guns. Seven TT. 10,500 tons. 360 × 70 × 26ft. 18 knots. Designed for Far East. Flagship China, Boxer Rising, 1900. Commissioned special service ship 1907. Sold 1910.

Crescent. 1st Class Cruiser. Armament as *Royal Arthur*. 7,700 tons. 388 × 60 × 24ft. North America & West Indies 1894-97. Training ship Queenstown 1913. Flagship 10th Cruiser Sq 1914. Depot ship Rosyth 1915. Sold 1921.

1893 *Fox.* 2nd Class Cruiser. Two 6-in, eight 4.7-in, ten 6-pdr guns. Four TT. 4,630 tons. 339 × 49 × 19ft. 19.5 knots. Naval brigade, Boer War. East Africa 1915, in action against ships supplying German cruiser *Konigsberg*. Sold 1920.

1895 *Majestic.* Battleship. Four 12-in, 12 6-in, 16 6-pdr guns. Five TT. 14,900 tons. 390 × 75 × 27ft. 17 knots. Flagship Channel Fleet until 1904. 1915 Dardanelles. Sunk by torpedoes from *U-21* 25 May 1915.

Prince George. 'Majestic' Class Battleship. Channel Fleet 1896. Collision with *Shannon* 1909. Flagship 7th Battle Sq Devonport 1912. Dardanelles 1915, damaged by shellfire. Hospital Ship Chatham 1916. Torpedo Boat depot Ship renamed *Victorious II* Devonport. Aground and total loss while on tow to breakers' yard 30 December 1921.

1896 *Caesar.* 'Majestic' Class Battleship. Mediterranean and Home Fleets. 7th Battle Sq at Devonport 1914. Atlantic patrols. West Indies. Depot ship Malta. Sold 1921.

Gladiator. 2nd Class Cruiser. Four 6-in, six 4.7-in, eight 12-pdr guns. Three TT. 5,750 tons. 342 × 58 × 20ft. 20 knots. Collision with American liner *St Paul* in a snowstorm in the Solent 25 April 1908. Turned over and stranded on shingle bank. Raised five months later. Sold 1909.

1897 *Canopus.* Battleship. Four 12-in, 12 6-in, ten 12-pdr, six 3-pdr guns. Four TT. 14,300 tons. 390 × 74 × 26ft. 18.3 knots. Home and Mediterranean. Falklands 1914. Dardanelles 1915. Accommodation ship Chatham 1916. Sold 1920.

1898 *Formidable.* Battleship. Four 12-in, 12 6-in, six 12-pdr guns. Four TT. 15,000 tons. 431 × 75 × 26ft. 18 knots. First battleship to cost more than a million pounds. Mediterranean 1901–8. 5th Battle Sq Portland 1914. Sunk by torpedo from *U-24* off Portland Bill, 1 January 1915.

1899 *London.* Battleship. Four 12-in, 12 6-in, 16 12-pdr guns. Four TT. 15,640 tons. 431 × 75 × 26ft. Mediterranean and Home Fleets. Converted for trials to launch aircraft from fore gun turret 1912. Mediterranean 1915. Converted to minelayer, 240 mines, 1918. Depot ship 1919. Sold 1920.

1900 *Pandora.* 3rd Class Cruiser. Eight 4-in, eight 3-pdr guns. Two TT. 2,200 tons. 313 × 36 × 16ft. Home Fleet. Sold 1913.

1901 *Kent.* 1st Class Armoured Cruiser. 14 6-in, 10 12-pdr guns. Two TT. 9,800 tons. 463 × 66 × 25ft. 23 knots. China Fleet 1903. Pacific Fleet. China 1918. Sold 1920.

1903 *Suffolk.* 'Kent' Class Cruiser. West Indies 1909. Falklands 1914. China Station 1917. Sold 1920.

1904 *Britannia.* 'King Edward VIII' ('Wobbly Eight') Class Battleship. Four 12-in, four 9.9-in, ten 6-in, 14 12-pdr and 14 3-pdr guns. Four TT. 16,350 tons. 452 × 78 × 26ft. 18 knots. Home and Mediterranean fleets. 3rd Battle Sq Grand Fleet 1914. Ran aground and badly damaged off Scottish coast January 1915. Sunk by two torpedoes from *UB-50* off Cape Trafalgar 9 November 1918.

New Zealand. 'Wobbly Eight' Class Battleship. Home fleet 1905. Renamed *Zealandia* 1911. Mediterranean Fleet 1912. 3rd Battle Sq Grand Fleet 1914. Dardanelles 1915. Accommodation ship Portsmouth 1919. Sold 1921.

1906 *Dreadnought.* Battleship. Ten 12-in in five twin turrets, 27 12-pdr guns. Five TT. 17,900 tons. 527 × 82 × 26ft. 21 knots. Designed by Constructor J. H. Narbeth. Total building time a year and a day. Biggest ship yet built at Portsmouth. Turbines replaced triple expansion engines. Rammed and sank *U-29* off Scapa Flow 18 March 1915. Refitting and missed Jutland. 3rd Battle Sq. Sold 1921.

1907 *Bellerophon.* Battleship. 'Improved Dreadnought'. 18,600 tons. 4th Battle Sq 1914. Jutland, May 1916. Gunnery Training ship Sheerness 1919. Sold 1922.

1908 *St Vincent.* Larger 'Bellerophon' Class. Ten 12-in, 20 4-in guns. Three TT. 19,560 tons. 536 × 84 × 28ft. Largest ship yet built at Portsmouth. 21 knots. Flagship 1st Battle Sq 1914. Jutland May 1916. Harbour gunnery training ship Portsmouth 1919. Sold 1922.

1909 *Neptune.* Battleship. Ten 12-in in five twin turrets, 16 4-in. Three TT. First British battleship to have superimposed turrets, one turret firing over the top of another, and first able to fire all her main armament on either side. 19,900 tons. 546 × 85 × 28ft. Largest ship yet built at Portsmouth. 21 knots. Flagship Home Fleet 1911. 1st Battle Sq Grand Fleet 1914. Jutland May 1916. Sold 1922.

1910 *Orion.* Battleship. Ten 13.5-in in five twin turrets, 16 4-in guns. Three TT. First to have turrets on centre line instead of in echelon. 22,500 tons. 581 × 88 × 28ft. Largest ship yet built at Portsmouth. 21 knots. 2nd Battle Sq Grand Fleet 1914. Jutland May 1916. sold 1922.

1911 *King George V.* Battleship. Ten 13.5-in, 16 4-in guns. Three TT. 23,000 tons. 597 × 89 × 28ft. Largest ship yet built at Portsmouth. 22 knots. Flagship 2nd Battle Sq Grand Fleet 1914. Jutland May 1916. Harbour training ship Devonport 1923. Sold 1926.

1912   *Iron Duke*. Battleship. Ten 13.5-in, 12 6-in guns. Four TT. 25,000 tons. 623 × 90 × 30ft. Largest ship yet built at Portsmouth. 21 knots. Last class of British battleship coal-fired. Flagship of Sir John Jellicoe, C-in-C Grand Fleet 1914. Jutland May 1916. Mediterranean until 1926. Converted to gunnery and boys' training ship 1931. Depot ship Scapa Flow 1939. Near missed by bombs 17 October 1939. Sank with most of hull above water. Continued as depot ship. Sold 1946.

1913   *Queen Elizabeth*. Battleship. Eight 15-in in four twin turrets (first to mount 15-in guns), 14 6-in guns. Four TT. 27,500 tons (with *Royal Sovereign*, the largest ship ever built in Portsmouth). 646 × 90 × 30ft. Dardanelles 1915. Joined Grand Fleet 1916, flagship Admiral Sir David Beatty. Accepted surrender of German fleet 1918. Mediterranean 1925. Atlantic Fleet 1927. Mediterranean Fleet 1930. Returned Portsmouth 1938 for extensive modernisation costing over a million pounds. Mediterranean Fleet 1941, flagship of Admiral Sir Andrew Cunningham. Damaged by Italian limpet mines in Alexandria December 1941. Refitted in US. Eastern Fleet flagship of Admiral Sir James Somerville 1943. Sabang 1944, Burma 1945. Sold 1948.

1915   *Royal Sovereign*. Battleship, last to be built in Portsmouth. Joined Grand Fleet 1916. Post war in Home Fleet. Convoy duties in Atlantic 1939-40. Action against Italian fleet Calabria, July 1940. Eastern Fleet 1941-43. Handed over to Red Navy and renamed *Archangelsk* July 1944. Handed back at Portsmouth 8 February 1949. Sold 1949.

       J1 and *J2*. Submarines. First built at Portsmouth. 1,210 tons. Six TT. 270 × 23 × 14ft. 20 knots on surface. 11th Flotilla Blyth 1916. Handed over to Royal Australian Navy and arrived Sydney 1919. *J1* scrapped 1924, and *J2* scuttled 1926.

1916   *K1, K2* and *K5*. Submarines. 1,780 tons. 340 × 27 × 16ft. Eight TT, two 4-in guns. Boilers and steam turbines gave surface speed of 25 knots. *K1* collided with *K4* off Danish coast 17 November and sunk by own forces. *K2* sold 1926. *K5* lost after accident in Bay of Biscay 20 January 1921.

1921   *Effingham*. Cruiser. Nine 6-in, four 4-in guns. Four TT. 9,750 tons. 565 × 58 × 20ft. 30 knots. 4th Cruiser Sq East Indies. 12th Cruiser Sq Scapa Flow 1939. Ran aground on Norwegian coast May 1940 and destroyed by own forces 21 May.

1926   *Suffolk*. Eight 8-in, four 4-in guns. Eight TT. 9,800 tons. 630 × 68 × 22ft. 31 knots. 5th Cruiser Sq China Station 1928. Major refit Portsmouth 1935-7. Damaged by German aircraft off Stavanger 17 April 1940. Returned Scapa and beached. May 1941 helped shadow *Bismarck*. Arctic convoys 1942. Eastern Fleet, Burma 1945. Sold 1948.

1927   *London*. Cruiser. Eight 8-in, four 4-in guns. Eight TT. 9,850 tons. 630 × 66 × 22ft. 32 knots. Mediterranean flagship 1st Cruiser Sq 1929. Convoys to Russia 1941-42. Eastern Fleet 1944. Damaged by gunfire from Chinese batteries while trying to reach *Amethyst* 1949. Sold 1950.

1931   *Comet*. Destroyer, first built at Portsmouth. Four 4.7-in guns. Eight TT. 1,375 tons. 326 × 33 × 9ft. 36 knots. Home Fleet 1932-38. Transferred Royal Canadian Navy renamed *Restigouche* 1938. North Atlantic convoys. D-Day landings, Normandy 1944. Sold 1946.

       Crusader. 'C' Class destroyer, as *Comet*. Transferred to Royal Canadian Navy renamed *Ottawa*. North Atlantic convoys. Sunk by *U-91* in Gulf of St Lawrence, 14 September 1942.

       Nightingale. Mining tender to *Vernon*. 298 tons. 100 × 24 × 8ft. 10 knots. Spent whole life in Portsmouth. Sold 1958.

1932   *Skylark*. Mining tender to *Vernon*. 302 tons. 98 × 25 × 8ft. 10 knots. Renamed *Vernon 9* 1938, *Vesuvius* 1941. Spent whole life in Portsmouth. Sold 1957.

       Duncan. Destroyer Leader. Four 4.7-in, two 2-pdr guns. Eight TT. 1,400 tons. 329 × 33 × 12ft. 36 knots. 8th Destroyer Flotilla China. Mediterranean Fleet. Spartivento 1940, Malta convoys 1941. Diego Suarez 1942. North Atlantic convoys. Sold 1945.

1933   *Neptune*. 'Leander' Class Cruiser. Eight 6-in, four 4-in guns. Eight TT. 7,270 tons. 554 × 56 × 20ft. 32 knots. One aircraft. 2nd Cruiser Sq Home Fleet 1934. 6th Cruiser Sq Africa 1937. Mediterranean Fleet, action with Italian Fleet off Calabria July 1940. *Bismarck* 1941. Malta convoys 1941. Mined off Tripoli 18 December 1941 and lost with only one survivor of 550 men.

1934 *Amphion*. 'Leander' Class Cruiser. 6,908 tons. 562 × 57 × 20ft. 32 knots. One aircraft. 6th Cruiser Sq Africa 1936. Transferred to Royal Australian Navy renamed *Perth* 1939. Mediterranean Fleet 1940. Cape Matapan March 1941. Evacuation from Crete May 1941. Java Sea February 1942. Sunk by Japanese Sunda Strait 1 March 1942.

Exmouth. Destroyer Leader, as *Duncan*. North Atlantic convoys 1939. Sunk by *U-22* Moray Firth 21 January 1940.

Aurora. Cruiser. Six 6-in, eight 4-in guns. Six TT. 5,270 tons. 506 × 51 × 14ft. 32 knots. Home Fleet 1937. Norway 1940, *Bismarck* 1941, Malta convoys 1941, North Africa landings 1942, Sicily landing 1943, Salerno landing 1943, Aegean 1943-44, South of France landing 1944. Sold Chinese 1948 renamed *Chung King*. Taken by Chinese communists 1949 renamed *Tchoung King*. Bombed and sunk by Chinese Nationalists March 1949. Salved by Communists 1951. Renamed *Hsuang Ho* then *Pei Ching*, as dockyard hulk. Renamed *Kuang Chou*. Not recorded after 1970s.

1940 *Sirius*. 'Dido' Class Anti-Aircraft Cruiser. Ten 5.25-in high angle guns. Six TT. 5,600 tons. 512 × 50 × 17ft. 32 knots. Home Fleet 1942. Arctic convoys, Malta convoys 1942, North Africa landing 1942, Sicily landing 1943, Salerno landing 1943, Aegean 1943-44, Normandy landings 1944, South of France landing 1944. Sold 1956.

1943 *Tireless* and *Token*. Submarines. 11 TT. 1,090 tons. 275 × 26 × 15ft. 16 knots surfaced, 9 knots dived. Both rebuilt in 1960s. *Tireless* sold 1967, *Token* 1970.

1955 *Leopard*. Type 41 Anti-Aircraft Frigate. First ship built at Portsmouth postwar. All welded. Four 4.5-in., one 40mm guns, one Squid A/S mortar. 2,300 tons. 340 × 40 × 16ft. 24 knots. Service all over the world. Sold 1978.

1960 *Nubian*. 'Tribal' Class Frigate. Two 4.5-in, two 20mm guns, one Limbo A/S mortar, and one Wasp helicopter — first to have helicopter embarked. 28 knots, one steam and one gas turbine. Service at home, Persian Gulf, and all over the world. Sold 1985.

1964 *Sirius*. 'Leander' Class Frigate. Two 4.5-in guns, two Seacat missile launchers, one Limbo A/S mortar, Wasp helicopter. 2,450 tons. 372 × 41 × 18ft. 30 knots. Devonport for conversion 1975-7, four Exocet missile launchers, two 40mm guns, three Seacat missile launchers, six A/S TT, Lynx helicopter. 1981-83 fitted with Towed Array Sonar Devonport. Still serving.

1967 *Andromeda*. 'Leander' Class Frigate. As *Sirius*. Devonport 1977-81 for conversion to anti-surface role, four Exocet missile launchers, one Seawolf missile launcher, two 40mm guns, six A/S TT, and Lynx helicopter. Falklands 1982. Led *Cardiff* and SS *Canberra* into Port Stanley after Argentine surrender, 15 June 1982. Last ship built at Portsmouth. Still serving.

BIBLIOGRAPHY AND SOURCES

Chapter 1
Anglo-Saxon Chronicle, Translated by G. N. Garmonsway, London: Dent Everyman's Library, 1954
Magoun, F. P., Jnr, 'King Alfred's Naval and Beach Battle with the Danes', *Modern Language Review*, Vol. 37
Thompson, Anthony, 'Note on a Roman Coin of Carausius (AD 287-93)', *The Mariner's Mirror*, Vol. XXV, No 1, February 1939, pp.119-120

Chapter 2
Nicolas, Sir Harry, KH, *History of the Battle of Agincourt*, Third Edition 1833, Rep. London: H. Pordes, 1971
Oppenheim, Michael, (Ed.), *Naval Accounts and Inventories of the Reign of Henry VII, 1485-8 and 1495-7*, Navy Records Society, 1896
Smith, Lucy Toulmin, (Ed.), *Itinerary of John Leland 1535-1543*, Vol. I, Arundel, Sussex: Centaur Press, 1964
Spont, Alfred, (Ed.), *Letters and Papers Relating to the War with France 1512-1513*, Navy Records Society, 1897

Chapter 3
Corbett, Julian S., *Drake and the Tudor Navy*, Vols I and II, London: Longmans Green & Co., 1898, Rep. Temple Smith, 1988
Hooker, John, *alias* Vowell, *Life of Sir Peter Carew*, Printed in *Archaeologia* xxviii, 96-151, (John Maclean, FSA, 'The Life and Times of Sir Peter Carew Kt.', London, 1857),
Kemp, Peter, *The Campaign of the Spanish Armada*, London: Phaidon, 1988
Laughton, L. G. Carr, (Ed. by Michael Lewis), 'Early Tudor Ship-Guns', *The Mariner's Mirror*, Vol. 46, No. 4, November 1960
Laughton, Professor John Knox, MA, RN, (Ed.), *State Papers Relating to the Defeat of the Spanish Armada Anno 1588*, Vols I and II, Navy Records Society, 1894
Lewis, Michael, *The Spanish Armada*, London: Batsford, 1960
Martin, Colin, and Geoffrey Parker, *The Spanish Armada*, London: Hamish Hamilton, 1988
Mattingly, Garrett, *The Defeat of the Spanish Armada*, London: Jonathan Cape, 1959
Oppenheim, Michael, *A History of the Administration of the Royal Navy 1509-1660*, London: John Lane The Bodley Head, 1896, Rep. Temple Smith, 1988
Raleigh, Sir Walter, *A Discourse of the Invention of Ships, Anchors, Compass &c.*, from an edition of The Works, pub. 1829, Rep. Burt Franklin, New York
Rodger, N. A. M., *The Armada in the Public Records*, HMSO, 1988
Rule, Margaret, *Mary Rose A Guide*, Portsmouth: Mary Rose Trust, 1986   —   *The Mary Rose*: The Excavation and Raising of Henry VIII's Flagship, London: Conway Maritime Press, 1982
Thomas, David A., *The Illustrated Armada Handbook*, London: Harrap, 1988

Chapters 4 and 5
Anderson, R. C., (Ed.), *The Journal of Edward Mountagu First Earl of Sandwich Admiral And General At Sea 1659-1665*, Navy Records Society, 1929
de Beer, E. S., (Ed.), *The Diary of John Evelyn*, Oxford University Press, 1959
Dymond, Dr. D., CBE, MA, *Captain John Mason and the Duke of Buckingham*, The Portsmouth Papers, No 17, Portsmouth City Council, 1972
Godwin, Rev. G. N., *The Civil War in Hampshire (1642-45) and the Story of Basing House*, Rev. Ed., Southampton: Henry Marsh Gilbert & Son, London: John & Edward Bumpus Ltd., 1904, London, 1904
McGowan, A. P., MA, PhD, *The Jacobean Commissions of Enquiry 1608 and 1618*, Navy Records Society. 1971
Perrin, W. G., (Editor), *The Autobiography of Phineas Pett*, Navy Records Society, 1918
Webb, John, MA, FRHistS, *The Siege of Portsmouth in the Civil War*, The Portsmouth Papers No 7, Portsmouth City Council, July 1969, Rev. 1977

Chapter 6

Defoe, Daniel, *The Great Storm*, 1704

Laughton, L. G. Carr, and Heddon, V., 'The Great Storm of 1703', *Great Storms*, London: Philip Allan, Nautilus Library No 13, 1930, Ch. IV

Hamilton, Admiral Sir R. Vesey, GCB, and Laughton, John Knox, MA, DLitt., (Eds.), *Recollections of James Anthony Gardner Commander RN, (1775-1814)*, Navy Records Society, 1906

Lloyd, Christopher, 'The Royal Naval Colleges at Portsmouth and Greenwich', *The Mariner's Mirror*, Vol. 52, No 2, May 1966, p. 145 — and Anderson, R. C., (Eds.), *A Memoir of James Trevenen*, Navy Records Society, 1954, Part I: Service in the British Navy, Ch. I The Naval Academy

Pope, Dudley, *At Twelve Mr Byng Was Shot*, London: Weidenfeld & Nicholson, 1962

Richmond, Captain H. W., RN, (Ed.), *Papers Relating To The Loss of Minorca in 1756*, Navy Records Society, 1913

Rodger, N. A. M., *The Wooden World*: An Anatomy of the Georgian Navy, London: Collins, 1986

Chapter 7

A Narrative of The Loss of H.M.S. Royal George of 108 Guns Sunk at Spithead, August 29th, 1782, Portsmouth: John Miller, June, 1840

Branch Johnson, W., *The English Prison Hulks*, Chichester: Phillimore Ltd., 1970

Hughes, Robert, *The Fatal Shore*, London: Collins Harvill, 1987

King, Jonathan, *The First Fleet*, Australia: Macmillan, 1982

Portsmouth Birthplace of Australia: Australian Bicentennial Celebrations 1787-1987, Fareham, Hants: Brian Masterson & Associates, 1987

Thomas, James H., BA, PhD, FRHistS, *Portsmouth and the First Fleet 1786-1787*, The Portsmouth Papers No 50, Portsmouth City Council, April 1987

Tuddenham, Mark, *Convicts Away!*, Southsea: EEP Environmental Education Project, 1987

Chapters 8 and 9

Beatty, William, MD, *The Death of Lord Nelson: The Authentic Narrative*, The Athenaeum Publishing Co. Ltd, 1985

Corbett, Julian S., LL.M, (Ed.), *Private Papers of George, Second Earl Spencer First Lord of the Admiralty 1794-1801*, Vol. II, Part II, Papers relating to the Mutinies at Spithead and the Nore, Navy Records Society. 1914

Dugan, James, *The Great Mutiny*, London: Andre Deutsch, 1966

Fraser, Edward, *The LONDONS of the British Fleet*, Ch. XVII, 'The Mutiny at Spithead: What Took Place on Board the *London*', London: John Lane The Bodley Head, 1907

Geddes, Alastair, *Portsmouth During the Great French Wars 1770-1800*, The Portsmouth Papers No 9, Portsmouth City Council, March 1970, Rep. 1980

Gill, Conrad, *The Naval Mutinies of 1797*, Manchester: The University Press, 1913

Manwaring, G. E., and Dobree, Bonamy, *The Floating Republic: An Account of the Mutinies at Spithead and the Nore in 1797*, London: Geoffrey Bles, 1935

Naish, George, P. B., FSA, (Ed.), *Nelson's Letters To His Wife And Other Documents 1785-1831*, Navy Records Society, 1958

Oman, Carola, *Nelson*, London: Hodder & Stoughton, 1947

Patterson, Professor A. Temple, MA, FRHistS, *The Naval Mutiny at Spithead 1797*, The Portsmouth Papers No 5, Portsmouth City Council, December 1968, Rep. 1978

Pocock, Tom, *Horatio Nelson*, London: The Bodley Head, 1987

Rawson, Geoffrey, (Ed.), *Nelson's Letters*, London: Dent, Everyman's Library No 1244, 1960

Chapter 10

Hoad, Margaret J., MA, and Professor A. Temple Patterson, *Portsmouth and the Crimean War*, The Portsmouth Papers No 19, Portsmouth City Council, June 1973

Horsey, S., Jun., *The Royal Visit to Portsmouth on Monday, February 28, 1842*, Portsea, 1842

Lant, Jeffrey L., 'The Spithead Naval Review of 1887', *The Mariner's Mirror*, Vol. 62, No 1, February 1976

Maxwell, Sir Herbert, Bart., MP, *Sixty Years A Queen: The Story of Her Majesty's Reign*, London: Harmsworth Bros Ltd, 1897

Moore, Pam, BA, *Sir Charles Ogle: A Worthy Admiral*, The Portsmouth Papers No 53, Portsmouth City Council, June 1988

The Visit of William IV when Duke of Clarence as Lord High Admiral to Portsmouth in the year 1827, with views of the Russian Squadron at Spithead, London: Henry Moses, 1827

Wade, G. R., BA, MLS, ALA, *The Wind of Change: Naval Reviews at Spithead 1842-56*, The Portsmouth Papers No 49, Portsmouth City Council, April 1987

Chapter 11

Ballard, Admiral G. A., Edited by G. A. Osbon and N. A. M. Rodger, *The Black Battle Fleet*, Lymington: Nautical Publishing Co., Greenwich: Society for Nautical Research, 1980 — 'The First Mastless Capital Ship: H.M.S. Devastation', *The Mariner's Mirror*, Vol. XXXII, 1946, pp. 1-20

Baynham, Henry, *Before the Mast*: Naval Ratings of the 19th Century, London: Hutchinson & Co., 1971

Capper, Lt Commander Henry D., OBE, RN, *Aft — From the Hawsehole*: Sixty-two Years of Sailors' Evolution, London: Faber & Gwyer, 1928

Gulliver, Doris, *Dame Agnes Weston*, Chichester: Phillimore Ltd, 1971

Hopkins, Gerard Manley, 'The Loss of the Eurydice', *Poems of Gerard Manley Hopkins*, London: Oxford University Press, 1960

May, Gunner James, RN, *The Narrative of the Loss of H.M.S. Captain*, Brompton, Kent: G. James Gale, 1872

Verney, Captain Edmund RN, *The Last Four Days of Eurydice*, Portsmouth: Griffin, 1878

Weston, Agnes, *My Life Among The Bluejackets*, London: James Nisbet & Co. Ltd., 1911

Winton, John, *Hurrah for the Life of a Sailor!*: Life on the Lower Deck of the Victorian Navy, London: Michael Joseph Ltd., 1977

Chapter 12

Bacon, Admiral Sir Reginald, KCB, KCVO, DSO, *From 1900 Onwards*, London: Hutchinson, 1940

Baynham, Henry, *Men From The Dreadnoughts*, London: Hutchinson, 1976

Drinkwater, William J., 'Mutiny at Pompey' (1906), *SEASCAPE International Maritime Magazine*, No 11, March 1988

Marquis of Lorne, KT, *VRI Her Life and Empire*, London: Harmsworth Bros Ltd, 1901

NAVAL BARRACKS RIOTS, *The Hampshire Telegraph*, Saturday, December 1st, 1906

Ponsonby, Sir Frederick, first Lord Sysonby, *Recollections of Three Reigns*, edited by Colin Welch, London: Eyre & Spottiswoode, 1951

The Navy and Army Illustrated, issues of February 2nd, 9th and 16th, 1901

Chapter 13

Everitt, Don, *The K Boats*, London: George Harrap, 1963

Gates, William G., *Portsmouth and the Great War*, Portsmouth: The Evening News and Hampshire Telegraph Co., 1919

JUTLAND REPORTS, *The Hampshire Telegraph*, June 9th and 16th, 1916

Murray, Commander John, RN, 'Hic Jacet' (Loss of *K5*), *Blackwood's Magazine*, No 1596, October 1948

Winton, John, *The Victoria Cross at Sea*, London: Michael Joseph, 1978

Wood, Walter, 'Famous Fighting Families II — The Holbrooks', *Navy and Army Illustrated*, Vol. III No 28, February 27th, 1915

Chapter 14

Burton, Lesley, *Gosport 1922*: An Impression in Word & Pictures, The Gosport Society, 1982

Carew, Anthony, *The Lower Deck of the Royal Navy 1900-39*: Invergordon in Perspective, Manchester: University Press, 1981

Cork & Orrery, Admiral of the Fleet The Earl, GCB, GCVO, *My Naval Life 1886-1941*, London: Hutchinson & Co. Ltd, 1942

Donaldson, Francis, *Edward VIII*, London: Weidenfeld & Nicholson, 1974

F. E. M., 'The Coronation Naval Review', *The Naval Review*, No 3 Vol. XXV, August 1937

Roskill, Captain Stephen W., DSC, RN, *Naval Policy between the Wars*, Vol. 2, The Period of Reluctant

Rearmament, 1930-1939, London: Collins, 1976
'The Coronation Naval Review', *The Illustrated London News*, 22 May and 29 May 1937
THE INVERGORDON MUTINY, *The Hampshire Telegraph*, 25 September 1931

Chapter 15

Burton, Lesley, *Gosport Goes to War: 1939-1945*, The Gosport Society, 1981
Front Line 1940-41: The Official Story of the Civil Defence of Britain, London, HMSO, 1942
James, Admiral Sir William, GCB, *The Sky Was Always Blue*, London: Methuen & Co. Ltd., 1951, Chs XVI and XVII, Commander-in-Chief Portsmouth, 1939-41, Admiralty House, and 1941-42, HMS *Victory*, and Ch. XVIII, Publicity and Parliament — 1943-46 — *The Portsmouth Letters*, London: Macmillan & Co. Ltd., 1946
Jenkins, Lt. Commander Paul, RN, *Battle Over Portsmouth*: A city at war in 1940, Midhurst, West Sussex: Middleton Press, 1986
Jubelin, Rear Admiral Andre, *The Flying Sailor*, London: Hurst and Blackett, 1953, Ch. 3, The Battleship *Courbet*
Lord, Walter, *The Miracle of Dunkirk*, London: Allen Lane, 1983
Masefield, John, *The Nine Days Wonder* (Operation DYNAMO), London: William Heinemann, 1941
Packer, Joy, *Pack And Follow*: One Person's Adventures in Four Different Worlds, London, Eyre & Spottiswoode, 1945 — *Grey Mistress*, London: Eyre & Spottiswoode, 1949
Peake, Nigel, *City at War: A Pictorial Memento of Portsmouth, Gosport, Fareham, Havant and Chichester during World War II*, Portsmouth: Milestone Publications and The News, Hilsea, 1986
Portsmouth at War, Vols I and II, WEA (Portsmouth Branch) Local History Group '*Smitten City'; The Story of Portsmouth in the Air Raids, 1940-1944*, The Evening News Portsmouth
Walsh, John, 'William Golding: a master of his craft', *The Sunday Times*, 29 March 1989

Chapter 16

Burton, Lesley, *D-Day Our Great Enterprise*, The Gosport Society, 1984
Glover, Lt Commander Denis, DSC, RNZNVR, '*It Was D-Day*', Penguin New Writing No 23, Penguin Books, 1945
Kemp, Anthony, *Springboard for Overlord*: Hampshire and the D-Day Landings, Horndean: Milestone Publications, 1984
Lipscomb, Commander Frank, OBE, RN, and Davies, John, ex-Lieutenant RNVR, *Up She Rises* (History of Admiralty Marine Salvage Service), London: Hutchinson, 1966, Ch. 5. The Day that almost never was
Morison, Samuel Eliot, *History of United States Naval Operations in World War II*, Vol. XI, The Invasion of France and Germany 1944-45, Boston: Little, Brown and Co., 1957
Ryan, Cornelius, *The Longest Day*, London: Victor Gollancz, 1960
Strutton, Bill, and Pearson, Michael, *The Secret Invaders* (The Story of the COPPs), London: Hodder & Stoughton, 1958, Ch. XI, Two Midgets to Normandy
Warren, C. E. T., and Benson, James, *Above Us The Waves*: The Story of Midget Submarines and Human Torpedoes, London: George G. Harrap & Co., 1953, Ch. 22, D-Day: First Across
Wilkes, Ted, Letter of 12 April 1989

Chapter 17

Burns, Ken, and Critchley, Mike, *HMS Bulwark 1948-1984*, Liskeard, Cornwall: Maritime Books, 1986
Grove, Eric J., *Vanguard to Trident*: British Naval Policy since World War II, London: The Bodley Head, 1987
Hampshire, A. Cecil, *The Royal Navy since 1945*: Its Transition to the nuclear age, London: William Kimber Ltd, 1975
Hutton, J. Bernard, *Commander Crabb is Alive*, London: Tandem Books, 1968
Naval Review Number, *The Illustrated London News*, June 20, 1953
Pugh, Marshall, *Commander Crabb*, London, Macmillan, 1956
'Requiescat H.M.S. Implacable: 2 December 1949', *The Mariner's Mirror*, Vol. 36, No 2, April 1950
The Times, 30 April 1956, Commander Crabb's Obituary
Winton, John, 'The Spithead Review', *The Illustrated London News*, August 1977

Chapter 18

Bateman, Michael, and Riley, Raymond, (Eds) *The Geography of Defence*, Beckenham, Kent: Croom Helm, 1987, Ch. 3, Military and Naval Land Use as a Determinant of Urban Development — The Case of Portsmouth, Ch. 4, The Defence Town in Crisis: The Paradox of the Tourism Strategy

Brown, David, *The Royal Navy And The Falklands War*, London: Leo Cooper, 1987

Dyson, Lt Commander Tony, RN, *HMS Hermes 1959-1984*, Liskeard: Maritime Books, 1984

Featherstone, Lt Commander E. H., (Ed.), *Falklands '82, HMS Fearless at war*: 100 days in the life of an Assault Ship, Bournemouth, Bourne Press Ltd, 1982

Flight Deck: The Fleet Air Arm Quarterly, Falklands Edition, 1982

Force 4 The Falklands: The Newsletter of the Royal Fleet Auxiliary, April 1983

Horlick, Vice Admiral Sir Ted, KBE, FIMechE, MIMarE, *Naval Engineering Achievements in the liberation of the Falklands*, Lecture to the Fellowship of Engineering at the Institute of Civil Engineers on 15 February 1983

Moore, Commander Peter, RN (Retd.), Chief Officer RFA, Personal Account of RFA *Stromness*, in typescript, 20 May 1984

NP 1810 MSV Stena Seaspread Falkland Islands 1982, Aberdeen: Stena (UK) Ltd, 1982

Ross, P. J. (Ed.) *HMS Invincible The Falklands Deployment 2nd April-17th September 1982*, Privately printed for HMS *Invincible* by Eyre & Spottiswoode Ltd, Her Majesty's Printers, at Grosvenor Press, Portsmouth, 1983

RFA *Stromness*, War Diary

Supply and Secretariat Newsletter, 1983, Ministry of Defence

The RNSTS Journal Nos 45 and 46, Summer and Autumn 1982

Villar, Captain Roger, DSC, RN, *Merchant Ships At War: The Falklands Experience*, London: Conway Maritime Press and Lloyd's of London Press, 1984

Winton, John, *Warrior: The First and The Last*, Liskeard: Maritime Press, 1987

Portsmouth Ships and Establishments

Callender, Geoffrey, MA, FSA, AINA, *The Story of H.M.S. Victory*, London: Philip Allan & Co., Nautilus Library, No 7, 1929

Dannreuther, Commodore H. E., (Ed.), *The Royal Naval Barracks Portsmouth and Its History*, Portsmouth: Charpentier Ltd, 1932

Dwyer, Inst. Lt. D. J., RN, (Ed. and Compiler), *A History of The Royal Naval Barracks Portsmouth*, Portsmouth: Gale & Polden, 1961

Lloyd, Christopher, 'The Origin of HMS *Excellent*', *The Mariner's Mirror*, Vol. 41, 1955

Oliver, Captain R. D., RN, (Ed.), *HMS Excellent: 1830-1930*, Portsmouth: Charpentier Ltd, 1930

Revell, Surg. Commander A. L., RN, FFARCS, *Haslar The Royal Hospital*, Gosport: The Gosport Society, 1978

Sayer, Lieutenant G. B., RN, *H.M.S. Vernon A History*, Portsmouth: The Mess Committee, Ward Room Mess, HMS *Vernon*, 1930

Schofield, Vice Admiral BB, CB, CBE, *The story of HMS Dryad*, Havant, Hants: Kenneth Mason, 1977

Statham, Commander E. P., RN, *The Story of the Britannia: The Training Ship for Naval Cadets*, Ch. I, The Good Old Times, Ch. II, The Royal Naval College, Ch. III, The 'Illustrious'

Warner, Commander W. E., DSC, RN, *A Short History of Fort Blockhouse: The British Submarine Head-quarters*, Portsmouth,: W. H. Barrell Ltd, 1947

Wells, Captain John G., CBE, DSC, RN, *Whaley: The Story of HMS Excellent 1830 to 1980*, Portsmouth: HMS *Excellent*, 1980

Young, Commander Robert Travers, OBE, RN, *The House That Jack Built: The Story of HMS Excellent*, Aldershot: Gale & Polden Ltd, 1955

Portsmouth Dockyard

Anon, *The Royal Dockyard at Portsmouth 1929*, Portsmouth Royal Dockyard Historical Society, 1984

Coad, Jonathan, 'Historical Architecture of H.M. Naval Base, Portsmouth, 1700-1850', *The Mariner's Mirror*, Vol. LXVII, February 1981, pp. 3-57

Holland, A. J., *The Rise and Decline of Wooden Shipbuilding in Hampshire*, Newton Abbot: David & Charles, 1971

King, Ivor, CBE, MINA, RCNC, 'Forty Years of Change at Portsmouth Dockyard', *The Naval*

Review, Vol. XLIII, No 3, August 1955

Kitson, Vice Admiral Sir Henry, 'The Early History of Portsmouth Dockyard, 1496-1800', *The Mariner's Mirror*, Vol. XXXIII, No 4, October 1947, Vol. XXXIV, Nos 1-4, 1948

Laing, E. A. M., *Steam Wooden Warship Building in Portsmouth Dockyard 1832-52*, The Portsmouth Papers No 42, Portsmouth City Council, March 1985

Patterson, B. H., and Riley, R. C., *Portsmouth Royal Dockyard: A Short Photographic History*, Portsmouth Royal Dockyard Historical Society, 1984

Richardson, H. E., 'Wages of Shipwrights in H.M. Dockyards, 1496-1788', *The Mariner's Mirror*, Vol. 33, No 4, October 1947

Riley, Dr R. C., BSc, (Econ), PhD, *The Evolution of the Docks and Industrial Buildings in Portsmouth Royal Dockyard 1698-1914*, The Portsmouth Papers No 44, Portsmouth City Council, November 1985

Portsmouth Harbour and Fortifications

Corney, Arthur, *Southsea Castle*, Portsmouth City Museums, 1967

Cunliffe, Professor Barry, *Portchester Castle*, The Portsmouth Papers No1, Portsmouth City Council, June 1967, Rep. 1984

Mitchell, Garry, with others, *Spit Bank and the Spithead Forts*, Solent Papers, No 1, West Wickham, Kent: G. H. Mitchell, 1987

Moore, David, *Fort Gilkicker*, Solent Papers No 5, Gosport: David Moore, 1988

Patterson, Professor A. Temple, MA, FRHistS, *'Palmerston's Folly' The Portsdown and Spithead Forts*, The Portsmouth Papers No 3, Portsmouth City Council, 1968, Rep. December 1985 — *Portsmouth - A French Gibraltar?*, The Portsmouth Papers No 10, Portsmouth City Council, September 1970

Ripley, Basil, BEM, ISM, *Horsea Island and The Royal Navy*, The Portsmouth Papers No 36, Portsmouth City Council, October 1982

Williams, G. H., CBE, MA, *The Western Defences of Portsmouth Harbour 1400-1800*, The Portsmouth Papers No 30, Portsmouth City Council, December 1979

Portsmouth Churches

Clissold, Peter, 'Ships and Monuments in Churches in the Solent Area', *The Mariner's Mirror*, Vol. 58, No 2, May 1972

Hubbock, Rodney, *Portsea Island Churches*, The Portsmouth Papers No 8, Portsmouth City Council, December 1969, Rev. 1976

Portsmouth Cathedral, Portsmouth: Grosvenor Press, 1968

Portsmouth and Southsea

Allen, Lake, *History of Portsmouth*, Portsmouth, 1817

Carson, Edward, MS, FIL, *Smugglers and Revenue Officers in the Portsmouth area in the Eighteenth Century*, The Portsmouth Papers No 22, Portsmouth City Council, July 1974

Curtis, William, *Southsea Its Story*, Alresford, Hants: Bay Tree Publishing Co., 1978

Gates, William G., *Illustrated History of Portsmouth*, Portsmouth: Charpentier & Co., The Evening News and Hampshire Telegraph Co., 1900 — *History of Portsmouth: A Naval Chronology*, Portsmouth: The Evening News and Hampshire Telegraph Co., 1931

Goss, James, *Portsmouth-built Warships 1497-1967*, Emsworth, Hants: Kenneth Mason, 1984

Hoad, Margaret, J., MA, *Portsmouth - As others have seen it*, Part I, 1540-1790, The Portsmouth Papers No 15, Portsmouth City Council, March 1972 — *Portsmouth - As others have seen it*, Part II, 1790-1900, The Portsmouth Papers No 20, Portsmouth City Council, November 1973

Lewis, Michael, *Spithead. An Informal History*, London: George Allen & Unwin, 1972

Lipscomb, F. W., *Heritage of Sea Power; The Story of Portsmouth*, London: Hutchinson, 1967

Murrell, R. J., and East, R., *Extrtacts from the Records of the borough of Portsmouth*, Portsmouth, 1884

Patterson, Professor A. Temple, MA, FRHistS., *Portsmouth Nineteenth-Centure Literary Figures*, The Portsmouth Papers No 14, Portsmouth City Council, January 1972 Portsmouth Navy Days Official Programmes, various years

Portsmouth Record Series. Borough Sessions Papers, 1653-1688, A Calendar, compiled by A. J. Willis and edited by Margaret J. Hoad, Chichester: Phillimore &Co., 1971

Powell, Michael, *Spithead The Navy's Anvil*, Redan & Vedette (Agencies) Ltd, 1977

Riley, Dr R. C., *The Growth of Southsea as a Naval Satellite and Victorian Resort*, The Portsmouth Papers No 16, Portsmouth City Council, July 1972

Rousham, Sally, *Historic Portsmouth*, Portsmouth City Museums, 1980

Smith, Peter, *Go To Blazes: The Story of Firefighting in Portsmouth*, Portsmouth: Milestone Publications, 1986

Southsea and Portsmouth Guide, London: Ward Lock & Co., Ltd., c. 1935

Sparks, Henry J., MA, *A Naval History of Portsmouth in Relation to British Naval Development*, Portsmouth: Charpentier & Co., 1912, Chapters first appeared in *The Hampshire Chronicle*

Thomas, James H., BA, PhD, FRHistS, *The Seaborne Trade of Portsmouth 1650-1800*, The Portsmouth Papers No 40, Portsmouth City Council, September 1984

Triggs, Anthony, *Portsmouth Past and Present*, Portsmouth; Milestone Publications, 1984

Webb, John, MA, FRHistS, *The City of Portsmouth and the Royal Navy*, London: Pitkin Pictorials Ltd, 1984

General

Burton, Lesley, (Ed.), *'Attentive to Our Duty': Aspects of Local Maritime History*, The Gosport Society, 1986

Clowes, Sir William Laird, *The Royal Navy: A History from the Earliest Times to the Present*, Vols I-VII, London: Sampson Low, Marston & Co., 1897-1903

Coad, Jonathan, *Historic Architecture of the Royal Navy*, London: Gollancz, 1983

Corbett, Sir Julian S., *History of the Great War: Naval Operations*, Vols I, II and III, London: Longmans, Green & Co., 1920-23

Eardley-Wilmot, Rear Admiral Sir Sydney M., *An Admiral's Memories: Sixty-Five Years Afloat and Ashore*, London: Sampson Low, Marston & Co. Ltd, 1927

Gosport Records, published by the Gosport Society, Issues Nos 10, 11, 13, 15 and 17

James, William, *The Naval History of Great Britain from the Declaration of War by France in 1793 to the Accession of George IV, and an account of the Burmese War and the Battle of Navarino*, by Captain Chamier, Vols I-VI, London: Richard Bentley, 1837

Lavery, Brian, *The Arming and Fitting of English Ships of War 1600-1815*, London: Conway Maritime Press, 1987

Mason, Ursula Stuart, *The Wrens 1917-77*: a history of the Women's Royal Naval Service, Reading: Educational Explorers, 1977

Mathews, Dame Vera Laughton, DBE, *Blue Tapestry*, London: Hollis & Carter, 1948

Newbolt, Henry, *History of the Great War: Naval Operations*, Vols IV and V, London: Longmans, Green & Co., 1928-31

Padfield, Peter, *Guns at Sea*, London: Hugh Evelyn, 1973

Parkes, Dr Oscar, OBE, AssINA, *British Battleships: Warrior 1860 to Vanguard 1950*, Revised Edition, London: Seeley Service & Co., 1973

Rance, Adrian B., (Ed.), *Sea Planes and Flying Boats of the Solent*, Southampton: Southampton University Industrial Archaeology Group, 1981 — *Southampton: An Illustrated History*, Horndean: Milestone Publications, 1986

Robertson, Frederick Leslie, Eng. Commander, RN, *The Evolution of Naval Armament*, Ch I, The Sailing Ship, Ch II, The Smooth-Bore Gun, London: Constable & Co., 1921, Rep. by Henry Storey, London, 1968

Robinson, Commander Charles N., RN, *The British Fleet*, London: George Bell & Sons, 1895 — *The British Tar In Fact And Fiction*, London and New York: Harper and Brothers, 1909

Roskill, Captain Stephen W., DSC, RN, *The War At Sea 1939-1945*, Vols I, II and III Parts I and II, London: HMSO, 1954-61

INDEX